GO MATH!

HOUGHTON MIFFLIN HARCOURT

HOUGHTON
MIFFLIN
HARCOURT

Printed in the U.S.A.

ISBN 978-0-547-58778-3

8 9 10 0877 20 19 18 17 16 15 14 13

4500403468   C D E F G

Dear Students and Families,

Welcome to **Go Math!**, Grade 6! In this exciting mathematics program, there are hands-on activities to do and real-world problems to solve. Best of all, you will write your ideas and answers right in your book. In **Go Math!**, writing and drawing on the pages helps you think deeply about what you are learning, and you will really understand math!

By the way, all of the pages in your **Go Math!** book are made using recycled paper. We wanted you to know that you can Go Green with **Go Math!**

Sincerely,

The Authors

GO MATH!

Authors

Juli K. Dixon
Professor of Mathematics Education
University of Central Florida
Orlando, Florida

Miriam A. Leiva
Founding President, TODOS:
    Mathematics for All
Distinguished Professor
    of Mathematics Emerita
University of North Carolina Charlotte
Charlotte, North Carolina

Matt Larson
Curriculum Specialist for Mathematics
Lincoln Public Schools
Lincoln, Nebraska

Thomasenia Lott Adams
Professor of Mathematics Education
University of Florida
Gainesville, Florida

The Number System

CRITICAL AREA

COMMON CORE **Critical Area** Completing understanding of division of fractions and extending the notion of number to the system of rational numbers, which includes negative numbers

DIGITAL PATH
Go online! Your math lessons are interactive. Use *i*Tools, Animated Math Models, the Multimedia *e*Glossary, and more.

Look for these:

Project Sweet Success

REAL WORLD

H.O.T.
Higher Order Thinking

Connect to Science
pp. 30, 42

Connect to Health
p. 60

GO MATH!

Use every day for Standards Practice.

Look for these:

REAL WORLD

H.O.T.
Higher Order Thinking

Connect to Reading
p. 122

Use every day
for Standards Practice.

Ratios and Rates

Project: Meet Me in St. Louis **144**

COMMON CORE **Critical Area** Connecting ratio and rate to whole number multiplication and division and using concepts of ratio and rate to solve problems

4 Ratios and Rates **145**

Domain Ratios and Proportional Reasoning
Common Core Standards CC.6.RP.1, CC.6.RP.2, CC.6.RP.3a, CC.6.RP.3b

5 Percents **185**

Domain Ratios and Proportional Reasoning
Common Core Standards CC.6.RP.3c

CRITICAL AREA

DIGITAL PATH
Go online! Your math lessons are interactive. Use *i*Tools, Animated Math Models, the Multimedia *e*Glossary, and more.

Look for these:

Project Meet Me in St. Louis

REAL WORLD

H.O.T.
Higher Order Thinking

Connect to Reading
p. 150

Connect to Art
p. 198

GO MATH!

Use every day for Standards Practice.

6 Units of Measure 217

Domain Ratios and Proportional Reasoning
Common Core Standards CC.6.RP.3d

Expressions and Equations

COMMON CORE   **Critical Area** Writing, interpreting, and using expressions and equations

7   Algebra: Expressions   247

Domain Expressions and Equations

Common Core Standards CC.6.EE.1, CC.6.EE.2a, CC.6.EE.2b, CC.6.EE.2c, CC.6.EE.3, CC.6.EE.4, CC.6.EE.6

DIGITAL PATH
Go online! Your math lessons are interactive. Use *i*Tools, Animated Math Models, the Multimedia *e*Glossary, and more.

Look for these:

Project The Great Outdoors

REAL WORLD

H.O.T.
Higher Order Thinking

Connect to Science
p. 252

Connect to Reading
p. 330

GO MATH!

Use every day for Standards Practice.

Geometry and Statistics

COMMON CORE | **Critical Area** Solve real-world and mathematical problems involving area, surface area, and volume; and developing understanding of statistical thinking

CRITICAL AREA

DIGITAL PATH
Go online! Your math lessons are interactive. Use *i*Tools, Animated Math Models, the Multimedia *e*Glossary, and more.

Look for these:

Project This Place Is a Zoo!

REAL WORLD

H.O.T.
Higher Order Thinking

Connect to Science
pp. 396, 440

Use every day for Standards Practice.

© Houghton Mifflin Harcourt Publishing Company

Look for these:

REAL WORLD

H.O.T.
Higher Order Thinking

Connect to Reading
p. 458

Connect to Science
p. 494

Use every day
for Standards Practice.

CRITICAL AREA

The Number System

COMMON CORE

CRITICAL AREA Completing understanding of division of fractions and extending the notion of number to the system of rational numbers, which includes negative numbers

Pennsylvania is one of the nation's largest growers of apples.

1

Project

Sweet Success

Businesses that sell food products need to combine ingredients in the correct amounts. They also need to determine what price to charge for the products they sell.

Get Started

A company sells Apple Cherry Mix. They make large batches of the mix that can be used to fill 250 bags each. Determine how many pounds of each ingredient should be used to make one batch of Apple Cherry Mix. Then decide how much the company should charge for each bag of Apple Cherry Mix, and explain how you made your decision.

Important Facts

Ingredients in Apple Cherry Mix (1 bag)
- $\frac{3}{4}$ pound of dried apples
- $\frac{1}{2}$ pound of dried cherries
- $\frac{1}{4}$ pound of walnuts

Cost of Ingredients
- dried apples: $2.80 per pound
- dried cherries: $4.48 per pound
- walnuts: $3.96 per pound

Completed by _____

Whole Numbers and Decimals

Show What You Know

Check your understanding of important skills.

Name _____

▶ **Factors** Find all of the factors of the number.

1. 16 _____

2. 27 _____

3. 30 _____

4. 45 _____

▶ **Round Decimals** Round to the place of the underlined digit.

5. 0.<u>3</u>23

6. <u>4</u>.096

7. 1<u>0</u>.67

8. 5.2<u>7</u>8

▶ **Multiply 3-Digit and 4-Digit Numbers** Multiply.

9. 2,143
   ×   6

10. 375
   ×   8

11. 3,762
   ×   7

12. 603
   ×   9

MATH DETECTIVE WITH CARMEN SANDIEGO™

Maxwell saved $18 to buy a fingerprinting kit that costs $99. He spent 0.25 of his savings to buy a magnifying glass. Be a Math Detective and help Maxwell find out how much more he needs to save to buy the fingerprinting kit.

Vocabulary Builder

▶ **Visualize It** •••••••••••••••••••••••••••••••••••••

Complete the Flow Map using the words with a ✓.

Estimation

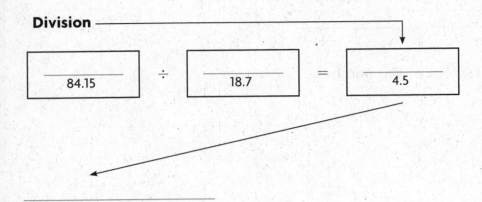

Division

| _____ 84.15 | ÷ | _____ 18.7 | = | _____ 4.5 |

| 80 | ÷ | 20 | = | 4 |

▶ **Understand Vocabulary** •••••••••••••••••••••••••••

Complete the sentences using the preview words.

1. The least number that is a common multiple of two or more

    numbers is the _____.

2. The greatest factor that two or more numbers have in common

    is the _____.

3. A number that is a factor of two or more numbers is a

    _____.

4. A number written as the product of its prime factors is the

    _____ of the number.

GO Online • eStudent Edition • Multimedia eGlossary

Divide Multi-Digit Numbers

Essential Question How do you divide multi-digit numbers?

COMMON CORE STANDARD **CC.6.NS.2**
Compute fluently with multi-digit numbers and find common factors and multiples.

UNLOCK the Problem REAL WORLD

When you watch a cartoon, the frames of film seem to blend together to form a moving image. A cartoon lasting just 92 seconds requires 2,208 frames. How many frames do you see each second when you watch a cartoon?

🔑 **Divide 2,208 ÷ 92.**

Estimate using compatible numbers. _____ ÷ _____ = _____

$$\begin{array}{r} 2 \\ 92\overline{)2{,}208} \\ -184\downarrow \\ \hline 368 \\ - \\ \hline \end{array}$$

Divide the tens.

Divide the ones.

Compare your estimate with the quotient. Since the estimate, _____,

is close to _____, the answer is reasonable.

So, you see _____ frames each second when you watch a cartoon.

🔑 **Example 1** Divide 12,749 ÷ 18.

Estimate using compatible numbers. _____ ÷ _____ = _____

STEP 1 Divide.

$$\begin{array}{r} 70\text{ r5} \\ 18\overline{)12{,}749} \\ -126\downarrow \\ \hline 14 \\ -0\downarrow \\ \hline 149 \\ - \\ \hline \end{array}$$

STEP 2 Check your answer.

$$\begin{array}{r} \\ \times 18 \\ \hline \\ + \\ \hline \\ + \\ \hline 12{,}749 \end{array}$$

Multiply the whole number part of the quotient by the divisor.

Add the remainder.

Math Idea

You can write a remainder with an r, as a fractional part of the divisor, or as a decimal. For 131 ÷ 5, the quotient can be written as 26 r1, $26\frac{1}{5}$, or 26.2.

So, 12,749 ÷ 18 = _____.

🔑 Example 2

Divide 59,990 ÷ 280. Write the remainder as a fraction.

Estimate using compatible numbers. _____ ÷ _____ = _____

STEP 1 Divide.

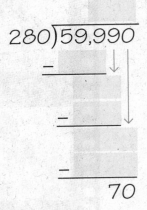

STEP 2 Write the remainder as a fraction.

$$\frac{remainder}{divisor} = \frac{\boxed{}}{280}$$ Write the remainder over the divisor.

$$\frac{70 \div \boxed{}}{280 \div \boxed{}} = \frac{\boxed{}}{\boxed{}}$$ Simplify.

Compare your estimate with the quotient. Since the estimate, _____

is close to _____, the answer is reasonable.

So, 59,990 ÷ 280 = _____.

- **Describe** two ways to check your answer in Example 2.

_____

_____

_____

Share and Show ·

Estimate. Then find the quotient. Write the remainder, if any, with an r.

1. 29)986   Think: 30 × 3 = 90

2. 37)3,786

_____

_____

Name _____

Share and Show . . . .

Estimate. Then find the quotient. Write the remainder, if any, as a fraction.

✅ **3.** $6{,}114 \div 63$

✅ **4.** $11{,}050 \div 26$

_____

_____

Math Talk   MATHEMATICAL PRACTICES
Explain why you can use multiplication to check a division problem.

On Your Own . . . .

Estimate. Then find the quotient. Write the remainder, if any, with an r.

5. $24\overline{)626}$

6. $24\overline{)28{,}536}$

7. $29\overline{)13{,}226}$

_____

_____

_____

Estimate. Then find the quotient. Write the remainder, if any, as a fraction.

8. $3{,}150 \div 9$

9. $2{,}115 \div 72$

10. $20{,}835 \div 180$

_____

_____

_____

Find the least whole number that can replace ■ **to make the statement true.**

11. ■ $\div\ 9 > 700$

12. ■ $\div\ 19 > 89$

13. $110 <$ ■ $\div\ 47$

_____

_____

_____

Problem Solving REAL WORLD

Use the table for 14–17.

14. A Boeing 747-400 jet carried 6,045 passengers last week, and all of its flights were full. How many flights did the jet make last week?

_____

15. Last month an airline made 6,322 reservations for flights from Newark, New Jersey, to Frankfurt, Germany. If there were 21 full flights and 64 reservations were cancelled, which airplane made the flights?

_____

16. **H.O.T.** An airline carries about 750 passengers from Houston to Chicago each day. How many McDonnell Douglas MD-90 jets would be needed to carry this many passengers, and how many empty seats would there be?

_____

17. **H.O.T. Pose a Problem** Look back at Problem 14. Use the information in the table to write a similar problem involving airplane passenger seats.

_____

_____

_____

18. ⭐ **Test Prep** A machine pasted labels on 8,316 soup cans in 27 minutes. How many cans did the machine label each minute?

Ⓐ $3\frac{4}{5}$

Ⓑ 38

Ⓒ 308

Ⓓ 380

Airplane Passenger Seats	
Type of Plane	**Seats**
Airbus A330-300	298
Boeing 747-400	403
McDonnell Douglas MD-90	160
Embraer 170	70

SHOW YOUR WORK

FOR MORE PRACTICE:
Standards Practice Book, pp. P3–P4

Name _____

Prime Factorization

Essential Question How do you write the prime factorization of a number?

COMMON CORE STANDARD CC.6.NS.4
Compute fluently with multi-digit numbers and find common factors and multiples.

UNLOCK the Problem REAL WORLD

Secret codes are often used to send information over the Internet. Many of these codes are based on very large numbers. For some codes, a computer must determine the prime factorization of these numbers to decode the information.

The **prime factorization** of a number is the number written as a product of all of its prime factors.

One Way Use a factor tree.

The key for a code is based on the prime factorization of 180. Find the prime factorization of 180.

Choose any two factors whose product is 180. Continue finding factors until only prime factors are left.

> **Remember**
> A prime number is a whole number greater than 1 that has exactly two factors: itself and 1.

A Use a basic fact.

Think: 10 times what number is equal to 180?

10 × _____ = 180

```
         180
        /   \
      10     ▢
     /  \
    2    ▢    6
        / \  / \
       2  ▢    3  ▢
```

180 = _____ × _____ × _____ × _____ × _____

So, the prime factorization of 180 is _____ × _____ × _____ × _____ × _____.

B Use a divisibility rule.

Think: 180 is even, so it is divisible by 2.

2 × _____ = 180

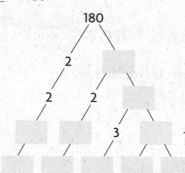

```
          180
         /   \
        2     ▢
       / \
      2   2   ▢
     /|       |\
    ▢ ▢   ▢   3  ▢
```

List the prime factors from least to greatest.

> **Math Talk** MATHEMATICAL PRACTICES
> **Explain** how you know whether a number is divisible by another number.

Another Way Use a ladder diagram.

The key for a code is based on the prime factorization of 140. Find the prime factorization of 140.

Choose a prime factor of 140. Continue dividing by prime factors until the quotient is 1.

A Use the divisibility rule for 2.

Think: 140 is even, so 140 is divisible by 2.

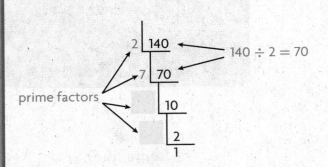

prime factors

$140 \div 2 = 70$

140 = _____ × _____ × _____ × _____

So, the prime factorization of 140 is _____ × _____ × _____ × _____.

B Use the divisibility rule for 5.

Think: The last digit is 0, so 140 is divisible by 5.

5 | 140
2 |
  | 14
  | 2

List the prime factors from least to greatest.

Math Talk MATHEMATICAL PRACTICES
How can you check whether the prime factorization of a number is correct?

Share and Show

Find the prime factorization.

1. 18

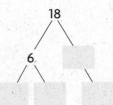

18 = _____ × _____ × _____

2. 42

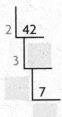

2 | 42
3 |
  | 7

42 = _____ × _____ × _____

Name _____

Share and Show

Find the prime factorization.

3. 75

☑ **4.** 12

☑ **5.** 65

Math Talk MATHEMATICAL PRACTICES
Explain why a prime number cannot be written as a product of prime factors.

On Your Own

Find the prime factorization.

6. 104

7. 225

8. 306

Write the number whose prime factorization is given.

9. $2 \times 2 \times 2 \times 7$

10. $2 \times 2 \times 5 \times 5$

11. $2 \times 2 \times 2 \times 2 \times 3 \times 3$

Practice: Copy and Solve Find the prime factorization.

12. 45

13. 50

14. 32

15. 76

16. 108

17. 126

Problem Solving REAL WORLD

Use the table and the information below for 18–20.

Agent Sanchez must enter a code on a keypad to unlock the door to her office.

18. In August, the digits of the code number are the prime factors of 150. What is the code number for the office door in August?

_____

19. In September, the digits of the code number are the prime factors of 375. What is the code number for the office door in September?

_____

20. **H.O.T.** One day in October, Agent Sanchez enters the code 3477. How do you know that this code is incorrect and will not open the door?

_____

_____

Code Number Rules

1. The code is a 4-digit number.

2. Each digit is a prime number.

3. The prime numbers are entered from least to greatest.

4. The code number is changed at the beginning of each month.

SHOW YOUR WORK

21. **Write Math** ▶ The prime factorization of 24 is $2 \times 2 \times 2 \times 3$. **Explain** how to find the prime factorization of 48 without using a factor tree or a ladder diagram.

_____

_____

_____

_____

_____

22. ⭐ **Test Prep** The key for a security code is based on the prime factorization of 90. What is the prime factorization of 90?

(A) $2 \times 2 \times 2 \times 3 \times 5$ (C) $3 \times 5 \times 6$

(B) $2 \times 5 \times 9$ (D) $2 \times 3 \times 3 \times 5$

Name _____

Least Common Multiple

Essential Question How can you find the least common multiple of two whole numbers?

COMMON CORE STANDARD CC.6.NS.4
Compute fluently with multi-digit numbers and find common factors and multiples.

 UNLOCK the Problem REAL WORLD

In an experiment, each flowerpot will get one seed. If the flowerpots are in packages of 6 and the seeds are in packets of 8, what is the least number of plants that can be grown without any seeds or pots left over?

The **least common multiple**, or **LCM**, is the least number that is a common multiple of two or more numbers.

- Explain why you cannot buy the same number of packages of each item.

  _____

  _____

  _____

One Way Use a list.

Make a list of the first eight nonzero multiples of 6 and 8. Circle the common multiples. Then find the least common multiple.

Multiples of 6: 6, 12, 18, _____ , _____ , _____ , _____ , _____

Multiples of 8: 8, 16, 24, _____ , _____ , _____ , _____ , _____

The least common multiple, or LCM, is _____ .

Another Way Use prime factorization and a Venn diagram.

Write the prime factorization of each number.

$6 = 2 \times$ _____

$8 = 2 \times$ _____ $\times$ _____

List the common prime factors of the numbers, if any.

6 and 8 have one prime factor of _____ in common.

Place the prime factors of the numbers in the appropriate parts of the Venn diagram.

To find the LCM, find the product of all of the prime factors in the Venn diagram.

$3 \times 2 \times 2 \times 2 =$ _____

The LCM is _____ .

So, the least number of plants is _____ .

Prime factors of 6   Prime factors of 8

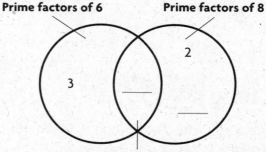

3   2

_____

_____

Common prime factors

Math Talk MATHEMATICAL PRACTICES
Explain how the diagram shows the prime factorization of 6 and 8.

Chapter 1 13

🔑 Example Use prime factorization to find the LCM of 12 and 18.

Write the prime factorization of each number.

$12 = 2 \times 2 \times$ _____

Line up the common factors.

$18 = 2 \quad \times \quad 3 \quad \times$ _____

Multiply one number from each column.

$2 \times 2 \times \quad 3 \quad \times \quad 3 = 36$

Math Idea

The factors in the prime factorization of a number are usually listed in order from least to greatest.

So, the LCM of 12 and 18 is _____.

Try This! Find the LCM.

Ⓐ 10, 15, and 25

Use prime factorization.

10 = _____

15 = _____

25 = _____

_____

The LCM is _____.

Ⓑ 3 and 12

Use a list.

Multiples of 3: _____

Multiples of 12: _____

The LCM is _____.

1. How can you tell whether the LCM of a pair of numbers is one of the numbers? Give an example.

_____

_____

2. Explain one reason why you might use prime factorization instead of making a list of multiples to find the LCM of 10, 15, and 25.

_____

_____

Share and Show ·

✅ **1.** List the first six nonzero multiples of 6 and 9. Circle the common multiples. Then find the LCM.

Multiples of 6: _____

Multiples of 9: _____   The LCM of 6 and 9 is _____.

Name _____

Share and Show

Find the LCM.

2. 3, 5

_____

3. 3, 9

_____

4. 9, 15

_____

Math Talk MATHEMATICAL PRACTICES
Explain what the LCM of two numbers represents.

On Your Own

Find the LCM.

5. 5, 10

_____

6. 3, 8

_____

7. 9, 12

_____

8. 8, 10

_____

9. 6, 16

_____

10. 8, 96

_____

11. 2, 7, 10

_____

12. 4, 27, 36

_____

13. 3, 8, 18

_____

 Algebra Write the unknown number for the ▓.

14. 5, 8   LCM: ▓

▓ = _____

15. 5, ▓   LCM: 15

▓ = _____

16. ▓, 6   LCM: 42

▓ = _____

UNLOCK the Problem — REAL WORLD

17. Katie is making hair clips to sell at the craft fair. To make each hair clip, she uses 1 barrette and 1 precut ribbon. The barrettes are sold in packs of 12, and the precut ribbons are sold in packs of 9. How many packs of each item does she need to buy to make the least number of hair clips with no supplies left over?

a. What information are you given? _____

_____

_____

b. What problem are you being asked to solve? _____

_____

_____

c. Show the steps you use to solve the problem.

d. Complete the sentences.

The least common multiple of

12 and 9 is _____.

Katie can make _____ hair clips with no supplies left over.

To get 36 barrettes and 36 ribbons, she

needs to buy _____ packs of barrettes

and _____ packs of precut ribbons.

18. ⭐ **Test Prep** Mailing labels are sold in packages of 16. Envelopes are sold in packages of 20. What is the least number of labels and envelopes you can buy so that there is one label for each envelope with none left over?

Ⓐ 4 labels and 4 envelopes

Ⓑ 80 labels and 80 envelopes

Ⓒ 160 labels and 160 envelopes

Ⓓ 320 labels and 320 envelopes

19. ⭐ **Test Prep** Which pair of numbers has an LCM of 60?

Ⓐ 15, 20

Ⓑ 6, 10

Ⓒ 30, 2

Ⓓ 4, 20

FOR MORE PRACTICE:
Standards Practice Book, pp. P7–P8

Greatest Common Factor

Essential Question How can you find the greatest common factor of two whole numbers?

COMMON CORE STANDARD CC.6.NS.4
Compute fluently with multi-digit numbers and find common factors and multiples.

A **common factor** is a number that is a factor of two or more numbers. The numbers 16 and 20 have 1, 2, and 4 as common factors.

Factors of 16: 1, 2, 4, 8, 16

Factors of 20: 1, 2, 4, 5, 10, 20

The **greatest common factor**, or **GCF**, is the greatest factor that two or more numbers have in common. The greatest common factor of 16 and 20 is 4.

> **Remember**
>
> A number that is multiplied by another number to find a product is a factor.
>
> Factors of 6: 1, 2, 3, 6
>
> Factors of 9: 1, 3, 9
>
> Every number has 1 as a factor.

UNLOCK the Problem REAL WORLD

Jim is cutting two strips of wood to make picture frames. The wood strips measure 12 inches and 18 inches. He wants to cut the strips into equal lengths that are as long as possible. Into what lengths should he cut the wood?

12 inches

18 inches

Find the greatest common factor, or GCF, of 12 and 18.

One Way Use a list.

Factors of 12: 1, 2, _____, _____, _____, 12

Factors of 18: 1, _____, _____, _____, _____, _____

The greatest common factor, or GCF, is _____.

> **Math Talk** MATHEMATICAL PRACTICES
> Into what other lengths could Jim cut the wood to obtain equal lengths?

Another Way Use prime factorization.

Write the prime factorization of each number.

$12 = 2 \times$ _____ $\times 3$

$18 =$ _____ $\times 3 \times$ _____

Place the prime factors of the numbers in the appropriate parts of the Venn diagram.

To find the GCF, find the product of the common prime factors.

$2 \times 3 =$ _____   The GCF is _____.

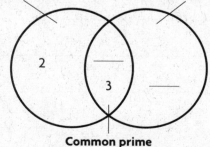

Prime factors of 12   **Prime factors of 18**

2   3

Common prime factors

So, Jim should cut the wood into _____-inch lengths.

Distributive Property

Multiplying a sum by a number is the same as multiplying each addend by the number and then adding the products.

$5 \times (8 + 6) = (5 \times 8) + (5 \times 6)$

You can use the Distributive Property to express the sum of two whole numbers as a product if the numbers have a common factor.

Example Use the GCF and the Distributive Property to express 36 + 27 as a product.

Find the GCF of 36 and 27.   GCF: _____

Write each number as the product $36 + 27$
of the GCF and another factor.
                                          $(9 \times \text{\_\_\_\_\_}) + (9 \times \text{\_\_\_\_\_})$

Use the Distributive Property to $9 \times (4 + \text{\_\_\_\_\_})$
write 36 + 27 as a product.

Check your answer. $36 + 27 = \text{\_\_\_\_\_}$

                                          $9 \times (4 + \text{\_\_\_\_\_}) = 9 \times \text{\_\_\_\_\_} = \text{\_\_\_\_\_}$

So, $36 + 27 = \text{\_\_\_\_\_} \times (\text{\_\_\_\_\_} + \text{\_\_\_\_\_})$.

---

1. Explain two ways to find the GCF of 36 and 27.

_____

_____

2. **Describe** how the figure at the right shows that
$36 + 27 = 9 \times (4 + 3)$.

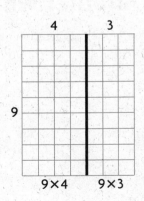

_____

_____

_____

_____

_____

Name _____

Share and Show

1. List the factors of 12 and 20. Circle the GCF.

   Factors of 12: _____

   Factors of 20: _____

Find the GCF.

2. 16, 18

   _____

3. 25, 40

   _____

✓ 4. 24, 40

   _____

5. 14, 35

   _____

Use the GCF and the Distributive Property to express the sum as a product.

6. 21 + 28

   _____

✓ 7. 15 + 27

   _____

8. 40 + 15

   _____

9. 32 + 20

   _____

Math Talk   MATHEMATICAL PRACTICES
Explain how to use the prime factorization of two numbers to find their GCF.

On Your Own

Find the GCF.

10. 8, 12

    _____

11. 27, 45

    _____

12. 30, 45

    _____

13. 42, 63

    _____

14. 8, 25

    _____

15. 31, 32

    _____

16. 56, 64

    _____

17. 150, 275

    _____

Use the GCF and the Distributive Property to express the sum as a product.

18. 24 + 30

    _____

19. 49 + 14

    _____

20. 63 + 81

    _____

21. 60 + 12

    _____

Problem Solving REAL WORLD

Use the table for 22–25. Teachers at the Scott School of Strings teach only one instrument in each class.

22. Francisco teaches group lessons to all of the violin and viola students at the Scott School of Strings. All of his classes have the same number of students. What is the greatest number of students he can have in each class?

_____

23. Amanda teaches music history lessons to all of the cello, viola, and violin students. All her classes have the same number of students. What is the greatest number of students she can have in each class?

_____

24. 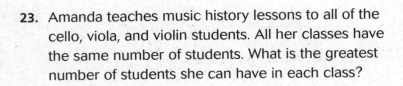 H.O.T. Mia teaches jazz classes. She has 9 students in each class, and she teaches all the students who play two instruments. How many students does she have, and which two instruments does she teach?

_____

25. Write Math ▶ **Explain** how you could use the GCF and the Distributive Property to express the sum of the number of bass students and the number of violin students as a product.

_____

_____

_____

_____

Scott School of Strings	
Instrument	**Number of Students**
Bass	20
Cello	27
Viola	30
Violin	36

SHOW YOUR WORK

26. ⭐ **Test Prep** Tina has 3 ribbons measuring 18 inches, 24 inches, and 36 inches. She wants to cut them into equal pieces that are as long as possible. Into what lengths should she cut the ribbons?

(A) 3 inches   (C) 6 inches

(B) 4 inches   (D) 12 inches

Name _____

Problem Solving • Apply the Greatest Common Factor

Essential Question How can you use the strategy *draw a diagram* to help you solve problems involving the GCF and the Distributive Property?

COMMON CORE STANDARD CC.6.NS.4
Compute fluently with multi-digit numbers and find common factors and multiples.

🔑 UNLOCK the Problem REAL WORLD

A trophy case at Riverside Middle School holds 18 baseball trophies and 24 soccer trophies. All shelves hold the same number of trophies. Only one sport is represented on each shelf. What is the greatest number of trophies that can be on each shelf? How many shelves are there for each sport?

Use the graphic organizer to help you solve the problem.

Read the Problem

What do I need to find?

I need to find _____

_____

_____

What information do I need to use?

I need to use _____

_____

How will I use the information?

I can find the GCF of _____ and use it to draw a diagram representing

the _____ of the trophy case.

Solve the Problem

Total trophies = baseball + soccer

$$18 + 24$$

Find the GCF of 18 and 24.   GCF: _____

Write each number as the product of the GCF and another factor.

$$18 + 24$$
$$(6 \times \text{\_\_\_\_}) + (6 \times \text{\_\_\_\_})$$

Use the Distributive Property to write 18 + 24 as a product.

$$6 \times (\text{\_\_\_\_} + \text{\_\_\_\_})$$

Use the product to draw a diagram of the trophy case. Use B's to represent baseball trophies. Use S's to represent soccer trophies.

B B B B B B
S S S S S S

Math Talk MATHEMATICAL PRACTICES
Explain how the Distributive Property helped you solve the problem.

So, there are _____ trophies on each shelf. There are _____ shelves of

baseball trophies and _____ shelves of soccer trophies.

🔑 Try Another Problem

Delia is bagging 24 onion bagels and 16 plain bagels for her bakery customers. Each bag will hold only one type of bagel. Each bag will hold the same number of bagels. What is the greatest number of bagels she can put in each bag? How many bags of each type of bagel will there be?

Use the graphic organizer to help you solve the problem.

Read the Problem	Solve the Problem
What do I need to find?	
What information do I need to use?	
How will I use the information?	

So, there will be _____ bagels in each bag. There will be

_____ bags of onion bagels and _____ bags of plain bagels.

- **Explain** how knowing that the GCF of 24 and 16 is 8 helped you solve the bagel problem.

_____

_____

Name _____

Share and Show

UNLOCK the Problem **Tips**

√ Circle important facts.
√ Check to make sure you answered the question.
√ Check your answer.

1. Toby is packaging 21 baseball cards and 12 football cards to sell at a flea market. Each packet will have the same number of cards. Each packet will have cards for only one sport. What is the greatest number of cards he can place in each packet? How many packets will there be for each sport?

   First, find the GCF of 21 and 12.

   _____

   Next, use the Distributive Property to write $21 + 12$ as a product, with the GCF as one of the factors.

   _____

   So, there will be _____ packets of baseball cards and

   _____ packets of football cards. Each packet will

   contain _____ cards.

SHOW YOUR WORK

2. **H.O.T.** **What if** Toby had decided to keep one baseball card for himself and sell the rest? How would your answers to the previous problem have changed?

   _____

   _____

   _____

   _____

3. Melissa bought 42 pine seedlings and 30 juniper seedlings to plant in rows on her tree farm. She wants each row to have the same number of seedlings. She wants only one type of seedling in each row. What is the greatest number of seedlings she can plant in each row? How many rows of each type of tree will there be?

   _____

   _____

   _____

© Houghton Mifflin Harcourt Publishing Company

On Your Own . . . .

Choose a STRATEGY

Use a Model
Draw a Diagram
Find a Pattern
Solve a Simpler Problem
Work Backward
Use a Formula

4. A drum and bugle marching band has 45 members who play bugles and 27 members who play drums. When they march, each row has the same number of players. Each row has only bugle players or only drummers. What is the greatest number of players there can be in each row? How many rows of each type of player can there be?

_____

_____

SHOW YOUR WORK

5. **H.O.T.** The "color guard" of a drum and bugle band consists of members who march with flags, hoops, and other props. How would your answers to Exercise 4 change if there were 21 color guard members marching along with the bugle players and drummers?

_____

_____

_____

6. **Write Math** ► What is the next number in the pattern below? Explain how you found the number.

1, 2, 4, 7, 11, 16, 22, ___?___

_____

_____

_____

_____

_____

7. ⭐ **Test Prep** A total of 36 math students and 54 science students are traveling to the Math-Science Olympiad. All buses will carry the same number of students. Each bus will carry either math students or science students. If buses are to carry the greatest possible number of students, how many buses will be needed?

(A) 5   (C) 15

(B) 10   (D) 30

FOR MORE PRACTICE:
Standards Practice Book, pp. P11–P12

✓ Mid-Chapter Checkpoint

▶ Vocabulary

Choose the best term from the box to complete the sentence.

Vocabulary
greatest common factor
least common multiple
prime number

1. The _____ of two numbers is greater than or equal to the numbers. (p.13)

2. The _____ of two numbers is less than or equal to the numbers. (p.17)

▶ Concepts and Skills

Estimate. Then find the quotient. Write the remainder, if any, with an r. (CC.6.NS.2)

3. $2,800 \div 25$

4. $19,129 \div 37$

5. $32,111 \div 181$

_____

_____

_____

Find the prime factorization. (CC.6.NS.4)

6. 44

7. 36

8. 90

_____

_____

_____

Find the LCM. (CC.6.NS.4)

9. 8, 10

10. 4, 14

11. 6, 9

_____

_____

_____

Find the GCF. (CC.6.NS.4)

12. 16, 20

13. 8, 52

14. 36, 54

_____

_____

_____

Fill in the bubble to show your answer.

★TEST PREP

15. A zookeeper divided 2,440 pounds of food equally among 8 elephants. How many pounds of food did each elephant receive? (CC.6.NS.2)

Ⓐ 35 pounds

Ⓑ 70 pounds

Ⓒ 305 pounds

Ⓓ 350 pounds

16. DVD cases are sold in packages of 20. Padded mailing envelopes are sold in packets of 12. What is the least number of cases and envelopes you could buy so that there is one case for each envelope with none left over? (CC.6.NS.4)

Ⓐ 32 cases and 32 envelopes

Ⓑ 60 cases and 60 envelopes

Ⓒ 120 cases and 120 envelopes

Ⓓ 240 cases and 240 envelopes

17. Max bought two deli sandwich rolls measuring 18 inches and 30 inches. He wants them to be cut into equal sections that are as long as possible. Into what lengths should the rolls be cut? (CC.6.NS.4)

Ⓐ 2 inches   Ⓒ 6 inches

Ⓑ 3 inches   Ⓓ 9 inches

18. Susan is buying supplies for a party. If spoons only come in bags of 8 and forks only come in bags of 6, what is the least number of spoons and the least number of forks she can buy so that she has the same number of each? (CC.6.NS.4)

Ⓐ 2 spoons and 2 forks

Ⓑ 12 spoons and 12 forks

Ⓒ 18 spoons and 18 forks

Ⓓ 24 spoons and 24 forks

19. Tina is placing 30 roses and 42 tulips in vases for table decorations in her restaurant. Each vase will hold the same number of flowers. Each vase will have only one type of flower. What is the greatest number of flowers she can place in each vase? (CC.6.NS.4)

Ⓐ 3   Ⓒ 12

Ⓑ 6   Ⓓ 18

Add and Subtract Decimals

Essential Question How do you add and subtract multi-digit decimals?

COMMON CORE STANDARD CC.6.NS.3
Compute fluently with multi-digit numbers and find common factors and multiples.

CONNECT The place value of a digit in a number shows the value of the digit. The number 2.358 shows 2 ones, 3 tenths, 5 hundredths, and 8 thousandths.

Place Value						
Thousands	Hundreds	Tens	Ones	Tenths	Hundredths	Thousandths
			2	3	5	8

🔑 UNLOCK the Problem — REAL WORLD

Amanda and three of her friends volunteer at the local animal shelter. One of their jobs is to weigh the puppies and kittens and chart their growth. Amanda's favorite puppy weighed 2.358 lb last month. If it gained 1.08 lb, how much does it weigh this month?

- How do you know whether to add or subtract the weights given in the problem?

_____

_____

🔒 **Add 2.358 + 1.08.**

Estimate the sum. _____ + _____ = _____

Add the thousandths first.

Then add the hundredths, tenths, and ones.

Regroup as needed.

$$\begin{array}{r} 2.358 \\ + 1.08 \\ \hline \end{array}$$

Compare your estimate with the sum. Since the estimate,

_____, is close to _____, the answer is reasonable.

So, the puppy weighs _____ lb this month.

1. Is it necessary to add a zero after 1.08 to find the sum? **Explain.**

_____

2. **Explain** how place value can help you add decimals.

_____

🔒 Example 1

A bee hummingbird, the world's smallest bird, has a mass of 1.836 grams. A new United States nickel has a mass of 5 grams. What is the difference in grams between the mass of a nickel and the mass of a bee hummingbird?

Subtract 5 − 1.836.

Estimate the difference. _____ − _____ = _____

Think: 5 = 5._____

Subtract the thousandths first.

Then subtract the hundredths, tenths, and ones.

Regroup as needed.

$$\begin{array}{r} 5. \\ -1.836 \\ \hline \end{array}$$

Compare your estimate with the difference. Since the estimate,

_____, is close to _____, the answer is reasonable.

So, the mass of a new nickel is _____ grams more than the mass of a bee hummingbird.

Bee hummingbird

U.S. Nickel

Math Talk MATHEMATICAL PRACTICES
Explain how to use inverse operations to check your answer to 5 − 1.836.

🔒 Example 2 Evaluate (6.5 − 1.97) + 3.461 using the order of operations.

Write the expression.

$$(6.5 - 1.97) + 3.461$$

Perform operations in parentheses.

$$\begin{array}{r} 6.50 \\ -1.97 \\ \hline \end{array}$$

Add.

$$\begin{array}{r} \\ +3.461 \\ \hline \end{array}$$

So, the value of the expression is _____.

Math Talk MATHEMATICAL PRACTICES
Describe how adding and subtracting decimals is like adding and subtracting whole numbers.

Name _____

Share and Show

1. Find $3.42 - 1.9$.

Estimate. _____

_____ − _____ = _____

Subtract the _____ first.

$$\begin{array}{r} 3.42 \\ -1.90 \\ \hline \end{array}$$

Estimate. Then find the sum or difference.

2. $2.3 + 5.68 + 21.047$

3. $33.25 - 21.463$

4. Evaluate $(8.54 + 3.46) - 6.749$.

Math Talk MATHEMATICAL PRACTICES
Explain why it is important to align the decimal points when you add or subtract decimals.

On Your Own

Estimate. Then find the sum or difference.

5. $57.08 + 34.71$

6. $20.11 - 13.27$

7. $62 - 9.817$

8. $35.1 + 4.89$

Practice: Copy and Solve Evaluate using the order of operations.

9. $8.01 - (2.2 + 4.67)$

10. $54 + (9.2 - 1.413)$

11. $(3.26 + 1.51) + 4.77$

12. $(2.4 + 13.913) - 0.92$

13. $21.3 - (19.1 - 3.22)$

14. $23.7 + (96.5 + 9.25)$

15. **H.O.T.** **What's the error?** A student subtracted $6.85 - 4.7$ and got 6.38. What is the correct answer? **Explain** the error.

Comparing Eggs

Different types of birds lay eggs of different sizes. Small birds lay eggs that are smaller than those that are laid by larger birds. The table shows the average lengths and widths of five different birds' eggs.

Canada Goose

Average Dimensions of Bird Eggs		
Bird	**Length (m)**	**Width (m)**
Canada Goose	0.086	0.058
Hummingbird	0.013	0.013
Raven	0.049	0.033
Robin	0.019	0.015
Turtledove	0.031	0.023

Use the table for 16–19.

16. What is the difference in average length between the longest egg and the shortest egg?

   _____

17. Which egg has a width that is eight thousandths of a meter shorter than its length?

   _____

18. How many robin eggs, laid end to end, would be about equal in length to two raven eggs? Justify your answer.

   _____

   _____

   _____

19. A perfectly spherical egg would have an equal length and width. Which egg is closest to spherical? Justify your answer.

   _____

   _____

FOR MORE PRACTICE:
Standards Practice Book, pp. P13–P14

Multiply Decimals

Essential Question How do you multiply multi-digit decimals?

COMMON CORE STANDARD CC.6.NS.3
Compute fluently with multi-digit numbers and find common factors and multiples.

UNLOCK the Problem REAL WORLD

Last summer Rachel worked 38.5 hours per week at a grocery store. She earned $9.70 per hour. How much did she earn in a week?

Multiply $9.70 × 38.5.

First estimate the product. $10 × 40 = _____

You can use the estimate to place the decimal in a product.

$$\begin{array}{r} \$9.70 \\ \times 38.5 \\ \hline \end{array}$$

Multiply as you would with whole numbers.

The estimate is about $ _____,

so the decimal point should be

placed after $ _____.

$$\begin{array}{r} + \underline{} \\ \$ \end{array}$$

• How can you estimate the product?

_____

_____

Since the estimate, _____, is close to _____, the answer is reasonable.

So, Rachel earned _____ per week.

---

1. **Explain** how your estimate helped you know where to place the decimal in the product.

_____

_____

Try This! **What if** Rachel gets a raise of $1.50 per hour? How much will she earn when she works 38.5 hours?

© Houghton Mifflin Harcourt Publishing Company

Counting Decimal Places Another way to place the decimal in a product is to add the numbers of decimal places in the factors.

🔑 Example 1 Multiply 0.084 × 0.096.

$$0.084$$
$$\times 0.096$$

_____ decimal places

_____ decimal places

Multiply as you would with whole numbers.

+ _____

_____ + _____, or _____ decimal places

🔑 Example 2 Evaluate 0.35 × (0.48 + 1.24) using the order of operations.

Write the expression.

$$0.35 \times (0.48 + 1.24)$$

Perform operations in parentheses.

$$0.35 \times \underline{\hspace{1.5cm}}$$

Multiply.

0.35   _____ decimal places

× _____   _____ decimal places

+ _____

_____ + _____, or _____ decimal places

So, the value of the expression is _____.

MATHEMATICAL PRACTICES

Math Talk Is the product of 0.5 and 3.052 greater than or less than 3.052? Explain.

2. Look for a pattern. **Explain.**

$0.645 \times 1 = 0.645$

$0.645 \times 10 = 6.45$ The decimal point moves _____ place to the right.

$0.645 \times 100 = $ _____   The decimal point moves _____ places to the right.

$0.645 \times 1,000 = $ _____   The decimal point moves _____ places to the right.

_____

_____

Name _____

Share and Show ....

Estimate. Then find the product.

1. 12.42 × 28.6

_____ × _____ = _____

$$12.42$$
$$\times\ 28.6$$

Estimate.

Think: The estimate is about _____, so the decimal point should be placed after _____.

✓ **2.** 32.5 × 7.4

_____

Algebra Evaluate using the order of operations.

3. 0.24 × (7.3 + 2.1)

✓ 4. 0.075 × (9.2 − 0.8)

5. 2.83 + (0.3 × 2.16)

_____

_____

_____

Math Talk MATHEMATICAL PRACTICES
Explain how estimation helps you know where to place the decimal in a product.

On Your Own ....

Estimate. Then find the product.

6. 29.14 × 5.2

7. 6.95 × 12

8. 0.055 × 1.82

_____

_____

_____

Algebra Evaluate using the order of operations.

9. (3.62 × 2.1) − 0.749

10. 5.8 − (0.25 × 1.5)

11. (0.83 + 1.27) × 6.4

_____

_____

_____

12. Sense or Nonsense? Reggie wrote that 21.5 × 5.4 = 11.61. Is Reggie's statement sense or nonsense? **Explain**.

_____

UNLOCK the Problem REAL WORLD

Use the table for 13–15.

The table shows some currency exchange rates for 2009. Read across each row to find equivalent amounts of each type of currency.

Major Currency Exchange Rates in 2009				
Currency	U.S. Dollar	Japanese Yen	European Euro	Canadian Dollar
U.S. Dollar	1	88.353	0.676	1.052
Japanese Yen	0.011	1	0.008	0.012
European Euro	1.479	130.692	1	1.556
Canadian Dollar	0.951	83.995	0.643	1

Different denominations of Euro

13. When Cameron went to Canada in 2007, he exchanged 40 U.S. dollars for 46.52 Canadian dollars. If Cameron exchanged 40 U.S. dollars in 2009, how much did he receive in Canadian dollars? Did he receive more or less than he received in 2007? How much more or less?

a. What do you need to find?

_____

_____

b. How will you use the table to solve the problem?

_____

_____

_____

_____

c. Complete the sentences.

40 U.S. dollars were worth _____ Canadian dollars in 2009.

So, Cameron would receive _____

_____ Canadian dollars in 2009.

14. **H.O.T.** Based on the exchange rates in the table, which is more valuable, 1 U.S. dollar or 1 euro? **Explain**.

_____

_____

_____

15. ★ **Test Prep** Mr. Jackson needs to exchange his euros for yen. How many yen will he receive if he exchanges 30 euros? Round your answer to the nearest yen.

(A)   0.24 yen   (C)   3,921 yen

(B) 3,900 yen   (D) 16,337 yen

Divide Decimals by Whole Numbers

Essential Question How do you divide decimals by whole numbers?

COMMON CORE STANDARD CC.6.NS.3
Compute fluently with multi-digit numbers and find common factors and multiples.

UNLOCK the Problem REAL WORLD

Dan opened a savings account at a bank to save for a new snowboard. He earned $3.48 interest on his savings account over a 3-month period. What was the average amount of interest Dan earned per month on his savings account?

 Divide $3.48 ÷ 3.

First estimate. 3 ÷ 3 = _____

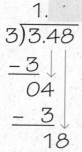

```
   1.
3)3.48
 -3 ↓
   04
  - 3 ↓
     18
    -18
      0
```

Remember

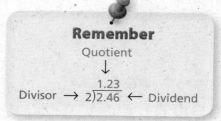

Quotient
↓
1.23
Divisor → 2)2.46 ← Dividend

Think: 3.48 is shared among 3 groups.

Divide the ones. Place a decimal point after the ones place in the quotient.

Divide the tenths and then the hundredths. When the remainder is zero and there are no more digits in the dividend, the division is complete.

Check your answer.

```
  $ 
×       3
 $3.48
```

Multiply the quotient by the divisor to check your answer.

So, Dan earned an average of _____ in interest per month.

Math Talk MATHEMATICAL PRACTICES
Explain how you know your answer is reasonable.

1. **What if** the same amount of interest was gained over 4 months?
   Explain how you would solve the problem.

_____

🔑 Example Divide 42.133 ÷ 7.

First estimate. 42 ÷ 7 = _____

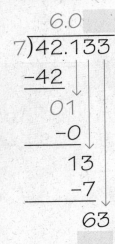

```
    6.0
  _____
7)42.133
 −42 ↓
  _____
   01
  −0 ↓
  _____
   13
  −7 ↓
  _____
    63
   −
  _____
```

Think: 42.133 is shared among 7 groups.

Divide the ones. Place a decimal point after the ones place in the quotient.

Divide the tenths. Since 1 tenth cannot be shared among 7 groups, write a zero in the quotient. Regroup the 1 tenth as 10 hundredths. Now you have 13 hundredths.

Continue to divide until the remainder is zero and there are no more digits in the dividend.

Check your answer.

```
  6.019
×     7
_____
```

Multiply the quotient by the divisor to check your answer.

So, 42.133 ÷ 7 = _____.

2. **Explain** how you know which numbers to multiply when checking your answer.

_____

_____

Share and Show . . . .

1. Estimate 24.186 ÷ 6. Then find the quotient. Check your answer.

Estimate. _____ ÷ _____ = _____

Think: Place a decimal point after the ones place in the quotient.

```
6)24.186        ×     6
```

Name _____

Share and Show

Estimate. Then find the quotient.

2. $7\overline{)\$17.15}$ ✓ 3. $4\overline{)1.068}$ 4. $12\overline{)60.84}$ ✓ 5. $18.042 \div 6$

Math Talk MATHEMATICAL PRACTICES
Explain how you know where to place the decimal point in the quotient when dividing a decimal by a whole number.

On Your Own

Estimate. Then find the quotient.

6. $9\overline{)461.7}$ 7. $15\overline{)45.75}$ 8. $8\overline{)0.744}$ 9. $19\overline{)8.17}$

10. $\$21.24 \div 6$ 11. $28.63 \div 7$ 12. $1.505 \div 35$ 13. $0.108 \div 18$

Algebra Evaluate using the order of operations.

14. $(3.11 + 4.0) \div 9$ 15. $(6.18 - 1.32) \div 3$ 16. $(18 - 5.76) \div 6$

Problem Solving  REAL WORLD

Pose a Problem

17. This table shows the average height in inches for girls and boys at ages 8, 10, 12, and 14 years.

Average Height (in.)				
	Age 8	Age 10	Age 12	Age 14
Girls	50.75	55.50	60.50	62.50
Boys	51.00	55.25	59.00	65.20

To find the average growth per year for girls from age 8 to age 12, Emma knew she had to find the amount of growth between age 8 and age 12, then divide that number by the number of years between age 8 and age 12.

Emma used this expression: $(60.50 - 50.75) \div 4$

She evaluated the expression using the order of operations.

Write the expression.	$(60.50 - 50.75) \div 4$
Perform operations in parentheses.	$9.75 \div 4$
Divide.	2.4375

So, the average annual growth for girls ages 8–12 is 2.4375 inches.

Write a new problem using the information in the table for the average height for boys. Use division in your problem.

Pose a Problem	**Solve Your Problem**
_____ _____ _____	

18. 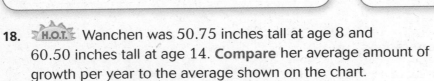 Wanchen was 50.75 inches tall at age 8 and 60.50 inches tall at age 14. **Compare** her average amount of growth per year to the average shown on the chart.

_____

_____

_____

FOR MORE PRACTICE:
Standards Practice Book, pp. P17–P18

Divide with Decimals

Essential Question How do you divide whole numbers and decimals by decimals?

COMMON CORE STANDARD CC.6.NS.3
Compute fluently with multi-digit numbers and find common factors and multiples.

CONNECT Find each quotient to discover a pattern.

$4 \div 2 =$ _____

$40 \div 20 =$ _____

$400 \div 200 =$ _____

When you multiply both the dividend and the divisor by the same

power of _____, the quotient is the _____. You can use this fact to help you divide decimals.

🔑 UNLOCK the Problem REAL WORLD

Tami is training for a triathlon. In a triathlon, athletes compete in three events: swimming, cycling, and running. She cycled 66.5 miles in 3.5 hours. If she cycled at a constant speed, how far did she cycle in 1 hour?

> **Remember**
> Compatible numbers are pairs of numbers that are easy to compute mentally.

🔑 **Divide 66.5 ÷ 3.5.**

Estimate using compatible numbers.

$60 \div 3 =$ _____

STEP 1

Make the divisor a whole number by multiplying the divisor and dividend by 10.

$3.5\overline{)66.5}$

Think: $3.5 \times 10 = 35$ $66.5 \times 10 = 665$

STEP 2

Divide.

$35\overline{)665}$

So, Tami cycled _____ in 1 hour.

• **Explain** whether your answer is reasonable.

_____

Example 1 Divide 17.25 ÷ 5.75. Check.

STEP 1

Make the divisor a whole number by multiplying the divisor and dividend by _____.

5.75 × _____ = _____

17.25 × _____ = _____

$$5.75\overline{)17.25}$$

STEP 2

Divide.

$$575\overline{)1{,}725}$$

STEP 3

Check.

So, 17.25 ÷ 5.75 = _____.

Example 2 Divide 37.8 ÷ 0.14.

STEP 1

Make the divisor a whole number by multiplying the divisor and dividend by _____.

_____ × _____ = _____

_____ × _____ = _____

$$0.14\overline{)37.80}$$

Think: Add a zero to the right of the dividend so that you can move the decimal point.

❗ ERROR Alert

Be careful to move the decimal point in the dividend the same number of places that you moved the decimal point in the divisor.

STEP 2

Divide.

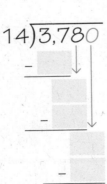

So, 37.8 ÷ 0.14 = _____.

Math Talk MATHEMATICAL PRACTICES
Explain how to check the quotient.

Name _____

Share and Show

1. Find the quotient.

Think: Make the divisor a whole number by

multiplying the divisor and dividend by _____.

$$14.8\overline{)99.456}$$

Estimate. Then find the quotient.

2. $10.80 ÷ $1.35

3. 26.4 ÷ 1.76

4. $8.7\overline{)53.07}$

> **Math Talk** MATHEMATICAL PRACTICES
> **Explain** how you know how many places to move the decimal point in the divisor and the dividend.

On Your Own

Estimate. Then find the quotient.

5. 75 ÷ 12.5

6. 544.6 ÷ 1.75

7. $2.7\overline{)22.41}$

Practice: Copy and Solve Find the quotient.

8. 2.64 ÷ 0.2

9. 1.43 ÷ 1.1

10. $0.3\overline{)3.15}$

11. $0.78\overline{)0.234}$

Algebra Evaluate using the order of operations.

12. 36.4 + (9.2 − 4.9 ÷ 7)

13. 16 ÷ 2.5 − 3.2 × 0.043

14. 142 ÷ (42 − 6.5) × 3.9

© Houghton Mifflin Harcourt Publishing Company

Amoebas

Amoebas are tiny one-celled organisms. Their flexible outer membranes enable them to constantly change the shape of their bodies. Amoebas can range in size from 0.01 mm to 5 mm in length. You can study amoebas by using a microscope or by studying photographic enlargements of them.

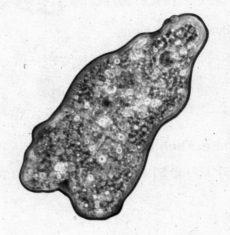

Jacob has a photograph of an amoeba that has been enlarged 1,000 times. The length of the amoeba in the photo is 60 mm. What is the actual length of the amoeba?

Divide 60 ÷ 1,000 by looking for a pattern.

60 ÷ 1 = 60

60 ÷ 10 = 6.0   The decimal point moves _____ place to the left.

60 ÷ 100 = _____   The decimal point moves _____ places to the left.

60 ÷ 1,000 = _____   The decimal point moves _____ places to the left.

So, the actual length of the amoeba is _____ mm.

15. **Explain** the pattern.

_____

_____

16. Jacob has a photograph of *Amoeba proteus* that has been enlarged 100 times. In the photo, the amoeba appears to have a length of 70 mm. What is its actual length? Explain your reasoning.

_____

_____

17. *Pelomyxa palustris* is the largest amoeba found in pond water. Some specimens are as large as 4.9 mm in length. How long would this amoeba appear in a photograph enlarged 1,000 times? Justify your answer.

_____

_____

FOR MORE PRACTICE:
Standards Practice Book, pp. P19–P20

Name _____

 Chapter 1 Review/Test

▶ Vocabulary

Choose the best term from the box to complete the sentence.

1. An example of _____ is 18 = 2 × 3 × 3. (p. 9)

2. The smallest number, other than zero, that is a common multiple of two or more numbers is the

   _____. (p. 13)

▶ Concepts and Skills

Find the LCM. (CC.6.NS.4)

3. 4, 16

4. 12, 8

5. 6, 10

6. 3, 5, 15

Find the GCF. (CC.6.NS.4)

7. 15, 18

8. 18, 27

9. 48, 56

10. 60, 72

Estimate. Then find the sum or difference. (CC.6.NS.3)

11. 7.6 + 3.2 + 22.8

12. 452.3 − 74.06

13. 520.85
    − 93.807

14. 54
     0.7
    + 11.23

Estimate. Then find the product or quotient. (CC.6.NS.3)

15. 375.1 × 0.9

16. 0.7 × 0.3

17. 3.276 ÷ 42

18. 9.2)619.16

GO Online · Assessment Options · Chapter Test

Fill in the bubble to show your answer.

19. Crackers come in packages of 24. Cheese slices come in packages of 18. You want one cheese slice for each cracker. What is the least number of crackers and cheese slices you can buy so that nothing is left over? (CC.6.NS.4)

Ⓐ 6 crackers and 6 cheese slices

Ⓑ 48 crackers and 48 cheese slices

Ⓒ 60 crackers and 60 cheese slices

Ⓓ 72 crackers and 72 cheese slices

20. A lumberyard worker is cutting three tree trunks into equal sections. The trunks measure 28 feet, 14 feet, and 42 feet. If the sections are as long as possible, how long should each section be? (CC.6.NS.4)

Ⓐ 3 feet

Ⓑ 7 feet

Ⓒ 14 feet

Ⓓ 16 feet

21. A movie theater has 250 seats. 3,250 tickets were sold at the theater last week. How many movies were shown at the theater last week if every person who bought a ticket saw a movie and every seat was filled for each feature? (CC.6.NS.2)

Ⓐ 11   Ⓒ 15

Ⓑ 13   Ⓓ 130

22. Lana paid $36.72 for 4 CDs. What was the average cost of each CD? (CC.6.NS.3)

Ⓐ $9.18

Ⓑ $9.28

Ⓒ $12.24

Ⓓ $148.88

23. Mr. DeLuca had $568.34 in a bank account. How much money did he have left in his bank account after he used his debit card two times, each time for $27.50? (CC.6.NS.3)

Ⓐ $513.34   Ⓒ $540.84

Ⓑ $523.34   Ⓓ $595.84

Fill in the bubble to show your answer.

24. The distance around the outside of Cedar Park is 0.8 mile. Joanie ran 0.25 of the distance during her lunch break. How far did she run? (CC.6.NS.3)

Ⓐ 0.2 mile   Ⓒ 1.05 miles

Ⓑ 0.25 mile   Ⓓ 2 miles

25. Zoe earned $28.38 working for 3.3 hours. How much did she earn per hour? (CC.6.NS.3)

Ⓐ $8.30

Ⓑ $8.33

Ⓒ $8.56

Ⓓ $8.60

26. A one-celled organism measures 32 millimeters in length in a photograph. If the photo has been enlarged by a factor of 100, what is the actual length of the organism? (CC.6.NS.3)

Ⓐ   0.32 millimeter

Ⓑ   3.2 millimeters

Ⓒ   320 millimeters

Ⓓ 3,200 millimeters

27. You can buy 5 T-shirts at Baxter's for the same price that you can buy 4 T-shirts at Bixby's. If one T-shirt costs $11.80 at Bixby's, how much does one T-shirt cost at Baxter's? (CC.6.NS.3)

Ⓐ $9.44

Ⓑ $10.80

Ⓒ $11.55

Ⓓ $14.75

28. The men's world record for the high jump is 2.45 meters. A puma can jump about 1.9 times as high. What is the height a puma can jump? (CC.6.NS.3)

Ⓐ 4.5 meters

Ⓑ 4.555 meters

Ⓒ 4.565 meters

Ⓓ 4.655 meters

29. Use prime factorization to find the LCM of 10 and 12. Explain how you determined your answer. (CC.6.NS.4)

_____

_____

_____

30. To estimate the quotient 98.3 ÷ 52.6, Brady used compatible numbers: 100 ÷ 5 = 20. Is his estimate reasonable? Explain.
(CC.6.NS.3)

_____

_____

_____

▶ **Performance Task** (CC.6.NS.4)

31. There are 16 sixth graders and 20 seventh graders in the Robotics Club. For the first project, the club sponsor wants to organize the club members into equal-size groups. Each group will have only sixth graders or only seventh graders.

A The club sponsor thinks there should be at least 3 students in each group to complete the project. Is this possible? Justify your answer.

_____

_____

B If each group has the greatest possible number of club members, how many groups of sixth graders and how many groups of seventh graders will there be? Explain.

_____

_____

C Explain how you could use the Distributive Property to show that your answer to Part B is correct. Show your work.

_____

_____

_____

Show What You Know ✓

Check your understanding of important skills.

Name _____

▶ **Compare and Order Whole Numbers** Compare.
Write <, >, or = for the ◯.

1. 289 ◯ 291

2. 476,225 ◯ 476,225

3. 5,823 ◯ 5,286

4. 30,189 ◯ 30,201

▶ **Benchmark Fractions** Write whether the fraction is closest to 0, $\frac{1}{2}$ or 1.

5. $\frac{3}{5}$ _____

6. $\frac{6}{7}$ _____

7. $\frac{1}{6}$ _____

8. $\frac{1}{3}$ _____

▶ **Multiply Fractions and Whole Numbers** Find the product. Write it in simplest form.

9. $\frac{2}{3} \times 21$

10. $\frac{1}{4} \times 10$

11. $6 \times \frac{2}{9}$

12. $\frac{3}{4} \times 14$

13. $35 \times \frac{2}{5}$

14. $\frac{3}{8} \times 12$

MATH DETECTIVE

WITH

CARMEN SANDIEGO™

Cyndi bought an extra large pizza, cut into 12 pieces, for today's meeting of the Mystery Club. She ate $\frac{1}{6}$ of the pizza yesterday afternoon. Her brother ate $\frac{1}{5}$ of what was left last night. Cyndi knows that she needs 8 pieces of pizza for the club meeting. Be a Math Detective and help Cyndi figure out if she has enough pizza left for the meeting.

Vocabulary Builder

▶ **Visualize It** ••

Complete the Bubble Map using review words that are related
to fractions.

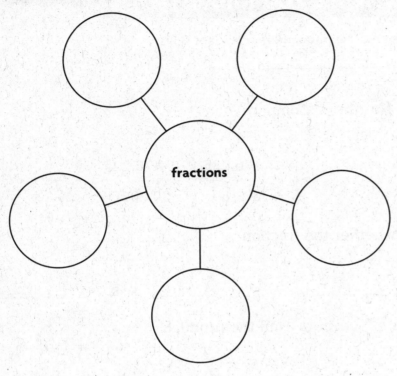

fractions

Review Words

✓ benchmark

✓ compatible numbers

denominator

equivalent fractions

fractions

mixed numbers

numerator

✓ simplest form

Preview Words

✓ multiplicative inverse

✓ reciprocal

✓ repeating decimal

✓ terminating decimal

▶ **Understand Vocabulary** •••••••••••••••••••••••••••••••••

Complete the sentences using the checked words.

1. _____ are numbers that are easy to
   compute with mentally.

2. One of two numbers whose product is 1 is a

   _____ or a _____.

3. A _____ is a reference point that is used for
   estimating fractions.

4. When the numerator and denominator of a fraction have only

   1 as a common factor, the fraction is in _____.

5. A _____ is a decimal representation of a
   number that has a repeating pattern that continues endlessly.

6. A _____ is a decimal representation of a
   number that eventually ends.

GO
Online

• eStudent Edition • Multimedia eGlossary

Name _____

Fractions and Decimals

Essential Question How can you convert between fractions and decimals?

COMMON CORE STANDARD CC.6.NS.6c
Apply and extend previous understandings of numbers to the system of rational numbers.

CONNECT You can use place value to write a decimal as a fraction or a mixed number.

Place Value			
Ones	**Tenths**	**Hundredths**	**Thousandths**
1 .	2	3	4

 UNLOCK the Problem REAL WORLD

The African pygmy hedgehog is a popular pet in North America. The average African pygmy hedgehog weighs between 0.5 lb and 1.25 lb. How can these weights be written as fractions or mixed numbers?

🔒 **Write 0.5 as a fraction and 1.25 as a mixed number in simplest form.**

• How do you know if a fraction is in simplest form?

_____

_____

_____

A 0.5

0.5 is five _____.

$$0.5 = \frac{5}{\quad}$$

Simplify using the GCF.

The GCF of 5 and 10 is _____.

$$\frac{5}{\quad} = \frac{5 \div \quad}{\quad \div \quad} = \frac{\quad}{\quad}$$

Divide the numerator and

the denominator by _____.

B 1.25

1.25 is one and

$$1.25 = 1\frac{\quad}{\quad}$$

_____.

Simplify using the GCF.

The GCF of 25 and 100 is _____.

$$1\frac{\quad}{\quad} = 1\frac{\quad \div \quad}{\quad \div \quad} = 1\frac{\quad}{\quad}$$

Divide the numerator and

the denominator by _____.

So, the average African pygmy hedgehog weighs between

_____ lb and _____ lb.

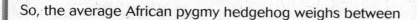

Math Talk MATHEMATICAL PRACTICES
Explain how you can use place value to write 0.05 and 0.005 as fractions. Then write the fractions in simplest form.

Terminating and Repeating Decimals You can use division to write a fraction or a mixed number as a decimal.

 Example Write the mixed number or fraction as a decimal. Tell whether the decimal terminates or repeats.

A $6\frac{3}{8}$

A **terminating decimal** eventually ends.

STEP 1

Use division to rename the fraction part as a decimal.

The quotient has _____ decimal places.

_____

$$8\overline{)3.000}$$

$$0$$

STEP 2

Add the whole number to the decimal.

$6 +$ _____ $=$ _____

So, $6\frac{3}{8} =$ _____ . The decimal form of $6\frac{3}{8}$ _____ .

> **Math Talk** MATHEMATICAL PRACTICES
> Explain why zeros were placed after the decimal point in the dividend.

B $\frac{5}{11}$

A **repeating decimal** has one or more digits that repeat endlessly.

STEP 1

Use division to rename the fraction as a decimal.

The digits _____ repeat in the quotient.

_____

$$
\begin{array}{r}
0.45 \\
11\overline{)5.0000} \\
-44 \\
\hline
60 \\
-55 \\
\hline
\\
\\
5
\end{array}
$$

STEP 2

Write the repeating decimal.

$\frac{5}{11} = 0.454545...$ $\frac{5}{11} = 0.\overline{45}$

So, $\frac{5}{11} =$ _____ or _____ .

The decimal form of $\frac{5}{11}$ _____ .

> **Math Idea**
> To write a repeating decimal, show the pattern and then three dots, or draw a bar over the repeating digits.

Name _____

Share and Show

Write as a fraction or as a mixed number in simplest form.

1. $95.5 = 95\dfrac{5}{\boxed{}} = \boxed{}$

2. 0.6

3. 5.75

Write as a decimal. Tell whether the decimal terminates or repeats.

4. $\dfrac{7}{8}$

5. $\dfrac{2}{3}$

6. $\dfrac{3}{25}$

Math Talk MATHEMATICAL PRACTICES
Explain how you know a fraction is equivalent to a repeating decimal.

On Your Own

Write as a fraction or as a mixed number in simplest form.

7. 0.27

8. 0.055

9. 2.45

Write as a decimal. Tell whether the decimal terminates or repeats.

10. $\dfrac{1}{6}$

11. $3\dfrac{1}{5}$

12. $2\dfrac{11}{20}$

Identify a decimal and a fraction in simplest form for the point.

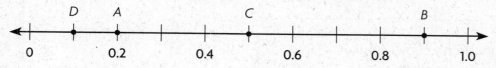

13. Point A

14. Point B

15. Point C

16. Point D

© Houghton Mifflin Harcourt Publishing Company

Problem Solving REAL WORLD

Use the table for 17–19.

17. Members of the Ozark Trail Hiking Club hiked a steep section of the trail in June and July. The table shows the distances club members hiked in miles. Write Maria's July distance as a decimal.

   _____

18. Write Kelsey's June hiking distance as a fraction or mixed number in simplest form.

   _____

19. How much farther did Zoey hike in July than in June? **Explain** how you found your answer.

   _____

   _____

20. **H.O.T.** **What's the Error?** Tabitha's hiking distance in July was $2\frac{1}{6}$ miles. She wrote the distance as 2.16 miles. What error did she make?

   _____

   _____

   _____

21. **Write Math** ▶ Write $\frac{4}{9}$, $\frac{5}{9}$, and $\frac{6}{9}$ as decimals. What pattern do you see? Use the pattern to predict the decimal form of $\frac{7}{9}$ and $\frac{8}{9}$.

   _____

   _____

   _____

22. ⭐ **Test Prep** Winona's measuring cup is $\frac{2}{3}$ full of water. What is this amount as a decimal?

   (A) 0.6   (C) 0.62

   (B) $0.\overline{6}$ (D) $0.6\overline{2}$

Ozark Trail Hiking Club

Hiker	June	July
Maria	2.95	$2\frac{5}{8}$
Devin	3.25	$3\frac{1}{8}$
Kelsey	3.15	$2\frac{7}{8}$
Zoey	2.85	$3\frac{3}{8}$

SHOW YOUR WORK

© Houghton Mifflin Harcourt Publishing Company

FOR MORE PRACTICE:
Standards Practice Book, pp. P25–P26

Compare and Order Fractions and Decimals

Essential Question How can you compare and order fractions and decimals?

COMMON CORE STANDARD CC.6.NS.6c
Apply and extend previous understandings of numbers to the system of rational numbers.

To compare fractions with the same denominators, compare the numerators. To compare fractions with the same numerators, compare the denominators.

Same Denominators

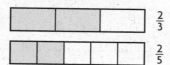

$\frac{2}{3}$

$\frac{1}{3}$

Two of three equal parts is greater than one of three equal parts.

So, $\frac{2}{3} > \frac{1}{3}$.

Same Numerators

$\frac{2}{3}$

$\frac{2}{5}$

Two of three equal parts is greater than two of five equal parts.

So, $\frac{2}{3} > \frac{2}{5}$.

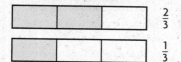 **UNLOCK the Problem** REAL WORLD

Three new flowering dogwood trees were planted in a park in Springfield, Missouri. The trees were $6\frac{1}{2}$ ft, $5\frac{2}{3}$ ft, and $5\frac{5}{8}$ ft tall. Order the plant heights from least to greatest.

To compare and order fractions with unlike denominators, write equivalent fractions with common denominators.

Remember
- Equivalent fractions are fractions that name the same amount or part.
- A common denominator is a denominator that is the same in two or more fractions.

 Order $6\frac{1}{2}$, $5\frac{2}{3}$, and $5\frac{5}{8}$ from least to greatest.

STEP 1

Compare the whole numbers first.

$6\frac{1}{2}$ $5\frac{2}{3}$ $5\frac{5}{8}$

5 ◯ 6

STEP 2

If the whole numbers are the same, compare the fractions.

Use common denominators to write equivalent fractions.

Think: _____ is a multiple of 3 and 8,

so _____ is a common denominator.

$5\dfrac{2 \times 8}{3 \times 8} = 5 \underline{}$ $5\dfrac{5 \times }{8 \times } = 5\underline{}$

STEP 3

Compare the numerators.

Order the fractions from least to greatest.

$5\underline{} < 5\underline{} < 6\dfrac{1}{2}$

So, from least to greatest, the order is _____ ft, _____ ft, _____ ft.

MATHEMATICAL PRACTICES

Math Talk Explain how you could compare $3\frac{3}{4}$ and $3\frac{3}{7}$.

Fractions and Decimals You can compare fractions and decimals.

🔑 One Way Compare to $\frac{1}{2}$.

Compare 0.92 and $\frac{2}{7}$. Write <, >, or =.

STEP 1 Compare 0.92 to $\frac{1}{2}$.

0.92 ◯ $\frac{1}{2}$

STEP 2 Compare $\frac{2}{7}$ to $\frac{1}{2}$.

$\frac{2}{7}$ ◯ $\frac{1}{2}$

So, 0.92 ◯ $\frac{2}{7}$.

Math Talk MATHEMATICAL PRACTICES
Explain how to compare $\frac{2}{7}$ to $\frac{1}{2}$.

🔑 Another Way Rewrite the fraction as a decimal.

Compare 0.8 and $\frac{3}{4}$. Write <, >, or =.

STEP 1 Write $\frac{3}{4}$ as a decimal.

$$4\overline{)3.00}$$

$$-\underline{}$$

$$-\underline{}$$

$$0$$

$\frac{3}{4} = \underline{}$

STEP 2 Use <, >, or = to compare the decimals.

0.80 ◯ _____

So, 0.8 ◯ $\frac{3}{4}$.

You can use a number line to order fractions and decimals.

🔑 Example Use a number line to order 0.95, $\frac{3}{10}$, $\frac{1}{4}$, and 0.45 from least to greatest.

STEP 1 Write each fraction as a decimal.

$$\frac{3}{10} \rightarrow 10\overline{)3.00} \qquad \frac{1}{4} \rightarrow 4\overline{)1.00}$$

Math Idea
- Numbers read from left to right on a number line are in order from least to greatest.
- Numbers read from right to left are in order from greatest to least.

STEP 2 Locate each decimal on a number line.

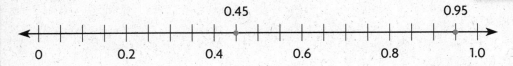

So, from least to greatest, the order is _____, _____, _____, _____.

Name _____

Share and Show

Order from least to greatest.

1. $3\frac{3}{6}$, $3\frac{5}{8}$, $2\frac{9}{10}$

Think: Compare the whole numbers first.

$3\frac{3 \times \_}{6 \times \_} = 3\,\underline{\hspace{1cm}}$ $3\frac{5 \times \_}{8 \times \_} = 3\,\underline{\hspace{1cm}}$

_____, _____, _____

Write <, >, or =.

2. $0.8 \bigcirc \frac{4}{12}$ | 3. $0.22 \bigcirc \frac{1}{4}$ | 4. $\frac{1}{20} \bigcirc 0.06$

Use a number line to order from least to greatest.

5. $1\frac{4}{5}$, 1.25, $1\frac{1}{10}$

_____

Math Talk MATHEMATICAL PRACTICES
Explain how to compare $\frac{3}{5}$ and 0.37 by comparing to $\frac{1}{2}$.

On Your Own

Order from least to greatest.

6. $1\frac{3}{4}$, $\frac{5}{7}$, $1\frac{3}{5}$ | 7. 0.6, $\frac{2}{3}$, 0.66 | 8. $\frac{1}{2}$, $\frac{2}{5}$, $\frac{7}{15}$

Write <, >, or =.

9. $\frac{7}{15} \bigcirc \frac{7}{10}$ | 10. $\frac{1}{8} \bigcirc 0.125$ | 11. $7\frac{1}{3} \bigcirc 6\frac{2}{3}$

Order from greatest to least.

12. $5\frac{1}{2}$, 5.05, $5\frac{5}{9}$ | 13. $\frac{37}{10}$, $3\frac{2}{5}$, $3\frac{1}{4}$ | 14. $\frac{5}{7}$, $\frac{5}{6}$, $\frac{5}{12}$

Problem Solving REAL WORLD

Use the table for 15–19.

15. In one week, Altoona, PA, and Bethlehem, PA, received snowfall every day, Monday through Friday. On which days did Altoona receive more snowfall than Bethlehem?

_____

16. **H.O.T. What if** Altoona received an additional 0.3 inch of snow on Thursday? How would the total amount of snow in Altoona compare to the amount received in Bethlehem that day?

_____

_____

17. **Explain** two ways you could compare the snowfall amounts in Altoona and Bethlehem on Monday.

_____

_____

_____

18. **Write Math** ▸ **Explain** how you could compare the snowfall amounts in Altoona on Thursday and Friday.

_____

_____

_____

19. ⭐ **Test Prep** The snowfall amounts recorded in inches in Reading, PA, on Monday through Friday during the same week were $2\frac{2}{5}$, $3\frac{1}{8}$, $2\frac{4}{5}$, $4\frac{2}{3}$, and $2\frac{7}{10}$. List the three cities in order of amount of snowfall received on Wednesday from least to greatest.

Ⓐ Reading, Altoona, Bethlehem

Ⓑ Bethlehem, Reading, Altoona

Ⓒ Bethlehem, Altoona, Reading

Ⓓ Reading, Bethlehem, Altoona

Altoona and Bethlehem Snowfall (inches)

Day	Altoona	Bethlehem
Monday	$2\frac{1}{4}$	2.6
Tuesday	$3\frac{1}{4}$	3.2
Wednesday	$2\frac{5}{8}$	2.5
Thursday	$4\frac{3}{5}$	4.8
Friday	$4\frac{3}{4}$	2.7

SHOW YOUR WORK

FOR MORE PRACTICE:
Standards Practice Book, pp. P27–P28

Name _____

Multiply Fractions

Essential Question How do you multiply fractions?

COMMON CORE STANDARD **CC.6.NS.4**
Compute fluently with multi-digit numbers and find common factors and multiples.

UNLOCK the Problem REAL WORLD

Sasha still has $\frac{4}{5}$ of a scarf left to knit. If she finishes $\frac{1}{2}$ of the remaining part of the scarf today, how much of the scarf will Sasha knit today?

Multiply $\frac{1}{2} \times \frac{4}{5}$. Write the product in simplest form.

Multiply the numerators.
Multiply the denominators.

$$\frac{1}{2} \times \frac{4}{5} = \frac{1 \times \_\_}{2 \times \_\_} = \_\_\_\_$$

Simplify using the GCF.

The GCF of 4 and 10 is _____.

Divide the numerator and the

$$= \frac{\_\_ \div \_\_}{10 \div \_\_} = \_\_\_\_$$

denominator by _____.

$\frac{1}{2} \times \frac{4}{5} =$ _____, so Sasha will knit _____ of the scarf today.

Remember

You can find the product of two fractions by multiplying the numerators and multiplying the denominators.

$$\frac{1}{3} \times \frac{2}{5} = \frac{1 \times 2}{3 \times 5} = \frac{2}{15}$$

Example 1

Multiply $1\frac{1}{4} \times 1\frac{2}{3}$. Write the product in simplest form.

Estimate. $1 \times$ _____ = _____

Write the mixed numbers as fractions greater than 1.

$$1\frac{1}{4} \times 1\frac{2}{3} = \frac{5}{4} \times \frac{\_\_}{3}$$

Multiply the fractions.

Write the product as a fraction or mixed number in simplest form.

$$= \frac{5 \times \_\_}{4 \times 3} = \_\_\_\_, \text{ or } _____$$

Since the estimate is _____, the answer is reasonable.

So, $1\frac{1}{4} \times 1\frac{2}{3} =$ _____, or _____.

Math Talk MATHEMATICAL PRACTICES
Explain whether the product $\frac{1}{3} \times \frac{3}{4}$ will be less than or greater than $\frac{3}{4}$.

Chapter 2 57

🔑 Example 2

Evaluate $\frac{4}{5} + \left(6 \times \frac{3}{8}\right)$ using the order of operations.

STEP 1

Estimate using benchmarks.

$$\boxed{} + \left(6 \times \frac{1}{2}\right) = \boxed{} + 3 = \boxed{}$$

STEP 2

Perform operations in parentheses.

$$\frac{4}{5} + \left(6 \times \frac{3}{8}\right) = \frac{4}{5} + \left(\frac{6 \times 3}{\boxed{} \times 8}\right)$$

$$= \frac{4}{5} + \frac{\boxed{}}{\boxed{}}$$

STEP 3

Write equivalent fractions using a common denominator.

Then add.

$$= \frac{4 \times 8}{5 \times 8} + \frac{\boxed{} \times 5}{\boxed{} \times 5}$$

$$= \frac{32}{40} + \frac{\boxed{}}{\boxed{}} = \frac{\boxed{}}{\boxed{}}$$

STEP 4

Simplify using the GCF.

$$= \frac{122 \div \boxed{}}{40 \div \boxed{}}$$

$$= \frac{\boxed{}}{\boxed{}}, \text{ or } \underline{\hspace{2cm}}$$

Since the estimate is _____, the answer is reasonable.

So, $\frac{4}{5} + \left(6 \times \frac{3}{8}\right) =$ _____, or _____.

1. What if you did not follow the order of operations and instead worked from left to right? How would that affect your answer?

_____

_____

2. **Explain** how you used benchmarks to estimate the answer.

_____

_____

Name _____

Share and Show

Find the product. Write it in simplest form.

1. $6 \times \frac{3}{8}$

$\frac{6}{1} \times \frac{3}{8} = $ _____

$\frac{ \div }{8 \div } = \frac{}{}$

or _____

2. $\frac{3}{8} \times \frac{8}{9}$

3. Sam and his friends ate $3\frac{3}{4}$ bags of fruit snacks. If each bag contained $2\frac{1}{2}$ ounces, how many ounces of fruit snacks did Sam and his friends eat?

Algebra Evaluate using the order of operations. Write the answer in simplest form.

4. $\left(\frac{3}{4} - \frac{1}{2}\right) \times \frac{3}{5}$

5. $\frac{1}{3} + \frac{4}{9} \times 12$

6. $\frac{5}{8} \times \frac{7}{10} - \frac{1}{4}$

7. $3 \times \left(\frac{5}{18} + \frac{1}{6}\right) + \frac{2}{5}$

Math Talk MATHEMATICAL PRACTICES
Explain why the product of two fractions has the same value before and after dividing the numerator and denominator by the GCF.

On Your Own

Practice: Copy and Solve Find the product. Write it in simplest form.

8. $1\frac{2}{3} \times 2\frac{5}{8}$

9. $\frac{4}{9} \times \frac{4}{5}$

10. $\frac{1}{6} \times \frac{2}{3}$

11. $4\frac{1}{7} \times 3\frac{1}{9}$

12. $\frac{5}{6}$ of the pets in the pet show are cats. $\frac{4}{5}$ of the cats are calico cats. What fraction of the pets are calico cats?

13. Five cats each ate $\frac{1}{4}$ cup of food. How much food did the five cats eat?

Algebra Evaluate using the order of operations. Write the answer in simplest form.

14. $\frac{1}{4} \times \left(\frac{3}{9} + 5\right)$

15. $\frac{9}{10} - \frac{3}{5} \times \frac{1}{2}$

16. $\frac{4}{5} + \left(\frac{1}{2} - \frac{3}{7}\right) \times 2$

17. $15 \times \frac{3}{10} + \frac{7}{8}$

18. H.O.T. **Pose a Problem** Write and solve a word problem for the expression $\frac{1}{3} \times \frac{2}{3}$.

_____

Changing Recipes

You can make a lot of recipes more healthful by reducing the amounts of fat, sugar, and salt.

Kelly has a recipe for muffins that calls for $1\frac{1}{2}$ cups of sugar. She wants to use $\frac{1}{2}$ that amount of sugar and more cinnamon and vanilla. How much sugar will she use?

Find $\frac{1}{2}$ of $1\frac{1}{2}$ cups to find what part of the original amount of sugar to use.

Write the mixed number as a fraction greater than 1.

$$\frac{1}{2} \times 1\frac{1}{2} = \frac{1}{2} \times \frac{}{2}$$

Multiply.

$$= \frac{}{}$$

So, Kelly will use _____ cup of sugar.

19. Michelle has a recipe that calls for $2\frac{1}{2}$ cups of vegetable oil. She wants to use $\frac{2}{3}$ that amount of oil and use applesauce to replace the rest. How much vegetable oil will she use?

_____

20. Tony's recipe for soup calls for $1\frac{1}{4}$ teaspoons of salt. He wants to use $\frac{1}{2}$ that amount. How much salt will he use?

_____

21. Jeffrey's recipe for oatmeal muffins calls for $2\frac{1}{4}$ cups of oatmeal and makes one dozen muffins. If he makes $1\frac{1}{2}$ dozen muffins for a club meeting, how much oatmeal will he use?

_____

22. Cara's muffin recipe calls for $1\frac{1}{2}$ cups of flour for the muffins and $\frac{1}{4}$ cup of flour for the topping. If she makes $\frac{1}{2}$ of the original recipe, how much flour will she use for the muffins and topping?

_____

FOR MORE PRACTICE:
Standards Practice Book, pp. P29–P30

Name _____

Simplify Factors

Essential Question How do you simplify fractional factors by using the greatest common factor?

COMMON CORE STANDARD CC.6.NS.4
Compute fluently with multi-digit numbers and find common factors and multiples.

🔑 UNLOCK the Problem · REAL WORLD

Some of the corn grown in the United States is used for making fuel. Suppose $\frac{7}{10}$ of a farmer's total crop is corn. He sells $\frac{2}{5}$ of the corn for fuel production. What fraction of the farmer's total crop does he sell for fuel production?

Multiply $\frac{2}{5} \times \frac{7}{10}$.

🔒 One Way Simplify the product.

Multiply the numerators.
Multiply the denominators.

$$\frac{2}{5} \times \frac{7}{10} = \frac{2 \times 7}{5 \times 10} = \underline{}$$

Write the product as a fraction in simplest form.

$$= \frac{ \div 2}{50 \div } = \underline{}$$

So, $\frac{2}{5} \times \frac{7}{10} = $ _____.

🔒 Another Way Simplify before multiplying.

Write the problem as a single fraction.

$$\frac{2}{5} \times \frac{7}{10} = \frac{2 \times 7}{5 \times 10}$$

Think: Do any numbers in the numerator have common factors with numbers in the denominator?

2 in the numerator and _____ in the denominator have a common factor other than 1.

Divide the numerator and the denominator by the GCF.

The GCF of 2 and 10 is _____.

$2 \div 2 = $ _____ $10 \div 2 = $ _____

$$\frac{\overset{1}{\cancel{2}} \times 7}{5 \times \cancel{10}}$$

Multiply the numerators.
Multiply the denominators.

$$\frac{1 \times 7}{5 \times } = \underline{}$$

$\frac{2}{5} \times \frac{7}{10} = $ _____, so the farmer sells _____ of his crop for fuel production.

Math Talk MATHEMATICAL PRACTICES
When you multiply two fractions, will the product be the same whether you multiply first or simplify first? **Explain.**

🔑 Example

Find $\frac{5}{8} \times \frac{14}{15}$. Simplify before multiplying.

Divide a numerator and a denominator by their GCF.

The GCF of 5 and 15 is _____.

$$\overset{1}{\cancel{5}} \times \frac{14}{\cancel{15}}$$

The GCF of 8 and 14 is _____.

$$\frac{\overset{1}{\cancel{5}}}{\cancel{8}} \times \frac{14}{\cancel{15}}_{3}$$

Multiply the numerators.
Multiply the denominators.

$$\frac{1}{\square} \times \frac{\square}{3} = \frac{\square}{\square}$$

> **! ERROR Alert**
>
> Be sure to divide both a numerator and a denominator by a common factor to write a fraction in simplest form.

So, $\frac{5}{8} \times \frac{14}{15} =$ _____.

Try This! Find the product. Simplify before multiplying.

Ⓐ $\frac{3}{8} \times \frac{2}{9}$

The GCF of 3 and 9 is _____.

The GCF of 2 and 8 is _____.

$$\frac{\cancel{3}}{\cancel{8}} \times \frac{\cancel{2}}{\cancel{9}} = \frac{\square}{\square}$$

Ⓑ $\frac{4}{7} \times \frac{7}{12}$

The GCF of 4 and 12 is _____.

The GCF of 7 and 7 is _____.

$$\frac{\cancel{4}}{\cancel{7}} \times \frac{\cancel{7}}{\cancel{12}} = \frac{\square}{\square}$$

1. **Explain** why you cannot simplify before multiplying when finding $\frac{3}{5} \times \frac{6}{7}$.

   _____

   _____

2. **What if** you divided by a common factor other than the GCF before you multiplied? How would that affect your answer?

   _____

   _____

Name _____

Share and Show

Find the product. Simplify before multiplying.

1. $\frac{5}{6} \times \frac{3}{10}$

$$\frac{\cancel{5}}{\cancel{6}} \times \frac{\cancel{3}}{\cancel{10}} = \frac{}{}$$

2. $\frac{3}{4} \times \frac{5}{9}$

3. $\frac{2}{3} \times \frac{9}{10}$

_____ _____ _____

4. After a picnic, $\frac{5}{12}$ of the cornbread is left over. Val eats $\frac{3}{5}$ of the leftover cornbread. What fraction of the cornbread does Val eat?

_____

5. The reptile house at the zoo has an iguana that is $\frac{5}{6}$ yd long. It has a Gila monster that is $\frac{4}{5}$ of the length of the iguana. How long is the Gila monster?

_____

Math Talk

MATHEMATICAL PRACTICES

Explain two ways to find the product $\frac{1}{6} \times \frac{2}{3}$ in simplest form.

On Your Own

Find the product. Simplify before multiplying.

6. $\frac{3}{4} \times \frac{1}{6}$

7. $\frac{7}{10} \times \frac{2}{3}$

8. $\frac{5}{8} \times \frac{2}{5}$

9. $\frac{9}{10} \times \frac{5}{6}$

10. $\frac{11}{12} \times \frac{3}{7}$

_____ _____ _____ _____ _____

11. Shelley's basketball team won $\frac{3}{4}$ of their games last season. In $\frac{1}{6}$ of the games they won, they outscored their opponents by more than 10 points. What fraction of their games did Shelley's team win by more than 10 points?

_____

12. Mr. Ortiz has $\frac{3}{4}$ pound of oatmeal. He uses $\frac{2}{3}$ of the oatmeal to bake muffins. How much oatmeal does Mr. Ortiz use to make the muffins?

_____

13. **H.O.T.** **Pose a Problem** Look back at Problem 12. Write and solve a similar problem by changing the amount of oatmeal and the fraction used for the muffins.

_____

_____

Problem Solving REAL WORLD

14. Three students each popped $\frac{3}{4}$ cup of popcorn kernels. The table shows the fraction of each student's kernels that did not pop. Which student had $\frac{1}{16}$ cup unpopped kernels?

_____

15. A recipe calls for 4 quarts popcorn and $\frac{1}{3}$ cup grated parmesan cheese. If you wanted to make $\frac{3}{4}$ of the recipe, how much popcorn and cheese would you need?

_____

16. The jogging track at Francine's school is $\frac{3}{4}$ mile long. Yesterday Francine completed two laps on the track. If she ran $\frac{1}{3}$ of the distance and walked the remainder of the way, how far did she walk?

_____

Popcorn Popping

Student	Fraction of Kernels not Popped
Katie	$\frac{1}{10}$
Mirza	$\frac{1}{12}$
Jawan	$\frac{1}{9}$

SHOW YOUR WORK

17. **H.O.T. Sense or Nonsense?** At a snack store, $\frac{7}{12}$ of the customers bought pretzels and $\frac{3}{10}$ of those customers bought low-salt pretzels. Bill states that $\frac{7}{30}$ of the customers bought low-salt pretzels. Is Bill's statement sense or nonsense? Explain.

_____

_____

_____

18. ⭐ **Test Prep** Mandy has a $\frac{5}{8}$-pound bag of blueberries. She uses $\frac{3}{10}$ of the bag to make pancakes for her friends. How many pounds of blueberries does Mandy use for the pancakes?

Ⓐ $\frac{3}{16}$ pound   Ⓒ $\frac{2}{5}$ pound

Ⓑ $\frac{4}{9}$ pound   Ⓓ $\frac{3}{4}$ pound

FOR MORE PRACTICE:
Standards Practice Book, pp. P31–P32

✓ Mid-Chapter Checkpoint

▶ **Vocabulary**

Choose the best term from the box to complete the sentence.

1. A _____ is a decimal representation of a number that has a repeating pattern that continues endlessly. (p. 50)

2. A _____ decimal is a decimal representation of a number that eventually ends. (p. 50)

▶ **Concepts and Skills**

Write as a decimal. Tell whether the decimal terminates or repeats. (CC.6.NS.6c)

3. $\frac{7}{12}$

4. $8\frac{39}{40}$

5. $1\frac{4}{9}$

6. $\frac{19}{25}$

Order from least to greatest. (CC.6.NS.6c)

7. $\frac{4}{5}, \frac{3}{4}, 0.88$

8. $0.65, 0.59, \frac{3}{5}$

9. $1\frac{1}{4}, 1\frac{2}{3}, \frac{11}{12}$

10. $0.9, \frac{8}{9}, 0.86$

Find the product. Write it in simplest form. (CC.6.NS.4)

11. $\frac{2}{3} \times \frac{1}{8}$

12. $\frac{4}{5} \times \frac{2}{5}$

13. $12 \times \frac{3}{4}$

14. Mia climbs $\frac{5}{8}$ of the height of the rock wall. Lee climbs $\frac{4}{5}$ of Mia's distance. What fraction of the wall does Lee climb?

Fill in the bubble to show your answer.

15. In Zoe's class, $\frac{4}{5}$ of the students have pets. Of the students who have pets, $\frac{1}{8}$ have rodents. What fraction of the students in Zoe's class have rodents? (CC.6.NS.4)

Ⓐ $\frac{1}{40}$

Ⓑ $\frac{1}{10}$

Ⓒ $\frac{2}{5}$

Ⓓ $\frac{1}{2}$

16. A recipe calls for $2\frac{2}{3}$ cups of flour. Terell wants to make $\frac{3}{4}$ of the recipe. How much flour should he use? (CC.6.NS.4)

Ⓐ $\frac{1}{2}$ cup

Ⓑ $\frac{2}{3}$ cup

Ⓒ $1\frac{1}{2}$ cups

Ⓓ 2 cups

17. Following the Baltimore Running Festival in 2009, volunteers collected and recycled 3.75 tons of trash. How can you write 3.75 as a mixed number in simplest form? (CC.6.NS.6c)

Ⓐ $3\frac{1}{2}$

Ⓑ $3\frac{2}{3}$

Ⓒ $3\frac{3}{4}$

Ⓓ $\frac{15}{4}$

18. Four students took an exam. The fraction of the total possible points that each received is given. Which student had the highest score? (CC.6.NS.6c)

Ⓐ Monica, $\frac{22}{25}$

Ⓑ Lily, $\frac{17}{20}$

Ⓒ Nikki, $\frac{4}{5}$

Ⓓ Sydney, $\frac{3}{4}$

Model Fraction Division

Essential Question How can you use a model to show division of fractions?

COMMON CORE STANDARD CC.6.NS.1
Apply and extend previous understandings of multiplication and division to divide fractions by fractions.

CONNECT There are two types of division problems. In one type you find how many or how much in each group, and in the other you find how many groups.

Investigate

Materials ■ fraction strips

A class is working on a community project to clear a path near the lake. They are working in teams on sections of the path.

A. Four students clear a section that is $\frac{2}{3}$ mi long. If each student clears an equal part, what fraction of a mile will each clear?

Divide $\frac{2}{3} \div 4$.

- Use fraction strips to model the division. Draw your model.

- What are you trying to find?

_____

_____

$\frac{2}{3} \div 4 =$ _____ , so each student will clear _____ of a mile.

B. Another team clears a section of the path that is $\frac{3}{4}$ mi long. If each student clears $\frac{1}{8}$ of a mile, how many students are on the team?

Divide $\frac{3}{4} \div \frac{1}{8}$.

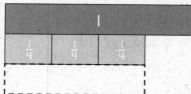

- Use fraction strips to model the division. Draw your model.

- What are you trying to find?

_____

$\frac{3}{4} \div \frac{1}{8} =$ _____ , so there are _____ students on the team.

Draw Conclusions

1. **Explain** how the model in problem A shows a related multiplication fact.

   _____

2. **Analysis** Suppose a whole number is divided by a fraction between 0 and 1. Is the quotient greater than or less than the dividend? **Explain** and give an example.

   _____

   _____

   _____

Make Connections

You can draw a model to help you solve a fraction division problem.

Jessica is making a recipe that calls for $\frac{3}{4}$ cup of flour. Suppose she only has a $\frac{1}{2}$ cup-size measuring scoop. How many $\frac{1}{2}$ cup scoops of flour does she need?

Divide $\frac{3}{4} \div \frac{1}{2}$.

STEP 1 Draw a model that represents the total amount of flour.

Think: Divide a whole into _____.

Jessica needs _____ cup.

STEP 2 Draw fraction parts that represent the scoops of flour.

Think: What are you trying to find?

_____

There is _____ full group of $\frac{1}{2}$ and _____ of a group of $\frac{1}{2}$.

So, there are _____ groups of $\frac{1}{2}$ in $\frac{3}{4}$.

$\frac{3}{4} \div \frac{1}{2} =$ _____, so Jessica will need _____ scoops of flour.

Math Talk Explain how you used the model to determine the number of groups of $\frac{1}{2}$ in $\frac{3}{4}$.

- **What if** Jessica's recipe calls for $\frac{1}{4}$ cup flour? How many $\frac{1}{2}$ cup scoops of flour does she need?

  _____

Name _____

Share and Show

Use the model to find the quotient.

1. $\frac{1}{2} \div 3 =$ _____

Think: $\frac{1}{2}$ is shared among 3 groups.

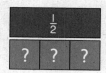

2. $\frac{3}{4} \div \frac{3}{8} =$ _____

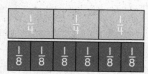

Use fraction strips to find the quotient. Then draw the model.

3. $\frac{1}{3} \div 4 =$ _____

4. $\frac{3}{5} \div \frac{3}{10} =$ _____

Draw a model to solve.

5. How many $\frac{1}{4}$ cup servings of raisins are in $\frac{3}{8}$ cup of raisins?

6. How many $\frac{1}{3}$ lb bags of trail mix can Josh make from $\frac{5}{6}$ lb of trail mix?

7. **Write Math** ▶ **Pose a Problem** Write and solve a problem for $\frac{3}{4} \div 3$ that represents how much in each of 3 groups.

_____

_____

Problem Solving > REAL WORLD

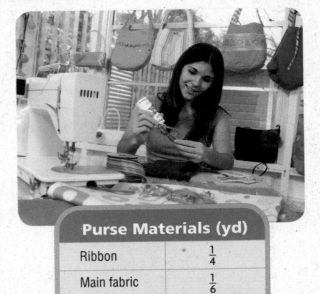

The table shows the amount of each material that students in a sewing class need for one purse.

Use the table for 8–11. Use models to solve.

8. Mrs. Brown has $\frac{2}{3}$ yd of denim. How many purses can be made using denim as the main fabric?

_____

9. **H.O.T.** One student brings $\frac{1}{2}$ yd of ribbon. If 3 students receive an equal length of the ribbon, how much ribbon will each student receive? Will each of them have enough ribbon for a purse? **Explain**.

_____

Purse Materials (yd)	
Ribbon	$\frac{1}{4}$
Main fabric	$\frac{1}{6}$
Trim fabric	$\frac{1}{12}$

· · · · **SHOW YOUR WORK** · · · · · · · ·

10. **What's the Error?** There was $\frac{1}{2}$ yd of purple and pink striped fabric. Jessie said she could only make $\frac{1}{24}$ of a purse using that fabric as the trim. Is she correct? **Explain** using what you know about the meanings of multiplication and division.

_____

_____

_____

11. **Pose a Problem** Use information in the table to write a new problem that represents how many groups of $\frac{1}{4}$ in $\frac{7}{8}$.

_____

_____

12. ⭐ **Test Prep** $\frac{2}{3}$ of the purses made by the class are blue. $\frac{1}{8}$ of the blue purses have red ribbon straps. What fraction of the purses are blue and have red ribbon straps?

Ⓐ $\frac{1}{24}$ Ⓒ $\frac{1}{6}$

Ⓑ $\frac{1}{12}$ Ⓓ $5\frac{1}{3}$

FOR MORE PRACTICE:
Standards Practice Book, pp. P33–P34

Name _____

Estimate Quotients

Essential Question How can you use compatible numbers to estimate quotients of fractions and mixed numbers?

COMMON CORE STANDARD CC.6.NS.1
Apply and extend previous understandings of multiplication and division to divide fractions by fractions.

CONNECT You have used compatible numbers to estimate quotients of whole numbers and decimals. You can also use compatible numbers to estimate quotients of fractions and mixed numbers.

Remember
Compatible numbers are pairs of numbers that are easy to compute mentally.

 UNLOCK the Problem REAL WORLD

Humpback whales have "songs" that they repeat continuously over periods of several hours. Eric is using an underwater microphone to record a $3\frac{5}{6}$ minute humpback song. He has $15\frac{3}{4}$ minutes of battery power left. About how many times will he be able to record the song?

- Which operation should you use to solve the problem? Why?

  _____

  _____

- How do you know that the problem calls for an estimate?

  _____

Estimate $15\frac{3}{4} \div 3\frac{5}{6}$ using compatible numbers.

Think: What whole numbers close to $15\frac{3}{4}$ and $3\frac{5}{6}$ are easy to divide mentally?

$15\frac{3}{4}$ is close to _____.

$3\frac{5}{6}$ is close to _____.

Rewrite the problem using compatible numbers.

$$15\frac{3}{4} \div 3\frac{5}{6}$$
$$\downarrow \qquad \downarrow$$

Divide.

$$16 \div 4 = \text{_____}$$

So, Eric will be able to record the complete whale song

about _____ times.

---

1. To estimate $15\frac{3}{4} \div 3\frac{5}{6}$, Martin used 15 and 3 as compatible numbers. Tina used 15 and 4. Were their choices good ones? **Explain** why or why not.

_____

_____

_____

🔒 Example   Estimate using compatible numbers.

A $5\frac{2}{3} \div \frac{5}{8}$

Rewrite the problem using compatible numbers.

$$5\frac{2}{3} \quad \div \quad \frac{5}{8}$$
$$\downarrow \qquad\qquad \downarrow$$
$$\underline{} \div \underline{}$$

Think: How many halves are there in 6? $6 \div \frac{1}{2} = \underline{}$

So, $5\frac{2}{3} \div \frac{5}{8}$ is about _____.

B $\frac{7}{8} \div \frac{1}{4}$

Rewrite the problem using compatible numbers.

$$\frac{7}{8} \quad \div \quad \frac{1}{4}$$
$$\downarrow \qquad\qquad \downarrow$$
$$\underline{} \div \quad \frac{1}{4}$$

Think: How many fourths are there in 1? $1 \div \frac{1}{4} = \underline{}$

So, $\frac{7}{8} \div \frac{1}{4}$ is about _____.

---

2. Will the actual quotient $5\frac{2}{3} \div \frac{5}{8}$ be greater than or less than the estimated quotient? **Explain**.

_____

_____

_____

3. Will the actual quotient $\frac{7}{8} \div \frac{1}{4}$ be greater than or less than the estimated quotient? **Explain**.

_____

_____

_____

4. **Explain** how you would estimate the quotient $14\frac{3}{4} \div 3\frac{9}{10}$ using compatible numbers.

_____

Name _____

Share and Show

Estimate using compatible numbers.

1. $22\frac{4}{5} \div 6\frac{1}{4}$

$\downarrow \qquad \downarrow$

_____ ÷ _____ = _____

2. $12 \div 3\frac{3}{4}$

☑ 3. $33\frac{7}{8} \div 5\frac{1}{3}$

☑ 4. $3\frac{7}{8} \div \frac{5}{9}$

5. $34\frac{7}{12} \div 7\frac{3}{8}$

6. $1\frac{2}{9} \div \frac{1}{6}$

Math Talk
MATHEMATICAL PRACTICES
Explain how using compatible numbers is different than rounding to estimate $35\frac{1}{2} \div 6\frac{5}{6}$.

On Your Own

Estimate using compatible numbers.

7. $\frac{13}{16} \div \frac{9}{10}$

8. $51\frac{5}{6} \div 5\frac{1}{2}$

9. $44\frac{1}{4} \div 11\frac{7}{9}$

10. $5\frac{11}{15} \div \frac{9}{19}$

11. $36\frac{2}{9} \div 2\frac{4}{5}$

12. $71\frac{11}{12} \div 8\frac{3}{4}$

13. $\frac{9}{10} \div \frac{1}{3}$

14. $13\frac{7}{8} \div \frac{1}{2}$

15. $1\frac{1}{6} \div \frac{1}{8}$

H.O.T. **Estimate to compare. Write <, >, or =.**

16. $21\frac{3}{10} \div 2\frac{5}{6} \bigcirc 35\frac{7}{9} \div 3\frac{2}{3}$

17. $29\frac{4}{5} \div 5\frac{1}{6} \bigcirc 27\frac{8}{9} \div 6\frac{5}{8}$

18. $55\frac{5}{6} \div 6\frac{7}{10} \bigcirc 11\frac{5}{7} \times \frac{5}{8}$

Problem Solving REAL WORLD

What's the Error?

19. Megan is making pennants from a piece of butcher paper that is $10\frac{3}{8}$ yards long. Each pennant requires $\frac{3}{8}$ yard of paper. To estimate the number of pennants she could make, Megan estimated the quotient $10\frac{3}{8} \div \frac{3}{8}$.

Look at how Megan solved the problem. Find her error.

Estimate:

$$10\frac{3}{8} \div \frac{3}{8}$$

$$\downarrow \quad \downarrow$$

$$10 \div \frac{1}{2} = 5$$

Correct the error. Estimate the quotient.

So, Megan can make about _____ pennants.

- Describe the error that Megan made.

_____

_____

- Tell which compatible numbers you used to estimate $10\frac{3}{8} \div \frac{3}{8}$. **Explain** why you chose those numbers.

_____

_____

- **What if** Megan wanted to make pennants that each required four times the amount of butcher paper? About how many pennants could she make? **Explain** your answer.

_____

_____

FOR MORE PRACTICE:
Standards Practice Book, pp. P35–P36

Divide Fractions

Essential Question How do you divide fractions?

COMMON CORE STANDARD CC.6.NS.1
Apply and extend previous understandings of multiplication and division to divide fractions by fractions.

🔑 UNLOCK the Problem REAL WORLD

Toby and his dad are building a doghouse. They need to cut a board that is $\frac{2}{3}$ yard long into $\frac{1}{6}$ yard pieces. How many $\frac{1}{6}$ yard pieces can they cut?

🔒 One Way Divide $\frac{2}{3} \div \frac{1}{6}$ by using a number line.

STEP 1 Draw a number line, and shade it to represent the total length of the board.

Think: Divide a whole into thirds.

Toby and his dad have $\frac{2}{3}$ yard, so shade $\frac{2}{3}$.

STEP 2 Show fraction parts that represent the pieces of board.

Think: Find the number of groups of $\frac{1}{6}$ in $\frac{2}{3}$.

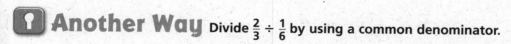

So, there are _____ $\frac{1}{6}$ yard pieces in $\frac{2}{3}$ yard.

🔒 Another Way Divide $\frac{2}{3} \div \frac{1}{6}$ by using a common denominator.

STEP 1 Write equivalent fractions using a common denominator.

Think: _____ is a multiple of 3 and 6,

so _____ is a common denominator.

$$\frac{2}{3} \div \frac{1}{6} = \frac{2 \times \quad}{3 \times \quad} \div \frac{1}{6} = \frac{\quad}{6} \div \frac{1}{6}$$

STEP 2 Divide.

Think: There are _____ groups of $\frac{1}{6}$ in $\frac{4}{6}$.

$$\frac{4}{6} \div \frac{1}{6} = \underline{\quad}$$

So, $\frac{2}{3} \div \frac{1}{6} =$ _____. Toby and his dad can cut _____ $\frac{1}{6}$ yard pieces.

Math Talk MATHEMATICAL PRACTICES
Explain how to find the quotient $\frac{2}{3} \div \frac{2}{9}$ by using a common denominator.

You can use reciprocals and inverse operations to divide fractions.

Two numbers whose product is 1 are **reciprocals** or **multiplicative inverses**.

$\frac{2}{3} \times \frac{3}{2} = 1$ $\frac{2}{3}$ and $\frac{3}{2}$ are reciprocals.

🔑 Activity Find a pattern.

- Complete the table by finding the products.

- How are each pair of division and multiplication problems the same, and how are they different?

_____

_____

_____

Division	Multiplication
$\frac{4}{7} \div \frac{2}{7} = 2$	$\frac{4}{7} \times \frac{7}{2} =$
$\frac{5}{6} \div \frac{4}{6} = \frac{5}{4}$	$\frac{5}{6} \times \frac{6}{4} =$
$\frac{1}{3} \div \frac{5}{9} = \frac{3}{5}$	$\frac{1}{3} \times \frac{9}{5} =$

- How could you use the pattern in the table to rewrite a division problem involving fractions as a multiplication problem?

_____

_____

🔑 Example

Winnie needs pieces of string for a craft project. How many $\frac{1}{12}$ yd pieces of string can she cut from a piece that is $\frac{3}{4}$ yd long?

Divide $\frac{3}{4} \div \frac{1}{12}$.

Estimate. _____ $\div \frac{1}{12} =$ _____

Use the reciprocal of the divisor to write a multiplication problem.

$$\frac{3}{4} \div \frac{1}{12} = \frac{3}{4} \times \frac{}{}$$

Simplify the factors.

$$= \frac{3}{4} \times \frac{\cancel{12}}{1}$$

Multiply. $=$ _____

Check your answer. $\frac{1}{12} \times$ _____ $=$ _____ $=$ _____

Since the estimate is _____, the answer is reasonable.

So, Winnie can cut _____ $\frac{1}{12}$ yd pieces of string.

Math Talk

MATHEMATICAL PRACTICES
Explain how you used multiplication to check your answer.

Name _____

Share and Show

Estimate. Then find the quotient.

1. $\dfrac{5}{6} \div 3$

Write the whole number as a fraction.

Use the reciprocal of the divisor to write a multiplication problem.

Estimate. _____ $\div 3 =$ _____

$\dfrac{5}{6} \div \dfrac{3}{\square}$

$\dfrac{5}{6} \times \dfrac{\square}{\square} = \dfrac{\square}{\square}$

Use a number line to find the quotient.

2. $\dfrac{3}{4} \div \dfrac{1}{8} =$ _____

3. $\dfrac{3}{5} \div \dfrac{3}{10} =$ _____

0   1

0   1

Estimate. Then write the quotient in simplest form.

4. $\dfrac{3}{4} \div \dfrac{5}{6}$

5. $3 \div \dfrac{3}{4}$

6. $\dfrac{1}{2} \div \dfrac{3}{4}$

7. $\dfrac{5}{12} \div 3$

_____

_____

8. Ben cuts a 5 ft board into $\dfrac{1}{3}$ ft pieces. How many $\dfrac{1}{3}$ ft pieces can he cut?

9. How many $\dfrac{1}{12}$ yd pieces of string can Maria cut from a piece that is $\dfrac{5}{6}$ yd long?

_____

_____

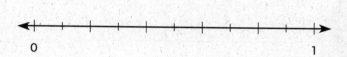

Math Talk MATHEMATICAL PRACTICES
Explain how to find a reasonable estimate for $\dfrac{11}{12} \div \dfrac{1}{4}$.

On Your Own

Practice: Copy and Solve **Estimate. Then write the quotient in simplest form.**

10. $2 \div \dfrac{1}{8}$

11. $\dfrac{3}{4} \div \dfrac{3}{5}$

12. $\dfrac{2}{5} \div 5$

13. $4 \div \dfrac{1}{7}$

14. Mari wants to cut a $\dfrac{2}{3}$ yd piece of ribbon into 6 equal pieces. How long will each piece be?

15. Yee puts $\dfrac{3}{4}$ lb of orange slices in bags that hold $\dfrac{1}{8}$ lb each. How many bags does she fill?

_____

_____

Practice: Copy and Solve **Evaluate using the order of operations. Write the answer in simplest form.**

16. $\left(\dfrac{3}{5} + \dfrac{1}{10}\right) \div 2$

17. $\dfrac{3}{5} + \dfrac{1}{10} \div 2$

18. $\dfrac{3}{5} + 2 \div \dfrac{1}{10}$

Problem Solving 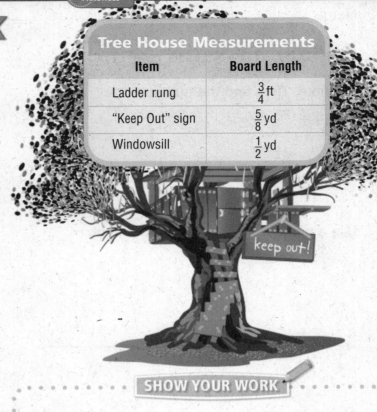 REAL WORLD

Model • Reason • Make Sense

Use the table for 19–23.

Tree House Measurements

Item	Board Length
Ladder rung	$\frac{3}{4}$ ft
"Keep Out" sign	$\frac{5}{8}$ yd
Windowsill	$\frac{1}{2}$ yd

19. Kristen wants to cut ladder rungs from a 6 ft board. How many ladder rungs can she cut?

_____

20. **H.O.T. Pose a Problem** Look back at Problem 19. Write and solve a new problem by changing the length of the board Kristen is cutting for ladder rungs.

_____

_____

_____

21. Dan paints a design that has 8 equal parts along the entire length of the windowsill. How long is each part of the design?

_____

22. Dan has a board that is $\frac{15}{16}$ yd. How many "Keep Out" signs can he make if the length of the sign is changed to half of the original length?

_____

23. **Write Math** ▶ Cade has a 4 yd board. The answer is 8. What's the question?

_____

_____

24. ⭐ **Test Prep** Hal has $\frac{3}{4}$ yard of string. How many $\frac{1}{12}$ yard pieces of string can he cut from $\frac{3}{4}$ yard?

Ⓐ 3

Ⓑ 6

Ⓒ 9

Ⓓ 12

SHOW YOUR WORK

FOR MORE PRACTICE:
Standards Practice Book, pp. P37–P38

Model Mixed Number Division

Essential Question How can you use a model to show division of mixed numbers?

COMMON CORE STANDARD CC.6.NS.1
Apply and extend previous understandings of multiplication and division to divide fractions by fractions.

Investigate

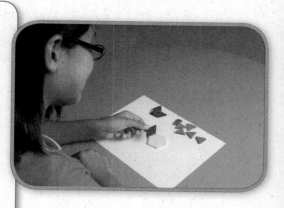

Materials ■ pattern blocks

A science teacher has $1\frac{2}{3}$ cups of baking soda. She performs an experiment for her students by mixing $\frac{1}{6}$ cup of baking soda with vinegar. If the teacher uses the same amount of baking soda for each experiment, how many times can she perform the experiment?

A. Which operation should you use to find the answer? Why?

_____

_____

B. Use pattern blocks to show $1\frac{2}{3}$.

Draw your model.

Think: A hexagon block is one whole, and a rhombus is

_____ of a whole.

- What type and number of blocks did you use to model $1\frac{2}{3}$?

_____

C. Cover $1\frac{2}{3}$ with blocks that represent $\frac{1}{6}$ to show dividing by $\frac{1}{6}$. Draw your model.

Think: One _____

block represents _____ of a whole.

_____ triangle blocks cover $1\frac{2}{3}$.

$1\frac{2}{3} \div \frac{1}{6} =$ _____

So, the teacher can perform the experiment _____ times.

Math Talk MATHEMATICAL PRACTICES
Explain how you could check that your answer is reasonable.

Draw Conclusions

1. **Tell** how your model shows a related multiplication problem.

   _____

2. **H.O.T.** **Evaluation** Suppose a mixed number is divided by a fraction between 0 and 1. Is the quotient greater than or less than the dividend? Explain and give an example.

   _____

   _____

   _____

   _____

Make Connections

You can use a model to divide a mixed number by a whole number.

Naomi has $2\frac{1}{4}$ quarts of lemonade. She wants to divide the lemonade equally between 2 pitchers. How many quarts of lemonade should she pour into each pitcher?

Divide $2\frac{1}{4} \div 2$.

STEP 1 Draw a model that represents the total amount of lemonade.

Think: Divide 3 wholes into _____.

Shade _____.

STEP 2 Draw parts that represent the amount in each pitcher.

Think: What are you trying to find?

_____

Think: In each of the two equal groups there is _____ whole and _____ of $\frac{1}{4}$.

$\frac{1}{2}$ of $\frac{1}{4}$ is _____.

So, $2\frac{1}{4} \div 2 =$ _____. Naomi should pour _____ quarts of lemonade into each pitcher.

Math Talk MATHEMATICAL PRACTICES
Explain how the quotient compares to the dividend when dividing a mixed number by a whole number greater than 1.

Name _____

Share and Show

Use the model to find the quotient.

1. $3\frac{1}{3} \div \frac{1}{3} =$ _____

2. $2\frac{1}{2} \div \frac{1}{6} =$ _____

Use pattern blocks to find the quotient. Then draw the model.

3. $2\frac{2}{3} \div \frac{1}{6} =$ _____

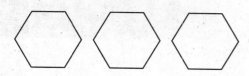

4. $3\frac{1}{2} \div \frac{1}{2} =$ _____

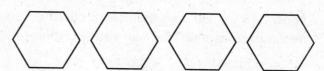

Draw a model to find the quotient.

5. $3\frac{1}{2} \div 3 =$ _____

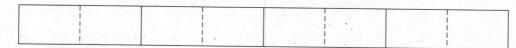

6. $1\frac{1}{4} \div 2 =$ _____

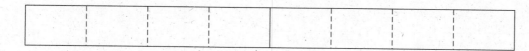

7. **Write Math** ▶ **Explain** how models can be used to divide mixed numbers by fractions or whole numbers.

_____

_____

_____

_____

Problem Solving **REAL WORLD**

Use a model to solve.

8. Eliza opens a box of bead kits. The box weighs $2\frac{2}{3}$ lb. Each bead kit weighs $\frac{1}{6}$ lb. How many kits are in the box?

_____

9. Hassan has two boxes of trail mix. Each box holds $1\frac{2}{3}$ lb of trail mix. He eats $\frac{1}{3}$ lb of trail mix each day. How many days can Hassan eat trail mix before he runs out?

_____

10. **H.O.T.** **Sense or Nonsense?** Steve made this model to show $2\frac{1}{3} \div \frac{1}{6}$. He says that the quotient is 7. Is his answer sense or nonsense? Explain your reasoning.

_____

_____

_____

11. **Pose a Problem** Write and solve a word problem for $3\frac{1}{4} \div 3$.

_____

_____

_____

_____

12. ⭐ **Test Prep** Joanna has a board that is $4\frac{3}{4}$ feet long. She cuts the board into 3 equal pieces. How long is each piece?

Ⓐ $1\frac{1}{4}$ feet 　Ⓒ $1\frac{7}{12}$ feet

Ⓑ $1\frac{1}{3}$ feet 　Ⓓ $1\frac{3}{4}$ feet

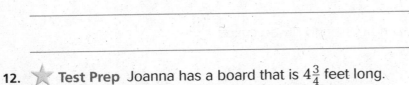

SHOW YOUR WORK

Name _____

Divide Mixed Numbers

Essential Question How do you divide mixed numbers?

COMMON CORE STANDARD CC.6.NS.1
Apply and extend previous understandings
of multiplication and division to divide
fractions by fractions.

 UNLOCK the Problem REAL WORLD

A box weighing $9\frac{1}{3}$ lb contains robot kits weighing $1\frac{1}{6}$ lb apiece. How many robot kits are in the box?

- Underline the sentence that tells you what you are trying to find.
- Circle the numbers you need to use to solve the problem.

🔑 Divide $9\frac{1}{3} \div 1\frac{1}{6}$.

Estimate the quotient. _____ ÷ _____ = _____

Write the mixed numbers as fractions.

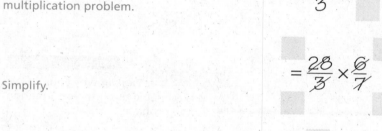
$$9\frac{1}{3} \div 1\frac{1}{6} = \frac{}{3} \div \frac{}{6}$$

Use the reciprocal of the divisor to write a multiplication problem.

$$= \frac{28}{3} \times \frac{}{}$$

Simplify.

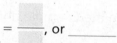
$$= \frac{28}{3} \times \frac{6}{7}$$

Multiply.

$$= \frac{}{}, \text{ or } \underline{}$$

Compare your estimate with the quotient. Since the estimate, _____,

is close to _____, the answer is reasonable.

So, there are _____ robot kits in the box.

Try This! Estimate. Then write the quotient in simplest form.

Think: Write the mixed numbers as fractions.

Ⓐ $2\frac{1}{3} \div \frac{1}{6}$

_____

Ⓑ $5\frac{3}{4} \div \frac{3}{8}$

_____

🔑 Example
Four hikers shared $3\frac{1}{3}$ qt of energy drink equally. How much did each hiker receive?

Divide $3\frac{1}{3} \div 4$. Check.

Estimate. _____ $\div 4 = 1$

Write the mixed number and the whole number as fractions.

$$3\frac{1}{3} \div 4 = \frac{\boxed{}}{3} \div \frac{\boxed{}}{}$$

Use the reciprocal of the divisor to write a multiplication problem.

$$= \frac{10}{3} \times \frac{\boxed{}}{\boxed{}}$$

Simplify.

$$= \frac{10}{3} \times \frac{1}{4}$$

Multiply.

$$= \underline{}$$

Check your answer.

$$4 \times \underline{} = \frac{}{} = \underline{}$$

So, each hiker received _____ qt.

Math Talk MATHEMATICAL PRACTICES
Explain why your answer is reasonable using the information in the problem.

1. **Describe** what you are trying to find in the Example above.

_____

2. **Explain** how dividing mixed numbers is similar to multiplying mixed numbers. How are they different?

_____

_____

_____

3. **H.O.T.** The divisor in a division problem is between 0 and 1 and the dividend is greater than 0. Will the quotient be greater than or less than the dividend? **Explain**.

_____

_____

Name _____

Share and Show

Estimate. Then write the quotient in simplest form.

1. $4\dfrac{1}{3} \div \dfrac{3}{4} = \dfrac{\boxed{}}{3} \div \dfrac{3}{4}$

$\qquad = \dfrac{13}{3} \times \dfrac{\boxed{}}{}$

$\qquad = \dfrac{\boxed{}}{}, \text{ or } 5\dfrac{\boxed{}}{9}$

2. Six hikers shared $4\dfrac{1}{2}$ lb of trail mix. How much trail mix did each hiker receive?

_____

3. $5\dfrac{2}{3} \div 3$

_____

4. $7\dfrac{1}{2} \div 2\dfrac{1}{2}$

_____

> **MATHEMATICAL PRACTICES**
> **Math Talk** Explain why you write a mixed number as a fraction before using it as a dividend or divisor.

On Your Own

Estimate. Then write the quotient in simplest form.

5. How many $3\dfrac{1}{3}$ yd pieces can Amanda get from a $13\dfrac{1}{3}$ yd ribbon?

_____

6. Samantha cut $6\dfrac{3}{4}$ yd of yarn into 3 equal pieces. How long was each piece?

_____

7. $5\dfrac{3}{4} \div 4\dfrac{1}{2}$

8. $5 \div 1\dfrac{1}{3}$

9. $6\dfrac{3}{4} \div 2$

10. $2\dfrac{2}{9} \div 1\dfrac{3}{7}$

11. $3\dfrac{3}{5} \div 2\dfrac{1}{4}$

12. $1\dfrac{5}{6} \div 1\dfrac{2}{9}$

13. $4\dfrac{1}{4} \div 12\dfrac{3}{4}$

14. $1\dfrac{1}{2} \div 1\dfrac{1}{4}$

Algebra Evaluate using the order of operations. Write the answer in simplest form.

15. $1\dfrac{1}{2} \times 2 \div 1\dfrac{1}{3}$

16. $1\dfrac{2}{5} \div 1\dfrac{13}{15} + \dfrac{5}{8}$

17. $3\dfrac{1}{2} - 1\dfrac{5}{6} \div 1\dfrac{2}{9}$

UNLOCK the Problem

TEST PREP

18. Dina hikes $\frac{1}{2}$ of the easy trail and stops for a break every $3\frac{1}{4}$ miles. How many breaks will she take?

(A) 1

(B) 3

(C) 6

(D) 10

Hiking Trails			
Park	**Trail**	**Length (mi)**	**Difficulty**
Cuyahoga Valley National Park, Ohio	Ohio and Erie Canal Towpath	$19\frac{1}{2}$	easy
	Brandywine Gorge	$1\frac{1}{4}$	moderate
	Buckeye Trail (Jaite to Boston)	$5\frac{3}{5}$	difficult

a. What problem are you asked to solve?

_____

_____

_____

b. How will you use the information in the table to solve the problem?

_____

_____

_____

c. How can you find the distance Dina hikes? How far does she hike?

_____

_____

_____

d. What operation will you use to find how many breaks Dina takes? How many does she take?

_____

e. Fill in the bubble for the correct answer choice above.

19. One weekend Michael hikes the $1\frac{1}{4}$ mile trail twice on Saturday and the $5\frac{3}{5}$ mile trail once on Sunday. How far does he hike that weekend?

(A) $2\frac{1}{2}$ miles

(B) $6\frac{17}{20}$ miles

(C) $8\frac{1}{10}$ miles

(D) $11\frac{1}{5}$ miles

20. Josh makes picture frames from old CD cases by gluing cases side-by-side to a strip of wood. If the length of a CD case is $4\frac{7}{8}$ inches, how many cases can Josh glue to a piece of wood that is $19\frac{1}{2}$ inches long?

(A) 2

(B) $3\frac{1}{2}$

(C) 4

(D) 6

FOR MORE PRACTICE:
Standards Practice Book, pp. P41–P42

Name _____

Problem Solving • Fraction Operations

Essential Question How can you use the strategy *use a model* to help you solve a division problem?

COMMON CORE STANDARD CC.6.NS.1
Apply and extend previous understandings of multiplication and division to divide fractions by fractions.

🔑 UNLOCK the Problem · REAL WORLD

Sam had $\frac{3}{4}$ lb of granola. Each day he took $\frac{1}{8}$ lb to school for a snack. If he had $\frac{1}{4}$ lb left over, how many days did Sam take granola to school?

Use the graphic organizer below to help you solve the problem.

Read the Problem

What do I need to find?	**What information do I need to use?**	**How will I use the information?**
I need to find _____ _____ _____ .	Sam started with _____ lb of granola and took _____ lb each day. He had _____ lb left over.	I will draw a bar model to find how much _____ _____ .

Solve the Problem

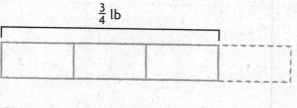

$\frac{3}{4}$ lb

used   left

The model shows that Sam used _____ lb of granola.

_____ groups of $\frac{1}{8}$ are equivalent to $\frac{1}{2}$

so $\frac{1}{2} \div \frac{1}{8} =$ _____ .

Math Talk MATHEMATICAL PRACTICES
Explain how you can justify your answer by solving the problem a different way.

So, Sam took granola to school for _____ days.

🔒 Try Another Problem

For a science experiment, Mr. Barrows divides $\frac{2}{3}$ cup of salt into small jars, each containing $\frac{1}{12}$ cup. If he has $\frac{1}{6}$ cup of salt left over, how many jars does he fill?

Read the Problem

What do I need to find?	What information do I need to use?	How will I use the information?

Solve the Problem

So, Mr. Barrows fills _____ jars.

1. Write an expression you could use to solve the problem.

_____

2. Suppose that Mr. Barrows starts with $1\frac{2}{3}$ cups of salt. **Explain** how you could find how many jars he fills.

_____

_____

_____

Name _____

Share and Show [MATH BOARD]

UNLOCK the Problem Tips

- Underline the question.
- Circle important information.
- Check to make sure you answered the question.

1. There is $\frac{4}{5}$ lb of sand in the class science supplies. If one scoop of sand weighs $\frac{1}{20}$ lb, how many scoops of sand can Maria get from the class supplies and still leave $\frac{1}{2}$ lb in the supplies?

   First, draw a bar model.

$\frac{4}{5}$ lb

   Next, find how much sand Maria gets.

   Maria will get $\frac{}{10}$ lb of sand.

   Finally, find the number of scoops.

   _____ groups of $\frac{1}{20}$ are equivalent to $\frac{}{10}$

   so $\frac{}{10} \div \frac{1}{20} =$ _____.

   So, Maria will get _____ scoops of sand.

2. **H.O.T.** **What if** Maria leaves $\frac{2}{5}$ lb of sand in the supplies? How many scoops of sand can she get?

   _____

3. There are 6 gallons of distilled water in the science supplies. If 10 students each use an equal amount of the distilled water and there is 1 gal left in the supplies, how much will each student get?

   _____

On Your Own.........

Choose a
STRATEGY

Use a Model
Draw a Diagram
Find a Pattern
Solve a Simpler Problem
Work Backward
Use a Formula

4. **H.O.T.** The total weight of the fish in a tank of tropical fish at Fish 'n' Fur was $\frac{7}{8}$ lb. Each fish weighed $\frac{1}{64}$ lb. After Eric bought some fish, the total weight of the fish remaining in the tank was $\frac{1}{2}$ lb. How many fish did Eric buy?

_____

5. An adult gerbil at Fish 'n' Fur weighed $\frac{1}{5}$ lb. A young gerbil weighed $\frac{1}{4}$ of that amount. How much did the young gerbil weigh?

_____

6. Fish 'n' Fur had a bin containing $2\frac{1}{2}$ lb of gerbil food. After selling bags of gerbil food that each held $\frac{3}{4}$ lb, $\frac{1}{4}$ lb of food was left in the bin. How many bags of gerbil food were sold?

_____

7. **Write Math** ➤ Niko bought 2 lb of dog treats. He gave his dog $\frac{3}{5}$ lb of treats one week and $\frac{7}{10}$ lb of treats the next week. Explain how Niko can find how much is left.

_____

_____

_____

_____

SHOW YOUR WORK

8. ⭐ **Test Prep** Keisha cut $\frac{35}{36}$ yard of fabric into 7 equal pieces. How long was each piece?

Ⓐ $\frac{1}{8}$ yard

Ⓑ $\frac{5}{36}$ yard

Ⓒ $\frac{1}{7}$ yard

Ⓓ $\frac{7}{36}$ yard

FOR MORE PRACTICE:
Standards Practice Book, pp. P43–P44

Name _____

 Chapter 2 Review/Test

▶ Vocabulary

Choose the best term from the box to complete the sentence.

1. A number is a _____ if it is one of two numbers

   whose product is 1. (p. 76)

2. Another term for one of two numbers whose product is 1 is

   _____. (p. 76)

▶ Concepts and Skills

Use the model to find the quotient. (CC.6.NS.1)

3. $\frac{3}{4} \div 3 = $ _____

4. $\frac{3}{4} \div \frac{3}{8} = $ _____

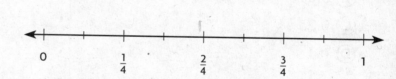

Find the product or quotient. Write it in simplest form.
(CC.6.NS.1, CC.6.NS.4)

5. $\frac{7}{8} \div \frac{3}{5}$

6. $\frac{1}{5} \times \frac{1}{4}$

7. Jon has $\frac{3}{4}$ cup of raisins. He puts the raisins into bags, each holding $\frac{1}{8}$ cup. How many bags will Jon use?

_____

Estimate. Then write the quotient in simplest form.
(CC.6.NS.1)

8. $2\frac{1}{10} \div 1\frac{1}{5}$

9. $3\frac{3}{4} \div 6$

10. Josiah cuts $13\frac{1}{8}$ yd of grape vines into 7 equal pieces to make wreaths. How long is each piece?

_____

GO Online **Assessment Options**
Chapter Test

Fill in the bubble to show your answer.

11. $\frac{2}{5}$ of the fish in Gary's fish tank are guppies. $\frac{1}{4}$ of the guppies are red. What fraction of the fish in Gary's tank are red guppies? (CC.6.NS.4)

Ⓐ $\frac{1}{10}$

Ⓑ $\frac{3}{20}$

Ⓒ $\frac{1}{5}$

Ⓓ $\frac{2}{9}$

12. One-third of the students at Finley High School play sports. Two-fifths of the students who play sports are girls. What fraction of all students are girls who play sports? (CC.6.NS.4)

Ⓐ $\frac{1}{15}$ Ⓒ $\frac{11}{15}$

Ⓑ $\frac{2}{15}$ Ⓓ $1\frac{1}{5}$

13. One twenty-fifth of the students at Westside Middle School were absent yesterday. How can you write $\frac{1}{25}$ as a decimal? (CC.6.NS.6c)

Ⓐ 0.025

Ⓑ 0.04

Ⓒ 0.25

Ⓓ 0.4

14. The table gives the heights of 4 trees. Which tree is tallest? (CC.6.NS.6c)

Type of Tree	Height (feet)
Sycamore	$15\frac{2}{3}$
Oak	$14\frac{3}{4}$
Maple	$15\frac{3}{4}$
Birch	15.72

Ⓐ oak

Ⓑ sycamore

Ⓒ maple

Ⓓ birch

15. Monty is making punch in a $\frac{7}{8}$ gallon container. How many cups of punch can he make? (1 cup $= \frac{1}{16}$ gallon) (CC.6.NS.1)

Ⓐ 2 cups   Ⓒ 14 cups

Ⓑ 7 cups   Ⓓ 16 cups

TEST PREP

16. Margie hiked a $17\frac{7}{8}$ mile trail. She stopped every $3\frac{2}{5}$ miles to take a picture. Which is the best estimate of the number of times she stopped? (CC.6.NS.1)

Ⓐ 4

Ⓑ 6

Ⓒ 7

Ⓓ 8

17. Sophie has $\frac{3}{4}$ quart of peanut butter. If she divides the peanut butter into containers that hold $\frac{1}{16}$ quart, how many containers can she fill?

(CC.6.NS.1)

Ⓐ $\frac{3}{32}$

Ⓑ 3

Ⓒ 12

Ⓓ 48

18. Brad and Wes are building a tree house. They cut a $12\frac{1}{2}$ foot piece of wood into 5 equally-sized pieces. How long is each piece of wood? (CC.6.NS.1)

Ⓐ $\frac{1}{2}$ foot

Ⓑ $2\frac{1}{4}$ feet

Ⓒ $2\frac{1}{2}$ feet

Ⓓ $12\frac{1}{2}$ feet

19. Sal had a board $\frac{5}{6}$ yard in length. He cut off $\frac{1}{3}$ yard, and then cut what remained into pieces each $\frac{1}{6}$ yard long. How many pieces were there? (CC.6.NS.1)

Ⓐ 2

Ⓑ 3

Ⓒ 4

Ⓓ 6

20. Ink cartridges weigh $\frac{1}{8}$ pound. The total weight of the cartridges in a box is $4\frac{1}{2}$ pounds. How many cartridges does the box contain? (CC.6.NS.1)

Ⓐ 18   Ⓒ 36

Ⓑ 32   Ⓓ 40

▶ Constructed Response

21. A bag contained $\frac{3}{4}$ pound of marbles. Each marble weighed $\frac{1}{36}$ pound. After Ashley removed some marbles from the bag, it weighed $\frac{1}{3}$ pound. How many marbles did Ashley remove? (CC.6.NS.1)

_____

22. Beth had 1 yard of ribbon. She used $\frac{1}{3}$ yard for a project. She wants to divide the rest of the ribbon into $\frac{1}{6}$ yard pieces. How many $\frac{1}{6}$ yard pieces of ribbon can she make? Explain your solution. (CC.6.NS.1)

_____

_____

_____

▶ Performance Task (CC.6.NS.1)

23. Brianna paints wooden birdhouses. She needs $\frac{3}{8}$ quart of paint to cover each birdhouse. She has 3 quarts of yellow paint and $4\frac{1}{4}$ quarts of blue paint.

Ⓐ Brianna plans to sell her birdhouses at a crafts fair. She wants to paint as many birdhouses as possible with the paint she has. Describe one way Brianna can use the yellow and blue paint she has to paint the greatest number of birdhouses.

_____

_____

_____

Ⓑ Suppose Brianna has $1\frac{3}{4}$ quart of red paint. Will she have enough to paint 4 birdhouses red? Explain two ways to solve the problem.

_____

_____

_____

_____

Rational Numbers

Show What You Know

Check your understanding of important skills.

Name _____

▶ **Compare Fractions** Compare. Write <, >, or =.

1. $\frac{3}{5}$ ◯ $\frac{1}{3}$

2. $\frac{3}{7}$ ◯ $\frac{1}{2}$

3. $\frac{3}{3}$ ◯ $\frac{5}{5}$

4. $\frac{6}{8}$ ◯ $\frac{2}{4}$

▶ **Equivalent Fractions** Write an equivalent fraction.

5. $\frac{3}{8}$ _____

6. $\frac{2}{5}$ _____

7. $\frac{10}{12}$ _____

8. $\frac{6}{9}$ _____

▶ **Compare Decimals** Compare. Write <, >, or =.

9. 0.3 ◯ 0.30

10. 4 ◯ 3.8

11. 0.4 ◯ 0.51

12. $2.61 ◯ $6.21

Angie finds a treasure map. Be a Math Detective and use the clues to find the location of the treasure. Write the location as an ordered pair.

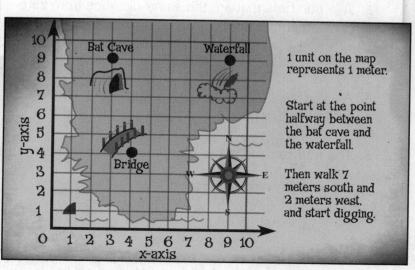

1 unit on the map represents 1 meter.

Start at the point halfway between the bat cave and the waterfall.

Then walk 7 meters south and 2 meters west, and start digging.

GO Online Assessment Options: **Soar to Success Math**

Vocabulary Builder

▶ **Visualize It**

Use the checked words to complete the flow map.

What is it?   What are some

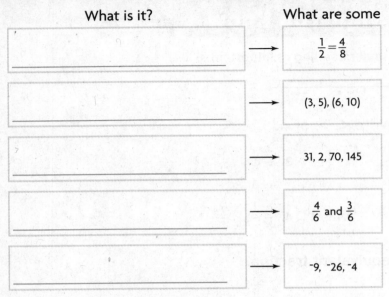

$\frac{1}{2} = \frac{4}{8}$

(3, 5), (6, 10)

31, 2, 70, 145

$\frac{4}{6}$ and $\frac{3}{6}$

⁻9, ⁻26, ⁻4

Review Words

compare

✓common denominator

✓equivalent fractions

order

✓whole numbers

Preview Words

absolute value

coordinate plane

integers

✓negative number

opposite

✓ordered pair

origin

positive number

quadrants

rational number

▶ **Understand Vocabulary**

Complete the sentences using the preview words.

1. The _____ are the set of whole numbers and their opposites.

2. The distance of a number from 0 on a number line is the number's _____.

3. Two numbers that are the same distance from zero on the number line, but on different sides of zero, are called _____.

4. A _____ is any number that can be written as $\frac{a}{b}$, where a and b are integers and $b \neq 0$.

5. The four regions of the coordinate plane that are separated by the x- and y-axes are called _____.

GO Online • eStudent Edition • Multimedia eGlossary

© Houghton Mifflin Harcourt Publishing Company

Name _____

Understand Positive and Negative Numbers

Essential Question How can you use positive and negative numbers to represent real-world quantities?

COMMON CORE STANDARDS CC.6.NS.5, CC.6.NS.6a
Apply and extend previous understandings of numbers to the system of rational numbers.

Integers are the set of all whole numbers and their opposites. Two numbers are **opposites** if they are the same distance from 0 on the number line, but on different sides of 0. For example, the integers ⁺3 and ⁻3 are opposites. Zero is its own opposite.

> **Math Idea**
> You do not need to write the + symbol for positive integers, so ⁺3 can also be written as 3.

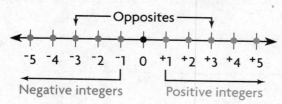

Positive numbers are located to the right of 0 on the number line, and negative numbers are located to the left of 0.

UNLOCK the Problem REAL WORLD

The temperature at the start of a 2009 Major League Baseball playoff game between the Colorado Rockies and the Philadelphia Phillies was 2°C. The temperature at the end of the game was ⁻4°C. What is the opposite of each temperature?

🔑 **Graph each integer and its opposite on a number line.**

A 2

The integer 2 is on the _____ side of 0.

Graph the opposite of 2 at _____.

So, the opposite of 2°C is _____.

B ⁻4

The integer ⁻4 is on the _____ side of 0.

Graph the opposite of ⁻4 at _____.

So, the opposite of ⁻4°C is _____.

- **What are you asked to find?**
  _____

- **Where can you find the opposite of a number on the number line?**
  _____

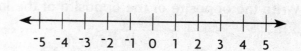

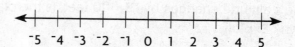

Math Talk MATHEMATICAL PRACTICES
Explain how to find the opposite of ⁻8 on a number line.

🔑 Example 1 Name the integer that represents the situation, and tell what 0 represents in that situation.

Situation	Integer	What Does 0 Represent?
A team loses 10 yards on a football play.	⁻10	the team neither gains nor loses yardage
A point in Yuma, Arizona, is 70 feet above sea level.		
A temperature of 40 degrees below zero was recorded in Missouri.		
Larry withdraws $30 from his bank account.		
Tricia's golf score was 7 strokes below par.		

🔑 Example 2 Use a number line to find ⁻(⁻3), the opposite of the opposite of 3.

STEP 1

Graph 3 on the number line. _____

⁻5 ⁻4 ⁻3 ⁻2 ⁻1 0 1 2 3 4 5

STEP 2

Use the number line to graph the opposite of 3. _____

STEP 3

Use the number line to graph the opposite of the number you graphed in Step 2.

So, ⁻(⁻3), or the opposite of the opposite of 3, equals _____.

Try This! Write the opposite of the opposite of the integer.

Ⓐ ⁺9 _____

Ⓑ ⁻12 _____

Ⓒ 0 _____

MATHEMATICAL PRACTICES

Math Talk Describe the pattern you see when finding the opposite of the opposite of a number.

- A plane's altitude changes by ⁻1,000 feet. Is the plane going up or down? **Explain.**

_____

_____

_____

Name _____

Share and Show

Graph the integer and its opposite on a number line.

1. ⁻7   opposite: _____

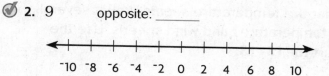

← + + + + + + + + + + →
⁻10 ⁻8 ⁻6 ⁻4 ⁻2 0 2 4 6 8 10

2. 9   opposite: _____

← + + + + + + + + + + →
⁻10 ⁻8 ⁻6 ⁻4 ⁻2 0 2 4 6 8 10

Name the integer that represents the situation, and tell what 0 represents in that situation.

Situation	Integer	What Does 0 Represent?
3. Kerri gained 24 points during a round of a game show.		
4. Ben lost 5 pounds during the summer.		
5. Marcy deposited $35 in her savings account.		

Math Talk MATHEMATICAL PRACTICES

Identify a real-world situation involving an integer and its opposite.

On Your Own

Write the opposite of the integer.

6. ⁻98 _____

7. 0 _____

8. ⁻53 _____

Name the integer that represents the situation, and tell what 0 represents in that situation.

Situation	Integer	What Does 0 Represent?
9. Desmond made $850 at his summer job.		
10. Miguel withdraws $300 from his checking account.		
11. Renee lost 18 points during her turn in the board game.		

Write the opposite of the opposite of the integer.

12. ⁻23 _____

13. 17 _____

14. ⁻125 _____

15. H.O.T. Suppose you know the distance from zero of a certain number on the number line. **Explain** how you could find the number's distance from its opposite.

_____

Problem Solving REAL WORLD

Wind makes the air temperature seem colder. The chart gives the wind chill temperature (what the temperature *seems* like) at several air temperatures and wind speeds. Use the chart for 16–18.

16. At 6 A.M., the air temperature was 20°F and the wind speed was 55 mi/hr. What was the wind chill temperature at 6 A.M.?

_____

17. At noon, the air temperature was 15°F and the wind speed was 45 mi/hr. At what air temperature and wind speed would the wind chill temperature be the opposite of what it was at noon?

_____

18. H.O.T. The wind was blowing 35 mi/hr in both Ashton and Fenton. The wind chill temperatures in the two towns were opposites. If the air temperature in Ashton was 25°F, what was the air temperature in Fenton?

_____

19. **Sense or Nonsense?** Claudia states that the opposite of any integer is always a different number than the integer. Is Claudia's statement sense or nonsense? Explain.

_____

20. ⭐ **Test Prep** Which situation could be represented by the integer ⁻10?

Ⓐ Anna spent $10 on a CD.

Ⓑ The temperature was 10 degrees above zero.

Ⓒ Dylan received a $10 gift certificate.

Ⓓ Cody got a 10-point bonus on his test.

Wind Chill Chart

		Air Temperature (°F)			
		30	25	20	15
Wind (mi/hr)	25	16	9	3	⁻4
	35	14	7	0	⁻7
	45	12	5	⁻2	⁻9
	55	11	3	⁻4	⁻11

SHOW YOUR WORK

© Houghton Mifflin Harcourt Publishing Company

FOR MORE PRACTICE:
Standards Practice Book, pp. P49–P50

Name _____

Compare and Order Integers

Essential Question How can you compare and order integers?

COMMON CORE STANDARDS CC.6.NS.7a, CC.6.NS.7b
Apply and extend previous understandings of numbers to the system of rational numbers.

You can use a number line to compare integers.

 UNLOCK the Problem REAL WORLD

On one play of a football game, the ball changed position by ⁻7 yards. On the next play, the ball changed position by ⁻4 yards. Compare ⁻7 and ⁻4.

🔑 **Use a number line to compare the numbers.**

STEP 1 Graph ⁻7 and ⁻4 on the number line.

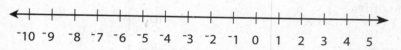

⁻10 ⁻9 ⁻8 ⁻7 ⁻6 ⁻5 ⁻4 ⁻3 ⁻2 ⁻1 0 1 2 3 4 5

STEP 2 Note the locations of the numbers.

⁻7 is to the _____ of ⁻4 on the number

line, so ⁻7 is _____ ⁻4.

> **Math Idea**
>
> As you move to the right on a horizontal number line, the values become greater. As you move to the left, values become less.

Try This! Use the number line to compare the numbers.

Ⓐ 5 and ⁻9

⁻10 ⁻9 ⁻8 ⁻7 ⁻6 ⁻5 ⁻4 ⁻3 ⁻2 ⁻1 0 1 2 3 4 5 6 7 8 9 10

5 is to the _____ of ⁻9 on the number line, so 5 is _____ ⁻9.

Ⓑ ⁻2 and 0

⁻10 ⁻9 ⁻8 ⁻7 ⁻6 ⁻5 ⁻4 ⁻3 ⁻2 ⁻1 0 1 2 3 4 5 6 7 8 9 10

_____ is to the left of _____ on the number line, so ⁻2 is _____ 0.

Math Talk MATHEMATICAL PRACTICES
Explain how you know that ⁻3 is less than 0 without using a number line.

You can also use a vertical number line to order integers.

Example The table gives the coldest temperatures recorded in seven cities in 2007.

Record Coldest Temperatures for 2007 (°F)					
Anchorage, AK ⁻17	Boise, ID 7	Duluth, MN ⁻25	Los Angeles, CA 35	Memphis, TN 18	Pittsburgh, PA ⁻5

A Order the temperatures from least to greatest.

STEP 1 Draw a dot on the number line to represent the record temperature of each city. Write the first letter of the city beside the dot.

_____

STEP 2 Write the record temperatures in order from least to greatest. Explain how you determined the order.

_____

_____

_____

B Use the table and the number line to answer each question.

• Which city had the colder record temperature, Memphis or Pittsburgh? How do you know?

_____

_____

• Which city had the warmest record temperature? How do you know?

_____

_____

• What are the record temperatures for Boise, Memphis, and Pittsburgh in order from least to greatest?

_____ < _____ < _____

• What are the record temperatures for Anchorage, Duluth, and Los Angeles in order from greatest to least?

_____ > _____ > _____

Record Coldest Temperatures (°F) for 2007

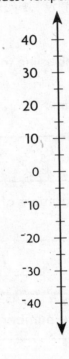

40
30
20
10
0
⁻10
⁻20
⁻30
⁻40

Remember
The symbol < means *less than*.
The symbol > means *greater than*.

MATHEMATICAL PRACTICES

Math Talk Generalize What rule can you use to compare numbers on a vertical number line?

Name _____

Share and Show

Compare the numbers. Write < or >.

1. ⁻8 ◯ 6   **Think:** ⁻8 is to the _____ of 6 on the number line, so ⁻8 is _____ 6.

✓ 2. 1 ◯ ⁻8

3. ⁻4 ◯ 0

4. 3 ◯ ⁻7

Order the numbers from least to greatest.

✓ 5. 4, ⁻3, ⁻7

_____ < _____ < _____

6. 0, ⁻1, 3

_____ < _____ < _____

7. ⁻5, ⁻3, ⁻9

_____ < _____ < _____

Order the numbers from greatest to least.

8. ⁻1, ⁻4, 2

_____ > _____ > _____

9. 5, 0, 10

_____ > _____ > _____

10. ⁻5, ⁻4, ⁻3

_____ > _____ > _____

Math Talk MATHEMATICAL PRACTICES
Explain how you can use a number line to compare numbers.

On Your Own

Order the numbers from least to greatest.

11. 2, 1, ⁻1

_____ < _____ < _____

12. ⁻6, ⁻12, 30

_____ < _____ < _____

13. 15, ⁻9, ⁻20

_____ < _____ < _____

Order the numbers from greatest to least.

14. ⁻13, 14, ⁻14

_____ > _____ > _____

15. ⁻20, ⁻30, ⁻40

_____ > _____ > _____

16. 9, ⁻37, 0

_____ > _____ > _____

17. Yesterday's low temperature was ⁻6°F. Today's low temperature was 3°F. Henri wrote ⁻6°F < 3°F to compare the temperatures. **Explain** what ⁻6°F < 3°F means and how you know that the statement is true.

_____

_____

_____

18. Write a comparison using < or > to show that South America's Valdes Peninsula (elevation ⁻131 ft) is lower than Europe's Caspian Sea (elevation ⁻92 ft).

_____

Problem Solving REAL WORLD

H.O.T. What's the Error?

19. In most games, the player with the highest score wins. In the game of golf, the player with the lowest score wins.

    Raheem, Erin, and Blake played a game of miniature golf. The table shows their scores compared to par.

Raheem	Erin	Blake
0	⁻5	⁻1

    At the end of the game, they wanted to know who had won.

Look at how they solved the problem. Find their error.

STEP 1: 0 is greater than both ⁻1 and ⁻5. Since Raheem had the highest score, he did not win.

STEP 2: ⁻1 is less than ⁻5, so Blake's score was less than Erin's score. Since Blake had the lowest score, he won the game.

Correct the error by ordering the scores from least to greatest.

So, _____ won. _____ came in second. _____ came in third.

• **Describe** the error that the players made.

_____

• **Explain** how you could check that your answer is correct.

_____

_____

_____

FOR MORE PRACTICE:
Standards Practice Book, pp. P51–P52

Rational Numbers and the Number Line

Essential Question How can you plot rational numbers on a number line?

COMMON CORE STANDARDS CC.6.NS.6a, CC.6.NS.6c
Apply and extend previous understandings of numbers to the system of rational numbers.

CONNECT A **rational number** is any number that can be written as $\frac{a}{b}$, where a and b are integers and $b \neq 0$. Decimals, fractions, and integers are all rational numbers.

UNLOCK the Problem REAL WORLD

The freezing point of a liquid is the temperature at which the liquid turns into a solid when it is cooled. The table shows the approximate freezing points of various liquids. Graph each temperature on a number line.

Liquid Freezing Points	
Liquid	**Freezing Point (°C)**
Carbonated water	⁻0.3
Fizzy lemonade	⁻0.5
Hydrazine	1.4

 Graph the values in the table.

STEP 1 Locate each number in relation to the nearest integers.

Think: ⁻0.3 is the opposite of _____.

0.3 is between the integers _____ and _____.
So, ⁻0.3 is between the opposites of these integers. ⁻0.3 is between _____ and _____.

⁻0.5 is between _____ and _____.   1.4 is between _____ and _____.

STEP 2 Graph each temperature.

⁻0.3°C   ⁻0.5°C   1.4°C

Think: ⁻0.3 is 3 tenths below 0 on the number line.

2 — | — 2 — | — 2 — | —
1 — | — 1 — | — 1 — | —
0 — | — 0 — | — 0 — | —
⁻1 — | — ⁻1 — | — ⁻1 — | —
⁻2 — | — ⁻2 — | — ⁻2 — | —

MATHEMATICAL PRACTICES
Math Talk How can you tell which number ⁻0.3 is closer to, 0 or ⁻1? **Explain.**

🔑 Example

City Hall is located at point 0 on a map of Maple Avenue. Other points of interest on Maple Avenue are indicated by their distances, in miles, to the right of City Hall (positive numbers) or to the left of City Hall (negative numbers). Graph each location on a number line.

Points of Interest	
Name	**Location**
City Park	$-\frac{3}{8}$
Fountain	$-1\frac{1}{2}$
Library	$1\frac{1}{4}$
Mall	$\frac{3}{4}$

STEP 1 Locate the numbers in relation to the nearest integers.

$-\frac{3}{8}$ is between _____ and _____. $-1\frac{1}{2}$ is between _____ and _____.

$1\frac{1}{4}$ is between _____ and _____. $\frac{3}{4}$ is between _____ and _____.

STEP 2 Graph each location on the number line.

City Park: $-\frac{3}{8}$ Think: $-\frac{3}{8}$ is three eighths to the left of 0 on the number line.

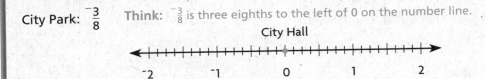

Fountain: $-1\frac{1}{2}$

Library: $1\frac{1}{4}$

Mall: $\frac{3}{4}$

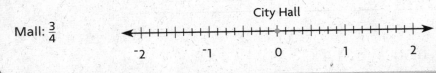

Math Talk MATHEMATICAL PRACTICES
Explain how you can use a horizontal or vertical number line to graph a rational number.

1. How did you identify the two integers that $-1\frac{1}{2}$ is between?

_____

_____

2. How do you know from looking at the table that City Hall is between the library and the mall?

_____

_____

_____

Name _____

Share and Show

Graph the number on the horizontal number line.

1. $^-2\frac{1}{4}$

The number is between the integers _____ and _____.

It is closer to the integer _____.

✅ 2. $^-1\frac{5}{8}$

✅ 3. $\frac{1}{2}$

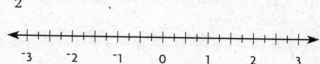

Math Talk   MATHEMATICAL PRACTICES
Two numbers are opposites. Zero is not one of the numbers. Do they lie on the same side or opposite sides of zero on a number line? **Explain.**

On Your Own

Practice: Copy and Solve Graph the number on a vertical number line.

4. 0.6

5. $^-1.25$

6. $^-1.5$

7. 0.3

8. $^-0.7$

9. 1.4

10. $^-0.5$

11. $^-0.25$

State whether the numbers are on the same or opposite sides of zero.

12. $^-1.38$ and 2.9

13. $^-3\frac{9}{10}$ and $^-0.99$

14. $\frac{5}{6}$ and $^-4.713$

_____

_____

_____

Write the opposite of the number.

15. $\frac{^-2}{3}$

16. 3.4

17. $^-5\frac{1}{2}$

18. $^-10.7$

_____

_____

_____

_____

19. Is $^-3.2$ less than $^-3$ or greater than $^-3$? How do you know?

_____

_____

Problem Solving

A star's *magnitude* is a number that measures the star's brightness. Use the table of star magnitudes for 20–22.

20. Between what two integers does the magnitude of Canopus lie?

_____

21. Graph the magnitude of Betelgeuse on the number line.

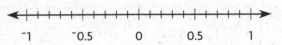

Magnitudes of Stars	
Star	**Magnitude**
Arcturus	⁻0.04
Betelgeuse	0.7
Canopus	⁻0.72
Deneb	1.25
Rigel Kentaurus A	⁻0.01
Sirius	⁻1.46

22. **H.O.T.** **What's the Error?** Jacob graphed the magnitude of Sirius on the number line. **Explain** his error. Then graph the magnitude correctly.

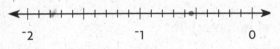

_____

_____

_____

23. **Write Math** How is a vertical number line like a horizontal number line?

_____

_____

_____

24. **Test Prep** Which fraction does NOT lie between 0 and ⁻1 on the number line?

(A) $\frac{^-17}{16}$

(B) $\frac{^-2}{3}$

(C) $\frac{^-7}{8}$

(D) $\frac{^-3}{4}$

SHOW YOUR WORK

FOR MORE PRACTICE:
Standards Practice Book, pp. P53–P54

Name _____

Compare and Order Rational Numbers

Essential Question How can you compare and order rational numbers?

COMMON CORE STANDARDS CC.6.NS.7a, CC.6.NS.7b
Apply and extend previous understandings of numbers to the system of rational numbers.

CONNECT You have used a number line to compare and order integers. You can also use a number line to compare other rational numbers, including decimals and fractions.

🔑 UNLOCK the Problem ⟩ REAL WORLD

The table shows the average December temperatures in five U.S. cities. Which city has the greater average December temperature, Indianapolis or Boise?

Average December Temperatures	
City	Temperature (°C)
Boise, ID	⁻1
Boston, MA	0.9
Indianapolis, IN	⁻0.6
Philadelphia, PA	2.1
Syracuse, NY	⁻2

🔒 One Way Use a number line.

Graph the temperatures for Indianapolis and Boise.

Think: As you move to the _____ on a horizontal number line, the numbers become greater.

⁻0.6 is to the _____ of ⁻1.

So, the city whose temperature is farther to the right is _____.

🔒 Another Way Use place value to compare the decimals.

STEP 1 Write the temperatures with their decimal points lined up.

Indianapolis: _____

Boise: _____

STEP 2 Compare the digits in the ones place. If the number is negative, include a negative sign with the digit.

Think: 0 is _____ than ⁻1.

⁻0.6 is _____ than ⁻1.

⁻0.6°C is _____ than ⁻1°C, so _____ has a greater average December temperature than _____.

Math Talk
MATHEMATICAL PRACTICES
Explain how you can order the average December temperatures of Boston, Philadelphia, and Syracuse from greatest to least.

The elevations of objects found at a dig site are recorded in the table. Which object was found at a lower elevation, the fossil of the shell or the fossil of the fish?

Fossils

Object	Elevation (ft)
shell	$^-3\frac{1}{2}$
fern	$\frac{1}{4}$
fish	$^-3\frac{1}{4}$

One Way Use a number line.

Graph the elevations for the fossil of the shell and the fossil of the fish.

Think: As you move _____ on a vertical number line, the numbers become less.

$^-3\frac{1}{2}$ is _____ $^-3\frac{1}{4}$ on the number line.

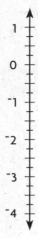

Another Way Use common denominators to compare fractions.

STEP 1 Write the elevations with a common denominator.

$$^-3\frac{1}{2} = {}^-3\frac{}{} \qquad {}^-3\frac{1}{4} = {}^-3\frac{}{}$$

STEP 2 Since the whole numbers are the same, you only need to compare the fractions. If the number is negative, include a negative sign with the fraction.

$^-\frac{2}{4}$ is _____ than $^-\frac{1}{4}$, so $^-3\frac{1}{2}$

is _____ than $^-3\frac{1}{4}$

So, the fossil of the _____ was found at a lower elevation than the fossil of the _____.

Example 2 Compare $^-0.1$ and $^-\frac{4}{5}$.

Convert to all fractions or all decimals.

fractions $^-0.1 = {}^-\dfrac{}{10} \qquad {}^-\dfrac{4}{5} = {}^-\dfrac{}{10}$

$^-8$ is _____ than $^-1$, so $^-\frac{4}{5}$ is less than $^-0.1$.

decimals $^-0.1 = {}^-0.1 \qquad {}^-\dfrac{4}{5} = {}^-0.$

$^-0.8$ is _____ than $^-0.1$, so $^-\frac{4}{5}$ is less than $^-0.1$.

Use a number line to check your answer.

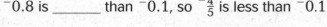

Math Talk

MATHEMATICAL PRACTICES **Explain** how you could use number sense to compare $^-0.1$ and $^-\frac{4}{5}$.

© Houghton Mifflin Harcourt Publishing Company

Name _____

Share and Show

Compare the numbers. Write < or >.

1. ⁻0.3 ◯ 0.2   Think: ⁻0.3 is to the _____ of 0.2 on the number line, so ⁻0.3 is _____ than 0.2.

2. $\frac{1}{3}$ ◯ ⁻$\frac{2}{5}$

3. ⁻0.8 ◯ ⁻0.5

✓4. ⁻$\frac{3}{4}$ ◯ ⁻0.7

Order the numbers from least to greatest.

5. 3.6, ⁻7.1, ⁻5.9

6. ⁻$\frac{6}{7}$, $\frac{1}{9}$, ⁻$\frac{2}{3}$

✓7. ⁻5$\frac{1}{4}$, ⁻6.5, ⁻5.3

_____ < _____ < _____

_____ < _____ < _____

_____ < _____ < _____

> **Math Talk** MATHEMATICAL PRACTICES
> Tell what the statement ⁻$\frac{1}{3}$ > ⁻$\frac{1}{2}$ means. Explain how you know that the statement is true.

On Your Own

Compare the numbers. Write < or >.

8. ⁻$\frac{1}{2}$ ◯ ⁻$\frac{3}{7}$

9. ⁻23.7 ◯ ⁻18.8

10. ⁻3$\frac{1}{4}$ ◯ ⁻4.3

Order the numbers from greatest to least.

11. ⁻2.4, 1.9, ⁻7.6

12. ⁻$\frac{2}{5}$, ⁻$\frac{3}{4}$, ⁻$\frac{1}{2}$

13. 3, ⁻6$\frac{4}{5}$, ⁻3$\frac{2}{3}$

_____ > _____ > _____

_____ > _____ > _____

_____ > _____ > _____

14. Yesterday's low temperature was ⁻4.5°F. Today's low temperature was ⁻5.25°F. Henri wrote ⁻4.5°F > ⁻5.25°F to compare the temperatures. **Explain** what ⁻4.5°F > ⁻5.25°F means and how you know that the statement is true.

_____

_____

_____

15. Write a comparison using < or > to show the relationship between an elevation of ⁻12$\frac{1}{2}$ ft and an elevation of ⁻16$\frac{5}{8}$ ft.

_____

MATHEMATICAL PRACTICES

Problem Solving REAL WORLD

Elevations, in miles, are given for the lowest points below sea level for 4 bodies of water. Use the table for 16–20.

16. The lowest point of which has the greater elevation, the Arctic Ocean or Lake Tanganyika?

   _____

17. Which has a lower elevation, the lowest point of Lake Superior or a point at an elevation of $-\frac{2}{5}$ mi?

   _____

18. List the elevations in order from least to greatest.

   _____

   _____

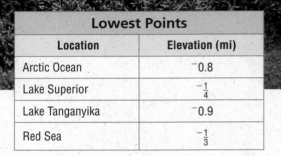

Lowest Points	
Location	**Elevation (mi)**
Arctic Ocean	-0.8
Lake Superior	$-\frac{1}{4}$
Lake Tanganyika	-0.9
Red Sea	$-\frac{1}{3}$

19. **H.O.T. What's the Error?** Kellie says that Lake Superior has a lower elevation than the Red Sea. Describe her error. Then write the comparison correctly.

   _____

   _____

   _____

SHOW YOUR WORK

20. **Write Math** A shipwreck is found at an elevation of $-\frac{3}{5}$ mi. Is it higher or lower than the lowest point in the Arctic Ocean? **Explain.**

   _____

   _____

   _____

   _____

21. ⭐ **Test Prep** Which temperature is coldest?

   (A) $-0.5°C$ **(C)** $1.4°C$

   (B) $-1.2°C$ **(D)** $0.8°C$

FOR MORE PRACTICE: Standards Practice Book, pp. P55–P56

Name _____

✓ Mid-Chapter Checkpoint

▶ **Vocabulary**

Choose the best term from the box to complete the sentence.

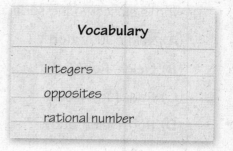

Vocabulary
integers
opposites
rational number

1. Any number that can be written as $\frac{a}{b}$, where a and b are integers and $b \neq 0$ is called a(n) _____. (p. 105)

2. The set of whole numbers and their opposites is the set of

_____. (p. 97)

▶ **Concepts and Skills**

Write the opposite of the integer. (CC.6.NS.6a)

3. ⁻72 _____

4. 0 _____

5. ⁻31 _____

6. 27 _____

Name the integer that represents the situation, and tell what 0 represents in that situation. (CC.6.NS.5)

Situation	Integer	What Does 0 Represent?
7. Greg scored 278 points during his turn in the video game.		
8. The temperature was 8 degrees below zero.		

Compare the numbers. Write < or >. (CC.6.NS.7a)

9. 3 ◯ ⁻4

10. ⁻6 ◯ ⁻5

11. 5 ◯ ⁻6

12. $\frac{1}{3}$ ◯ $\frac{-1}{2}$

13. ⁻3.1 ◯ ⁻4.3

14. $1\frac{3}{4}$ ◯ $-2\frac{1}{2}$

Order the numbers. (CC.6.NS.7a)

15. 5, ⁻2, ⁻8

_____ < _____ < _____

16. 0, ⁻3, 1

_____ < _____ < _____

17. ⁻7, ⁻6, ⁻11

_____ > _____ > _____

18. 2.5, ⁻1.7, ⁻4.3

_____ < _____ < _____

19. $\frac{2}{3}$, $\frac{-1}{4}$, $\frac{5}{12}$

_____ < _____ < _____

20. ⁻5.2, ⁻3.8, ⁻9.4

_____ > _____ > _____

Fill in the bubble to show your answer.

21. Judy is scuba diving at ⁻7 meters, Nelda is scuba diving at ⁻9 meters, and Rod is scuba diving at ⁻3 meters. Which list shows the divers in order from the deepest diver to the diver who is closest to the surface? (CC.6.NS.7b)

    (A) Nelda, Judy, Rod

    (B) Nelda, Rod, Judy

    (C) Rod, Judy, Nelda

    (D) Rod, Nelda, Judy

22. A football team gains 8 yards on their first play. They lose 12 yards on the next play. Which pair of integers represents the two plays? (CC.6.NS.5)

    (A) ⁻8, ⁻12

    (B) 8, ⁻12

    (C) ⁻8, 12

    (D) 8, 12

23. The player who scores the closest to 0 points wins the game. The scores of four players are given. Who won the game? (CC.6.NS.7b)

    (A) Myra, ⁻1.93 points

    (B) Amari, ⁻$1\frac{2}{3}$ points

    (C) Justine, ⁻1.8 points

    (D) Donavan, ⁻$1\frac{1}{2}$ points

24. Which point on the graph represents ⁻$3\frac{3}{4}$? (CC.6.NS.6c)

    (A) Point A

    (B) Point B

    (C) Point C

    (D) Point D

Absolute Value

Essential Question How can you find and interpret the absolute value of rational numbers?

COMMON CORE STANDARD CC.6.NS.7c
Apply and extend previous understandings of numbers to the system of rational numbers.

The **absolute value** of a number is the number's distance from 0 on a number line. The absolute value of ⁻3 is 3.

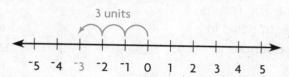

3 units

⁻5 ⁻4 ⁻3 ⁻2 ⁻1 0 1 2 3 4 5

The absolute value of ⁻3 is written symbolically as |⁻3|.

 UNLOCK the Problem REAL WORLD

In 1934, a cargo ship called the *Mohican* sank off the coast of Florida. Divers today can visit the ship at an elevation of ⁻32 feet. Use a number line to find |⁻32|.

🔑 **Graph ⁻32. Then find its absolute value.**

Graph ⁻32 on the number line.

Think: The distance from 0 to the point I graphed

is _____ units.

So, |⁻32| = _____.

10

0

⁻10

⁻20

⁻30

⁻40

⁻50

Math Idea
Since distance can never be negative, the absolute value of a number can never be negative.

Math Talk   MATHEMATICAL PRACTICES
Compare the absolute values of two numbers that are opposites. Explain your reasoning.

1. The depth of a diver is her distance below sea level. Because depth represents a distance, it is never negative. Find the depth of a diver visiting the *Mohican*, and explain how her depth is related to the ship's elevation of ⁻32 ft.

_____

_____

2. **Explain** how the expression |⁻32| relates to the diver's depth.

_____

_____

_____

You can find the absolute values of decimals, fractions, and other rational numbers just as you found the absolute values of integers.

🔑 Example 1

A food scientist tested a new dog food on five dogs. Each dog's weight was monitored during the course of the test. The results are shown in the table. Positive values indicate weight gains in pounds. Negative values indicate weight losses in pounds.

Graph the weight changes on the number line. Then find their absolute values.

Food Test Results	
Name	**Weight Change (lb)**
Buck	$\frac{3}{4}$
Goldie	$\frac{-5}{8}$
Mackerel	$-1\frac{7}{16}$
Paloma	$2\frac{1}{8}$
Spike	$\frac{-3}{8}$

```
<-+--+--+--+--+--+--+--+--+--+--+--+--+--+--+->
  ⁻3    ⁻2    ⁻1     0     1     2     3
```

Think: The distance from 0 to the point I graphed is $\frac{3}{4}$. $\left|\frac{3}{4}\right| = \frac{3}{4}$

$\left|\frac{-5}{8}\right| = $ _____ $\left|-1\frac{7}{16}\right| = $ _____ $\left|2\frac{1}{8}\right| = $ _____ $\left|\frac{-3}{8}\right| = $ _____

3. **Explain** how the absolute values of the positive and negative weight changes relate to the starting weights of the dogs.

_____

_____

_____

🔑 Example 2 Find all integers with an absolute value of 7.

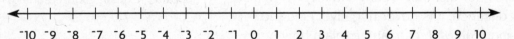

```
<-+--+--+--+--+--+--+--+--+--+--+--+--+--+--+--+--+--+--+--+--+->
 ⁻10 ⁻9 ⁻8 ⁻7 ⁻6 ⁻5 ⁻4 ⁻3 ⁻2 ⁻1  0  1  2  3  4  5  6  7  8  9  10
```

Think: The distance from 0 to integers with an absolute value of 7 is _____ units.

Graph integers located 7 units from 0 on the number line.

|_____| = 7 and |_____| = 7

So, both _____ and _____ have an absolute value of 7.

4. Paula says that there are always two numbers that have a given absolute value. Is she correct? **Explain.**

_____

Name _____

Share and Show

Find the absolute value.

1. $|{}^-2|$ Graph $^-2$ on the number line.

   $^-2$ is _____ units from 0.

   $|{}^-2| =$ _____

2. $|6|$ ☑ 3. $|{}^-5|$ 4. $|{}^-11|$ ☑ 5. $|9|$ 6. $|{}^-15|$

_____   _____   _____   _____   _____

Math Talk MATHEMATICAL PRACTICES
Can a number have a negative absolute value? **Explain.**

On Your Own

Find the absolute value.

7. $|{}^-37|$ 8. $|1.8|$ 9. $\left|\dfrac{-2}{3}\right|$ 10. $|{}^-6.39|$ 11. $\left|{}^-5\dfrac{7}{8}\right|$

_____   _____   _____   _____   _____

Find all numbers with the given absolute value.

12. 13 13. $\dfrac{5}{6}$ 14. 14.03 15. 0.59 16. $3\dfrac{1}{7}$

_____   _____   _____   _____   _____

H.O.T. **Algebra** Find the missing number or numbers to make the statement true.

17. $|\blacksquare| = 10$ 18. $|\blacksquare| = 1.78$ 19. $|\blacksquare| = 0$ 20. $|\blacksquare| = \dfrac{15}{16}$

_____   _____   _____   _____

21. On Monday, Melinda's bank account showed a change of $^-\$26$. Find $|{}^-\$26|$, and tell what the absolute value represents in this situation.

_____

_____

UNLOCK the Problem

22. The Blue Ridge Trail starts at Park Headquarters in Big Bear Park and goes up the mountain. The Green Creek Trail starts at Park Headquarters and goes down the mountain. The table gives elevations of various points of interest in relation to Park Headquarters. How many points of interest are less than 1 kilometer above or below Park Headquarters?

Point of Interest	Elevation Compared to Park Headquarters (km)
A	1.9
B	1.1
C	0.7
D	0.3
E	⁻0.2
F	⁻0.5
G	⁻0.9
H	⁻1.6

(A) 1   (C) 5

(B) 3   (D) 7

a. How can you find how far above or below Park Headquarters a given point of interest is located?

_____

_____

b. How can you find the number of points of interest that are less than 1 km above or below Park Headquarters?

_____

_____

_____

c. Find how far above or below Park Headquarters each point of interest is located. How many are less than 1 km above or below Park Headquarters?

_____

_____

_____

_____

d. Fill in the bubble for the correct answer choice above.

23. Which of the following has a value less than 0?

(A) $|6|$

(B) $|{}^-6|$

(C) ⁻6

(D) 6

24. In the third round of a board game, Desmond scored ⁻13 points. What does $|{}^-13|$ represent in this situation?

(A) the decrease in Desmond's score

(B) the increase in Desmond's score

(C) the number of points Desmond has at the end of the round

(D) the number of points Desmond had at the beginning of the round

Compare Absolute Values

Essential Question How can you interpret comparisons involving absolute values?

COMMON CORE STANDARD CC.6.NS.7d
Apply and extend previous understandings of numbers to the system of rational numbers.

🔑 UNLOCK the Problem REAL WORLD

🔒 Activity

Carmen is taking a one-day scuba diving class. Completion of the class will allow her to explore the ocean at elevations of less than ⁻25 feet. Use absolute value to describe the depths to which Carmen will be able to dive after taking the class.

- Graph an elevation of ⁻25 feet on the number line.

- List three elevations less than ⁻25 feet. Then graph these elevations.

  _____

- Elevations less than ⁻25 feet are found _____ ⁻25 feet.

- Because depth represents a distance below sea level, it is never

  negative. In this situation, |⁻25| ft represents a depth of _____ feet.

- Write each elevation as a depth.

Elevation (ft)	Depth (ft)
⁻30	
⁻35	
⁻40	

- An elevation of less than |⁻25| feet is a depth _____ than 25 feet.

So, Carmen will be able to dive to depths _____ than 25 feet after taking the class.

Elevation (feet)

```
30 ─┼
20 ─┼
10 ─┼
 0 ─┼
⁻10 ─┼
⁻20 ─┼
⁻30 ─┼
⁻40 ─┼
⁻50 ─┼
```

---

1. Compare a ⁻175-foot elevation and a 175-foot depth. Explain your reasoning.

_____

_____

🔓 Example Cole has an online account for buying video games.

His account balance has always been greater than ⁻$16. Use absolute value to describe Cole's account balance as a debt.

STEP 1 Graph an account balance of ⁻$16 on the number line.

Account balance ($)

STEP 2 List three account balances greater than ⁻$16. Then graph these account balances on the number line above.

_____

Balances greater than ⁻$16 are found to the _____ of ⁻$16.

STEP 3 Express an account balance of ⁻$16 as a debt.

In this situation |⁻$16| represents a debt of _____.

STEP 4 Complete the table.

Balances Greater Than ⁻$16	Debt
⁻$15	
⁻$14	
	$13

Each debt in the table is _____ than $16.

Cole's account balance is always greater than ⁻$16, so his debt

on the account is always _____ than $16.

> **MATHEMATICAL PRACTICES**
> **Math Talk** The temperature at the North Pole was ⁻35°F at noon. Explain how you can use absolute value to express a temperature of ⁻35°F.

2. **Explain** how you can describe a debt as an absolute value.

_____

_____

3. List three numbers greater than |⁻28|. **Describe** how you determined your answer.

_____

_____

Name _____

Share and Show

1. On Monday, Allie's bank account balance was ⁻$24. On Tuesday, her account balance was less than it was on Monday. Use absolute value to describe Allie's balance on Tuesday as a debt.

   In this situation |⁻$24| represents a debt

   of _____.

   On Tuesday, Allie had a debt of _____ than $24.

2. Matthew scored ⁻36 points in his turn at a video game. In Genevieve's turn, she scored fewer points than Matthew. Use absolute value to describe Genevieve's score as a loss.

   Genevieve lost _____ than 36 points.

Math Talk

MATHEMATICAL PRACTICES

Compare a negative bank balance and the size of the debt owed to the bank. Explain.

On Your Own

3. The surface of the water in Mike's well is at an elevation greater than ⁻92 meters. Use absolute value to describe the depth of the water's surface.

   The water's surface is at a depth of _____ than 92 meters.

4. The temperature in Saint Paul is ⁻13°F. Duluth is colder than Saint Paul. Use absolute value to describe the temperature in Duluth as a temperature below zero.

   The temperature in Duluth is _____ than 13°F below zero.

5. The table shows the changes in the weights of four cats. Which cat had the greatest decrease in weight? By how much did the cat's weight decrease?

   _____

Cat	Weight Change (ounces)
Missy	3.8
Angel	⁻3.2
Frankie	⁻2.6
Spot	⁻3.4

Compare. Write <, >, or =.

6. ⁻8 ◯ |⁻8|

7. 13 ◯ |⁻13|

8. |⁻23| ◯ |⁻24|

9. 15 ◯ |⁻14|

10. 34 ◯ |⁻36|

11. ⁻5 ◯ |⁻6|

Compare and Contrast

When you *compare and contrast*, you look for ways that two or more subjects are alike (compare) and ways they are different (contrast). This helps you to discover information about each subject that you might not have known otherwise. As you read the following passage, think about how the main topics are alike and how they are different.

Trevor mows lawns after school to raise money for a new mountain bike. Last week, it rained every day, and he couldn't work. While waiting for better weather, he spent some of his savings on lawnmower repairs. As a result, his savings balance changed by ⁻$45. This week, the weather was better, and Trevor was back at work. His savings balance changed by ⁺$45 this week.

12. The passage has two main parts. **Describe** them.

_____

_____

_____

13. **Describe** the two changes in Trevor's savings balance.

_____

_____

14. **Compare** the two changes in Trevor's savings balance. How are they alike?

_____

_____

15. ⬡ H.O.T. **Contrast** the two changes in Trevor's savings balance. How are they different?

_____

_____

_____

_____

FOR MORE PRACTICE:
Standards Practice Book, pp. P59–P60

Rational Numbers and the Coordinate Plane

COMMON CORE STANDARD CC.6.NS.6c
Apply and extend previous understandings of
numbers to the system of rational numbers.

Essential Question How do you plot ordered pairs of rational numbers
on a coordinate plane?

A **coordinate plane** is a plane formed by a horizontal number
line called the **x-axis** that intersects a vertical number line
called the **y-axis**. The axes intersect at 0 on both number lines.
The point where the axes intersect is the **origin**.

An **ordered pair** is a pair of numbers, such as (3, 2), that can
be used to locate a point on the coordinate plane. The first
number is the **x-coordinate**; it tells the distance to move left or
right from the origin. The second number is the **y-coordinate**;
it tells the distance to move up or down from the origin. The
ordered pair for the origin is (0, 0).

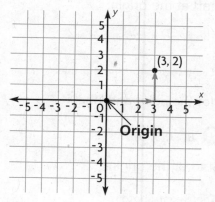

UNLOCK the Problem REAL WORLD

A screen in a video game shows a coordinate
plane. The points *P*, *Q*, *R*, and *S* represent treasure
chests. Write the ordered pair for each treasure
chest's location.

• If a point is to the left of the *y*-axis, is its
  x-coordinate positive or negative?

_____

 Find the coordinates of each point.

To find the coordinates of point *P*, start at the origin.

To find the *x*-coordinate, move right   **Move 2 units to the _____.**
(positive) or left (negative).

To find the *y*-coordinate, move up   **Move _____ units up.**
(positive) or down (negative).

Point *P* is located at ($^-$2, _____).

Point *Q* is located at (_____, _____).

Point *R* is located at (_____, _____).

Point *S* is located at (_____, _____).

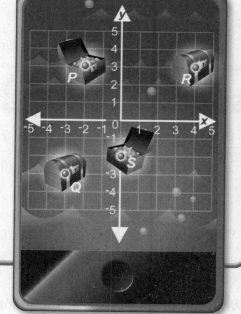

1. **Make a conjecture** about the *x*-coordinate of any point that
   lies on the *y*-axis.

   _____

2. **Explain** why (2, 4) represents a different location than (4, 2).

   _____

🔒 **Example** Graph and label the point on the coordinate plane.

Ⓐ $A\left(2, \frac{-1}{2}\right)$

Start at the origin.

The x-coordinate is positive.   Move _____ units to the right.

The y-coordinate is negative.   Move $\frac{1}{2}$ unit _____.

Plot the point and label it A.

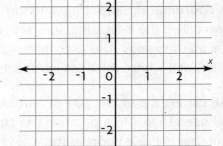

Ⓑ $B(^-0.5, 0)$

Start at the origin.

The x-coordinate is _____.   Move _____ unit to the _____.

The y-coordinate is 0.   The point lies on the _____-axis.

Plot the point and label it B.

Ⓒ $C\left(2\frac{1}{2}, \frac{3}{4}\right)$

Start at the origin.

Move _____ units to the _____.

Move _____ unit _____.

Plot the point and label it C.

Ⓓ $D(^-1.25, ^-1.75)$

Start at the origin.

Move _____ units to the _____.

Move _____ units _____.

Plot the point and label it D.

> **MATHEMATICAL PRACTICES**
>
> **Math Talk** Describe the location of a point that has a positive x-coordinate and a negative y-coordinate.

Share and Show 🖊️MATH BOARD ⋅

1. Write the ordered pair for point J.

   Start at the origin. Move _____ units to the _____

   and _____ units _____.

   The ordered pair is _____.

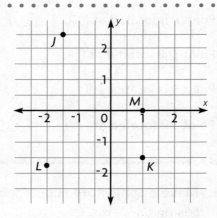

Write the ordered pair for the point.

2. K

✓ 3. L

4. M

Name _____

Share and Show

Graph and label the point on the coordinate plane.

5. $P(^-2.5, 2)$

6. $Q(^-2, \frac{1}{4})$

7. $R(0, 1.5)$

8. $S(^-1, \frac{-1}{2})$

✓ 9. $T(1\frac{1}{2}, ^-2)$

10. $U(0.75, 1.25)$

11. $V(^-0.5, 0)$

12. $W(2, 0)$

13. $X(0, ^-2)$

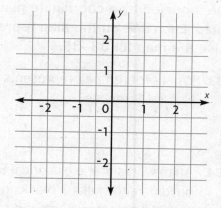

On Your Own

Math Talk **MATHEMATICAL PRACTICES** **Explain** how graphing $(3, 2)$ is similar to and different from graphing $(3, ^-2)$.

Write the ordered pair for the point. Give approximate coordinates when necessary.

14. A

_____

15. B

_____

16. C

_____

17. D

_____

18. E

_____

19. F

_____

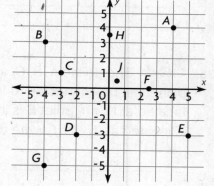

20. G

_____

21. H

_____

22. J

_____

Graph and label the point on the coordinate plane.

23. $M(^-4, 0)$

24. $N(2, 2)$

25. $P(^-3, 3)$

26. $Q(0, 2\frac{1}{2})$

27. $R(0.5, 0.5)$

28. $S(^-5, \frac{1}{2})$

29. $T(0, 0)$

30. $U(3\frac{1}{2}, 0)$

31. $V(^-2, ^-4)$

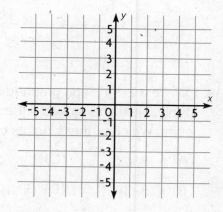

32. A point lies to the left of the y-axis and below the x-axis. What can you conclude about the coordinates of the point?

_____

Problem Solving REAL WORLD

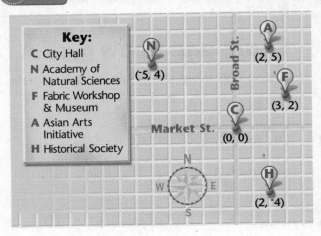

Key:
C City Hall
N Academy of Natural Sciences
F Fabric Workshop & Museum
A Asian Arts Initiative
H Historical Society

Many of the streets in downtown Philadelphia can be modeled by a coordinate plane, as shown on the map. Each unit on the map represents one block. Use the map for 33–35.

33. What ordered pair represents the Academy of Natural Sciences?

_____

34. Anita works at the Historical Society. She leaves the building and walks 3 blocks north to a restaurant. What ordered pair represents the restaurant?

_____

35. **H.O.T. Pose a Problem** Write and solve a new problem that uses a location on the map of Philadelphia.

_____

_____

_____

SHOW YOUR WORK

36. **H.O.T.** The points *A*, *B*, *C*, and *D* on a coordinate plane can be connected to form a rectangle. Point *A* is located at (2, 0), point *B* is located at (6, 0), and point *C* is located at (6, 2.5). Write the ordered pair for point *D*.

_____

37. **Write Math** ▶ **Explain** how you can tell that the line segment connecting two points is vertical without graphing the points.

_____

_____

38. ⭐ **Test Prep** Zena graphed a point by starting at the origin. Next she moved left and then up to plot the point. Which of these points could she have graphed?

Ⓐ (⁻3, ⁻5) Ⓒ (3, ⁻5)

Ⓑ (⁻5, 3) Ⓓ (5, 3)

FOR MORE PRACTICE:
Standards Practice Book, pp. P61–P62

Ordered Pair Relationships

Essential Question How can you identify the relationship between points on a coordinate plane?

COMMON CORE STANDARD CC.6.NS.6b
Apply and extend previous understandings of numbers to the system of rational numbers.

The four regions of the coordinate plane that are separated by the x- and y-axes are called **quadrants**. Quadrants are numbered with the Roman numerals I, II, III, and IV. If you know the signs of the coordinates of a point, you can determine the quadrant where the point is located.

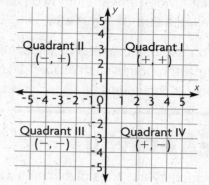

🔑 UNLOCK the Problem REAL WORLD

The point ($^-$3, 4) represents the location of a bookstore on a map of a shopping mall. Identify the quadrant where the point is located.

- What is the x-coordinate of the point? _____
- What is the y-coordinate of the point? _____

🔑 **Find the quadrant that contains ($^-$3, 4).**

STEP 1 Examine the x-coordinate.

Think: The x-coordinate is _____, so the point is _____ units to the _____ of the origin.

Since the point is to the left of the origin, it must be located in either

Quadrant _____ or Quadrant _____.

_____

STEP 2 Examine the y-coordinate.

Think: The y-coordinate is _____, so the point is _____ units _____ from the origin.

Since the point is above the origin, it must be located in

Quadrant _____.

Check by graphing the point ($^-$3, 4) on the coordinate plane.

So, the point representing the bookstore is located in

Quadrant _____.

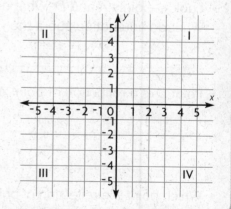

- Look at the signs of the coordinates of points in Quadrants I and II. What do they have in common? How are they different?

_____

_____

A figure has **line symmetry** if it can be folded about a line so that its two parts match exactly. If you cut out the isosceles triangle at the right and fold it along the dashed line, the two parts would match. A line that divides a figure into two halves that are reflections of each other is called a **line of symmetry**.

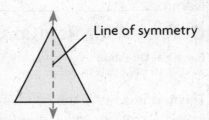

Line of symmetry

You can use the idea of line symmetry to analyze the relationship between points such as (5, ⁻1) and (⁻5, ⁻1) whose coordinates differ only in their signs.

🔑 Activity

- Identify the lines of symmetry in the rectangle.

  The _____ -axis is a horizontal line of symmetry, and the _____ -axis is a vertical line of symmetry.

- Look at points *A* and *B*. What do you notice about the *x*-coordinates? What do you notice about the *y*-coordinates?

  _____

  _____

- Point *B* is a reflection of point *A* across which axis? How do you know?

  _____

  _____

- Look at points *A* and *D*. What do you notice about the *x*-coordinates? What do you notice about the *y*-coordinates?

  _____

- Point *D* is a reflection of point *A* across which axis? How do you know?

  _____

  _____

- Which point is a reflection of point *B* across the *x*-axis and then the *y*-axis?

  _____

- Compare the coordinates of point *B* with the coordinates of point *D*.

  _____

  _____

Math Talk

Describe how the coordinates of a point change if it is reflected across the *x*-axis.

Name _____

Share and Show

Identify the quadrant where the point is located.

1. (2, ⁻5)

To graph the point, first move to the _____ from the origin.

Then move _____.

Quadrant: _____

2. (4, 1)

Quadrant: _____

☑ **3.** (⁻6, ⁻2)

Quadrant: _____

4. (⁻7, 3)

Quadrant: _____

5. (8, 8)

Quadrant: _____

6. (1, ⁻1)

Quadrant: _____

The two points are reflections of each other across the *x*- or *y*-axis. Identify the axis.

☑ **7.** (⁻1, 3) and (1, 3)

axis: _____

8. (4, 4) and (4, ⁻4)

axis: _____

9. (2, ⁻9) and (2, 9)

axis: _____

10. (8, 1) and (⁻8, 1)

axis: _____

On Your Own

Math Talk MATHEMATICAL PRACTICES
Explain how you can identify the quadrant where a given point is located.

Identify the quadrant where the point is located.

11. (⁻8, ⁻9)

Quadrant: _____

12. (12, 1)

Quadrant: _____

13. (⁻13, 10)

Quadrant: _____

14. (5, ⁻20)

Quadrant: _____

The two points are reflections of each other across the *x*- or *y*-axis. Identify the axis.

15. (⁻9, ⁻10) and (⁻9, 10)

axis: _____

16. (21, ⁻31) and (21, 31)

axis: _____

17. (15, ⁻20) and (⁻15, ⁻20)

axis: _____

Give the reflection of the point across the given axis.

18. (⁻7, ⁻7), *y*-axis

_____

19. (⁻15, 18), *x*-axis

_____

20. (11, 9), *x*-axis

_____

Problem Solving > REAL WORLD

Use the map of Gridville for 21–24.

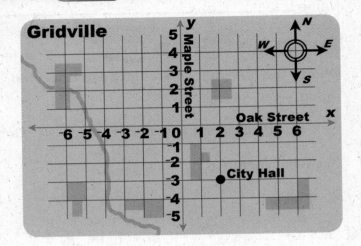

Gridville

21. The mayor of Gridville lives at point $(^-3, 4)$. In which quadrant of the town does the mayor live?

_____

22. The library's location has the same y-coordinate as City Hall but the opposite x-coordinate. Across which street could you reflect City Hall's location to find the library's location?

_____

23. **H.O.T.** Each unit on the map represents 1 mile. Gregory leaves his house at $(^-5, 4)$, cycles 4 miles east, 6 miles south, and 1 mile west. In which quadrant of the city is he now?

_____

24. The bus station has the same x-coordinate as City Hall but the opposite y-coordinate. In which quadrant of the city is the bus station located?

_____

25. **Write Math** ▸ Describe the relationship between the location of the points $(2, 5)$ and $(2, ^-5)$ on the coordinate plane.

_____

_____

26. ⭐ **Test Prep** What are the coordinates of the point $(^-2, ^-3)$ if it is reflected first across the x-axis and then across the y-axis on a coordinate grid?

    Ⓐ $(2, 3)$ Ⓒ $(2, ^-3)$

    Ⓑ $(^-2, 3)$ Ⓓ $(^-2, ^-3)$

SHOW YOUR WORK

Name _____

Distance on the Coordinate Plane

Essential Question How can you find the distance between two points that lie on a horizontal or vertical line on a coordinate plane?

COMMON CORE STANDARD CC.6.NS.8
Apply and extend previous understandings of numbers to the system of rational numbers.

🔓 UNLOCK the Problem REAL WORLD

The map of Foggy Mountain Park is marked on a coordinate grid in units of 1 mile. There are two campgrounds in the park. Camp 1 is located at (‾4, 3). Camp 2 is located at (5, 3). How far is it from Camp 1 to Camp 2?

 Find the distance from Camp 1 to Camp 2.

STEP 1 Graph the points.

Think: The points have the same _____ -coordinate, so they are located on a horizontal line.

STEP 2 Find the horizontal distance from Camp 1 to the y-axis.

Find the distance between the x-coordinates of the point (_____, 3) and the point (0, 3).

The distance of a number from 0 is the _____ of the number.

$$|{}^-4| = 4$$

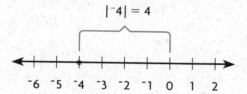

The distance from (‾4, 3) to (0, 3) is $|{}^-4| =$ _____ miles.

STEP 3 Find the horizontal distance from Camp 2 to the y-axis.

Find the distance between the x-coordinates of (_____, 3) and (_____, 3).

The distance from (5, 3) to (0, 3) is $|$_____$| =$ _____ miles.

STEP 4 Add to find the total distance: _____ + _____ = _____ miles.

So, the distance from Camp 1 to Camp 2 is _____ miles.

> **⚠ ERROR Alert**
>
> Remember that distance is never negative. You can find the distance between a negative number and 0 by using absolute value.

Math Talk MATHEMATICAL PRACTICES
Explain how you could check that you found the distance correctly.

1. **Explain** how you could use absolute value to find the distance from Camp 2 to the Eagle Nest. What is the distance?

_____

_____

In the problem on the previous page, you used absolute value to find the distance between points in different quadrants. You can also use absolute value to find the distance between points in the same quadrant.

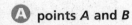 **Example** Find the distance between the pair of points on the coordinate grid.

A points *A* and *B*

STEP 1 Look at the coordinates of the points.

The _____ -coordinates of the points are the same, so the points lie on a horizontal line.

Think of the horizontal line passing through *A* and *B* as a number line.

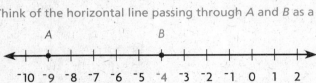

STEP 2 Find the distances of *A* and *B* from 0.

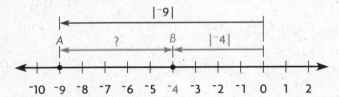

Distance of *A* from 0:

$|^-9| =$ _____ units

Distance of *B* from 0:

$|$ _____ $| =$ _____ units

STEP 3 Subtract to find the distance from *A* to *B*: _____ − _____ = _____ units.

So, the distance from *A* to *B* is _____ units.

B points *C* and *D*

STEP 1 Look at the coordinates of the points.

The _____ -coordinates of the points are the same, so the points lie on a vertical line.

Think of the vertical line passing through *C* and *D* as a number line.

STEP 2 Find the distances of *C* and *D* from 0 on the vertical number line.

Distance of *C* from 0: $|10| =$ _____ units

Distance of *D* from 0: $|$ _____ $| =$ _____ units

STEP 3 Subtract to find the distance from *C* to *D*:

_____ − _____ = _____ units.

So, the distance between *C* and *D* is _____ units.

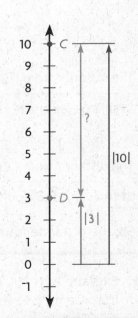

Math Talk

Explain how to find the distance from $M(^-5, 1)$ to $N(^-5, 7)$.

Name _____

Share and Show

Find the distance between the pair of points.

1. ($^-$3, 1) and (2, 1)

   Horizontal distance from ($^-$3, 1) to y-axis:

   |_____| = _____

   Horizontal distance from (2, 1) to y-axis: |_____| = _____

   Distance from ($^-$3, 1) to (2, 1): _____

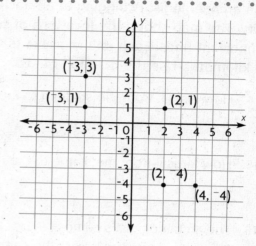

2. (2, 1) and (2, $^-$4)

3. (2, $^-$4) and (4, $^-$4)

4. ($^-$3, 3) and ($^-$3, 1)

_____   _____   _____

Math Talk MATHEMATICAL PRACTICES
Explain how you can find the distance between two points that have the same y-coordinate.

On Your Own

Practice: Copy and Solve Graph the pair of points. Then find the distance between them.

5. (0, 5) and (0, $^-$5)

6. (1, 1) and (1, $^-$3)

7. ($^-$2, $^-$5) and ($^-$2, $^-$1)

_____   _____   _____

8. ($^-$7, 3) and (5, 3)

9. (3, $^-$6) and (3, $^-$10)

10. (8, 0) and (8, $^-$8)

_____   _____   _____

Algebra Write the coordinates of a point that is the given distance from the given point.

11. 4 units from (3, 5)

12. 6 units from (2, 1)

13. 7 units from ($^-$4, $^-$1)

(3, ☐)

(☐, 1)

($^-$4, ☐)

Problem Solving > REAL WORLD

An archaeologist is digging at an ancient city. The map shows the locations of several important finds. Each unit represents 1 kilometer. Use the map for 14–18.

14. How far is it from the stadium to the statue?

_____

15. How far is it from the statue to the market?

_____

16. The archaeologist's campsite is located at (⁻9, ⁻3). How far is it from the campsite to the market?

_____

Archaeological Site

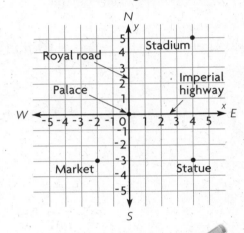

17. **H.O.T.** The archaeologist rode east on a donkey from the Great Gate, at (⁻11, 4), to the Royal Road. Then he rode south to the palace. How far did the archaeologist ride?

_____

18. **Write Math** > Explain how you could find the distance from the palace to any point on the Imperial Highway.

SHOW YOUR WORK

_____

_____

_____

_____

19. ⭐ **Test Prep** What is the distance between the points (2, ⁻6) and (⁻6, ⁻6)?

(A) 4 units

(B) 8 units

(C) 12 units

(D) 16 units

FOR MORE PRACTICE:
Standards Practice Book, pp. P65–P66

Problem Solving • The Coordinate Plane

Essential Question How can you use the strategy *draw a diagram* to help you solve a problem on the coordinate plane?

COMMON CORE STANDARD CC.6.NS.8
Apply and extend previous understandings of numbers to the system of rational numbers.

🔑 UNLOCK the Problem › REAL WORLD

An artist is using an illustration program. The program uses a coordinate plane, with the origin (0, 0) located at the center of the computer screen. The artist draws a dinosaur centered on the point (4, 6). Then she moves it 10 units to the left and 12 units down. What ordered pair represents the dinosaur's new location?

Use the graphic organizer to help you solve the problem.

Read the Problem

What do I need to find?	**What information do I need to use?**	**How will I use the information?**
I need to find the _____ for the dinosaur's new location.	The dinosaur started at the point _____. Then the artist moved it _____ to the left and _____ down.	I can draw a diagram to graph the information on a _____.

Solve the Problem

- Start by graphing and labeling the point _____.

- From this point, count _____ to the left.

- Then count _____ down.

- Graph and label the point at this location, and

  write its coordinates: _____.

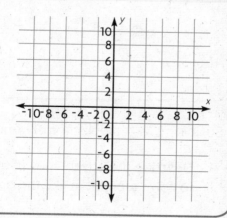

So, the dinosaur's new location is _____.

Math Talk **MATHEMATICAL PRACTICES**
Explain how you could check that your answer is correct.

🔑 Try Another Problem

Tyrone and Kyra both walk home from school. Kyra walks 4 blocks east and 3 blocks south to get home. Tyrone lives 3 blocks west and 3 blocks south of the school. How far apart are Tyrone's and Kyra's homes?

Use the graphic organizer to help you solve the problem.

Read the Problem	Solve the Problem
What do I need to find?	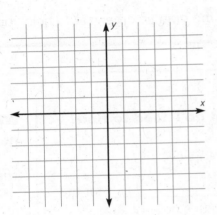
What information do I need to use?	
How will I use the information?	

So, it is _____ blocks from Tyrone's house to Kyra's house.

- **Describe** the advantages of using a coordinate plane to solve a problem like the one above.

_____

_____

Math Talk MATHEMATICAL PRACTICES **Explain** how you know that your answer is reasonable.

Name _____

Share and Show ![MATH BOARD]

UNLOCK the Problem Tips

√ Draw a diagram of the situation.
√ Use absolute value to find distance.

✓ **1.** Busby County is rectangular. A map of the county on a
coordinate plane shows the vertices of the county at
($^-$5, 8), (8, 8), (8, $^-$10), and ($^-$5, $^-$10). Each unit on
the map represents 1 mile. What is the county's perimeter?

First, draw a diagram of Busby County.

Busby County

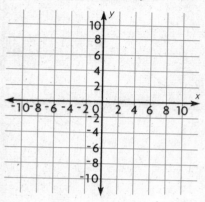

Next, use the diagram to find the length of each side of
the rectangle. Then add.

_____

So, the perimeter of Busby County is _____.

2. 🌟H.O.T. What if the vertices of the county were ($^-$5, 8),
(8, 8), (8, $^-$6) , and ($^-$5, $^-$6) ? What would the
perimeter of the county be?

_____

✓ **3.** On a coordinate map of Melville, a pizza restaurant is
located at ($^-$9, $^-$5). A laundry business is located 3
units to the left of the pizza restaurant on the map. What
are the map coordinates of the laundry business?

_____

4. The library is 4 blocks north and 9 blocks east of the
school. The museum is 9 blocks east and 11 blocks
south of the school. How far is it from the library to
the museum?

_____

SHOW YOUR WORK

© Houghton Mifflin Harcourt Publishing Company

On Your Own......

5. Diana left her campsite at (2, 6) on a map of Big Trees Park, hiked to Redwood Grove at ($^-$5, 6), and continued on to Bass Lake at ($^-$5, $^-$3). Each unit on the map represents 1 kilometer. How far did Diana hike?

_____

6. **H.O.T.** Hector left his house at ($^-$6, 13) on a map of Coleville and walked to the zoo at ($^-$6, 2). From there he walked east to his friend's house. He walked a total distance of 25 blocks. If each unit on the map represents one block, what are the coordinates of Hector's friend's house?

_____

SHOW YOUR WORK

7. In November, the price of a GizmoPhone was double the price in March. In December, the price was $57, which was $29 less than the price in November. What was the price of a GizmoPhone in March?

_____

8. **Write Math** ▸ A group of 12 boys and 16 girls are divided into teams with the same number of boys on each team and the same number of girls on each team. What is the greatest number of teams that can be made if each person is on a team? **Explain.**

_____

_____

_____

9. ⭐ **Test Prep** Which point is **not** 5 units from (1, 2) on the coordinate plane?

Ⓐ (1, 7)

Ⓑ (4, 2)

Ⓒ (1, $^-$3)

Ⓓ ($^-$4, 2)

Name _____

✓ Chapter 3 Review/Test

▶ Vocabulary

Choose the best term from the box to complete the sentence.

1. The _____ of a number is the distance of the number from 0 on a number line. (p. 115)

2. The four regions of the coordinate plane that are separated by the

   x- and y-axes are called _____. (p. 127)

▶ Concepts and Skills

Find the absolute value. (CC.6.NS.7c)

3. $|^-23|$

4. $|4.1|$

5. $\left|\dfrac{^-3}{4}\right|$

6. $|^-3.78|$

7. $\left|^-6\dfrac{3}{5}\right|$

_____ | _____ | _____ | _____ | _____

Compare. Write <, >, or =. (CC.6.NS.7a, CC.6.NS.7c)

8. $^-16 \bigcirc 0$

9. $|^-26| \bigcirc 26$

10. $|^-31| \bigcirc {}^-41$

11. $^-2 \bigcirc {}^-22$

Write a number that makes the statement true. (CC.6.NS.7d)

12. $|^-8| < \blacksquare$

13. $|11| > \blacksquare$

14. $\left|^-1\dfrac{1}{3}\right| < \blacksquare$

15. $|^-8.4| > \blacksquare$

_____ | _____ | _____ | _____

Graph and label the point on the coordinate plane. Identify the quadrant where the point is located (CC.6.NS.6b, CC.6.NS.6c)

16. $A\left(^-1\dfrac{1}{2}, 2\right)$

   Quadrant _____

17. $B(2, {}^-1.5)$

   Quadrant _____

18. $C\left(^-2\dfrac{1}{4}, {}^-2\dfrac{1}{4}\right)$

   Quadrant _____

19. $D(2.5, 1)$

   Quadrant _____

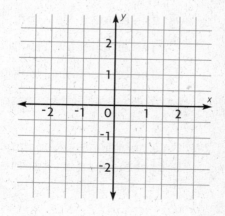

The two points are reflections of each other across the x- or y-axis. Identify the axis. (CC.6.NS.6b)

20. $(^-2, 1)$ and $(2, 1)$

   axis: _____

21. $(3, 3)$ and $(3, {}^-3)$

   axis: _____

22. $(5, {}^-6)$ and $(5, 6)$

   axis: _____

GO Online Assessment Options
Chapter Test

Fill in the bubble to show your answer.

23. Which set of integers is written in order from least to greatest? (CC.6.NS.7a)

    (A) ⁻9, 10, 12, ⁻15

    (B) 3, 5, ⁻7, ⁻8

    (C) ⁻2, ⁻3, 0, 4

    (D) ⁻5, ⁻1, 0, 1

24. Which situation can best be represented by a negative integer? (CC.6.NS.5)

    (A) Denver is 1 mile above sea level.

    (B) Eve withdrew $100 from her savings account.

    (C) The temperature rose 17 degrees.

    (D) The Rockets scored 21 points in the second half.

25. The average January temperatures in four towns are given. Which temperature is highest? (CC.6.NS.7b)

    (A) Fenton, ⁻0.7°F

    (B) Dexter, ⁻1.3°F

    (C) Millville, ⁻0.65°F

    (D) Wesley, ⁻2.8°F

26. The account balance in Ms. Hampton's checking account is ⁻$12. What does |⁻$12| represent in this situation? (CC.6.NS.7c)

    (A) The amount Ms. Hampton owes the bank

    (B) The amount Ms. Hampton has available to spend

    (C) The amount Ms. Hampton deposited in her account

    (D) The amount of increase in Ms. Hampton's account

27. On a coordinate plane map, Tyler Park is located at (5, ⁻12). Badger Stadium is located at (5, ⁻3). If each unit on the map represents 1 mile, how far apart are the two points? (CC.6.NS.8)

    (A) 7 miles

    (B) 8 miles

    (C) 9 miles

    (D) 15 miles

TEST PREP

Fill in the bubble to show your answer.

28. Renee has an account balance greater than ⁻$24. Which statement best describes her balance as a debt? (CC.6.NS.7d)

Ⓐ Her debt is greater than ⁻$24.

Ⓑ Her debt is less than ⁻$24.

Ⓒ Her debt is greater than $24.

Ⓓ Her debt is less than $24.

29. On a coordinate plane map, the town of Franklin is located at the point $F(3, 9)$. The town of Washington is located at the reflection of point F across the x-axis. What are the coordinates of Washington? (CC.6.NS.6b)

Ⓐ (9, 3)

Ⓑ (3, ⁻9)

Ⓒ (⁻3, 9)

Ⓓ (⁻3, ⁻9)

30. A drawing program uses a coordinate plane system to locate objects. An artist draws an owl centered on the point (2, 6). Then she moves the owl 4 units to the left and 4 units down. Which ordered pair represents the new location of the owl? (CC.6.NS.8)

Ⓐ (⁻2, 2)

Ⓑ (⁻2, 10)

Ⓒ (6, 2)

Ⓓ (6, 10)

31. Which point on the number line represents $-2\frac{1}{2}$? (CC.6.NS.6c)

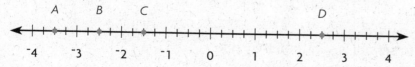

Ⓐ Point A

Ⓑ Point B

Ⓒ Point C

Ⓓ Point D

► Constructed Response

32. Jeremy says that the absolute value of 6 is ⁻6. Is he correct? Explain. (CC.6.NS.7c)

_____

_____

_____

_____

33. Shayla says the opposite of the opposite of ⁻4 is ⁻4. Is she correct? Explain. (CC.6.NS.6a)

_____

_____

► Performance Task (CC.6.NS.7c, CC.6.NS.8)

34. The map shows the location of Marc's house at point *M* and his school at point *S*. Each unit on the map represents 1 block.

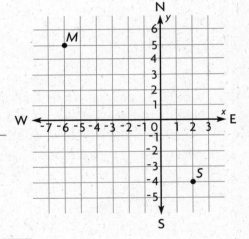

A Marc leaves his house and rides his bike 8 blocks east to the park. What ordered pair represents the park? Graph and label the point that represents the park.

_____

B The grocery store is 9 blocks south of Marc's house. What ordered pair represents the grocery store? Graph and label the point that represents the grocery store.

_____

C Marc usually rides his bike to school. He leaves his house and goes east to the park and then turns south and continues until he reaches school. How many blocks does he ride to get to school?

_____

D Marc's brother thinks the trip to school is shorter if they ride south to the grocery store and then east to school. Is he correct? Explain.

_____

_____

_____

CRITICAL AREA Ratios and Rates

CRITICAL AREA Connecting ratio and rate to whole number multiplication and division and using concepts of ratio and rate to solve problems

COMMON CORE

The St. Louis Cardinals, based in St. Louis, Missouri, were founded in 1882.

Project

Meet Me in St. Louis

Baseball teams, like the St. Louis Cardinals, record information about each player on the team. These statistics are used to describe a player's performance.

Get Started

A batting average is calculated from the ratio of a player's hits to the number of at bats. Batting averages are usually recorded as a decimal to the thousandths place. The table shows the batting results of three baseball players who received the Most Valuable Player award while playing for the St. Louis Cardinals. Write each batting ratio as a fraction. Then write the fraction as a decimal to the thousandths place and as a percent.

Important Facts

Player Name	Batting Results
Albert Pujols (2008)	187 hits in 524 at bats
Stan Musial (1948)	230 hits in 611 at bats
Rogers Hornsby (1925)	203 hits in 504 at bats

The players on a baseball team take their turns batting in the same order or sequence throughout a game. The manager sets the batting order. Suppose you are the manager of a team that includes Pujols, Musial, and Hornsby. What batting order would you use for those three players? Explain your answer.

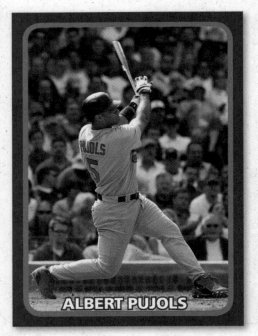

ALBERT PUJOLS

_____

_____

_____

_____

_____

_____

_____

_____

Completed by _____

Show What You Know

Check your understanding of important skills.

Name _____

▶ **Multiply or Divide to Find Equivalent Fractions** Multiply or divide to find two equivalent fractions for the given fraction.

1. $\frac{1}{2}$

_____

2. $\frac{5}{6}$

_____

3. $\frac{12}{18}$

_____

▶ **Extend Patterns** Write a description of the pattern. Then find the missing numbers.

4. 3, _____, 48, 192, 768, _____

_____

5. 625, 575, 525, _____, _____, 375

_____

▶ **Multiply by 2-Digit Numbers** Find the product.

6. 52
   × 19

7. 14
   × 88

8. 37
   × 21

9. 45
   × 62

MATH DETECTIVE WITH CARMEN SANDIEGO™

The student council should have 1 representative for every 25 students. Be a Math Detective and determine which of these situations fits the description. Explain your answer.

a. 5 representatives for 100 students

b. 10 representatives for 250 students

c. 15 representatives for 300 students

Vocabulary Builder

▶ **Visualize It** ....

Complete the bubble map with review words that are related to fractions.

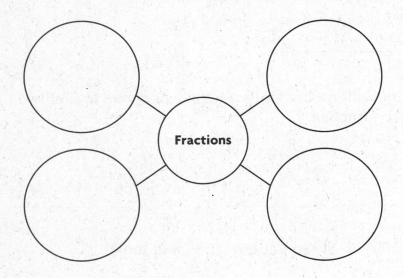

Review Words

coordinate plane

denominator

✓ equivalent fractions

numerator

✓ ordered pair

pattern

simplify

x-coordinate

y-coordinate

Preview Words

✓ equivalent ratios

✓ rate

✓ ratio

✓ unit rate

▶ **Understand Vocabulary** ....

Complete the sentences using the checked words.

1. A comparison of one number to another by division is a

   _____.

2. _____ are ratios that name the same comparison.

3. _____ are fractions that name the same amount or part.

4. A ratio that compares quantities with different units is a

   _____.

5. A _____ is a rate that compares a quantity to 1 unit.

6. In an _____ the first number is the *x*-coordinate and the second number is the *y*-coordinate.

GO Online • eStudent Edition • Multimedia eGlossary

Model Ratios

Essential Question How can you model ratios?

COMMON CORE STANDARD CC.6.RP.1
Understand ratio concepts and use ratio reasoning to solve problems.

The drawing shows 5 blue squares and 1 red square. You can compare the number of blue squares to the number of red squares by using a ratio. A **ratio** is a comparison of two quantities by division.

The ratio that compares blue squares to red squares is 5 to 1.
The ratio 5 to 1 can also be written as 5:1.

Investigate

Materials ■ two-color counters

Julie makes 3 bracelets for every 1 bracelet Beth makes. Use ratios to compare the number of bracelets Julie makes to the number Beth makes.

A. Use red and yellow counters to model the ratio that compares the number of bracelets Julie makes to the number of bracelets Beth makes.

> **Think:** Julie makes _____ bracelets when Beth makes 1 bracelet.

The ratio is _____:1.

B. Model the ratio that shows the number of bracelets Julie makes when Beth makes 2 bracelets. Write the ratio and explain how you modeled it.

_____

_____

C. How could you change the model from Part B to show the number of bracelets Julie makes when Beth makes 3 bracelets? Write the ratio.

_____

_____

Math Talk MATHEMATICAL PRACTICES
For each ratio, divide the number of bracelets Julie makes by the number of bracelets Beth makes. **Describe** a pattern you notice in the quotients.

Draw Conclusions

1. **Explain** how you used counters to compare the number of bracelets Julie makes to the number of bracelets Beth makes.

_____

_____

2. **Describe** a rule that you can use to find the number of bracelets Julie makes when you know the number of bracelets Beth makes.

_____

3. **H.O.T.** **Application** How can you use counters to find how many bracelets Beth makes if you know the number Julie makes? Explain and give an example.

_____

_____

_____

Make Connections

You can use a table to compare quantities and write ratios.

A bakery uses 1 packing box for every 4 muffins. Draw a model and make a table to show the ratio of boxes to muffins.

STEP 1 Draw a model to show the ratio that compares boxes to muffins.

Think: There is _____ box for every _____ muffins.

The ratio is _____ : _____.

STEP 2 Complete the table to show the ratio of boxes to muffins.

Think: Each time the number of boxes increases by 1,

the number of muffins increases by _____.

Number of Boxes	1	2	3	4
Number of Muffins	4			

+1

+

What is the ratio of boxes to muffins when there are 2 boxes? _____

Write another ratio shown by the table. Explain what the ratio represents.

_____

_____

Math Talk MATHEMATICAL PRACTICES Describe the pattern you see in the table comparing the number of boxes to the number of muffins.

Name _____

Share and Show

Write the ratio of yellow counters to red counters.

1.

_____ : _____

2.

_____

Draw a model of the ratio.

3. 3:2

4. 1:5

Use the ratio to complete the table.

5. Wen is arranging flowers in vases. For every 1 rose she uses, she uses 6 tulips. Complete the table to show the ratio of roses to tulips.

Roses	1	2	3	4
Tulips	6			

6. On the sixth-grade field trip, there are 8 students for every 1 adult. Complete the table to show the ratio of students to adults.

Students	8		24	
Adults	1	2		4

7. **Write Math** ▶ Joe reads 2 books for every 3 books Sam reads. **Describe** how to use ratios and counters to find the number of books Sam reads if Joe reads 6 books.

_____

_____

_____

_____

Draw Conclusions

The reading skill *draw conclusions* can help you analyze and make sense of information.

Hikers take trail mix as a snack on long hikes because it is tasty, nutritious, and easy to carry. There are many different recipes for trail mix, but it is usually made from different combinations of dried fruit, raisins, seeds, and nuts. Tanner and his dad make trail mix that has 1 cup of raisins for every 3 cups of sunflower seeds.

8. What is the ratio of cups of raisins to cups of sunflower seeds in the trail mix?

_____

9. **Explain** how you could model the ratio that compares cups of raisins to cups of sunflower seeds when Tanner uses 2 cups of raisins.

_____

_____

_____

_____

The table shows the ratio of cups of raisins to cups of sunflower seeds for different amounts of trail mix. Model each ratio as you complete the table.

Trail Mix					
Raisins (cups)	1	2	3	4	5
Sunflower Seeds (cups)	3				

10. Describe the pattern you see in the table.

_____

_____

11. What conclusion can Tanner draw from this pattern?

_____

_____

Ratios and Rates

Essential Question How do you write ratios and rates?

COMMON CORE STANDARD CC.6.RP.1
Understand ratio concepts and use ratio reasoning to solve problems.

🔑 UNLOCK the Problem · REAL · WORLD

A bird rescue group is caring for 3 eagles, 2 hawks, and 5 owls in their rescue center.

You can compare the numbers of different types of birds using ratios. There are three ways to write the ratio of owls to eagles in the rescue center.

Using words	As a fraction	With a colon
5 to 3	$\frac{5}{3}$	5:3

Ratios can be written to compare a part to a part, a part to a whole, or a whole to a part.

🔒 **Write each ratio using words, as a fraction, and with a colon.**

Ⓐ Owls to hawks

_____ to _____ | ——— | _____ : _____   Part to part

Ⓑ Eagles to total birds in the rescue center

_____ to _____ | ——— | _____ : _____   Part to whole

Ⓒ Total birds in the rescue center to hawks

_____ to _____ | ——— | _____ : _____   Whole to part

1. The ratio of owls to total number of birds is 5:10. **Explain** what this ratio means.

_____

🔑 Example

A restaurant sells veggie burgers at the rate of $4 for 1 burger. What rate gives the cost of 5 veggie burgers? Write the rate for 5 burgers using words, as a fraction, and with a colon.

A **rate** is a ratio that compares two quantities that have different units of measure.

A **unit rate** is a rate that makes a comparison to 1 unit. The unit rate for cost per veggie burger is $4 to 1 burger or $\frac{\$4}{1\text{ burger}}$.

Complete the table to find the rate that gives the cost of 5 veggie burgers.

Think: 1 veggie burger costs $4, so 2 veggie burgers cost $4 + _____ , or 2 × _____ .

	Unit Rate	2 · $4 ↓	3 · $4 ↓	▢ · $4 ↓	▢ · $4 ↓
Cost	$4	$8			
Veggie Burgers	1	2	3	4	

2 · 1   ▢ · 1   4 · 1   ▢ · 1

The table shows that 5 veggie burgers cost _____ .

So, the rate that gives the cost for 5 veggie burgers is

$ _____ to _____ burgers, $\frac{\$\,\square}{\square\text{ burgers}}$, or $ _____ : _____ burgers.

MATHEMATICAL PRACTICES

Math Talk Describe two other ways to say "$4 per burger".

Try This! Write the rate in three different ways.

Ⓐ The rate that gives the cost of 3 veggie burgers

_____

Ⓑ The rate that gives the cost of 4 veggie burgers

_____

2. **Explain** why the ratio $\frac{\$4}{1\text{ burger}}$ is a unit rate.

_____

3. **Explain** the pattern you see in the table in the Example.

_____

_____

Name _____

Share and Show

1. Write the ratio of the number of red bars to blue stars.

Write the ratio in two different ways.

2. 8 to 16

3. $\frac{4}{24}$

4. 1:3

5. 7 to 9

_____ _____ _____ _____

6. Marilyn saves $15 per week. Complete the table to find the rate that gives the amount saved in 4 weeks. Write the rate in three different ways.

Savings		$30	$45		$75
Weeks	1	2	3	4	5

_____

Math Talk MATHEMATICAL PRACTICES
Explain whether the ratios 5:2 and 2:5 are the same or different.

On Your Own

Write the ratio in two different ways.

7. $\frac{16}{40}$

8. 8:12

9. 4 to 11

10. 2:13

_____ _____ _____ _____

11. There are 24 baseball cards in 4 packs. Complete the table to find the rate that gives the number of cards in 2 packs. Write this rate in three different ways.

Cards			18	24
Packs	1	2	3	4

_____

12. Explain how the statement "There are 6 apples per bag" represents a rate.

_____

_____

_____

Problem Solving REAL WORLD

Use the diagram of a birdhouse for 13–15.

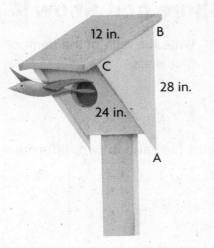

12 in. B

C

28 in.

24 in.

A

13. Write the ratio of *AB* to *BC* in three different ways.

_____

14. Write the ratio of the shortest side length of triangle *ABC* to the perimeter of the triangle in three different ways.

_____

15. Write the ratio of the perimeter of triangle *ABC* to the longest side length of the triangle in three different ways.

_____

SHOW YOUR WORK

16. Leandra places 6 photos on each page in a photo album. Find the rate that gives the number of photos on 2 pages. Write the rate in three different ways.

_____

17. **H.O.T. What's the Question?** The ratio of total students in Ms. Murray's class to students in the class who have an older brother is 3 to 1. The answer is 1:2. What is the question?

_____

_____

18. **Write Math** ▸ What do all unit rates have in common?

_____

_____

19. ⭐ **Test Prep** Two smoothies at Smoothie Haven cost $6. What is the unit rate for the cost per smoothie at Smoothie Haven?

Ⓐ $\dfrac{\$1}{3\text{ smoothies}}$

Ⓑ $\dfrac{\$6}{2\text{ smoothies}}$

Ⓒ $\dfrac{\$3}{1\text{ smoothie}}$

Ⓓ $\dfrac{\$6}{1\text{ smoothie}}$

FOR MORE PRACTICE:
Standards Practice Book, pp. P75–P76

Equivalent Ratios and Multiplication Tables

Essential Question How can you use a multiplication table to find equivalent ratios?

COMMON CORE STANDARD CC.6.RP.3a
Understand ratio concepts and use ratio reasoning to solve problems.

The table below shows two rows from the multiplication table: the row for 1 and the row for 6. The ratios shown in each column of the table are equivalent to the original ratio. Ratios that name the same comparison are **equivalent ratios**.

	Original ratio	$2 \cdot 1$ ↓	$3 \cdot 1$ ↓	$4 \cdot 1$ ↓	$5 \cdot 1$ ↓
Bags	1	2	3	4	5
Apples	6	12	18	24	30
		↑ $2 \cdot 6$	↑ $3 \cdot 6$	↑ $4 \cdot 6$	↑ $5 \cdot 6$

×	1	2	3	4	5
1	1	2	3	4	5
2	2	4	6	8	10
3	3	6	9	12	15
4	4	8	12	16	20
5	5	10	15	20	25
6	6	12	18	24	30

You can use a multiplication table to find equivalent ratios.

UNLOCK the Problem REAL WORLD

The ratio of adults to students on a field trip is $\frac{3}{8}$.

Write two ratios that are equivalent to $\frac{3}{8}$.

 Use the multiplication table.

STEP 1 Shade the rows that show the original ratio.

Think: The original ratio is ——. Shade the row for _____ and

the row for _____ on the multiplication table.

_____

STEP 2 Circle the column that shows the original ratio.

Think: There is one group of 3 adults for every group of 8 students.

_____

STEP 3 Circle two columns that show equivalent ratios.

The column for 2 shows there are $2 \cdot 3$, or _____ adults when

there are $2 \cdot 8$, or _____ students.

The column for 3 shows there are $3 \cdot 3$, or _____ adults when

there are $3 \cdot 8$, or _____ students.

So, _____ and _____ are equivalent to $\frac{3}{8}$.

×	1	2	3	4	5	6	7	8	9
1	1	2	3	4	5	6	7	8	9
2	2	4	6	8	10	12	14	16	18
3	3	6	9	12	15	18	21	24	27
4	4	8	12	16	20	24	28	32	36
5	5	10	15	20	25	30	35	40	45
6	6	12	18	24	30	36	42	48	54
7	7	14	21	28	35	42	49	56	63
8	8	16	24	32	40	48	56	64	72
9	9	18	27	36	45	54	63	72	81

Math Talk MATHEMATICAL PRACTICES

Explain whether the multiplication table shown represents all of the ratios that are equivalent to 3:8.

CONNECT You can find equivalent ratios by using a table or by multiplying or dividing by a form of one.

🔑 One Way Use a table.

Jessa made fruit punch by mixing 2 pints of orange juice with 5 pints of pineapple juice. To make more punch, she needs to mix orange juice and pineapple juice in the same ratio. Write three equivalent ratios for $\frac{2}{5}$.

Think: Use rows from the multiplication table to help you complete a table of equivalent ratios.

×	1	2	3	4	5
1	1	2	3	4	5
2	2	4	6	8	10
3	3	6	9	12	15
4	4	8	12	16	20
5	5	10	15	20	25

→

	Original ratio	2 · 2 ↓	3 · 2 ↓	☐ · 2 ↓
Orange juice (pints)	2			8
Pineapple juice (pints)	5		15	
		↑ 2 · 5	↑ ☐ · 5	↑ 4 · 5

So, $\frac{2}{5}$, _____, _____, and _____ are equivalent ratios.

🔑 Another Way Multiply or divide by a form of one.

Write two equivalent ratios for $\frac{6}{8}$.

Ⓐ Multiply by a form of one.

Multiply the numerator and denominator by the same number.

$$\frac{6 \cdot \ \boxed{\ }}{8 \cdot \ \boxed{\ }} = \frac{\boxed{\ }}{\boxed{\ }}$$

Ⓑ Divide by a form of one.

Divide the numerator and denominator by the same number.

$$\frac{6 \div \ \boxed{\ }}{8 \div \ \boxed{\ }} = \frac{\boxed{\ }}{\boxed{\ }}$$

So, $\frac{6}{8}$, _____, and _____ are equivalent ratios.

ERROR Alert

Be sure to multiply or divide the numerator and the denominator by the same number.

- **Explain** how ratios are similar to fractions. Explain how they are different.

_____

_____

Name _____

Share and Show

Write two equivalent ratios.

1. Use a multiplication table to write two ratios that are equivalent to $\frac{4}{7}$.

   Find the rows that show $\frac{4}{7}$.

   Find columns that show equivalent ratios. $\frac{4}{7} =$ _____ = _____

 2.

3		
7		

3.

5		
2		

4.

	2	
	10	

5. $\frac{4}{5}$

_____

 6. $\frac{12}{30}$

_____

7. $\frac{2}{9}$

_____

Math Talk   MATHEMATICAL PRACTICES
Explain how the multiplication table helps you find equivalent ratios.

On Your Own

Write two equivalent ratios.

8.

9		
8		

9.

5		
4		

10.

	6	
	9	

11. $\frac{8}{7}$

_____

12. $\frac{2}{6}$

_____

13. $\frac{4}{11}$

_____

Determine whether the ratios are equivalent.

14. $\frac{2}{3}$ and $\frac{8}{12}$

_____

15. $\frac{8}{10}$ and $\frac{6}{10}$

_____

16. $\frac{16}{60}$ and $\frac{4}{15}$

_____

17. $\frac{3}{14}$ and $\frac{8}{28}$

_____

Problem Solving REAL WORLD

Use the multiplication table for 18–20.

×	1	2	3	4	5	6	7	8	9
1	1	2	3	4	5	6	7	8	9
2	2	4	6	8	10	12	14	16	18
3	3	6	9	12	15	18	21	24	27
4	4	8	12	16	20	24	28	32	36
5	5	10	15	20	25	30	35	40	45
6	6	12	18	24	30	36	42	48	54
7	7	14	21	28	35	42	49	56	63
8	8	16	24	32	40	48	56	64	72
9	9	18	27	36	45	54	63	72	81

18. In Keith's baseball games this year, the ratio of times he has gotten on base to the times he has been at bat is $\frac{4}{14}$. Write two ratios that are equivalent to $\frac{4}{14}$.

_____

19. A radio station plays 24 minutes of music out of every 30 minutes. Write two ratios that are equivalent to the ratio $\frac{24}{30}$.

_____

SHOW YOUR WORK

20. **H.O.T.** **Pose a Problem** Use the multiplication table to write a new problem involving equivalent ratios. Then solve the problem.

_____

_____

_____

21. **Write Math** ▶ **Describe** how to write an equivalent ratio for $\frac{9}{27}$ without using a multiplication table.

_____

_____

_____

_____

22. ⭐ **Test Prep** Of the 21 people polled about the election for mayor, 12 said they planned to vote for the current mayor. Which ratio is equivalent to $\frac{12}{21}$?

(A) $\frac{12}{28}$ (C) $\frac{3}{5}$

(B) $\frac{4}{7}$ (D) $\frac{2}{3}$

FOR MORE PRACTICE:
Standards Practice Book, pp. P77–P78

Name _____

Problem Solving •
Use Tables to Compare Ratios

Essential Question How can you use the strategy *find a pattern* to help you compare ratios?

COMMON CORE STANDARD CC.6.RP.3a
Understand ratio concepts and use ratio reasoning to solve problems.

🔑 UNLOCK the Problem REAL WORLD

A paint store makes rose-pink paint by mixing 3 parts red paint to 8 parts white paint. A clerk mixes 4 parts red paint to 7 parts white paint. Did the clerk mix the paint correctly to make rose-pink paint? Use tables of equivalent ratios to support your answer.

Use the graphic organizer to help you solve the problem.

Read the Problem

What do I need to find?	**What information do I need to use?**	**How will I use the information?**
I need to find whether the ratio used by the clerk is _____ to the ratio for rose-pink paint.	I need to use the rose-pink paint ratio and the ratio used by the clerk.	I will make tables of equivalent ratios to compare the ratios _____ to _____ and _____ to _____.

Solve the Problem

Rose-Pink Paint				
Parts Red	3	6	9	12
Parts White	8			

Clerk's Paint Mixture				
Parts Red	4			
Parts White	7	14	21	28

Look for a pattern to determine whether the ratios in the first table are equivalent to the ratios in the second table.

Think: The number 12 appears in the first row of both tables.

__12__ is/is not equivalent to __12__.

The ratios have the same numerator and _____ denominators.

So, the clerk _____ mix the paint correctly.

Math Talk MATHEMATICAL PRACTICES
Explain how you can check that your answer is correct.

🔑 Try Another Problem

In Amy's art class, the ratio of brushes to students is 6 to 4. In Traci's art class, the ratio of brushes to students is 9 to 6. Is the ratio of brushes to students in Amy's class equivalent to the ratio of brushes to students in Traci's class? Use tables of equivalent ratios to support your answer.

Read the Problem

What do I need to find?	What information do I need to use?	How will I use the information?

Solve the Problem

So, the ratio of brushes to students in Amy's class is/is not equivalent to the ratio of brushes to students in Traci's class.

1. **Explain** how you used a pattern to determine whether the ratios in the two tables are equivalent.

   _____

   _____

   _____

2. **Tell** how writing the ratios in simplest form can help you justify your answer.

   _____

Name _____

Share and Show

❗ UNLOCK the Problem **Tips**

✓ Circle the question.

✓ Underline important facts.

✓ Check to make sure you answered the question.

1. In Jawan's school, 4 out of 10 students chose basketball as a sport they like to watch, and 3 out of 5 students chose football. Is the ratio of students who chose basketball (4 to 10) equivalent to the ratio of students who chose football (3 to 5)?

   First, make tables to show the ratios.

Basketball			

Football			

   Next, compare the ratios in the tables. Find a ratio in the first table that has the same numerator as a ratio in the second table.

   $\dfrac{12}{}$ _____ equivalent to $\dfrac{12}{}$.

   So, the ratios _____ equivalent.

2. **H.O.T.** **What if** 20 out of 50 students chose baseball as a sport they like to watch? Is this ratio equivalent to the ratio for either basketball or football? Explain.

   _____

   _____

   _____

3. The table shows the results of the quizzes Hannah took in one week. Did Hannah get the same score on her math and science quizzes? **Explain.**

   _____

   _____

Hannah's Quiz Results	
Subject	**Questions Correct**
Social Studies	4 out of 5
Math	8 out of 10
Science	3 out of 4
English	10 out of 12

4. Did Hannah get the same score on the quizzes in any of her classes? **Explain.**

   _____

   _____

On Your Own

5. For every $10 that Julie makes, she saves $3. For every $15 Liam makes, he saves $6. Is Julie's ratio of money saved to money earned equivalent to Liam's ratio of money saved to money earned?

_____

6. **H.O.T.** **Analyze** Thad, Joey, and Mia ran in a race. The finishing times were 4.56 minutes, 3.33 minutes, and 4.75 minutes. Thad did not finish last. Mia had the fastest time. What was each runner's time?

_____

_____

7. **Write Math** Gisele and her father went shopping. Gisele spent $32 on a dress. Her father gave her $20 more. Then she spent $19.50 on a pair of shoes. After she finished shopping, she had $12.75 left. **Explain** how you could find how much money Gisele had before she went shopping.

_____

_____

_____

_____

_____

_____

8. ⭐ **Test Prep** The list shows the ratio of pieces of fruit to cups of juice for different smoothie flavors. Which smoothies have equivalent ratios?

(A) banana and strawberry

(B) orange and strawberry

(C) orange, banana, and peach

(D) strawberry, banana, and peach

Choose a
STRATEGY

Use a Model
Draw a Diagram
Find a Pattern
Solve a Simpler Problem
Work Backward
Use a Formula

SHOW YOUR WORK

Smoothie Ratios

Orange smoothie
3 pieces of fruit to 4 cups of juice
Strawberry smoothie
2 pieces of fruit to 3 cups of juice
Banana smoothie
6 pieces of fruit to 8 cups juice
Peach smoothie
9 pieces of fruit to 12 cups of juice

© Houghton Mifflin Harcourt Publishing Company

Name _____

Use Equivalent Ratios

Essential Question How can you use tables to solve problems involving equivalent ratios?

COMMON CORE STANDARD CC.6.RP.3a
Understand ratio concepts and use ratio reasoning to solve problems.

🔑 UNLOCK the Problem 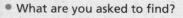 REAL WORLD

In warm weather, the Anderson family likes to spend time on the family's boat. The boat uses 2 gallons of gas to travel 12 miles on the lake. How much gas would the boat use to travel 48 miles?

 Solve by finding equivalent ratios.

Let ■ represent the unknown number of gallons.

$$\frac{\text{gallons}}{\text{miles}} \rightarrow \frac{2}{12} = \frac{\blacksquare}{48} \leftarrow \frac{\text{gallons}}{\text{miles}}$$

Make a table of equivalent ratios.

	Original ratio	$2 \cdot 2$ ↓	$\blacksquare \cdot 2$ ↓	$\blacksquare \cdot 2$ ↓
Gas used (gallons)	2		6	
Distance (miles)	12	24		48

↑ $\blacksquare \cdot 12$ ↑ $3 \cdot 12$ ↑ $\blacksquare \cdot 12$

The ratios $\frac{2}{12}$ and _____ are equivalent ratios,

so $\frac{2}{12} = \frac{\blacksquare}{48}$.

So, the boat will use _____ gallons of gas to travel 48 miles.

* **What if** the boat uses 14 gallons of gas? Explain how you can use equivalent ratios to find the number of miles the boat travels when it uses 14 gallons of gas.

_____

_____

_____

What are you asked to find?

_____

_____

🔑 Example · Use equivalent ratios to find the unknown value.

Ⓐ $\frac{3}{4} = \frac{\blacksquare}{20}$

Use common denominators to write equivalent ratios.

_____ is a multiple of 4, so _____ is a common denominator.

Multiply the _____ and denominator by _____ to write the ratios using a common denominator.

The _____ are the same, so the _____ are equal to each other.

$$\frac{3}{4} = \frac{\blacksquare}{20}$$

$$\frac{3 \times \blacksquare}{4 \times \blacksquare} = \frac{\blacksquare}{20}$$

$$\frac{\blacksquare}{20} = \frac{\blacksquare}{20}$$

So, the unknown value is _____ and $\frac{3}{4} = \frac{\blacksquare}{20}$.

Check your answer by making a table of equivalent ratios.

Original ratio   ▨ · 3   ▨ · 3   ▨ · 3   ▨ · 3

3	6			
4	8			

    ▨ · 4   ▨ · 4   ▨ · 4   ▨ · 4

Ⓑ $\frac{56}{42} = \frac{8}{\blacksquare}$

Write an equivalent ratio with 8 in the numerator.

Think: Divide 56 by _____ to get 8.

So, divide the denominator by _____ as well.

The _____ are the same, so the _____ are equal to each other.

$$\frac{56}{42} = \frac{8}{\blacksquare}$$

$$\frac{56 \div \blacksquare}{42 \div \blacksquare} = \frac{8}{\blacksquare}$$

$$\frac{8}{\blacksquare} = \frac{8}{\blacksquare}$$

So, the unknown value is _____ and $\frac{56}{42} = \frac{8}{\blacksquare}$.

Check your answer by making a table of equivalent ratios.

Original ratio   ▨ · 8   ▨ · 8   ▨ · 8   ▨ · 8   ▨ · 8   ▨ · 8

8	16					
6	12					

    ▨ · 6   ▨ · 6   ▨ · 6   ▨ · 6   ▨ · 6   ▨ · 6

Math Talk MATHEMATICAL PRACTICES

Give an example of two equivalent ratios. **Explain** how you know that they are equivalent.

Name _____

Share and Show

Use equivalent ratios to find the unknown value.

1. $\dfrac{\blacksquare}{10} = \dfrac{4}{5}$

$\dfrac{\blacksquare}{10} = \dfrac{4 \cdot \square}{5 \cdot \square}$

$\dfrac{\blacksquare}{10} = \dfrac{\square}{10}$

So, the unknown value is _____.

2. $\dfrac{18}{24} = \dfrac{6}{\blacksquare}$

$\dfrac{18 \div \square}{24 \div \square} = \dfrac{6}{\blacksquare}$

$\dfrac{6}{\square} = \dfrac{6}{\blacksquare}$

So, the unknown value is _____.

3. $\dfrac{3}{6} = \dfrac{15}{\blacksquare}$

_____

4. $\dfrac{\blacksquare}{5} = \dfrac{8}{10}$

_____

☑ 5. $\dfrac{7}{4} = \dfrac{\blacksquare}{12}$

_____

☑ 6. $\dfrac{10}{\blacksquare} = \dfrac{40}{12}$

_____

Math Talk MATHEMATICAL PRACTICES **Explain** whether you can always find an equivalent ratio by subtracting the same number from the numerator and denominator. Give an example to support your answer.

On Your Own

Use equivalent ratios to find the unknown value.

7. $\dfrac{2}{6} = \dfrac{\blacksquare}{30}$

_____

8. $\dfrac{5}{\blacksquare} = \dfrac{55}{110}$

_____

9. $\dfrac{3}{9} = \dfrac{9}{\blacksquare}$

_____

10. $\dfrac{\blacksquare}{6} = \dfrac{16}{24}$

_____

11. $\dfrac{18}{15} = \dfrac{6}{\blacksquare}$

_____

12. $\dfrac{\blacksquare}{16} = \dfrac{4}{8}$

_____

13. $\dfrac{14}{\blacksquare} = \dfrac{7}{9}$

_____

14. $\dfrac{42}{54} = \dfrac{\blacksquare}{9}$

_____

Problem Solving REAL WORLD

Solve by finding an equivalent ratio.

15. It takes 8 minutes for Sue to make 2 laps around the go-kart track. How many laps can Sue complete in 24 minutes?

_____

16. The width of Jay's original photo is 8 inches. The length of the original photo is 10 inches. He prints a smaller version that has an equivalent ratio of width to length. The width of the smaller version is 4 inches. What is the length of the smaller version?

_____

SHOW YOUR WORK

17. Ariel bought 3 raffle tickets for $5. How many tickets could Ariel buy for $15?

_____

18. **H.O.T. Reasoning** Is the unknown value in $\frac{2}{3} = \frac{\blacksquare}{18}$ the same as the unknown value in $\frac{3}{2} = \frac{18}{\blacksquare}$? **Explain.**

_____

_____

19. **What's the Error?** Greg used the steps shown to find the unknown value. Describe his error and give the correct solution.

$$\frac{2}{6} = \frac{\blacksquare}{12}$$

$$\frac{2+6}{6+6} = \frac{\blacksquare}{12}$$

$$\frac{8}{12} = \frac{\blacksquare}{12}$$

The unknown value is 8.

_____

_____

_____

20. ⭐ **Test Prep** A speedboat can travel 24 miles on 3 gallons of gas. How many miles could the boat travel on 12 gallons of gas?

Ⓐ 6 miles   Ⓒ 72 miles

Ⓑ 33 miles   Ⓓ 96 miles

FOR MORE PRACTICE:
Standards Practice Book, pp. P81–P82

Name _____

✓ Mid-Chapter Checkpoint

▶ **Vocabulary**

Choose the best term from the box to complete the sentence.

Vocabulary
equivalent ratios
rate
ratio
unit rate

1. A _____ is a rate that makes a comparison to 1 unit. (p. 152)

2. Two ratios that name the same comparison are

   _____. (p. 155)

▶ **Concepts and Skills**

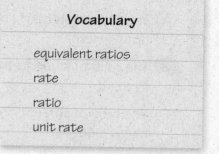

3. Write the ratio of red circles to blue squares. (CC.6.RP.1)

   _____

Write the ratio in two different ways. (CC.6.RP.1)

4. 8 to 12

   _____

5. 7:2

   _____

6. $\frac{5}{9}$

   _____

7. 11 to 3

   _____

Write two equivalent ratios. (CC.6.RP.3a)

8. $\frac{2}{7}$

   _____

9. $\frac{6}{5}$

   _____

10. $\frac{9}{12}$

    _____

11. $\frac{18}{6}$

    _____

Find the unknown value. (CC.6.RP.3a)

12. $\frac{15}{\blacksquare} = \frac{5}{10}$

    _____

13. $\frac{\blacksquare}{9} = \frac{12}{3}$

    _____

14. $\frac{48}{16} = \frac{\blacksquare}{8}$

    _____

15. $\frac{9}{36} = \frac{3}{\blacksquare}$

    _____

16. There are 36 students in the chess club, 40 students in the drama club, and 24 students in the film club. Which ratio is equivalent to 5:3? (CC.6.RP.3a)

(A) The ratio of students in the chess club to students in the drama club

(B) The ratio of students in the chess club to students in the film club

(C) The ratio of students in the drama club to students in the chess club

(D) The ratio of students in the drama club to students in the film club

17. A trail mix has 4 cups of raisins, 3 cups of chocolate, 6 cups of peanuts, and 2 cups of cashews. Which ingredients are in the same ratio as cashews to raisins? (CC.6.RP.3a)

(A) raisins to peanuts

(B) cashews to chocolate

(C) chocolate to peanuts

(D) cashews to peanuts

18. There are 32 adults and 20 children at a school play. Which of these ratios is not equivalent to the ratio of adults to children? (CC.6.RP.3a)

(A) 16 to 10

(B) 24 to 15

(C) 48 to 25

(D) 64 to 40

19. Sonya got 8 out of 10 questions right on a quiz. She got the same score on a quiz that had 20 questions. How many questions did Sonya get right on the second quiz? (CC.6.RP.3a)

(A) 10

(B) 16

(C) 18

(D) 20

Name _____

Find Unit Rates

Essential Question How can you use unit rates to make comparisons?

COMMON CORE STANDARD CC.6.RP.2
Understand ratio concepts and use ratio reasoning
to solve problems.

 **UNLOCK the Problem** REAL WORLD

The star fruit, or carambola, is the fruit of a tree that is native to Indonesia, India, and Sri Lanka. Slices of the fruit are in the shape of a five-pointed star. Lara paid $9.60 for 16 ounces of star fruit. Find the price of 1 ounce of star fruit.

Recall that a unit rate makes a comparison to 1 unit. You can find a unit rate by dividing the numerator and denominator by the number in the denominator.

- Underline the sentence that tells you what you are trying to find.
- Circle the numbers you need to use to solve the problem.

 Write the unit rate for the price of star fruit.

Write a ratio that compares _____

to _____.

Divide the numerator and denominator by

the number in the _____.

$$\frac{price}{weight} \rightarrow \frac{\$\quad}{\quad oz}$$

$$\frac{\$9.60 \div \quad}{16\,oz \div \quad}$$

$$\frac{\$\quad}{1\,oz}$$

So, the unit rate is _____. The price is _____ per ounce.

Math Talk MATHEMATICAL PRACTICES
Explain the difference between a ratio and a rate.

1. **Explain** why the unit rate is equivalent to the original rate.

_____

_____

2. **Explain** how you could check that you found the unit rate correctly.

_____

_____

🔑 Example

A During migration, a hummingbird can fly 210 miles in 7 hours, and a goose can fly 165 miles in 3 hours. Which bird flies at a faster rate?

Write the rate for each bird.

Hummingbird: $\dfrac{\text{_____ miles}}{\text{7 hours}}$ Goose: $\dfrac{165 \text{ miles}}{\text{_____ hours}}$

Write the unit rates.

$$\dfrac{210 \text{ mi} \div \text{_____}}{7 \text{ hr} \div \text{_____}} \qquad \dfrac{165 \text{ mi} \div \text{_____}}{3 \text{ hr} \div \text{_____}}$$

$$\dfrac{\text{_____ mi}}{1 \text{ hr}} \qquad \dfrac{\text{_____ mi}}{1 \text{ hr}}$$

Compare the unit rates.   _____ miles per hour is faster than _____ miles per hour.

So, the _____ flies at a faster rate.

B A 64-ounce bottle of apple juice costs $5.76. A 15-ounce bottle of apple juice costs $1.80. Which item costs less per ounce?

Write the rate for each bottle.

64-ounce bottle: $\dfrac{\text{_____}}{64 \text{ ounces}}$ 15-ounce bottle: $\dfrac{\text{_____}}{\text{_____ ounces}}$

Write the unit rates.

$$\dfrac{\text{_____} \div \text{_____}}{64 \text{ oz} \div \text{_____}} \qquad \dfrac{\$1.80 \div \text{_____}}{\text{_____ oz} \div \text{_____}}$$

$$\dfrac{\text{_____}}{1 \text{ oz}} \qquad \dfrac{\text{_____}}{1 \text{ oz}}$$

Compare the unit rates.   _____ per ounce is less expensive than _____ per ounce.

So, the _____-ounce bottle costs less per ounce.

Try This! At one grocery store, a dozen eggs cost $1.20. At another store, $1\frac{1}{2}$ dozen eggs cost $2.16. Which is the better buy?

Store 1:   Store 2:

The unit price is lower at Store _____, so a dozen eggs for _____ is the better buy.

© Houghton Mifflin Harcourt Publishing Company

Name _____

Share and Show

Write the rate as a fraction. Then find the unit rate.

1. Sara drove 72 miles on 4 gallons of gas.

   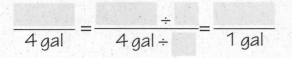

   $$\frac{\boxed{}}{4\text{ gal}} = \frac{\boxed{} \div \boxed{}}{4\text{ gal} \div \boxed{}} = \frac{\boxed{}}{1\text{ gal}}$$

✓ 2. Dean paid $27.00 for 4 movie tickets.

   _____

3. Amy and Mai have to read *Bud, Not Buddy* for a class. Amy reads 20 pages in 2 days. Mai reads 35 pages in 3 days. Who reads at a faster rate?

   _____

✓ 4. An online music store offers 5 downloads for $6.25. Another online music store offers 12 downloads for $17.40. Which store offers the better deal?

   _____

Math Talk MATHEMATICAL PRACTICES
Explain how to find a unit rate.

On Your Own

Write the rate as a fraction. Then find the unit rate.

5. A company packed 108 items in 12 boxes.

   _____

6. There are 112 students for 14 teachers.

   _____

7. Geoff charges $27 for 3 hours of swimming lessons. Anne charges $32 for 4 hours of swimming lessons. Which swimming instructor offers a better deal?

   _____

8. One florist made 16 bouquets in 5 hours. A second florist made 40 bouquets in 12 hours. Which florist makes bouquets at a faster rate?

   _____

Tell which rate is faster by comparing unit rates.

9. $\dfrac{160\text{ mi}}{2\text{ hr}}$ and $\dfrac{210\text{ mi}}{3\text{ hr}}$

10. $\dfrac{270\text{ ft}}{9\text{ min}}$ and $\dfrac{180\text{ ft}}{9\text{ min}}$

11. $\dfrac{250\text{ m}}{10\text{ s}}$ and $\dfrac{120\text{ m}}{4\text{ s}}$

   _____

🔑 UNLOCK the Problem — REAL WORLD

12. Ryan wants to buy treats for his puppy. If Ryan wants to buy the treats that cost the least per pack, which treat should he buy? Explain.

a. What do you need to find?

_____

_____

Cost of Dog Treats		
Name	**Cost**	**Number of Packs**
Pup Bites	$5.76	4
Doggie Treats	$7.38	6
Pupster Snacks	$7.86	6
Nutri-Biscuits	$9.44	8

b. Find the price per pack for each treat.

_____

_____

_____

_____

_____

_____

c. Complete the sentences.

The treat with the highest price per pack is

_____.

The treat with the lowest price per pack is

_____.

Ryan should buy _____

because _____

_____

_____.

13. 🔆 H.O.T. **Write Math** ▶ What information do you need to consider in order to decide whether one product is a better deal than another? When might the lower unit rate not be the best choice? **Explain.**

_____

_____

_____

_____

_____

14. ⭐ **Test Prep** A 32-ounce box of cereal costs $3.84. What is the unit rate?

(A) $0.12 for 1 ounce

(B) $1.92 for 16 ounces

(C) $0.24 for 1 ounce

(D) $3.84 for 32 ounces

FOR MORE PRACTICE:
Standards Practice Book, pp. P83–P84

Name _____

Use Unit Rates

Essential Question How can you solve problems using unit rates?

COMMON CORE STANDARD CC.6.RP.3b
Understand ratio concepts and use ratio reasoning to solve problems.

🔓 UNLOCK the Problem · REAL WORLD

The Champies are traveling from Arizona to Texas. On the first leg of the trip, they drove 500 miles in 10 hours. If they continue driving at the same rate, how many hours will it take them to drive 750 miles?

You can use equivalent ratios to find the number of hours it will take the Champie family to drive 750 miles. You may need to find a unit rate before you can write equivalent ratios.

🔑 Find equivalent ratios by using a unit rate.

Write ratios that compare miles to hours.

750 is not a multiple of 500.

Write the known ratio as a unit rate.

$$\frac{miles \rightarrow}{hours \rightarrow} \quad \frac{500}{10} = \frac{750}{\blacksquare} \quad \begin{matrix} \leftarrow \ miles \\ \leftarrow \ hours \end{matrix}$$

$$\frac{500 \div \blacksquare}{10 \div 10} = \frac{750}{\blacksquare}$$

$$\frac{\blacksquare}{1} = \frac{750}{\blacksquare}$$

Write an equivalent rate by multiplying the

_____ and _____ by the same value.

Think: Multiply 50 by _____ to get 750.

So, multiply the denominator by _____ also.

$$\frac{50 \cdot \blacksquare}{1 \cdot \blacksquare} = \frac{750}{\blacksquare}$$

The _____ are the same, so the

_____ are equal to each other.

$$\frac{\blacksquare}{15} = \frac{750}{\blacksquare}$$

The unknown value is _____.

So, it will take the Champies _____ hours to drive 750 miles.

Math Talk MATHEMATICAL PRACTICES
Explain why you needed to find a unit rate first.

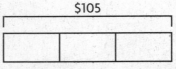

Kenyon earns $105 for mowing 3 yards. How much would Kenyon earn for mowing 10 yards?

STEP 1 Draw a bar model to represent the situation:

$105

$?

STEP 2 Solve the problem.

The model shows that 3 units represent $105.

You need to find the value represented by _____ units.

Write a unit rate:

1 unit represents $_____.

10 units are equal to 10 times 1 unit,

so 10 units = 10 × $_____.

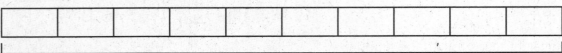
$$\frac{\$105}{3} = \frac{\$105 \div }{3 \div } = \frac{\$}{1}$$

10 × $_____ = $_____

So, Kenyon will earn $_____ for mowing 10 yards.

Try This!

Last summer, Kenyon earned $210 for mowing 7 yards. How much did he earn for mowing 5 yards last summer?

STEP 1 Draw a bar model to represent the situation.

STEP 2 Solve the problem.

Name _____

Share and Show

Use a unit rate to find the unknown value.

1. $\dfrac{10}{\blacksquare} = \dfrac{6}{3}$

$\dfrac{10}{\blacksquare} = \dfrac{6 \div \blacksquare}{3 \div 3}$

$\dfrac{10}{\blacksquare} = \dfrac{\blacksquare}{1}$

$\dfrac{10}{\blacksquare} = \dfrac{2 \cdot \blacksquare}{1 \cdot \blacksquare}$

$\dfrac{10}{\blacksquare} = \dfrac{10}{\blacksquare}$

$\blacksquare = $ _____

2. $\dfrac{6}{8} = \dfrac{\blacksquare}{20}$

$\dfrac{6 \div \blacksquare}{8 \div 8} = \dfrac{\blacksquare}{20}$

$\dfrac{\blacksquare}{1} = \dfrac{\blacksquare}{20}$

$\dfrac{0.75 \cdot 20}{1 \cdot \blacksquare} = \dfrac{\blacksquare}{20}$

$\dfrac{\blacksquare}{20} = \dfrac{\blacksquare}{20}$

$\blacksquare = $ _____

Draw a bar model to find the unknown value.

3. $\dfrac{6}{30} = \dfrac{14}{\blacksquare}$

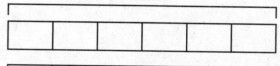

The unknown value is _____.

Math Talk MATHEMATICAL PRACTICES
Explain how to find an unknown value in a ratio by using a unit rate.

On Your Own

Use a unit rate to find the unknown value.

4. $\dfrac{40}{8} = \dfrac{45}{\blacksquare}$

5. $\dfrac{42}{14} = \dfrac{\blacksquare}{5}$

6. $\dfrac{\blacksquare}{2} = \dfrac{56}{8}$

7. $\dfrac{\blacksquare}{4} = \dfrac{26}{13}$

_____

Practice: Copy and Solve Draw a bar model to find the unknown value.

8. $\dfrac{4}{32} = \dfrac{9}{\blacksquare}$

9. $\dfrac{9}{3} = \dfrac{\blacksquare}{4}$

10. $\dfrac{\blacksquare}{14} = \dfrac{9}{8}$

11. $\dfrac{3}{\blacksquare} = \dfrac{2}{1.25}$

Problem Solving 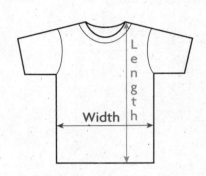 REAL WORLD

H.O.T. Pose a Problem

12. Josie runs a T-shirt printing company. The table shows the length and width of four sizes of T-shirts. The measurements of each size T-shirt form equivalent ratios.

What is the length of an extra-large T-shirt?

Write two equivalent ratios and find the unknown value:

Adult T-Shirt Sizes		
Size	Length (inches)	Width (inches)
Small	27	18
Medium	30	20
Large	?	22
X-large	?	24

$$\frac{\text{Length of medium}}{\text{Width of medium}} \rightarrow \frac{30}{20} = \frac{\blacksquare}{24} \leftarrow \frac{\text{Length of X-large}}{\text{Width of X-large}}$$

$$\frac{30 \div 20}{20 \div 20} = \frac{\blacksquare}{24} \rightarrow \frac{1.5}{1} = \frac{\blacksquare}{24} \rightarrow \frac{1.5 \cdot 24}{1 \cdot 24} = \frac{\blacksquare}{24} \rightarrow \frac{36}{24} = \frac{\blacksquare}{24}$$

The length of an extra-large T-shirt is 36 inches.

Write a problem that can be solved by using the information in the table and could be solved by using equivalent ratios.

Pose a Problem

_____

_____

_____

_____

_____

_____

_____

Solve Your Problem

- **Describe** how you could draw a bar model to solve your problem.

_____

_____

_____

FOR MORE PRACTICE:
Standards Practice Book, pp. P85–P86

Equivalent Ratios and Graphs

Essential Question How can you use a graph to represent equivalent ratios?

COMMON CORE STANDARD CC.6.RP.3a
Understand ratio concepts and use ratio reasoning to solve problems.

🔑 UNLOCK the Problem REAL WORLD

A car travels at a rate of 50 miles per hour. Use equivalent ratios to graph the distance the car travels over time. Graph time on the *x*-axis and distance on the *y*-axis.

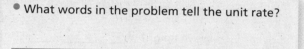
- What words in the problem tell the unit rate?

_____

 Write and graph equivalent ratios.

STEP 1 Use the unit rate to write equivalent ratios.

Write the unit rate.

$$\frac{\boxed{} \text{ miles}}{1 \text{ hour}}$$

Write an equivalent ratio.

$$\frac{\boxed{} \text{ mi} \times 2}{1 \text{ hr} \times 2}$$

$$= \frac{\boxed{} \text{ mi}}{\boxed{} \text{ hr}}$$

Complete the table of equivalent ratios.

Distance (mi)			150	200	
Time (hr)	1	2			5

STEP 2 Use an ordered pair to represent each ratio in the table.

Let the *x*-coordinate represent time in hours and the *y*-coordinate represent distance in miles.

$$\frac{50 \text{ mi}}{1 \text{ hr}} \rightarrow (1, 50)$$

(1, _____)

(2, _____)

(_____ , 150)

(_____ , 200)

(5, _____)

Remember

The first number in an ordered pair is the *x*-coordinate, and the second number is the *y*-coordinate.

STEP 3 Use the ordered pairs to graph the car's distance over time.

Think: The graph represents the same relationship as the unit rate.

For every 1 hour the car travels, the distance increases by

_____ miles.

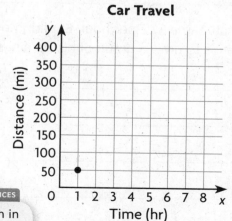

Car Travel

Math Talk MATHEMATICAL PRACTICES
Identify a pattern in the graph.

🔑 Example
During a heavy rainstorm, the waters of the Blue River rose at a steady rate for 8 hours. The graph shows the river's increase in height over time. Use the graph to complete the table of equivalent ratios. How many inches did the river rise in 8 hours?

Increase in Blue River Height

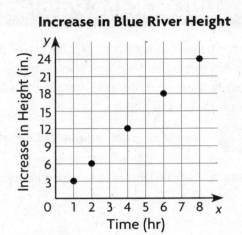

Think: On the graph, x-coordinates represent

time in _____, and y-coordinates represent

the river's increase in height in _____.

The ordered pair (1, _____) means that after _____

hour, the river rose _____ inches.

Increase in height (in.)	3				
Time (hr)	1	2	4	6	8

So, the river rose _____ inches in 8 hours.

---

1. **Describe** the pattern you see in the graph and the table.

   _____

   _____

2. **Explain** how you know that the ratios in the table are equivalent.

   _____

   _____

3. Matt earns $12 per hour. **Explain** how you could use equivalent ratios to draw a graph of his earnings over time.

   _____

   _____

   _____

   _____

Name _____

Share and Show

A redwood tree grew at a rate of 4 feet per year. Use this information for 1–3.

1. Complete the table of equivalent ratios for the first 5 years.

Height (ft)					
Time (yr)	1	2			

2. Write ordered pairs, letting the *x*-coordinate represent time in years and the *y*-coordinate represent height in feet.

(1, _____), (2, _____), (_____, _____),

(_____, _____), (_____, _____)

3. Use the ordered pairs to graph the tree's growth over time.

Redwood Tree Growth

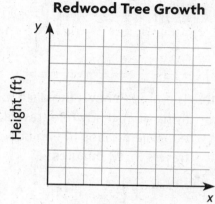

Time (yr)

MATHEMATICAL PRACTICES

Math Talk Explain what the point (1, 4) represents on the graph of the redwood tree's growth.

On Your Own

The graph shows the rate at which Luis's car uses gas, in miles per gallon. Use the graph for 4–8.

4. Complete the table of equivalent ratios.

Distance (mi)	30				
Gas (gal)	1	2	3	4	5

5. Find the car's unit rate of gas usage. $\dfrac{\text{miles}}{\text{gallon}}$

6. How far can the car go on 5 gallons of gas? _____

7. Estimate the amount of gas needed to travel 50 miles.

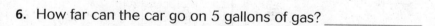
_____

8. **H.O.T.** Ellen's car averages 35 miles per gallon of gas. If you used equivalent ratios to graph her car's gas usage, how would the graph differ from the graph of Luis's car's gas usage?

_____

_____

Gas Usage in Luis's Car

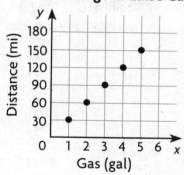

Gas (gal)

© Houghton Mifflin Harcourt Publishing Company

Problem Solving REAL WORLD

9. The graph shows the depth of a submarine over time. Use equivalent ratios to find the number of minutes it will take the submarine to descend 1,600 feet.

Submarine Depth

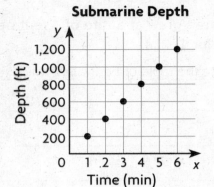

_____

10. The graph shows the distance that a plane flying at a steady rate travels over time. Use equivalent ratios to find how far the plane travels in 13 minutes.

Plane Travel

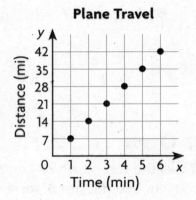

_____

11. **H.O.T.** **Sense or Nonsense?** Emilio types at a rate of 84 words per minute. He claims that he can type a 500-word essay in 5 minutes. Is Emilio's claim sense or nonsense? Use a graph to help explain your answer.

Emilio's Typing Rate

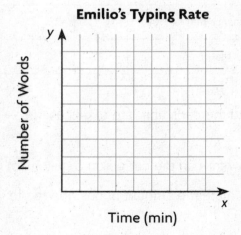

_____

_____

_____

_____

_____

12. **Test Prep** Meg's job pays her at a rate of $\frac{\$16}{1 \text{ hour}}$. Which is an equivalent ratio?

(A) $\frac{\$20}{4 \text{ hours}}$ (C) $\frac{\$48}{3 \text{ hours}}$

(B) $\frac{\$32}{16 \text{ hours}}$ (D) $\frac{\$96}{4 \text{ hours}}$

FOR MORE PRACTICE:
Standards Practice Book, pp. P87–P88

✓ Chapter 4 Review/Test

▶ Vocabulary

Choose the best term from the box to complete the sentence.

1. A _____ compares two quantities by division. (p. 147)

2. A _____ is a ratio that compares two quantities that have different units. (p. 152)

Vocabulary
ordered pair
rate
ratio

▶ Concepts and Skills

Write the rate as a fraction. Then find the unit rate. (CC.6.RP.2, CC.6.RP.3b)

3. Julian played 16 notes in 4 seconds.

_____

4. Brianna types 165 words in 5 minutes.

_____

Tell which rate is faster by comparing unit rates. (CC.6.RP.2)

5. $\dfrac{240 \text{ mi}}{4 \text{ hr}}$ and $\dfrac{330 \text{ mi}}{6 \text{ hr}}$

_____

6. $\dfrac{45 \text{ m}}{15 \text{ s}}$ and $\dfrac{24 \text{ m}}{6 \text{ s}}$

_____

7. $\dfrac{168 \text{ ft}}{21 \text{ min}}$ and $\dfrac{108 \text{ ft}}{12 \text{ min}}$

_____

Find the unknown value. (CC.6.RP.3a, CC.6.RP.3b)

8. $\dfrac{12}{16} = \dfrac{\blacksquare}{4}$

_____

9. $\dfrac{18}{\blacksquare} = \dfrac{6}{7}$

_____

10. $\dfrac{5}{25} = \dfrac{13}{\blacksquare}$

_____

11. $\dfrac{\blacksquare}{21} = \dfrac{27}{9}$

_____

12. $\dfrac{\blacksquare}{5} = \dfrac{6}{15}$

_____

13. $\dfrac{3}{4} = \dfrac{18}{\blacksquare}$

_____

14. $\dfrac{7}{\blacksquare} = \dfrac{21}{9}$

_____

15. $\dfrac{8}{3} = \dfrac{\blacksquare}{12}$

_____

GO Online Assessment Options **Chapter Test**

TEST PREP

16. An animal shelter houses 11 cats, 9 dogs, and 5 birds. Which of the following shows the ratio of dogs to birds? (CC.6.RP.1)

    (A)   9:5

    (B)   11:5

    (C)   9:25

    (D)   11:25

17. A movie theater sells about 3 bags of popcorn for every 4 people who buy tickets to the movie. If 300 people buy tickets, how many bags of popcorn can the theater be expected to sell? (CC.6.RP.3a)

    (A) 225

    (B) 300

    (C) 400

    (D) 700

18. An aquarium contains 12 guppies and 16 swordtail fish. Which ratio is not equivalent to the ratio of guppies to swordtail fish? (CC.6.RP.3a)

    (A) $\frac{3}{4}$

    (B) $\frac{6}{8}$

    (C) $\frac{8}{10}$

    (D) $\frac{24}{32}$

19. The ratio of dahlias to tulips in a flower arrangement is 2 to 5. Which of these could be the number of dahlias and tulips in the arrangement? (CC.6.RP.3a)

    (A)   8 dahlias, 25 tulips

    (B) 12 dahlias, 30 tulips

    (C) 14 dahlias, 17 tulips

    (D) 20 dahlias, 40 tulips

20. Jasmine is painting picture frames. She uses 1 tube of red paint and 2 tubes of yellow paint for every 5 frames. How many tubes of paint will she use for 20 picture frames? (CC.6.RP.3a)

    (A)   3

    (B) 10

    (C) 12

    (D) 15

Fill in the bubble to show your answer.

21. The ratio of adults to children at a museum is usually 5:2. There are currently 35 adults at the museum. How many children do you expect to be at the museum? (CC.6.RP.3a)

Ⓐ 10

Ⓑ 14

Ⓒ 21

Ⓓ 32

22. A 3-pound bag of almonds costs $16.50, a 5-pound bag of walnuts costs $28.75, and a 4-pound bag of cashews costs $24.80. Which list shows the items in order from the best deal to the worst deal? (CC.6.RP.2, CC.6.RP.3b)

Ⓐ cashews, walnuts, almonds

Ⓑ cashews, almonds, walnuts

Ⓒ almonds, cashews, walnuts

Ⓓ almonds, walnuts, cashews

23. A large bumblebee beats its wings 2,340 times in 13 seconds. A honeybee beats its wings 1,470 times in 7 seconds. Which beats its wings at a faster rate? (CC.6.RP.3b)

Ⓐ honeybee at 147 beats per second

Ⓑ honeybee at 210 beats per second

Ⓒ bumblebee at 280 beats per second

Ⓓ bumblebee at 234 beats per second

24. Marci bought 4 yards of ribbon for $6. How much should Marci expect to pay for 10 yards of the ribbon? (CC.6.RP.3b)

Ⓐ $12 Ⓒ $18

Ⓑ $15 Ⓓ $24

25. A waterfall erodes the land beneath it by 3 inches per month. Which of the following is equivalent to the ratio comparing inches to months? (CC.6.RP.3a)

Ⓐ 51 inches:17 months

Ⓑ 39 inches:42 months

Ⓒ 17 inches:51 months

Ⓓ 42 inches:39 months

▶ Constructed Response

26. A cat's heart beats 30 times in 12 seconds, an elephant's heart beats 20 times in 40 seconds, and a monkey's heart beats 32 times in 10 seconds. List the animals in order from the fastest heart rate to the slowest heart rate. (CC.6.RP.2, CC.6.RP.3b)

_____

27. Joshua saves $325 every 5 months. How long will it take him to save $845? Explain how you determined your answer. (CC.6.RP.3b)

_____

_____

_____

_____

▶ Performance Task (CC.6.RP.3a)

28. An electronics store sells an average of 45 laptops every 3 weeks.

Ⓐ Make a table of equivalent ratios.

Laptops			45		
Time (weeks)	1	2	3	4	5

Ⓑ Write ordered pairs for the ratios in the table. Let the x-coordinate represent time in weeks and the y-coordinate represent number of laptops.

_____

Ⓒ Graph the number of laptops sold over time.

Ⓓ The store has 83 laptops in stock. If sales continue at the same rate, will there be enough laptops to last for 6 weeks? Use the graph to explain your answer.

_____

_____

_____

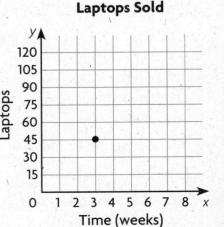

Laptops Sold

Show What You Know

Check your understanding of important skills.

Name _____

▶ **Decimal Models** Shade the model to show the decimal.

1. 0.31

2. 0.7

3. 1.7

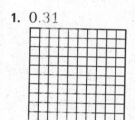 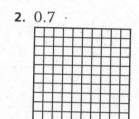 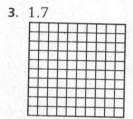 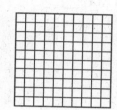

▶ **Division** Find the quotient.

4. 2,002 ÷ 91

5. 98)3,038

6. 24,487 ÷ 47

7. 22)2,332

_____   _____   _____   _____

▶ **Multiply Whole Numbers by Decimals** Find the product.

8. 2.38
    × 4

9. 32.06
    × 7

10. 4.60
     × 18

11. 7.04
     × 32

_____   _____   _____   _____

MATH DETECTIVE

WITH

CARMEN SANDIEGO™

Esmeralda likes to listen to music while she works out. She had a playlist on her MP3 player that lasted 40 minutes, but she accidentally deleted 25% of the music. Be a Math Detective and figure out if Esmeralda has enough music left on her playlist for a 30-minute workout. Explain your answer.

Vocabulary Builder

▶ Visualize It

Complete the bubble map with review and preview words that are related to ratios.

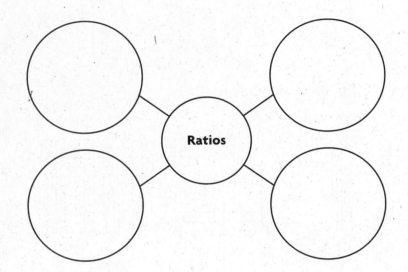

Review Words
decimal
equivalent ratios
factor
quotient
rate
ratio
simplify

Preview Word

percent

▶ **Understand Vocabulary**

Complete the sentences using review and preview words.

1. A comparison of one number to another by division is a

   _____.

2. _____ name the same comparison.

3. A ratio that compares quantities with different units is a

   _____.

4. A _____ is a ratio, or rate, that compares a
   number to 100.

5. _____ a fraction or a ratio by dividing the
   numerator and denominator by a common factor.

GO Online • eStudent Edition • Multimedia eGlossary

Model Percents

Essential Question How can you use a model to show a percent?

COMMON CORE STANDARD CC.6.RP.3c
Understand ratio concepts and use ratio reasoning to solve problems.

Investigate

Materials ■ 10-by-10 grids

Not many people drive electric cars today. But one expert estimates that by 2025, 35 percent of all cars will be powered by electricity.

A **percent** is a ratio, or rate, that compares a number to 100. Percent means "per hundred." The symbol for percent is %.

A. Model 35% on the 10-by-10 grid. Then tell what the percent represents.

The large square represents the whole, or 100%. Each small square represents 1%.

- Shade the grid to show 35%.

   Think: 35% is _____ out of 100.

- Write 35% as a ratio comparing 35 to 100.

   Think: 35 out of 100 squares is $\dfrac{}{100}$.

- $35\% = \dfrac{}{}$

So, by 2025, _____ out of _____ cars may be powered by electricity.

B. Model 52% on a 10-by-10 grid.

- _____ out of _____ squares is $\dfrac{}{100}$.

- $52\% = \dfrac{}{100}$

C. Model 18% on a 10-by-10 grid.

- _____ out of _____ squares is $\dfrac{}{100}$.

- $18\% = \dfrac{}{100}$

Draw Conclusions

1. **Explain** how you would use a 10-by-10 grid to model 7%.

   _____

2. **Model** $\frac{1}{4}$ on a 10-by-10 grid. What percent is shaded? **Explain**.

   _____

3. **Explain** how you could model 0.5% on a 10-by-10 grid.

   _____

   _____

4. **H.O.T.** **Apply** How would you model 181% using 10-by-10 grids?

   _____

Make Connections

The table shows the types of meteorites in Meg's collection. Shade a grid to show the ratio comparing the number of each type to the total number. Then write the ratio as a percent.

Think: A percent is a ratio that compares a number to _____.

Meg's Meteorite Collection

Type	Number
Iron	21
Stone	76
Stony-iron	3

Iron

_____ out of _____ meteorites are iron.

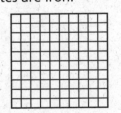

$\dfrac{\quad}{100}$ = _____ %

Stone

_____ out of _____ meteorites are stone.

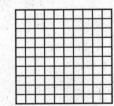

$\dfrac{\quad}{\quad}$ = _____ %

Stony-iron

_____ out of _____ meteorites are stony-iron.

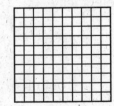

$\dfrac{\quad}{\quad}$ = _____ %

Math Talk MATHEMATICAL PRACTICES
Explain what this statement means: 13% of the students at Harding Middle School are left-handed.

Name _____

Share and Show MATH BOARD ·

Write a ratio and a percent to represent the shaded part.

1.

ratio: _____ percent: _____

2.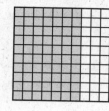

ratio: _____ percent: _____

3.

ratio: _____ percent: _____

4.

ratio: _____ percent: _____

5.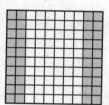

ratio: _____ percent: _____

6.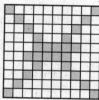

ratio: _____ percent: _____

Model the percent and write it as a ratio.

7. 30%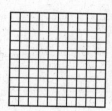

ratio: _____

8. 5%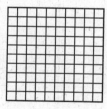

ratio: _____

9. 75%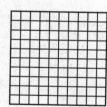

ratio: _____

10. **Write Math** ▸ **Explain** how to model 32% on a 10-by-10 grid. How does the model represent the ratio of 32 to 100?

_____

_____

_____

Problem Solving REAL WORLD

Pose a Problem

11. Javier designed a mosaic wall mural using 100 tiles in 3 different colors: yellow, blue, and red. If 64 of the tiles are yellow, what percent of the tiles are either red or blue?

To find the number of tiles that are either red or blue, count the red and blue squares. Or subtract the number of yellow squares, 64, from the total number of squares, 100.

36 out of 100 tiles are red or blue.

The ratio of red or blue tiles to all tiles is $\frac{36}{100}$.

So, the percent of the tiles that are either red or blue is 36%.

Write another problem involving a percent that can be solved by using the mosaic wall mural.

Pose a Problem	**Solve Your Problem**

12. **Describe** how you could change the original problem by changing the number of tiles of one or more colors. Then solve the problem.

Name _____

Write Percents as Fractions and Decimals

Essential Question How can you write percents as fractions and decimals?

COMMON CORE STANDARD CC.6.RP.3c
Understand ratio concepts and use ratio reasoning to solve problems.

To write a percent as a fraction or a decimal, first write the percent as a ratio that compares a number to 100. For example, $37\% = \frac{37}{100}$.

🔑 UNLOCK the Problem REAL WORLD

Carlos eats a banana, an orange, and a blueberry muffin for breakfast. What fraction of the daily value of vitamin C does each item contain?

Vitamin C Content	
Item	**Percent of Daily Value**
Banana	15%
Orange	113%
Blueberry Muffin	0.5%

🗝 **Write each percent as a fraction.**

A Write 15% as a fraction.

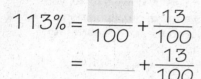 $= \dfrac{}{100} = \dfrac{}{}$

15% is 15 out of 100.

Write the fraction in simplest form.

So, 15% = _____.

B Write 113% as a fraction.

$113\% = \dfrac{}{100} + \dfrac{13}{100}$

$= \underline{} + \dfrac{13}{100}$

113% is 100 out of 100 plus 13 out of 100.

$\frac{100}{100} = 1$

So, 113% = _____.

Write the sum as a mixed number.

C Write 0.5% as a fraction.

$0.5\% = \dfrac{}{100}$

$= \dfrac{0.5 \cdot 10}{100 \cdot 10} = \dfrac{}{1{,}000}$

$= \dfrac{1}{}$

0.5% is 0.5 out of 100.

Multiply the numerator and denominator by 10 to get a whole number in the numerator.

Write the fraction in simplest form.

So, 0.5% = _____.

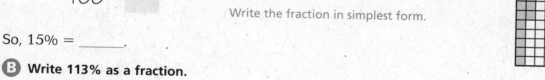

- **Explain** why two 10-by-10 grids were used to show 113%.

_____

_____

🔑 Example

Ⓐ Write 72% as a decimal.

$$72\% = \dfrac{}{100}$$

$$= \underline{\hspace{3cm}}.$$

So, 72% = _____.

72% is 72 out of 100.

Use place value to write 72 hundredths as a decimal.

Ⓑ Write 4% as a decimal.

$$4\% = \dfrac{}{100}$$

```
        .
100 ) 4.00
     -0 ↓
      40
     - 0 ↓
      400
     -400
        0
```

So, 4% = _____.

4% is 4 out of 100.

Use division to write 4% as a decimal.

Divide the ones. Since 4 ones cannot be shared among 100 groups, write a zero in the quotient.

Place a decimal point after the ones place in the quotient.

📌 Remember

When you divide decimal numbers by powers of 10, you move the decimal point one place to the left for each factor of 10.

Ⓒ Write 25.81% as a decimal.

$$25.81\% = \dfrac{}{100}$$

$$= \underline{\hspace{3cm}}$$

So, 25.81% = _____.

25.81% is 25.81 out of 100.

To divide by 100, move the decimal point 2 places to the left: 0.2581

Share and Show . . . .

Write the percent as a fraction.

1. 80%

$$80\% = \dfrac{}{100} = \dfrac{}{}$$

2. 150%

_____

✅ **3.** 0.2%

_____

Write the percent as a decimal.

✅ **4.** 58%

_____

5. 9%

_____

MATHEMATICAL PRACTICES

Math Talk Explain how to use estimation to check that your answer is reasonable when you write a percent as a fraction or decimal.

Name _____

On Your Own ·····································

Write the percent as a fraction or mixed number.

6. 17%

7. 20%

8. 125%

_____

_____

_____

9. 355%

10. 0.1%

11. 2.5%

_____

_____

_____

Write the percent as a decimal.

12. 89%

13. 30%

14. 2%

_____

_____

_____

15. 122%

16. 3.5%

17. 6.33%

_____

_____

_____

18. About 21.6% of the population of Canada speaks French. Write 21.6% as a decimal.

19. Georgianne completed 60% of her homework assignment. Write the portion of her homework that she still needs to complete as a fraction.

_____

_____

Problem Solving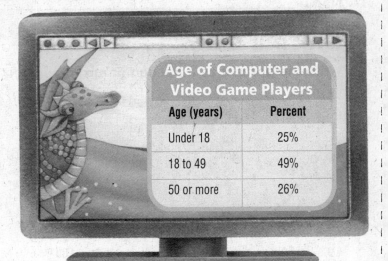

Use the table for 20 and 21.

20. What fraction of computer and video game players are 50 years old or more?

    _____

21. What fraction of computer and video game players are 18 years old or more?

    _____

Age of Computer and Video Game Players

Age (years)	Percent
Under 18	25%
18 to 49	49%
50 or more	26%

22. **H.O.T.** Box A and Box B each contain black tiles and white tiles. They have the same total number of tiles. In Box A, 45% of the tiles are black. In Box B, $\frac{11}{20}$ of the tiles are white. Compare the number of black tiles in the boxes. Explain your reasoning.

    _____

    _____

    _____

    _____

23. **What's the Error?** About 8.4% of the students at Jenna's school are in the drama club. Jenna says 0.84 of the students are in the drama club. Is she correct? Explain.

    _____

    _____

    _____

24. ⭐ **Test Prep** A large carrot contains 41% of the daily value of vitamin A. Which is the best estimate of the fraction of the daily value of vitamin A in a large carrot?

    (A) $\frac{1}{4}$ (C) $\frac{3}{4}$

    (B) $\frac{2}{5}$ (D) $\frac{4}{5}$

SHOW YOUR WORK

FOR MORE PRACTICE:
Standards Practice Book, pp. P95–P96

Write Fractions and Decimals as Percents

Essential Question How can you write fractions and decimals as percents?

COMMON CORE STANDARD CC.6.RP.3c
Understand ratio concepts and use ratio reasoning to solve problems.

UNLOCK the Problem REAL WORLD

During the 2008–2009 season of the National Basketball Association (NBA), the Phoenix Suns won about $\frac{11}{20}$ of their games. The Miami Heat won about 0.524 of their games. Which team was more successful during the season?

- Underline the sentence that tells you what you are trying to find.
- Circle the numbers you need to use.

To compare the season performances of the Suns and the Heat, it is helpful to write the fraction and the decimal as a percent.

Write the fraction or decimal as a percent.

Ⓐ $\frac{11}{20}$

Multiply the _____ and

_____ by the same value to write an equivalent fraction with a denominator of 100.

A percent is a ratio comparing a number

to _____. Write the ratio

as a _____.

$$\frac{11}{20} = \frac{11 \times \boxed{}}{20 \times \boxed{}}$$

$$= \frac{\boxed{}}{100}$$

$$= \underline{}$$

So, the percent of games won by the Phoenix Suns is _____.

Ⓑ 0.524

To write a percent as a decimal, divide by _____.

To write a decimal as a percent,

_____ by 100.

To multiply by 100, move the decimal

point 2 places to the _____.

$0.524 \times 100 = 52.4$

$0.524 = \underline{}$ %

So, the percent of games won by the Miami Heat is _____.

Because they won a greater percentage of their games, the _____ were more successful during the 2008–2009 season.

CONNECT You can use what you know about fractions, decimals, and percents to write numbers in different forms.

🔑 Example

A Write 0.7 as a fraction and as a percent.

0.7 means 7 _____. Write 0.7 as a fraction.

$0.7 = \dfrac{7}{}$

To write as a percent, first write an equivalent fraction with a denominator

$= \dfrac{7 \times }{10 \times }$

of _____.

Write the ratio of _____ to

$= \dfrac{}{100}$

_____ as a percent.

$= \underline{}$

So, 0.7 written as a fraction is _____, and

0.7 written as a percent is _____.

B Write $\frac{3}{40}$ as a decimal and as a percent.

Since 40 is not a factor of 100, it is more difficult to find an equivalent fraction with a denominator of 100.

Use division to write $\frac{3}{40}$ as a decimal.

Divide 3 by 40.

```
        .
40)3.000
   -0↓
    30
   - 0↓
    300
   -280↓
     200
    -200
       0
```

To write a decimal as a percent,

_____ by 100.

Move the decimal point 2 places to the

_____.

$\frac{3}{40} = 0.075$

$0.075 = $ _____

So, $\frac{3}{40}$ written as a decimal is _____, and

$\frac{3}{40}$ written as a percent is _____.

Math Talk MATHEMATICAL PRACTICES
Explain why it makes sense that $\frac{3}{40}$ is less than 10%.

Name _____

Share and Show

Write the fraction or decimal as a percent.

1. $\dfrac{3}{25}$

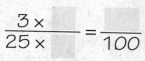
$$\dfrac{3 \times \boxed{}}{25 \times \boxed{}} = \dfrac{\boxed{}}{100}$$

_____

2. $\dfrac{3}{10}$

_____

3. 0.717

_____

4. 0.02

_____

Write the number in two other forms (fraction, decimal, or percent).

5. 0.9

_____

6. $\dfrac{3}{8}$

_____

7. 0.45

_____

8. $\dfrac{5}{16}$

_____

Math Talk MATHEMATICAL PRACTICES

Explain how you know that $\frac{5}{4}$ is greater than 100%.

On Your Own

Write the fraction or decimal as a percent.

9. $\dfrac{7}{50}$

_____

10. $\dfrac{4}{5}$

_____

11. 0.902

_____

12. 1.25

_____

Write the number in two other forms (fraction, decimal, or percent).

13. 0.01

_____

14. $\dfrac{13}{40}$

_____

15. $\dfrac{6}{5}$

_____

16. 0.008

_____

Sand Sculptures

Every year, dozens of teams compete in the U.S. Open Sandcastle Competition. Recent winners have included complex sculptures in the shape of flowers, elephants, and racing cars.

Teams that participate in the contest build their sculptures using a mixture of sand and water. Finding the correct ratios of these ingredients is essential for creating a stable sculpture.

The table shows the recipes that three teams used. Which team used the greatest percent of sand in their recipe?

Convert to percents. Then order from least to greatest.

Team A	$\dfrac{30}{30+10} = \dfrac{30}{40} = 0.75 = \underline{}$ %
Team B	$\dfrac{19}{20} = \dfrac{19 \times \boxed{}}{20 \times \boxed{}} = \dfrac{\boxed{}}{100} = \underline{}$ %
Team C	$0.84 = \boxed{}$ %

Sand Sculpture Recipes

Team	Sand	Water
A	30 cups	10 cups
B	$\dfrac{19}{20}$	$\dfrac{1}{20}$
C	0.84	0.16

From least to greatest, the percents are _____.

So, Team _____ used the greatest percent of sand.

Solve.

17. Which team used the greatest percent of water in their recipe?

_____

18. Some people say that the ideal recipe for sand sculptures contains 88.9% sand. Which team's recipe is closest to the ideal recipe?

_____

19. H.O.T. Team D used a recipe that consists of 20 cups of sand, 2 cups of flour, and 3 cups of water. How does the percent of sand in Team D's recipe compare to that of the other teams?

_____

_____

✓ Mid-Chapter Checkpoint

▶ **Vocabulary**

Choose the best term from the box to complete the sentence.

1. A _____ is a ratio that compares a quantity to 100. (p. 187)

▶ **Concepts and Skills**

Write a ratio and a percent to represent the shaded part. (CC.6.RP.3c)

2.

_____

3.

_____

4.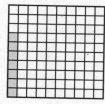

_____

5.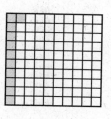

_____

6.

_____

7.

_____

Write the number in two other forms (fraction, decimal, or percent). (CC.6.RP.3c)

8. 0.04

_____

9. $\frac{3}{10}$

_____

10. 1%

_____

11. $1\frac{1}{5}$

_____

12. 0.9

_____

13. 0.5%

_____

14. $\frac{7}{8}$

_____

15. 355%

_____

16. About $\frac{9}{10}$ of the avocados grown in the United States are grown in California. About what percent of the avocados grown in the United States are grown in California? (CC.6.RP.3c)

Ⓐ 9%
Ⓒ 40%
Ⓑ 10%
Ⓓ 90%

17. Morton made 36 out of 48 free throws last season. What percent of his free throws did Morton make? (CC.6.RP.3c)

Ⓐ 36%
Ⓒ 48%
Ⓑ 40%
Ⓓ 75%

18. Sarah answered 85% of the trivia questions correctly. What fraction describes this percent? (CC.6.RP.3c)

Ⓐ $\frac{17}{25}$
Ⓑ $\frac{3}{4}$
Ⓒ $\frac{17}{20}$
Ⓓ $\frac{9}{10}$

19. About $\frac{4}{5}$ of all the orange juice in the world is produced in Brazil. About what percent of all the orange juice in the world is produced in Brazil? (CC.6.RP.3c)

Ⓐ 8%
Ⓑ 80%
Ⓒ 85%
Ⓓ 90%

20. If you eat 4 medium strawberries, you get 48% of your daily recommended amount of vitamin C. What fraction of your daily amount of vitamin C do you still need? (CC.6.RP.3c)

Ⓐ $\frac{12}{25}$
Ⓑ $\frac{1}{2}$
Ⓒ $\frac{13}{25}$
Ⓓ $\frac{3}{5}$

Percent of a Quantity

Essential Question How do you find a percent of a quantity?

COMMON CORE STANDARD CC.6.RP.3c
Understand ratio concepts and use ratio reasoning to solve problems.

 UNLOCK the Problem REAL WORLD

A typical family of four uses about 400 gallons of water each day, and 30% of this water is for outdoor activities, such as gardening. How many gallons of water does a typical family of four use each day for outdoor activities?

> • Will the number of gallons of water for outdoor activities be greater than or less than 200 gallons? Explain.
>
> _____
>
> _____

🔓 One Way Use ratio reasoning.

Draw a bar model.

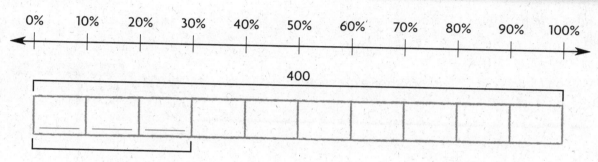

The model shows that 100% represents 400 gallons.

Think: 30% is 3 groups of 10%, so divide the model into 10 equal groups.

Find the value of 10% of 400.

$$10\% \text{ of } 400 = \frac{1}{10} \times 400 = \frac{400}{} = \underline{}$$

Find the value of 30% of 400.

$$30\% = 3 \times \underline{} = \underline{}$$

🔓 Another Way Multiply.

You can find 30% of 400 by multiplying.

Write the percent as a rate per 100.

$$30\% = \frac{30}{100}$$

Multiply to find $\frac{30}{100}$ of 400.

$$\frac{30}{100} \times 400 = \underline{}$$

So, 30% of 400 gallons is _____ gallons.

> **MATHEMATICAL PRACTICES**
> **Math Talk** How can you find the number of gallons of water used for indoor activities?

Try This! Find 65% of 300.

$$65\% = \underline{}$$

$$\underline{} \times 300 = \underline{}$$

Example

Charla earns $4,000 per month. She spends 40% of her salary on rent and 15% of her salary on groceries. How much money does Charla have left for other expenses?

STEP 1 Add to find the total percent of Charla's salary that is used for rent and groceries.

40% + _____ % = _____ %

STEP 2 Subtract the total percent from 100% to find the percent that is left for other expenses.

100% − _____ % = 45%

STEP 3 Write the percent from Step 2 as a rate per 100 and multiply.

45% = _____

_____ × 4,000 = _____

So, Charla has $_____ left for other expenses.

Math Talk MATHEMATICAL PRACTICES Explain how you could solve the problem a different way.

Share and Show MATH BOARD

Find the percent of the quantity.

0%   25%   50%   75%   100%

320

1. 25% of 320

   $25\% = \frac{1}{4}$, so use _____ equal groups.

   $\frac{1}{4} \times 320 = \frac{320}{\text{ }} =$ _____

2. 80% of 50

3. 175% of 24

4. 60% of 210

5. A jar contains 125 marbles. Given that 4% of the marbles are green, 60% of the marbles are blue, and the rest are red, how many red marbles are in the jar?

6. There are 32 students in Mr. Moreno's class and 62.5% of the students are girls. How many boys are in the class?

Math Talk MATHEMATICAL PRACTICES Explain how you could estimate 49.3% of 3,000.

Name _____

On Your Own ·

Find the percent of the quantity.

7. 75% of 52

8. 60% of 90

9. 1% of 750

10. 17% of 100

11. 40% of 18

12. 25% of 32.4

13. 110% of 300

14. 0.2% of 6,500

15. A baker made 60 muffins for a cafe. By noon, 45% of the muffins were sold. How many muffins were sold by noon?

16. There are 30 treasures hidden in a castle in a video game. LaToya found 80% of them. How many of the treasures did LaToya find?

17. A school library has 260 DVDs in its collection. Given that 45% of the DVDs are about science and 40% are about history, how many of the DVDs are about other subjects?

18. Mitch planted cabbage, squash, and carrots on his 150-acre farm. He planted half the farm with squash and 22% of the farm with carrots. How many acres did he plant with cabbage?

Compare. Write <, >, or =.

19. 45% of 60 ◯ 60% of 45

20. 10% of 90 ◯ 90% of 100

21. 75% of 8 ◯ 8% of 7.5

22. **H.O.T.** Sarah had 12 free throw attempts during a game and made at least 75% of the free throws. What is the greatest number of free throws Sarah could have missed during the game?

🔑 UNLOCK the Problem

23. One-third of the juniors in the Linwood High School Marching Band play the trumpet. The band has 50 members and the table shows what percent of the band members are freshmen, sophomores, juniors, and seniors. How many juniors play the trumpet?

Ⓐ 4   Ⓒ 8

Ⓑ 6   Ⓓ 12

Linwood High School Marching Band

Freshmen	26%
Sophomores	30%
Juniors	24%
Seniors	20%

a. What do you need to find?

_____

_____

b. How can you use the table to help you solve the problem?

_____

_____

_____

c. What operation can you use to find the number of juniors in the band?

_____

d. Show the steps you use to solve the problem.

e. Complete the sentences.

The band has _____ members. There are

_____ juniors in the band. The number of juniors who

play the trumpet is _____.

f. Fill in the bubble for the correct answer choice above.

Use the information in Problem 23 and the above table for 24–25.

24. How many more sophomores than freshmen are in the band?

Ⓐ 1   Ⓒ 4

Ⓑ 2   Ⓓ 6

25. The seniors in the band line up in 2 rows, with the same number of seniors in each row. How many seniors are in each row?

Ⓐ 2   Ⓒ 10

Ⓑ 5   Ⓓ 20

FOR MORE PRACTICE:
Standards Practice Book, pp. P99–P100

Name _____

Problem Solving • Percents

Essential Question How can you use the strategy *use a model* to help you solve a percent problem?

🔑 UNLOCK the Problem REAL WORLD

The recommended daily amount of protein is about 50 grams. One Super Protein Cereal Bar contains 16% of that amount of protein. If Stefon eats one Super Protein Cereal Bar per day, how much protein will he need to get from another source to meet the recommended daily amount?

Use the graphic organizer to help you solve the problem.

Read the Problem

What do I need to find?	**What information do I need to use?**	**How will I use the information?**
Write what you need to find.	Write the important information.	What strategy can you use?
_____		_____
_____	_____	_____
_____	_____	_____
	_____	_____

Solve the Problem

Draw a bar model.

```
                    100%
Recommended  ┌─────────────────────────┐
Daily Amount │          50 g           │
             └─────────────────────────┘
             ┌───┬─────────────────────┐
Cereal Bar   │   ┊                     ┊
             └───┴─────────────────────┘
              └─┘
             16%
```

The model shows that 100% = 50 grams,

so 1% of $50 = \dfrac{50}{100} =$ _____.

16% of $50 = 16 \times$ _____ = _____

So, the cereal bar contains _____ of protein.

$50 -$ _____ = _____

So, _____ of protein should come from another source.

Math Talk MATHEMATICAL PRACTICES How can you use estimation to show that your answer is reasonable?

Try Another Problem

Lee has saved 65% of the money she needs to buy a pair of jeans that cost $24. How much money does Lee have, and how much more money does she need to buy the jeans?

Read the Problem

What do I need to find?	What information do I need to use?	How will I use the information?

Solve the Problem

1. Does your answer make sense? Explain how you know.

_____

_____

2. **Explain** how you could solve this problem in a different way.

_____

_____

Math Talk MATHEMATICAL PRACTICES
Compare the model you used to solve this problem with the model on page 205.

Name _____

Share and Show MATH BOARD

1. A geologist visits 40 volcanoes in Alaska and California. 15% of the volcanoes are in California. How many volcanoes does the geologist visit in California and how many in Alaska?

   First, draw a bar model.

SHOW YOUR WORK

100%

Total Volcanoes	40

California

15%

Next, find 1%.

$100\% = 40$, so 1% of $40 = \dfrac{40}{100} = $ _____

Then, find 15%, the number of volcanoes in California.

15% of $40 = 15 \times$ _____ = _____

Finally, subtract to find the number of volcanoes in Alaska.

So, the geologist visited _____ volcanoes in California

and _____ volcanoes in Alaska.

2. **H.O.T. What if** 30% of the volcanoes were in California? How many volcanoes would the geologist have visited in California and how many in Alaska?

_____

3. Ricardo has $25 to spend on school supplies. He spends 72% of the money on a backpack and the rest on a large binder. How much does he spend on the backpack? How much does he spend on the binder?

_____

4. **H.O.T. Sense or Nonsense** A diner ordered 144 bagels. The order was for 80% plain and 20% sesame bagels. An employee says that the diner should receive 43 sesame bagels. Explain whether the employee's statement is sense of nonsense.

_____

_____

On Your Own · · · · · · · · · · · · · · ·

5. Jordan takes 50% of the cherries from a bowl. Then Mei takes 50% of the remaining cherries. Finally, Greg takes 50% of the remaining cherries. There are 3 cherries left. How many cherries were in the bowl before Jordan arrived?

_____

6. Kevin is hiking on a trail that is 4.2 miles long. So far, he has hiked 80% of the total distance. How many more miles does Kevin have to hike in order to complete the trail?

_____

7. **H.O.T.** An employee at a state park has 53 photos of animals found at the park. She wants to arrange the photos in rows so that every row except the bottom row has the same number of photos. She also wants there to be at least 5 rows. Describe two different ways she can arrange the photos.

_____

_____

· · · · · **SHOW YOUR WORK** · · · · · · · ·

8. **Write Math** ► Maya wants to mark a length of 7 inches on a sheet of paper, but she does not have a ruler. She has pieces of wood that are 4 inches, 5 inches, and 6 inches long. Explain how she can use these pieces to mark a length of 7 inches.

_____

_____

_____

_____

9. ⭐ **Test Prep** At basketball practice, Tony took 60 foul shots and made 70% of them. He had hoped to make 50 shots. By how many shots did he fall short of his goal?

(A) 8 shots   (C) 12 shots

(B) 10 shots   (D) 15 shots

FOR MORE PRACTICE:
Standards Practice Book, pp. P101–P102

Find the Whole From a Percent

Essential Question How can you find the whole given a part and the percent?

COMMON CORE STANDARD CC.6.RP.3c
Understand ratio concepts and use ratio reasoning to solve problems.

A percent is equivalent to the ratio of a part to a whole. Suppose there are 20 marbles in a bag and 5 of them are blue. The *whole* is the total number of marbles, 20. The *part* is the number of blue marbles, 5. The ratio of the part to the whole, $\frac{5}{20}$, is equal to the *percent* of marbles that are blue, 25%.

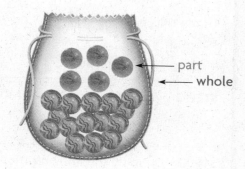
part
whole

$$\frac{\text{part} \rightarrow}{\text{whole} \rightarrow} \frac{5}{20} = \frac{5 \times 5}{20 \times 5} = \frac{25}{100} = 25\% \leftarrow \text{percent}$$

You can use the relationship among the part, the whole, and the percent to solve problems.

🔓 UNLOCK the Problem REAL WORLD

Emily has sent 28 text messages so far this week. That is 20% of the total number of text messages she is allowed in one week. What is the total number of text messages Emily can send in one week?

🔑 One Way Use a double number line.

Think: The *whole* is the total number of messages Emily can send. The *part* is the number of messages Emily has sent so far.

The double number line shows that 20% represents 28 messages.

Find the number of messages represented by 100%.

Think: I want to find 100%. What can I multiply 20 by to get 100?

$20 \times \boxed{} = 100$

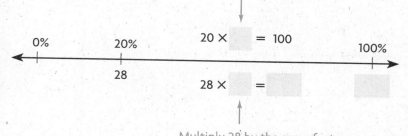

0%   20%   100%

28

$28 \times \boxed{} = \boxed{}$ $\boxed{}$

Multiply 28 by the same factor.

So, 28 is 20% of _____. Emily can send

_____ messages in one week.

Math Talk MATHEMATICAL PRACTICES
Explain the relationship among the part, the whole, and the percent using the information in this problem.

🔑 Another Way Use equivalent ratios.

STEP 1 Write the relationship among the percent, part, and whole.

$$\text{percent} = \frac{\text{part}}{\text{whole}}$$

Think: The percent is _____ %. The part is _____ messages. The _____ is unknown.

$$20\% = \frac{}{\boxed{}}$$

> **Math Idea**
> The denominator of the percent ratio will always be 100 because 100% represents the whole.

STEP 2 Write the percent as a ratio.

$$\frac{20}{\boxed{}} = \frac{28}{\boxed{}}$$

STEP 3 Simplify the known ratio.

$$\frac{20 \div 20}{100 \div \boxed{}} = \frac{1}{\boxed{}} = \frac{28}{\boxed{}}$$

STEP 4 Write an equivalent ratio.

$$\frac{1 \times 28}{5 \times \boxed{}} = \frac{28}{\boxed{}}$$

Think: The numerator should be _____.

$$\frac{28}{\boxed{}} = \frac{28}{\boxed{}}$$

So, 28 is 20% of _____. Emily can send _____ messages in one week.

🔑 Example 24 is 5% of what number?

STEP 1 Write the relationship among the percent, part, and whole.

$$\text{percent} = \frac{\text{part}}{\text{whole}}$$

Think: The percent is _____ %. The part is _____. The _____ is unknown.

$$5\% = \frac{}{\boxed{}}$$

STEP 2 Write the percent as a ratio.

$$\frac{5}{\boxed{}} = \frac{24}{\boxed{}}$$

STEP 3 Simplify the known ratio.

$$\frac{5 \div \boxed{}}{100 \div \boxed{}} = \frac{1}{\boxed{}} = \frac{24}{\boxed{}}$$

STEP 4 Write an equivalent ratio.

$$\frac{1 \times \boxed{}}{20 \times \boxed{}} = \frac{24}{\boxed{}}$$

Think: The numerator should be _____.

$$\frac{24}{\boxed{}} = \frac{24}{\boxed{}}$$

So, 24 is 5% of _____.

Math Talk

Explain how you could check your answer to the Example.

Name _____

Share and Show MATH BOARD

Find the unknown value.

✓**1.** 9 is 25% of _____

0%   25%   25 × ▢ = 100   100%

9

9 × ▢ = ▢   ▢

2. 14 is 10% of _____

✓**3.** 3 is 5% of _____

4. 12 is 60% of _____

Math Talk MATHEMATICAL PRACTICES
Explain how to solve a problem involving a part, a whole, and a percent.

On Your Own

Find the unknown value.

5. 16 is 20% of _____

0%   100%

6. 42 is 50% of _____

7. 28 is 40% of _____

8. 60 is 75% of _____

9. 27 is 30% of _____

10. 21 is 60% of _____

11. 12 is 15% of _____

Solve.

12. 40% of the students in the sixth grade at Andrew's school participate in sports. If 52 students participate in sports, how many sixth graders are there at Andrew's school?

_____

13. There were 170 people at the concert. If 85% of the seats were filled, how many seats are in the auditorium?

_____

Algebra Find the unknown value.

14. $40\% = \dfrac{32}{▢}$

15. $65\% = \dfrac{91}{▢}$

16. $45\% = \dfrac{54}{▢}$

_____   _____   _____

Problem Solving REAL WORLD

Use the advertisement for 17 and 18.

17. Corey spent 20% of his savings on a printer at Louie's Electronics. How much did Corey have in his savings account before he bought the printer?

_____

18. Kai spent 90% of his money on a laptop that cost $423. Does he have enough money left to buy a scanner? Explain.

_____

19. Maurice has completed 17 pages of the research paper he is writing. That is 85% of the required length of the paper. What is the required length of the paper?

_____

20. **H.O.T.** Of 250 seventh-grade students, 175 walk to school. What percent of seventh-graders do not walk to school?

_____

21. **What's the Error?** Kate has made 20 free throws in basketball games this year. That is 80% of the free throws she has attempted. To find the total number of free throws she attempted, Kate wrote the equation $\frac{80}{100} = \frac{\blacksquare}{20}$. What error did Kate make?

_____

_____

22. ⭐ **Test Prep** Of the students at Washington Middle School, 320 signed up for the school picnic. That was 80% of all the students in the school. How many students attend Washington Middle School?

Ⓐ 250   Ⓒ 360

Ⓑ 256   Ⓓ 400

SHOW YOUR WORK

FOR MORE PRACTICE:
Standards Practice Book, pp. P103–P104

Name _____

✓ Chapter 5 Review/Test

▶ **Vocabulary**

Choose the best term from the box to complete the sentence.

1. A _____ is equivalent to the ratio of a part to a whole. (p. 187)

▶ **Concepts and Skills**

Write the number in two other forms (fraction, decimal, or percent). (CC.6.RP.3c)

2. $\frac{5}{8}$

_____

3. 44%

_____

4. 0.75

_____

5. $\frac{3}{5}$

_____

Find the percent of the quantity. (CC.6.RP.3c)

6. 35% of 125

_____

7. 6% of 78

_____

8. 20% of 282

_____

9. 23% of 60

_____

10. 98% of 76

_____

11. 1.5% of 400

_____

12. 0.1% of 48

_____

13. 125% of 302

_____

Find the unknown value. (CC.6.RP.3c)

14. 27 is 30% of _____

15. 63 is 150% of _____

16. 14 is 40% of _____

17. 28 is 7% of _____

18. 45 is 60% of _____

19. 60 is 40% of _____

GO Online Assessment Options Chapter Test

Fill in the bubble to show your answer.

20. Kate wants to buy a new sled. She has already saved 35% of the amount she needs. What fraction describes this percent? (CC.6.RP.3c)

Ⓐ $\frac{3}{10}$

Ⓑ $\frac{7}{20}$

Ⓒ $\frac{7}{10}$

Ⓓ $\frac{4}{5}$

21. In a survey of sixth graders in an after-school theater program, $\frac{3}{5}$ of the students said they attend a theater class. What percent of students surveyed do not attend a theater class? (CC.6.RP.3c)

Ⓐ 40%

Ⓑ 50%

Ⓒ 60%

Ⓓ 70%

22. One cup of cooked spinach contains 377% of the recommended daily value of vitamin A. What fraction of the recommended daily value of vitamin A is in one cup of cooked spinach? (CC.6.RP.3c)

Ⓐ $37\frac{7}{10}$

Ⓑ $3\frac{77}{100}$

Ⓒ $3\frac{7}{10}$

Ⓓ $\frac{377}{1,000}$

23. About $\frac{4}{10}$ of the population has blood type O+. What percent of the population has blood type O+? (CC.6.RP.3c)

Ⓐ 0.04%

Ⓑ 0.4%

Ⓒ 4%

Ⓓ 40%

24. At a frozen yogurt shop, $\frac{7}{25}$ of sales are chocolate, 0.09 of sales are mocha, 23% of sales are strawberry, and $\frac{2}{5}$ of sales are vanilla. Which flavor is most popular? (CC.6.RP.3c)

Ⓐ Chocolate

Ⓑ Mocha

Ⓒ Strawberry

Ⓓ Vanilla

Fill in the bubble to show your answer.

25. A magazine has 96 pages. There are advertisements on 75% of the pages. How many of the magazine's pages do not have advertisements? (CC.6.RP.3c)

Ⓐ 12

Ⓑ 24

Ⓒ 71

Ⓓ 72

26. An electrician has a piece of wire that is 18 feet long. He cuts off 20% of the wire. Then he cuts the remaining piece of wire into 6 equal pieces. What is the length of each piece? (CC.6.RP.3c)

Ⓐ 0.6 feet

Ⓑ 2.4 feet

Ⓒ 3.6 feet

Ⓓ 14.4 feet

27. There are 90 students in Grade 5, and 10% of them were absent today. In Grade 6, 15% of the 80 students were absent today. What was the total number of students in the two grades who were present today? (CC.6.RP.3c)

Ⓐ 17

Ⓑ 21

Ⓒ 149

Ⓓ 153

28. Annette has finished 20 of her homework problems. That is 80% of the total assigned by her math teacher. How many problems were assigned? (CC.6.RP.3c)

Ⓐ 16   Ⓒ 30

Ⓑ 25   Ⓓ 32

29. The sixth grade is raising money for the local animal shelter. So far they have raised $320, which is 40% of their goal. How much money do they hope to raise? (CC.6.RP.3c)

Ⓐ $400

Ⓑ $640

Ⓒ $800

Ⓓ $1,280

▶ Constructed Response

30. According to the Motion Picture Association of America, 4% of all movie advertising is on the Internet and $\frac{1}{10}$ of all movie advertising is in newspapers. Which form of advertising is used more often? Explain. (CC.6.RP.3c)

_____

31. Alex spent 25% of his money on a sports drink. Then he spent 25% of the remaining money on trail mix. He had $9 left. How much money did Alex have to begin with? (CC.6.RP.3c)

_____

▶ Performance Task (CC.6.RP.3c)

32. Snow season at Whitecap Ski Resort lasts from November through April. The table shows the amount of snow received each month during the most recent snow season and the percent of the total snowfall.

Ⓐ Use the information from December to find the total amount of snowfall received by Whitecap last snow season.

_____

Ⓑ Use your answer from A to complete the table.

Whitecap Ski Resort Snowfall		
Month	Amount of snow (in.)	Percent of total snowfall
November		14%
December	60	20%
January		
February		22%
March	42	
April	21	

Ⓒ Two snow seasons ago, Whitecap received 320 inches of snow. That season it received 10% of the total season's snowfall in November. Officials at Whitecap like to have at least 40 inches of snowfall by the end of November. Did Whitecap receive enough snowfall to meet that goal? Explain how you determined your answer.

_____

Show What You Know ✓

Check your understanding of important skills.

Name _____

▶ **Choose the Appropriate Unit** Circle the more reasonable unit to measure the object.

1. the length of a car
   inches or feet

2. the length of a soccer field
   meters or kilometers

▶ **Multiply and Divide by 10, 100, and 1,000** Use mental math.

3. 2.51×10

_____

4. 5.3×100

_____

5. $0.71 \times 1,000$

_____

6. $3.25 \div 10$

_____

7. $8.65 \div 100$

_____

8. $56.2 \div 1,000$

_____

▶ **Convert Units** Complete.

9. 12 lb = ▮ oz
   Think: 1 lb = 16 oz

_____

10. 8 c = ▮ pt
    Think: 2 c = 1 pt

_____

11. 84 in. = ▮ ft
    Think: 12 in. = 1 ft

_____

MATH DETECTIVE

WITH

CARMEN SANDIEGO™

A cheetah can run at a rate of 105,600 yards per hour. Be a math detective and find the number of miles the cheetah could run at this rate in 5 minutes.

Vocabulary Builder

▶ **Visualize It** •

Sort the review words into the Venn diagram. One word has been filled in for you.

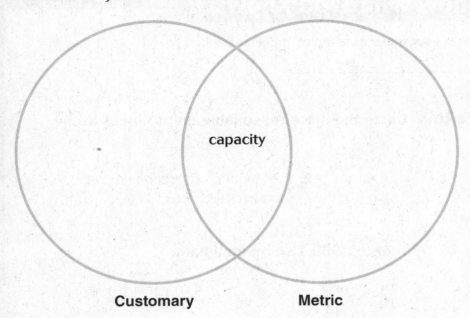

Customary   **Metric**

Review Words

✓ gallon

  gram

✓ length

  liter

✓ mass

  meter

  ounce

  pint

  pound

✓ quart

  ton

✓ weight

Preview Words

✓ capacity

✓ conversion factor

▶ **Understand Vocabulary** •

Complete the sentences by using the checked words.

1. A rate in which the two quantities are equal but use different

   units is called a _____.

2. _____ is the the amount of matter in an object.

3. _____ is the amount a container can hold.

4. The _____ of an object tells how heavy the
   object is.

5. Inches, feet, and yards are all customary units used to measure

   _____.

6. A _____ is a larger unit of capacity than a
   quart.

GO Online • eStudent Edition • Multimedia eGlossary

Convert Units of Length

Essential Question How can you use ratio reasoning to convert from one unit of length to another?

COMMON CORE STANDARD CC.6.RP.3d
Understand ratio concepts and use ratio reasoning to solve problems.

In the customary measurement system, some of the common units of length are inches, feet, yards, and miles. You can multiply by an appropriate conversion factor to convert between units. A **conversion factor** is a rate in which the two quantities are equal, but use different units.

Customary Units of Length

1 foot (ft) = 12 inches (in.)
1 yard (yd) = 36 inches
1 yard = 3 feet
1 mile (mi) = 5,280 feet
1 mile = 1,760 yards

🔑 UNLOCK the Problem REAL WORLD

In a soccer game, Kyle scored a goal from a corner kick. Kyle was 33 feet from the goal. How many yards from the goal was he?

Math Idea

When the same unit appears in a numerator and a denominator, you can divide out the common unit before multiplying as you would with a common factor.

 Convert 33 feet to yards.

Choose a conversion factor. **Think:** I'm converting to yards *from* feet.

1 yard = 3 feet, so use the rate $\frac{1\text{ yd}}{3\text{ ft}}$.

Multiply 33 feet by the conversion factor. Units of *feet* appear in a numerator and a denominator, so you can divide out these units before multiplying.

$33\text{ ft} \times \frac{1\text{ yd}}{3\text{ ft}} = \frac{33\ \cancel{\text{ft}}}{1} \times \frac{1\text{ yd}}{3\ \cancel{\text{ft}}} = $ _____ yd

So, Kyle was _____ yards from the goal.

 How many inches from the goal was Kyle?

Choose a conversion factor. **Think:** I'm converting to inches *from* feet.

12 inches = 1 foot, so use the rate $\frac{12\text{ in.}}{1\text{ ft}}$.

Multiply 33 ft by the conversion factor.

$33\text{ ft} \times \frac{12\text{ in.}}{1\text{ ft}} = \frac{33\ \cancel{\text{ft}}}{1} \times \frac{12\text{ in.}}{1\ \cancel{\text{ft}}} = $ _____ in.

So, Kyle was _____ inches from the goal.

Math Talk

MATHEMATICAL PRACTICES

Explain how you know which unit to use in the numerator and which unit to use in the denominator of a conversion factor.

Metric Units You can use a similar process to convert metric units. Metric units are used throughout most of the world. One advantage of using the metric system is that the units are related by powers of 10.

Example

A Boeing 777-300 passenger airplane measures 73.9 meters from nose to tail. What is the length of the airplane in centimeters? What is the length in kilometers?

 One Way Use a conversion factor.

! ERROR Alert

Be sure to use the correct conversion factor. The units you are converting from should divide out, leaving only the units you are converting to.

73.9 meters = ▩ centimeters

Choose a conversion factor.

100 cm = 1 m, so use the rate $\dfrac{\text{cm}}{\text{m}}$.

Multiply 73.9 meters by the conversion factor. Divide out the common units before multiplying.

$$\dfrac{73.9 \, \cancel{m}}{1} \times \dfrac{\text{cm}}{\cancel{m}} = \underline{\hspace{2cm}} \, cm$$

So, 73.9 meters is equal to _____ centimeters.

 Another Way Use powers of 10.

Metric units are related to each other by factors of 10.

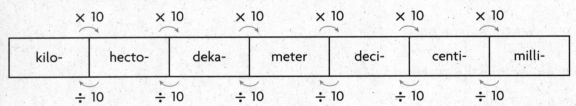

	× 10	× 10	× 10	× 10	× 10	× 10
kilo-	hecto-	deka-	meter	deci-	centi-	milli-
	÷ 10	÷ 10	÷ 10	÷ 10	÷ 10	÷ 10

73.9 meters = ▩ kilometers

Use the chart.

Kilometers are 3 places to the left of meters in the chart. Move the decimal point 3 places to the left. This is the same as dividing by 1,000.

73.9   0.0739

So, 73.9 meters is equal to _____ kilometer.

Math Talk

MATHEMATICAL PRACTICES

If you convert 285 centimeters to decimeters, will the number of decimeters be greater or less than the number of centimeters? **Explain.**

Name ______________________________

Share and Show

MATH BOARD

Convert to the given unit.

1. 3 miles = ▒ yards

conversion factor: $\frac{\square \text{ yd}}{\square \text{ mi}}$

3 miles = $\frac{3 \text{ mi}}{1} \times \frac{1{,}760 \text{ yd}}{1 \text{ mi}}$ = ________ yd

2. 43 dm = ________ hm

✓3. 9 yd = ________ in.

4. 72 ft = ________ yd

✓5. 7,500 mm = ________ dm

Math Talk MATHEMATICAL PRACTICES **Explain** how to convert from inches to yards and yards to inches.

On Your Own

6. Jason used 9 yards of ribbon while wrapping gifts for a local charity. How many inches of ribbon did he use?

____

7. The smallest known frog species can reach a maximum length of 12.4 millimeters. What is the maximum length of this frog species in centimeters?

____

8. The height of the Empire State Building measured to the top of the lightning rod is approximately 443.1 meters. What is this height in hectometers?

____

9. H.O.T. A snail moves at a speed of 2.5 feet per minute. How many yards will the snail have moved in half an hour?

____

Practice: Copy and Solve **Compare. Write <, >, or =.**

10. 32 feet ◯ 11 yards

11. 537 cm ◯ 5.37 m

12. 75 inches ◯ 6 feet

Problem Solving  REAL WORLD

What's the Error?

13. The Redwood National Park is home to some of the largest trees in the world. Hyperion is the tallest tree in the park, with a height of approximately 379 feet. Tom wants to find the height of the tree in yards.

Tom converted the height this way:

$$3 \text{ feet} = 1 \text{ yard}$$

$$\text{conversion factor: } \frac{3 \text{ ft}}{1 \text{ yd}}$$

$$\frac{379 \text{ ft}}{1} \times \frac{3 \text{ ft}}{1 \text{ yd}} = 1{,}137 \text{ yd}$$

Find and describe Tom's error.

Show how to correctly convert from 379 feet to yards.

So, 379 feet = _____ yards.

- Explain how you knew Tom's answer was incorrect.

_____

_____

_____

- Stratosphere Giant, located in Humboldt State Park in California, is 4,446 inches tall. **Compare** the heights of Hyperion and Stratosphere Giant.

_____

_____

_____

FOR MORE PRACTICE:
Standards Practice Book, pp. P109–P110

Convert Units of Capacity

Essential Question How can you use ratio reasoning to convert from one unit of capacity to another?

COMMON CORE STANDARD CC.6.RP.3d
Understand ratio concepts and use ratio reasoning to solve problems.

Capacity measures the amount a container can hold when filled. In the customary measurement system, some common units of capacity are fluid ounces, cups, pints, quarts, and gallons. You can convert between units by multiplying the given units by an appropriate conversion factor.

Customary Units of Capacity

8 fluid ounces (fl oz) = 1 cup (c)
2 cups = 1 pint (pt)
2 pints = 1 quart (qt)
4 cups = 1 quart
4 quarts = 1 gallon (gal)

UNLOCK the Problem REAL WORLD

Each dairy cow in the United States produces, on average, 25 quarts of milk per day. How many gallons of milk does a cow produce each day?

- How are quarts and gallons related?

  _____

- Why can you multiply a quantity by $\frac{1 \text{ gal}}{4 \text{ qt}}$ without changing the value of the quantity?

  _____

  _____

 Convert 25 quarts to gallons.

Choose a conversion factor. **Think:** I'm converting *to* gallons *from* quarts.

1 gallon = 4 quarts, so use the rate $\frac{1 \text{ gal}}{4 \text{ qt}}$.

Multiply 25 qt by the conversion factor.

$$25 \text{ qt} \times \frac{1 \text{ gal}}{4 \text{ qt}} = \frac{25 \text{ qt}}{1} \times \frac{1 \text{ gal}}{4 \text{ qt}} = 6\,\frac{\boxed{}}{4} \text{ gal}$$

The fractional part of the answer can be renamed using the smaller unit.

$$6\,\frac{\boxed{}}{4} \text{ gal} = \underline{\hspace{1cm}} \text{ gallons}, \underline{\hspace{1cm}} \text{ quart}$$

So, a cow produces _____ gallons, _____ quart of milk each day.

 How many pints of milk does a cow produce each day?

Choose a conversion factor. **Think:** I'm converting *to* pints *from* quarts.

2 pints = 1 quart, so use the rate $\dfrac{\boxed{} \text{ pt}}{\boxed{} \text{ qt}}$.

Multiply 25 qt by the conversion factor.

$$25 \text{ qt} \times \frac{\boxed{} \text{ pt}}{\boxed{} \text{ qt}} = \frac{25 \text{ qt}}{1} \times \frac{\boxed{} \text{ pt}}{\boxed{} \text{ qt}} = \underline{\hspace{1cm}} \text{ pt}$$

So, a cow produces _____ pints of milk each day.

Metric Units You can use a similar process to convert metric units of capacity. Just like metric units of length, metric units of capacity are related by powers of 10.

Example

A piece of Native American pottery has a capacity of 1.7 liters. What is the capacity of the pot in dekaliters? What is the capacity in milliliters?

One Way Use a conversion factor.

1.7 liters = ▢ dekaliters

Choose a conversion factor.

1 dekaliter = 10 liters, so use the rate

$$\frac{\boxed{}\ \text{daL}}{\boxed{}\ \text{L}}.$$

Multiply 1.7 L by the conversion factor.

$$\frac{1.7\ \cancel{L}}{1} \times \frac{\boxed{}\ \text{daL}}{\boxed{}\ \cancel{L}} = \underline{}\ \text{daL}$$

So, 1.7 liters is equivalent to _____ dekaliter.

Another Way Use powers of 10.

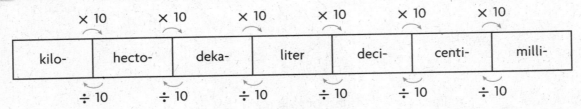

1.7 liters = ▢ milliliters

Use the chart.

Milliliters are 3 places to the right of liters. So, move the decimal point 3 places to the right.

1.7   1700.

So, 1.7 liters is equal to _____ milliliters.

Math Talk MATHEMATICAL PRACTICES

Explain why you cannot convert between units in the customary system by moving the decimal point left or right.

- **Describe** how you would convert kiloliters to milliliters.

Name _____

Share and Show

Convert to the given unit.

1. 5 quarts = ▮ cups

   conversion factor: $\dfrac{\ c\ }{qt}$

   5 quarts = $\dfrac{5\ qt}{1} \times \dfrac{4\ c}{1\ qt}$ = _____ c

2. 6.7 liters = _____ hectoliters

3. 5.3 kL = _____ L

4. 36 qt = _____ gal

5. 5,000 mL = _____ cL

Math Talk MATHEMATICAL PRACTICES Compare the customary and metric systems. In which system is it easier to convert from one unit to another?

On Your Own

6. It takes 41 gallons of water for an average washing machine to wash a load of laundry. How many quarts of water does it take to wash one load?

   _____

7. Sam squeezed 237 milliliters of juice from 4 oranges. How many liters of juice did Sam squeeze?

   _____

8. Anthony filled a bottle with 3.78 liters of water. How many deciliters of water are in the bottle?

   _____

9. A recipe calls for 16 ounces of milk. If Tonya is going to triple the recipe, how many cups of milk will she need?

   _____

Practice: Copy and Solve **Compare. Write <, >, or =.**

10. 700,000 L ◯ 70 kL

11. 6 gal ◯ 30 qt

12. 54 kL ◯ 540,000 dL

13. 10 pt ◯ 5 qt

14. 500 mL ◯ 50 L

15. 14 c ◯ 4 qt

© Houghton Mifflin Harcourt Publishing Company

🔑 UNLOCK the Problem

16. Jeffrey is loading cases of bottled water onto a freight elevator. Each case holds 24 one-pint bottles. The maximum weight that the elevator can carry is 1,000 pounds. If 1 gallon of water weighs 8.35 pounds, what is the maximum number of full cases Jeffrey can load onto the elevator?

Ⓐ 39 cases

Ⓑ 39.9 cases

Ⓒ 40 cases

Ⓓ 119 cases

a. What do you need to find?

_____

_____

_____

b. How do you know that the answer cannot be choice B?

_____

_____

c. How can you find the weight of 1 case of bottled water? What is the weight?

_____

_____

_____

_____

d. How can you find the number of cases that Jeffrey can load onto the elevator?

_____

_____

_____

_____

_____

_____

_____

e. Fill in the bubble for the correct answer choice above.

---

17. Each day, a dripping faucet dripped 1 gallon, 1 quart, 1 pint, and 1 cup of water. How many total cups of water did the faucet drip in one day?

Ⓐ 23 cups

Ⓑ 30 cups

Ⓒ 45 cups

Ⓓ 52 cups

18. A warehouse holds 100 barrels in storage. Each barrel has a capacity of 50 liters. If all the barrels are filled with water, how many kiloliters (kL) of water will they hold?

Ⓐ   5 kL

Ⓑ   50 kL

Ⓒ   5,000 kL

Ⓓ 5,000,000 kL

Convert Units of Weight and Mass

Essential Question How can you use ratio reasoning to convert from one unit of weight or mass to another?

COMMON CORE STANDARD CC.6.RP.3d
Understand ratio concepts and use ratio reasoning to solve problems.

The weight of an object is a measure of how heavy it is. Common units of weight in the customary measurement system include ounces, pounds, and tons.

> **Customary Units of Weight**
> 1 pound (lb) = 16 ounces (oz)
> 1 ton (T) = 2,000 pounds

UNLOCK the Problem REAL WORLD

The largest pearl ever found weighed 226 ounces. What was the pearl's weight in pounds?

- How are ounces and pounds related?

  _____

- Will you expect the number of pounds to be greater than 226 or less than 226? Explain.

  _____

 Convert 226 ounces to pounds.

Choose a conversion factor.
Think: I'm converting *to* pounds *from* ounces.

1 lb = 16 oz, so use the rate $\dfrac{\boxed{}\ \text{lb}}{\boxed{}\ \text{oz}}$.

Multiply 226 ounces by the conversion factor.

$$226\ oz \times \frac{1\ lb}{16\ oz} = \frac{226\ \cancel{oz}}{1} \times \frac{1\ lb}{16\ \cancel{oz}} = \frac{\boxed{}}{16}\ lb$$

Think: The fractional part of the answer can be renamed using the smaller unit.

$$\frac{\boxed{}}{16}\ lb = \underline{\quad}\ lb,\ \underline{\quad}\ oz$$

So, the largest pearl weighed _____ pounds, _____ ounces.

 The largest emerald ever found weighed 38 pounds. What was its weight in ounces?

Choose a conversion factor.
Think: I'm converting *to* ounces *from* pounds.

16 oz = 1 lb, so use the rate $\dfrac{\boxed{}\ \text{oz}}{\boxed{}\ \text{lb}}$.

Multiply 38 lb by the conversion factor.

$$38\ lb \times \frac{16\ oz}{1\ lb} = \frac{38\ \cancel{lb}}{1} \times \frac{16\ oz}{1\ \cancel{lb}} = \underline{\qquad}\ oz$$

So, the emerald weighed _____ ounces.

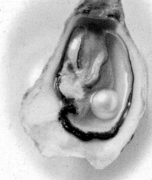

1. **Explain** how you could convert the emerald's weight to tons.

_____

Metric Units The amount of matter in an object is called the mass. Metric units of mass are related by powers of 10.

Example Corinne caught a rainbow trout with a mass of 2,570 grams. What was the mass of the trout in centigrams? What was the mass in kilograms?

One Way Use a conversion factor.

2,570 grams to centigrams

Choose a conversion factor.   100 cg = 1 g, so use the rate $\dfrac{\boxed{}\ cg}{g}$.

Multiply 2,570 g by the conversion factor. $\dfrac{2{,}570\ \cancel{g}}{1} \times \dfrac{100\ cg}{1\ \cancel{g}} = \underline{\hspace{2cm}}\ cg$

So, the trout's mass was _____ centigrams.

Another Way Use powers of 10.

Recall that metric units are related to each other by factors of 10.

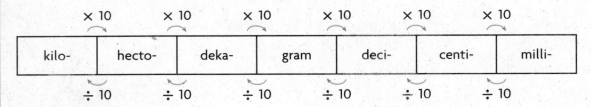

	× 10	× 10	× 10	× 10	× 10	× 10
kilo-	hecto-	deka-	gram	deci-	centi-	milli-
	÷ 10	÷ 10	÷ 10	÷ 10	÷ 10	÷ 10

2,570 grams to kilograms

Use the chart.

Kilograms are 3 places to the left of grams.   2570.   2.570
Move the decimal point 3 places to the left.

So, 2,570 grams = _____ kilograms.

Math Talk Compare objects with masses of 1 dg and 1 dag. Which has a greater mass? **Explain.**

2. Suppose hoots and floops are units of weight, and 2 hoots = 4 floops. Which is heavier, a hoot or a floop? **Explain.**

_____

_____

Name _____

Share and Show

Convert to the given unit.

1. 9 pounds = ☐ ounces

   conversion factor: ☐ $\frac{oz}{lb}$

   9 pounds = 9 lb × $\frac{16\ oz}{1\ lb}$ = _____ oz

2. 3.77 grams = _____ dekagram

3. Amanda's netbook weighs 56 ounces. How many pounds does it weigh?

   _____

4. A honeybee can carry a 40 mg load of nectar to the hive. How many grams of nectar can a honeybee carry?

   _____

Math Talk MATHEMATICAL PRACTICES
Compare metric units of capacity and mass. How are they alike? How are they different?

On Your Own

Convert to the given unit.

5. 4 lb = _____ oz

6. 7.13 g = _____ cg

7. 3 T = _____ lb

8. The African Goliath frog can reach weights up to 7 pounds. How many ounces can the Goliath frog weigh?

   _____

9. The mass of a standard hockey puck must be at least 156 grams. What is the minimum mass of 8 hockey pucks in kilograms?

   _____

Practice: Copy and Solve. Compare. Write <, >, or =.

10. 250 lb ◯ 0.25 T

11. 65.3 hg ◯ 653 dag

12. 5 T ◯ 5,000 lb

13. **H.O.T.** Masses of precious stones are measured in carats, where 1 carat = 200 milligrams. What is the mass of a 50-dg diamond in carats?

   _____

Problem Solving REAL WORLD

Use the table for 14–18.

14. Express the weight range for bowling balls in pounds.

_____

15. By how many pounds does the maximum allowable weight for a soccer ball exceed the maximum allowable weight for a baseball? Round your answer to the nearest hundredth.

_____

16. **H.O.T.** A manufacturer produces 3 tons of baseballs per day and packs them in cartons of 24 baseballs each. If all of the balls are the minimum allowable weight, how many cartons of balls does the company produce each day?

_____

17. **Write Math** ▶ **Explain** how you could use mental math to estimate the number of soccer balls it would take to produce a total weight of 1 ton.

_____

_____

_____

18. ⭐ **Test Prep** A tennis ball must weigh at least 0.4 times the minimum allowable weight for a baseball. What is a tennis ball's minimum allowable weight?

Ⓐ 1.25 oz

Ⓑ 2 oz

Ⓒ 12.5 oz

Ⓓ 20 oz

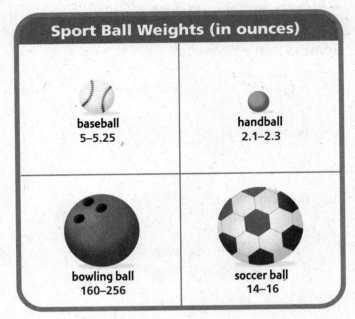

Sport Ball Weights (in ounces)

baseball 5–5.25	handball 2.1–2.3
bowling ball 160–256	soccer ball 14–16

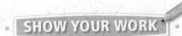

SHOW YOUR WORK

FOR MORE PRACTICE:
Standards Practice Book, pp. P113–P114

© Houghton Mifflin Harcourt Publishing Company

Name _____

✓ Mid-Chapter Checkpoint

▶ **Vocabulary**

Choose the best term from the box to complete the sentence.

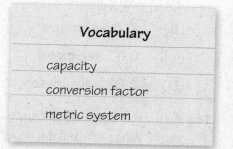

Vocabulary
capacity
conversion factor
metric system

1. A _____ is a rate in which the two quantities are equal, but use different units. **(p. 219)**

2. _____ is the amount a container can hold. **(p. 223)**

▶ **Concepts and Skills**

Convert units to solve. (CC.6.RP.3d)

3. A professional football field is 160 feet wide. What is the width of the field in yards?

_____

4. Julie drinks 8 cups of water per day. How many quarts of water does she drink per day?

_____

5. The mass of Riley's math book is 4,458 grams. What is the mass of 4 math books in kilograms?

_____

6. Turning off the water while brushing your teeth saves 379 centiliters of water. How many liters of water can you save if you turn off the water while you brush 3 times?

_____

Convert to the given unit. (CC.6.RP.3d)

7. 34.2 mm = _____ cm

8. 42 in. = _____ ft

9. 1.4 km = _____ hm

10. 4 gal = _____ qt

11. 53 dL = _____ daL

12. 28 c = _____ pt

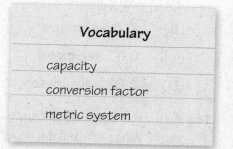

Fill in the bubble to show your answer.

13. Quentin's laptop is 32 centimeters wide. What is the width of the laptop in decimeters? (CC.6.RP.3d)

Ⓐ 320 decimeters

Ⓑ 3.2 decimeters

Ⓒ 0.32 decimeter

Ⓓ 0.032 decimeter

14. A truck is carrying 8 cars weighing an average of 4,500 pounds each. What is the total weight in tons of the cars on the truck?
(CC.6.RP.3d)

Ⓐ 18 tons

Ⓑ 30 tons

Ⓒ 36 tons

Ⓓ 180 tons

15. Ben's living room is a rectangle measuring 10 yards by 168 inches. By how many feet does the length of the room exceed the width?
(CC.6.RP.3d)

Ⓐ 9 feet

Ⓑ 12 feet

Ⓒ 16 feet

Ⓓ 21 feet

16. Jessie served 13 pints of orange juice at her party. How many quarts of orange juice did she serve? (CC.6.RP.3d)

Ⓐ 1 quart 5 pints

Ⓑ 3 quarts 1 pint

Ⓒ 6 quarts 1 pint

Ⓓ 12 quarts 1 pint

17. Cassidy's cell phone has a mass of 50,000 centigrams. What is the mass of her phone in grams? (CC.6.RP.3d)

Ⓐ 5,000,000 grams

Ⓑ 500,000 grams

Ⓒ 5,000 grams

Ⓓ 500 grams

Name _____

Transform Units

Essential Question How can you transform units to solve problems?

COMMON CORE STANDARD CC.6.RP.3d
Understand ratio concepts and use ratio reasoning to solve problems.

You can sometimes use the units of the quantities in a problem to help you decide how to solve the problem.

UNLOCK the Problem REAL WORLD

A car's gas mileage is the average distance the car can travel on 1 gallon of gas. Maria's car has a gas mileage of 20 miles per gallon. How many miles can Maria travel on 9 gallons of gas?

- Would you expect the answer to be greater or less than 20 miles? Why?

_____

_____

_____

 Analyze the units in the problem.

STEP 1 Identify the units.

You know two quantities: the car's gas mileage and the amount of gas.

Gas mileage: 20 miles per gallon = $\dfrac{20\ \rule{1cm}{0.4pt}}{1\ \rule{1cm}{0.4pt}}$

Amount of gas: 9 _____

You want to know a third quantity: the distance the car can travel.

Distance: ▪ _____

STEP 2 Determine the relationship among the units.

Think: The answer needs to have units of miles. If I multiply $\frac{20\text{ miles}}{1\text{ gallon}}$ by 9 gallons, I can divide out units of gallons. The product will have units of

_____, which is what I want.

STEP 3 Use the relationship.

$$\frac{20\text{ mi}}{1\text{ gal}} \times 9\text{ gal} = \frac{20\text{ mi}}{1\ \cancel{\text{gal}}} \times \frac{9\ \cancel{\text{gal}}}{1} = \underline{\hspace{3cm}}$$

So, Maria can travel _____ on 9 gallons of gas.

1. **Explain** why the units of gallons are crossed out in the multiplication step above.

_____

_____

Sometimes you may need to convert units before solving a problem.

 Example

The material for a rectangular awning has an area of 315 square feet. If the width of the material is 5 yards, what is the length of the material in feet? (Recall that the area of a rectangle is equal to its length times its width.)

STEP 1   Identify the units.

You know two quantities: the area of the material and the width of the material.

Area: 315 sq ft = 315 ft × ft

Width: 5 _____

You want to know a third quantity: the length of the material.

Length: ▇ ft

> **Math Idea**
>
> You can write units of area as products.
>
> sq ft = ft × ft

STEP 2   Determine the relationship among the units.

Think: The answer needs to have units of feet. So, I should convert the width from yards to feet.

Width: $\dfrac{5 \text{ yd}}{1} \times \dfrac{\boxed{} \text{ ft}}{1 \text{ yd}} = \boxed{}$ ft

Think: If I divide the area by the width I can divide out units of feet. The quotient will have units of _____, which is what I want.

STEP 3   Use the relationship.

Divide the area by the width.

315 sq ft ÷ _____ ft

Write the division using a fraction bar.

$\dfrac{\boxed{} \text{ sq ft}}{15 \text{ ft}}$

Write the units of area as a product and divide out the common units.

$\dfrac{\boxed{} \text{ ft} \times \cancel{ft}}{\cancel{ft}} = \boxed{}$ ft

So, the length of the material is _____.

2. **Explain** how knowing how to find the area of a rectangle could help you solve the problem above.

_____

_____

3. **Explain** why the answer is in feet even though units of feet are divided out.

_____

_____

234

Name _____

Share and Show

1. A dripping faucet leaks 12 gallons of water per day. How many gallons does the faucet leak in 6 days?

   Quantities you know: $\dfrac{12}{1}$ _____ and _____ days

   Quantity you want to know: ▓ _____

   $\dfrac{ \text{gal}}{1 \text{ day}} \times$ ▓ days = _____

   So, the faucet leaks _____ in 6 days.

2. Bananas sell for $0.44 per pound. How much will 7 pounds of bananas cost?

   _____

3. Grizzly Park is a rectangular park with an area of 24 square miles. The park is 3 miles wide. What is its length in miles?

   _____

> **Math Talk** MATHEMATICAL PRACTICES
> Discuss how examining the units in a problem can help you solve the problem.

On Your Own

Multiply or divide the quantities.

4. $\dfrac{24 \text{ kg}}{1 \text{ min}} \times 15 \text{ min}$

   _____

5. 216 sq cm ÷ 8 cm

   _____

6. $\dfrac{17 \text{ L}}{1 \text{ hr}} \times 9 \text{ hr}$

   _____

7. A bamboo plant grew at a rate of 16 inches per day. How many inches did it grow in 8 days?

   _____

8. Orlando's new hybrid car gets 45 miles per gallon. How many gallons of gas did he use to drive 180 miles?

   _____

9. The rectangular rug in Marcia's living room measures 12 feet by 108 inches. What is the rug's area in square feet?

   _____

10. A box-making machine makes cardboard boxes at a rate of 72 boxes per minute. How many minutes does it take to make 360 boxes?

    _____

Connect to Reading

Make Predictions

A *prediction* is a guess about something in the future. A prediction is more likely to be accurate if it is based on facts and logical reasoning.

The Hoover Dam is one of America's largest producers of hydroelectric power. During periods of peak electricity production, 300,000 gallons of water move through the dam's generators every second. Predict the amount of water that moves through the generators in half an hour.

FACT		PREDICTION
300,000 gallons per second	→	? gallons in half an hour

Use what you know about transforming units to make a prediction.

You know the rate of the water through the generators, and you are given an amount of time.

Rate of flow: $\dfrac{\boxed{} \text{ gal}}{1 \text{ sec}}$; time: $\dfrac{1}{2}$ _____

You want to find the amount of water.

Amount of water: ■ gallons

Convert the amount of time to seconds to match the units in the rate.

$\dfrac{1}{2}$ hr = _____ min

$\dfrac{30 \text{ min}}{1} \times \dfrac{\boxed{} \text{ sec}}{1 \text{ min}} =$ _____ sec

Multiply the rate by the amount of time to find the amount of water.

$\dfrac{\boxed{} \text{ gal}}{\text{sec}} \times \dfrac{\boxed{} \text{ sec}}{1} =$ _____ gal

So, a good prediction of the amount of water that moves through the

generators in half an hour is _____ .

Convert units to solve.

11. An average of 19,230 people tour the Hoover Dam each week. Predict the number of people touring the dam in a year.

12. H.O.T. The Hoover Dam generates an average of about 11,506,000 kilowatt-hours of electricity per day. Predict the number of kilowatt-hours generated in 7 weeks.

FOR MORE PRACTICE: Standards Practice Book, pp. P115–P116

Name _____

Problem Solving • Distance, Rate, and Time Formulas

Essential Question How can you use the strategy *use a formula* to solve problems involving distance, rate, and time?

COMMON CORE STANDARD CC.6.RP.3d
Understand ratio concepts and use ratio reasoning to solve problems.

You can solve problems involving distance, rate, and time by using the formulas below. In each formula, *d* represents distance, *r* represents rate, and *t* represents time.

Distance, Rate, and Time Formulas		
To find distance, use $d = r \times t$	To find rate, use $r = d \div t$	To find time, use $t = d \div r$

🔑 UNLOCK the Problem   REAL WORLD

Helen drives 220 miles to visit Niagara Falls. She drives at an average speed of 55 miles per hour. How long does the trip take?

Use the graphic organizer to help you solve the problem.

Read the Problem

What do I need to find?

I need to find the _____ the trip takes.

What information do I need to use?

I need to use the _____ Helen travels and

the _____ of speed her car is moving.

How will I use the information?

First I will choose the formula _____ because

I need to find time. Next I will substitute for *d* and *r*.

Then I will _____ to find the time.

Solve the Problem

- First write the appropriate formula.

  $t = d \div r$

- Next substitute the values for *d* and *r*.

  $t = \underline{\quad}$ mi $\div \dfrac{\underline{\quad} \text{ mi}}{1 \text{ hr}}$

- Rewrite the division as multiplication by the reciprocal of $\dfrac{55 \text{ mi}}{1 \text{ hr}}$.

  $t = \dfrac{\underline{\quad} \text{ mi}}{1} \times \dfrac{1 \text{ hr}}{\underline{\quad} \text{ mi}} = \underline{\quad}$ hr

So, the trip takes _____ hours.

Math Talk
MATHEMATICAL PRACTICES
Explain how you know which formula to use.

🔑 Try Another Problem

Zachary's class traveled to the Museum of Natural Science for a field trip. To reach the destination, the bus traveled at a rate of 65 miles per hour for 2 hours. What distance did Zachary's class travel?

Choose the appropriate formula.

$$d = r \times t \qquad r = d \div t \qquad t = d \div r$$

Use the graphic organizer to help you solve the problem.

Read the Problem	Solve the Problem
What do I need to find?	
What information do I need to use?	
How will I use the information?	

So, Zachary's class traveled _____ miles.

Math Talk   MATHEMATICAL PRACTICES   Explain how you could check your answer by solving the problem a different way.

1. **What if** the bus traveled at a rate of 55 miles per hour for 2.5 hours? How would the distance be affected?

   _____

2. **Describe** how to find the rate if you are given the distance and time.

   _____

   _____

Name _____

Share and Show

⚷ UNLOCK the Problem Tips

√ Choose the appropriate formula.
√ Include the unit in your answer.

1. McKenzie runs at a rate of 180 meters per minute. How far does she run in 5 minutes?

   First, choose the appropriate formula.

   _____

   Next, substitute the values into the formula and solve.

   _____

   So, McKenzie runs _____ in 5 minutes.

2. ☀H.O.T.☀ **What if** McKenzie runs for 20 minutes? How many kilometers will she run if she maintains the same rate of speed?

   _____

3. A car traveled 130 miles in 2 hours. How fast did the car travel?

   _____

4. A subway car travels at a rate of 32 feet per second. How far does it travel in 16 seconds?

   _____

5. A garden snail travels at a rate of 2.6 feet per minute. At this rate, how long will it take for the snail to travel 65 feet?

   _____

6. A squirrel can run at a maximum speed of 12 miles per hour. At this rate, how long will it take the squirrel to run 3 miles?

   _____

7. A cyclist rides 8 miles in 32 minutes. What is the speed of the cyclist in miles per minute?

   _____

SHOW YOUR WORK

On Your Own.........

MATHEMATICAL PRACTICES

Choose a STRATEGY

Use a Model
Draw a Diagram
Find a Pattern
Solve a Simpler Problem
Work Backward
Use a Formula

8. A pilot flies 441 kilometers in 31.5 minutes. What is the speed of the airplane?

_____

9. Chris spent half of his money on a pair of headphones. Then he spent half of his remaining money on recordable CDs. Finally, he spent his remaining $12.75 on a book. How much money did Chris have to begin with?

_____

SHOW YOUR WORK

10. **H.O.T.** Jeremy and Cynthia leave at the same time and travel 75 miles to a fair. Jeremy drives 11 miles in 12 minutes. Cynthia drives 26 miles in 24 minutes. If they continue at the same rates, who will arrive at the fair first? **Explain**.

_____

_____

_____

11. **Sense or Nonsense?** Bonnie says that if she drives at an average rate of 40 miles per hour, it will take her about 2 hours to drive 20 miles across town. Does Bonnie's statement make sense? **Explain**.

_____

_____

_____

12. ⭐ **Test Prep** Shane rows for exercise. He rows 18 kilometers at a rate of 9 kilometers per hour. How long does it take Shane to row 18 kilometers?

Ⓐ $\frac{1}{2}$ hour

Ⓑ 2 hours

Ⓒ 20 hours

Ⓓ 162 hours

✓ Chapter 6 Review/Test

▶ **Vocabulary**

Choose the best term from the box to complete the sentence.

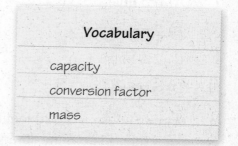

Vocabulary
capacity
conversion factor
mass

1. _____ is the amount a container can hold. (p. 223)

2. A _____ is a rate in which the two quantities are equal but use different units. (p. 219)

▶ **Concepts and Skills**

Convert to the given unit. (CC.6.RP.3d)

3. 27 yd = _____ ft

4. 3.60 cg = _____ g

5. 68.2 L = _____ dL

6. 4,000 m = _____ km

7. 26 c = _____ qt

8. 8,000 lb = _____ T

Find the product or quotient. (CC.6.RP.3d)

9. $\dfrac{28 \text{ miles}}{\text{gallon}} \times 4$ gallons

_____

10. 72 sq cm ÷ 8 cm

_____

11. 104 sq ft ÷ 13 ft

_____

12. $\dfrac{45 \text{ quarts}}{1 \text{ minute}} \times 4$ minutes

_____

Use the formula to complete. (CC.6.RP.3d)

13. $d = r \times t$

$d =$ _____

$r = 6$ cm per sec

$t = 7$ sec

14. $r = d \div t$

$d = 320$ mi

$r =$ _____

$t = 4$ hr

15. $t = d \div r$

$d = 72$ m

$r = 3$ m per sec

$t =$ _____

GO Online | Assessment Options
Chapter Test

Fill in the bubble to show your answer.

16. A passenger jet flew at an average rate of 540 miles per hour. How long did it take to fly 270 miles? (CC.6.RP.3d)

   (A) 0.5 hour

   (B) 2 hours

   (C) 2.5 hours

   (D) 5 hours

17. Marcy's house is 1,320 feet from the city library. How many miles does she live from the library? (CC.6.RP.3d)

   (A) 0.25 mile

   (B) 0.5 mile

   (C) 0.75 mile

   (D) 3 miles

18. Tina's aquarium has a capacity of 40 gallons of water. She plans to stock her aquarium with 0.25 inches of fish per quart of capacity. Mollies are 2 inches in length. How many mollies can she have in her aquarium? (CC.6.RP.3d)

   (A) 10 mollies

   (B) 20 mollies

   (C) 40 mollies

   (D) 80 mollies

19. A greyhound ran a distance of 1,200 feet in 30 seconds. Find the greyhound's average rate of speed. (CC.6.RP.3d)

   (A) 25 feet per second

   (B) 36 feet per second

   (C) 40 feet per second

   (D) 400 feet per second

20. Becky used 8 gallons of gas driving to visit her friend. Her car used gas at the rate of 24 miles per gallon. How far did she drive? (CC.6.RP.3d)

   (A) 3 miles   (C) 192 miles

   (B) 32 miles   (D) 300 miles

Fill in the bubble to show your answer.

21. Fran's snowmobile weighs 0.3 ton. Mike's weighs 500 pounds. What is the difference in the weights of the two vehicles? (CC.6.RP.3d)

Ⓐ 100 pounds

Ⓑ 200 pounds

Ⓒ 250 pounds

Ⓓ 400 pounds

22. Eric competed in the 400-meter run. His average rate of speed was 5 meters per second. How long did it take Eric to finish the race? (CC.6.RP.3d)

Ⓐ 8 seconds

Ⓑ 80 seconds

Ⓒ 125 seconds

Ⓓ 200 seconds

23. Kevin bought 6 hectograms of cheese selling for $9 per kilogram. What was the total cost? (CC.6.RP.3d)

Ⓐ $0.54

Ⓑ $4.50

Ⓒ $5.40

Ⓓ $54.00

24. A case of bottled water contains twenty-four 500 milliliter bottles. How many liters of water are in the case? (CC.6.RP.3d)

Ⓐ 5 liters

Ⓑ 12 liters

Ⓒ 5,000 liters

Ⓓ 12,000 liters

25. The screen of Angelo's eBook reader has a width of 12 centimeters and an area of 228 square centimeters. What is the length of the screen in centimeters? (CC.6.RP.3d)

Ⓐ 19 centimeters

Ⓑ 216 centimeters

Ⓒ 240 centimeters

Ⓓ 2,736 centimeters

▶ Constructed Response

26. Which has the greater capacity, a container that holds 50 hectoliters or a container that holds 10 kiloliters? Explain. (CC.6.RP.3d)

_____

_____

_____

27. Explain how you can find the distance that a runner ran if you know the runner's average rate of speed and the total time it took the runner to run the distance. (CC.6.RP.3d)

_____

▶ Performance Task (CC.6.RP.3d)

28. Carina is planning a trip to visit her parents.

A Carina will drive 4.5 hours at an average speed of 55 miles per hour to reach her parents' house. How many miles will she drive?

_____

B How many miles will Carina travel to get to her parents house and back?

_____

C The gas tank in Carina's car has a capacity of 64 quarts. If gas costs $2.58 per gallon, can Carina fill her tank for less than $40? Explain.

_____

_____

D Carina's car averages 25 miles per gallon. Will she be able to make the round trip on one tank of gas? Explain how you found your answer.

_____

_____

_____

CRITICAL AREA

Expressions and Equations

COMMON CORE

CRITICAL AREA Writing, interpreting, and using expressions and equations

Great Smoky Mountains National Park is located in the states of North Carolina and Tennessee.

Project

The Great Outdoors

The Moores are planning a family reunion in Great Smoky Mountains National Park. This park includes several campgrounds and over 800 miles of hiking trails. Some trails lead to stunning views of the park's many waterfalls.

Get Started

The Moores want to camp at the park during their reunion. They will have 17 people in their group, and they want to spend no more than $100 on camping fees.

Decide how many and what type of campsites the Moores should reserve, and determine how many nights *n* the Moores can camp without going over budget. Show your work, and support your answer by writing and evaluating algebraic expressions.

Important Facts

Group Campsite
- Fee of $35 per night
- Holds up to 25 people

Individual Campsite
- Fee of $14 per night
- Holds up to 6 people

Completed by _____

© Houghton Mifflin Harcourt Publishing Company

Algebra: Expressions

Show What You Know

Check your understanding of important skills.

Name _____

▶ **Addition Properties** Find the unknown number. Tell whether you used the Identity (or Zero) Property, Commutative Property, or Associative Property of Addition.

1. $128 + \underline{\hspace{2cm}} = 128$

    _____

2. $(17 + 36) + 14 = 17 + (\underline{\hspace{1.5cm}} + 14)$

    _____

3. $23 + 15 = \underline{\hspace{1.5cm}} + 23$

    _____

4. $9 + (11 + 46) = (9 + \underline{\hspace{1.5cm}}) + 46$

    _____

▶ **Multiply with Decimals** Find the product.

5. 1.5×7

6. 5.83×6

7. 3.7×0.8

8. 0.27×0.9

▶ **Use Parentheses** Identify which operation to do first. Then find the value of the expression.

9. $5 \times (3 + 6)$ _____

10. $(24 \div 3) - 2$ _____

11. $40 \div (20 - 16)$ _____

12. $(7 \times 6) + 5$ _____

Greg just moved into an old house and found a mysterious trunk in the attic. The lock on the trunk has a dial numbered 1 to 60. Greg found the note shown at right lying near the trunk. Be a Math Detective and help him figure out the three numbers needed to open the lock.

Lock Combination
Top Secret!

1st number: $3x$

2nd number: $5x - 1$

3rd number: $x^2 + 4$

Hint: $x = 6$

GO Online Assessment Options: **Soar to Success Math**

Vocabulary Builder

▶ **Visualize It** ·

Sort the review words into the bubble map.

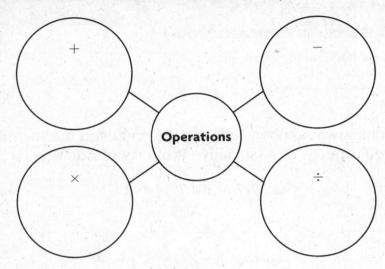

Review Words

addition

difference

division

multiplication

product

quotient

subtraction

sum

Preview Words

algebraic expression

base

coefficient

evaluate

numerical expression

terms

variable

▶ **Understand Vocabulary** ·

Complete the sentences using the preview words.

1. An exponent is a number that tells how many times a(n)

   _____ is used as a factor.

2. In the expression 4*a*, the number 4 is a(n)

   _____.

3. To _____ an expression, substitute
   numbers for the variables in the expression.

4. A mathematical phrase that uses only numbers and operation

   symbols is a(n) _____.

5. A letter or symbol that stands for one or more numbers is a(n)

   _____.

6. The parts of an expression that are separated by an addition

   or subtraction sign are the _____ of the
   expression.

GO Online · eStudent Edition · Multimedia eGlossary

Exponents

Essential Question How do you write and find the value of expressions involving exponents?

COMMON CORE STANDARD CC.6.EE.1
Apply and extend previous understandings of arithmetic to algebraic expressions.

You can use an exponent and a base to show repeated multiplication of the same factor. An **exponent** is a number that tells how many times a number called the **base** is used as a repeated factor.

$$\underbrace{5 \times 5 \times 5}_{\text{3 repeated factors}} = 5\overset{\leftarrow \text{ exponent}}{\underset{\leftarrow \text{ base}}{3}}$$

Math Idea

- 5^2 can be read "the 2nd power of 5" or "5 squared."
- 5^3 can be read "the 3rd power of 5" or "5 cubed."

🔑 UNLOCK the Problem   REAL WORLD

The table shows the number of bonuses a player can receive in each level of a video game. Use an exponent to write the number of bonuses a player can receive in level D.

🔑 **Use an exponent to write 3 × 3 × 3 × 3.**

The number _____ is used as a repeated factor.

3 is used as a factor _____ times.

Write the base and exponent. _____

So, a player can receive _____ bonuses in level D.

Level	Bonuses
A	3
B	3 × 3
C	3 × 3 × 3
D	3 × 3 × 3 × 3

Math Talk MATHEMATICAL PRACTICES
Explain how you know which number to use as the base and which number to use as the exponent.

Try This! Use one or more exponents to write the expression.

Ⓐ 7 × 7 × 7 × 7 × 7

The number _____ is used as a repeated factor.

7 is used as a factor _____ times.

Write the base and exponent. _____

Ⓑ 6 × 6 × 8 × 8 × 8

The numbers _____ and _____ are used as repeated factors.

6 is used as a factor _____ times.

8 is used as a factor _____ times.

Write each base with its own exponent.   6 ▢ × 8 ▢

Chapter 7 249

🔑 Example 1 Find the value.

Ⓐ 10^3

STEP 1 Use repeated multiplication to write 10^3.

The repeated factor is _____ . $10^3 =$ _____ × _____ × _____

Write the factor _____ times.

_____

STEP 2 Multiply.

Multiply each pair of factors, working from left to right. $10 \times 10 \times 10 =$ _____ × 10

= _____

Ⓑ 7^1

The repeated factor is _____ . $7^1 =$ _____ .

Write the factor _____ time.

Math.Talk In 10^3, what do you notice about the value of the exponent and the product? Is there a similar pattern in other powers of 10? **Explain.**

MATHEMATICAL PRACTICES

🔑 Example 2 Write 81 with an exponent by using 3 as the base.

STEP 1 Find the correct exponent.

Try 2. $3^2 = 3 \times 3 =$ _____

Try 3. $3^3 =$ _____ × _____ × _____ = _____

Try 4. $3^4 =$ _____ × _____ × _____ × _____ = _____

STEP 2 Write using the base and exponent.

$81 =$ _____

1. **Explain** how to write repeated multiplication of a factor by using an exponent.

_____

_____

2. **H.O.T.** Is 5^2 equal to 2^5? **Explain** why or why not.

_____

3. **Describe** how you could have solved the problem in Example 2 by using division.

_____

_____

_____

Name _____

Share and Show

1. Write 2^4 by using repeated multiplication. Then find the value of 2^4.

   $2^4 = 2 \times 2 \times$ _____ $\times$ _____ = _____

Use one or more exponents to write the expression.

2. $7 \times 7 \times 7 \times 7$

   _____

✓ 3. $5 \times 5 \times 5 \times 5 \times 5$

   _____

4. $3 \times 3 \times 4 \times 4$

   _____

Find the value.

5. 11^2

   _____

✓ 6. 9^3

   _____

7. 4^4

   _____

8. Write 64 with an exponent by using 4 as the base.

   _____

Math Talk MATHEMATICAL PRACTICES
In Exercise 7, does it matter in what order you multiply the factors when finding the value? Explain.

On Your Own

Use one or more exponents to write the expression.

9. $25 \times 25 \times 25$

   _____

10. $2 \times 2 \times 2 \times 4 \times 4$

    _____

11. $8 \times 8 \times 8 \times 8 \times 8$

    _____

Find the value.

12. 20^2

    _____

13. 82^1

    _____

14. 3^5

    _____

15. Write 32 with an exponent by using 2 as the base.

    _____

Complete the statement with the correct exponent.

16. $5^{\boxed{}} = 125$

17. $16^{\boxed{}} = 16$

18. $30^{\boxed{}} = 900$

Bacterial Growth

Bacteria are tiny one-celled organisms that live almost everywhere on Earth. Although some bacteria cause disease, other bacteria are helpful to humans, other animals, and plants. For example, bacteria are needed to make yogurt and many types of cheese.

Under ideal conditions, a certain type of bacterium cell grows larger and then splits into 2 "daughter" cells. After 20 minutes, the daughter cells split, resulting in 4 cells. This splitting can happen again and again as long as conditions remain ideal.

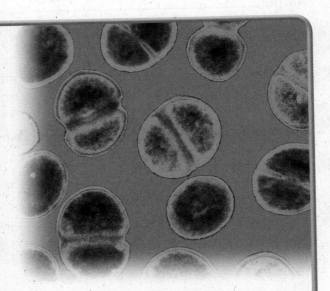

Complete the table.

Bacterial Growth	
Number of Cells	Time (min)
1	0
$2^1 = 2$	20
$2^2 = 2 \times 2 = 4$	40
$2^3 = \underline{} \times \underline{} \times \underline{} = \underline{}$	60
$2^{} = 2 \times 2 \times 2 \times 2 = 16$	80
$2^5 = \underline{} \times \underline{} \times \underline{} \times \underline{} \times \underline{} = \underline{}$	100
$2^{} = \underline{} \times \underline{} \times \underline{} \times \underline{} \times \underline{} \times \underline{} = \underline{}$	120
$2^7 = 2 \times 2 \times 2 \times 2 \times 2 \times 2 \times 2 = \underline{}$	\underline{}

Extend the pattern in the table above to answer 19 and 20.

19. What power of 2 shows the number of cells after 3 hours? How many cells are there after 3 hours?

20. How many minutes would it take to have a total of 4,096 cells?

Name _____

Evaluate Expressions Involving Exponents

Essential Question How do you use the order of operations to evaluate expressions involving exponents?

COMMON CORE STANDARD CC.6.EE.1
Apply and extend previous understandings of arithmetic to algebraic expressions.

A **numerical expression** is a mathematical phrase that uses only numbers and operation symbols.

$$3 + 16 \times 2^2 \qquad 4 \times (8 + 5^1) \qquad 2^3 + 4$$

You **evaluate** a numerical expression when you find its value. To evaluate an expression with more than one operation, you must follow a set of rules called the **order of operations**.

Order of Operations
1. Perform operations in parentheses.
2. Find the values of numbers with exponents.
3. Multiply and divide from left to right.
4. Add and subtract from left to right.

 UNLOCK the Problem REAL WORLD

An archer shoots 6 arrows at a target. Two arrows hit the ring worth 8 points, and 4 arrows hit the ring worth 4 points. Evaluate the expression $2 \times 8 + 4^2$ to find the archer's total number of points.

Follow the order of operations.

Write the expression. There are no parentheses. $2 \times 8 + 4^2$

Find the value of numbers with exponents. $2 \times 8 +$ _____

_____ from left to right.   _____ $+ 16$

Then add.   _____

So, the archer scores a total of _____ points.

Math Talk MATHEMATICAL PRACTICES
Explain the order you should perform the operations to evaluate the expression $30 - 10 + 5^2$.

Try This! Evaluate the expression $24 \div 2^3$.

There are no parentheses.	$24 \div 2^3$
Find the value of numbers with exponents.	$24 \div$ _____
Then divide.	_____

Example 1 Evaluate the expression $72 \div (13 - 4) + 5 \times 2^3$.

Write the expression.	$72 \div (13 - 4) + 5 \times 2^3$
Perform operations in _____.	$72 \div \underline{\hspace{1cm}} + 5 \times 2^3$
Find the values of numbers with _____.	$72 \div 9 + 5 \times \underline{\hspace{1cm}}$
Multiply and _____ from left to right.	$\underline{\hspace{1cm}} + 5 \times 8$
	$8 + \underline{\hspace{1cm}}$
Then add.	$\underline{\hspace{1cm}}$

Example 2

Last month, an online bookstore had approximately 10^5 visitors to its website. On average, each visitor bought 2 books. Approximately how many books did the bookstore sell last month?

STEP 1 Write an expression.

Think: The number of books sold is equal to the number of visitors times the number of books each visitor bought.

(number of visitors) (times) (number of books bought)

$\quad 10^5 \qquad\qquad \times \qquad\qquad \underline{\hspace{1.5cm}}$

STEP 2 Evaluate the expression.

Write the expression. There are no parentheses.	$10^5 \times 2$
Find the values of numbers with _____.	$\underline{\hspace{2.5cm}} \times 2$
Multiply.	$\underline{\hspace{2.5cm}}$

So, the bookstore sold approximately _____ books last month.

- **Explain** why the order of operations is necessary.

_____

_____

_____

Name _____

Share and Show ....

1. Evaluate the expression $9 + (5^2 - 10)$.

   $9 + (5^2 - 10)$ Write the expression.

   $9 + ($ _____ $- 10)$ Follow the order of operations within the parentheses.

   $9 +$ _____

   _____   Add.

Evaluate the expression.

2. $6 + 3^3 \div 9$

   3. $(15 - 3)^2 \div 9$

   4. $(8 + 9^2) - 4 \times 10$

_____   _____   _____

Math Talk   MATHEMATICAL PRACTICES

Explain how the parentheses make the values of these expressions different: $(2^2 + 8) \div 4$ and $2^2 + (8 \div 4)$.

On Your Own ....

Evaluate the expression.

5. $10 + 6^2 \times 2 \div 9$

6. $6^2 - (2^3 + 5)$

7. $16 + 18 \div 9 + 3^4$

_____   _____   _____

H.O.T.   **Place parentheses in the expression so that it equals the given value.**

8. $10^2 - 50 \div 5$
   value: 10

9. $20 + 2 \times 5 + 4^1$
   value: 38

10. $28 \div 2^2 + 3$
    value: 4

_____   _____   _____

Problem Solving REAL WORLD

Use the table for 11–13.

11. To find the cost of a window, multiply its area in square feet by the price per square foot. Write and evaluate an expression to find the cost of a knot window.

_____

12. A builder installs 4 rose windows in a home. Write and evaluate an expression to find the combined area of the windows.

_____

13. **H.O.T.** **Pose a Problem** Use the data in the table to write a new problem that involves using exponents and the order of operations. Then solve the problem.

_____

_____

_____

_____

_____

Art Glass Windows		
Type	Area (square feet)	Price per square foot
Knot	2^2	$27
Rose	3^2	$30
Tulip	4^2	$33

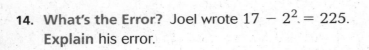
SHOW YOUR WORK

14. **What's the Error?** Joel wrote $17 - 2^2 = 225$. **Explain** his error.

_____

_____

_____

_____

15. ⭐ **Test Prep** What is the value of the expression $(4.2 + 1.3) \times 4^3$?

(A) 352   (C) 66

(B) 87.4   (D) 19.8

Name _____

Write Algebraic Expressions

Essential Question How do you write an algebraic expression to represent a situation?

COMMON CORE STANDARD CC.6.EE.2a
Apply and extend previous understandings of arithmetic to algebraic expressions.

An **algebraic expression** is a mathematical phrase that includes at least one variable. A **variable** is a letter or symbol that stands for one or more numbers.

$x + 10$ $3 \times y$ $3 \times (a + 4)$
↑   ↑   ↑
variable   variable   variable

Math Idea

There are several ways to show multiplication with a variable. Each expression below represents "3 times y."

$3 \times y$ $3y$ $3(y)$ $3 \cdot y$

UNLOCK the Problem REAL WORLD

An artist charges $5 for each person in a cartoon drawing. Write an algebraic expression for the cost in dollars for a drawing that includes p people.

🔒 **Write an algebraic expression for the cost.**

Think: [cost for each person] [times] [number of _____]
     ↓   ↓   ↓
    _____   × p

So, the cost in dollars is _____.

Math Talk MATHEMATICAL PRACTICES Discuss why p is an appropriate variable for this problem. Would it be appropriate to select a different variable? Explain.

Try This! On Mondays, a bakery adds 2 extra muffins for free with every muffin order. Write an algebraic expression for the number of muffins customers will receive on Mondays when they order m muffins.

Think: [muffins ordered] [_____] [extra muffins on Mondays]
     ↓   ↓   ↓
    _____   +   2

So, customers will receive _____ muffins on Mondays.

🔑 Example 1
The table shows the number of points that items on a quiz are worth. Write an algebraic expression for the quiz score of a student who gets m multiple-choice items and s short-answer items correct.

Quiz Scoring	
Item Type	**Points**
Multiple-choice	2
Short-answer	5

points for multiple-choice items		points for short-answer items
↓	↓	↓
$(2 \times m)$	$+$	$(\underline{\hspace{2cm}})$

So, the student's quiz score is _____ points.

🔑 Example 2
Write an algebraic expression for the word expression.

Ⓐ 30 more than the product of 4 and x

Think: Start with the product of 4 and x. Then find 30 more than the product.

the product of 4 and x $\underline{\hspace{1.5cm}} \times \underline{\hspace{1.5cm}}$

30 more than the product $\underline{\hspace{1.5cm}} + 4x$

Ⓑ 4 times the sum of x and 30

Think: Start with the sum of x and 30. Then find 4 times the sum.

the sum of x and 30 $\underline{\hspace{1.5cm}} + \underline{\hspace{1.5cm}}$

4 times the sum $\underline{\hspace{1.5cm}} \times (x + 30)$

1. When you write an algebraic expression with two operations, how can you show which operation to do first?

   _____

2. **H.O.T.** One student wrote $4 + x$ for the word expression "4 more than x." Another student wrote $x + 4$ for the same word expression. Are both students correct? **Justify** your answer.

   _____

   _____

   _____

Name _____

Share and Show

MATH BOARD

1. Write an algebraic expression for the product of 6 and *p*.

   What operation does the word "product" indicate?

   _____

   The expression is _____ × _____.

Write an algebraic expression for the word expression.

2. 11 more than *e*

3. 9 less than the quotient of *n* and 5

4. Jake is 5 years older than his brother Kevin. Kevin is *k* years old. Write an algebraic expression for Jake's age.

5. At a restaurant, 6 people can fit at a large table and 4 people can fit at a small table. Write an algebraic expression for the number of people who can fit at *ℓ* large tables and *s* small tables.

Math Talk   MATHEMATICAL PRACTICES
Explain why 3*x* is an algebraic expression.

On Your Own

Write an algebraic expression for the word expression.

6. 20 divided by *c*

7. 8 times the product of 5 and *t*

8. There are 12 eggs in a dozen. Write an algebraic expression for the number of eggs in *d* dozen.

9. A state park charges a $6.00 entry fee plus $7.50 per night of camping. Write an algebraic expression for the cost in dollars of entering the park and camping for *n* nights.

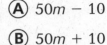 **UNLOCK the Problem**

10. Martina signs up for the cell phone plan described at the right. Which expression gives the total cost of the plan in dollars if Martina uses it for *m* months?

Ⓐ $50m - 10$

Ⓑ $50m + 10$

Ⓒ $50 \times (m - 10)$

Ⓓ $50 \times (m + 10)$

SPECIAL OFFER
CELL PHONE PLAN!

Pay a low monthly fee of **$50.**

Receive **$10** off your first month's fee.

a. What information do you know about the cell phone plan?

_____

_____

b. Write an expression for the monthly fee in dollars for *m* months.

_____

c. What operation can you use to show the discount of $10 for the first month?

_____

d. How do you know that the correct answer cannot be choice B?

_____

_____

_____

e. Write an expression for the total cost of the plan in dollars for *m* months.

_____

f. Fill in the bubble for the correct answer choice above.

11. The Computer Club has 4 fewer than twice the number of students in the band. Let *n* represent the number of students in the band. Which expression gives the number of students in the Computer Club?

Ⓐ $4n - 2$

Ⓑ $2n - 4$

Ⓒ $2 \times (n - 4)$

Ⓓ $4 \times (n - 2)$

12. At a bookstore, comic books are on sale for $2 each and graphic novels are on sale for $8 each. Which expression gives the cost in dollars of *c* comic books and *g* graphic novels?

Ⓐ $(2 + c) + (8 + g)$

Ⓑ $(2 + c) \times (8 + g)$

Ⓒ $2c + 8g$

Ⓓ $2c \times 8g$

FOR MORE PRACTICE:
Standards Practice Book, pp. P127–P128

Identify Parts of Expressions

Essential Question How can you describe the parts of an expression?

COMMON CORE STANDARD CC.6.EE.2b
Apply and extend previous understandings of arithmetic to algebraic expressions.

🔑 UNLOCK the Problem REAL WORLD

At a gardening store, seed packets cost $2 each. Martin bought 6 packets of lettuce seeds and 7 packets of pea seeds. The expression $2 \times (6 + 7)$ represents the cost in dollars of Martin's seeds. Identify the parts of the expression. Then write a word expression for $2 \times (6 + 7)$.

• Explain how you could find the cost of each type of seed.

_____

_____

 Describe the parts of the expression $2 \times (6 + 7)$.

Identify the operations in the expression.

multiplication and _____

Describe the part of the expression in parentheses, and tell what it represents.

• The part in parentheses shows the _____ of 6 and _____.

• The sum represents the number of packets of _____ seeds plus the number of packets of _____ seeds.

Describe the multiplication, and tell what it represents.

• One of the factors is _____. The other factor is the _____ of 6 and 7.

• The product represents the _____ per packet times the number of _____ Martin bought.

So, a word expression for $2 \times (6 + 7)$ is "the _____ of 2 and the _____ of _____ and 7."

• **Explain** how the expression $2 \times (6 + 7)$ differs from $2 \times 6 + 7$. Then write a word expression for $2 \times 6 + 7$.

_____

_____

_____

The **terms** of an expression are the parts of the expression that are separated by an addition or subtraction sign. A **coefficient** is a number that is multiplied by a variable.

$4k + 5$

The expression has two terms, $4k$ and 5. The coefficient of the term $4k$ is 4.

🔑 Example Identify the parts of the expression. Then write a word expression for the algebraic expression.

A $2x + 8$

Identify the terms in the expression.

The expression is the sum of _____ terms.

The terms are _____ and 8.

Describe the first term.

The first term is the product of the coefficient

_____ and the variable _____.

Describe the second term.

The second term is the number _____.

A word expression for $2x + 8$ is "8 more than the _____

of _____ and x."

Math Talk MATHEMATICAL PRACTICES
Explain why the terms of the expression are $2x$ and 8, not x and 8.

B $3a - 4b$

Identify the terms in the expression.

The expression is the _____ of

2 terms. The terms are _____ and _____.

Describe the first term.

The first term is the product of the

_____ 3 and the variable _____.

Describe the second term.

The second term is the product of the

coefficient _____ and the variable _____.

A word expression for the algebraic expression is "the difference of

_____ times _____ and 4 _____ b.

Math Talk MATHEMATICAL PRACTICES
Identify the coefficient of y in the expression $12 + y$. Explain your reasoning.

© Houghton Mifflin Harcourt Publishing Company

Name _____

Share and Show MATH BOARD

Identify the parts of the expression. Then write a word expression for the numerical or algebraic expression.

1. $7 \times (9 - 4)$

   The part in parentheses shows the _____ of _____ and _____.

   One factor of the multiplication is _____, and the other factor is $9 - 4$.

   Word expression: _____

✓ 2. $6 + 20 \div 4$

   _____

   _____

   _____

   _____

   _____

✓ 3. $5m + 2n$

   _____

   _____

   _____

   _____

   _____

Math Talk   MATHEMATICAL PRACTICES
Describe the expression $9 \times (a + b)$ as a product of two factors.

On Your Own

Practice: Copy and Solve Identify the parts of the expression. Then write a word expression for the numerical or algebraic expression.

4. $8 + (10 - 7)$

6. $b + 12x$

5. $1.5 \times 6 + 8.3$

7. $4a \div 6$

Identify the terms of the expression. Then give the coefficient of each term.

8. $k - 3d$

   _____

   _____

9. $0.5x + 2.5y$

   _____

   _____

© Houghton Mifflin Harcourt Publishing Company

Problem Solving REAL WORLD

Use the table for 10–12.

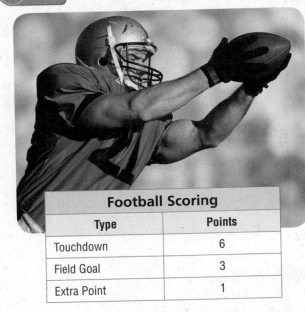

Football Scoring	
Type	Points
Touchdown	6
Field Goal	3
Extra Point	1

10. A football team scored 3 touchdowns and 3 extra points. Write a numerical expression for the team's score, and identify the parts of the expression.

_____

_____

11. Write an algebraic expression for the number of points scored by a football team that makes t touchdowns, f field goals, and e extra points.

_____

12. Identify the parts of the expression you wrote in Exercise 11.

_____

_____

_____

13. **H.O.T.** **Write Math** ▶ Give an example of an expression involving multiplication in which one of the factors is a sum. **Explain** why you do or do not need parentheses in your expression.

_____

_____

_____

_____

14. ⭐ **Test Prep** There are 12 girls and 18 boys in a sixth grade class. The students are sharing a group of 90 test tubes equally. The expression $90 \div (12 + 18)$ gives the number of test tubes each student will receive. What is the divisor in this expression?

   (**A**) 12   (**C**) $12 + 18$

   (**B**) 90   (**D**) $90 \div 12$

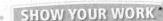

SHOW YOUR WORK

FOR MORE PRACTICE:
Standards Practice Book, pp. P129–P130

Name _____

Evaluate Algebraic Expressions and Formulas

Essential Question How do you evaluate an algebraic expression or a formula?

COMMON CORE STANDARD CC.6.EE.2c
Apply and extend previous understandings of arithmetic to algebraic expressions.

To evaluate an algebraic expression, substitute numbers for the variables and then follow the order of operations.

🔑 UNLOCK the Problem REAL WORLD

Mitchell is saving money to buy an MP3 player that costs $120. He starts with $25, and each week he saves $9. The expression $25 + 9w$ gives the amount in dollars that Mitchell will have saved after w weeks.

A **How much will Mitchell have saved after 8 weeks?**

🔑 **Evaluate the expression for $w = 8$.**

Write the expression. $25 + 9w$

Substitute 8 for w. $25 + 9 \times$ _____

Multiply. $25 +$ _____

Add.   _____

So, Mitchell will have saved $ _____ after 8 weeks.

- Which operations does the expression $25 + 9w$ include?

  _____

- In what order should you perform the operations?

  _____

B **After how many weeks will Mitchell have saved enough money to buy the MP3 player?**

🔑 **Make a table to find the week when the amount saved is at least $120.**

Week	Value of $25 + 9w$	Amount Saved
9	$25 + 9 \times 9 = 25 +$ _____ $= 106$	
10	$25 + 9 \times 10 = 25 +$ _____ $=$ _____	
11	$25 + 9 \times 11 = 25 +$ _____ $=$ _____	

So, Mitchell will have saved enough money for the

MP3 player after _____ weeks.

Math Talk MATHEMATICAL PRACTICES
Explain what it means to substitute a value for a variable.

Chapter 7 265

🔑 Example 1 Evaluate the expression for the given value of the variable.

A $4 \times (m - 8) \div 3$ for $m = 14$

Write the expression.	$4 \times (m - 8) \div 3$
Substitute 14 for m.	$4 \times (\underline{\hspace{1cm}} - 8) \div 3$
Perform operations in parentheses.	$4 \times \underline{\hspace{1cm}} \div 3$
Multiply and divide from left to right.	$\underline{\hspace{1cm}} \div 3$
	$\underline{\hspace{1cm}}$

B $3 \times (y^2 + 2)$ for $y = 4$

Write the expression.	$3 \times (y^2 + 2)$
Substitute 4 for y.	$3 \times (\underline{\hspace{1cm}}^2 + 2)$
Follow the order of operations within the parentheses.	$3 \times (\underline{\hspace{1cm}} + 2)$
	$3 \times \underline{\hspace{1cm}}$
Multiply.	$\underline{\hspace{1cm}}$

> ⚠️ **ERROR Alert**
>
> When squaring a number, be sure to multiply the number by itself.
>
> $4^2 = 4 \times 4$

Recall that a *formula* is a set of symbols that expresses a mathematical rule.

🔑 Example 2

The formula $P = 2\ell + 2w$ gives the perimeter P of a rectangle with length ℓ and width w. What is the perimeter of a rectangular vegetable garden with a length of 2.4 meters and a width of 1.2 meters?

Write the expression for the perimeter of a rectangle.	$2\ell + 2w$
Substitute 2.4 for ℓ and $\underline{\hspace{1cm}}$ for w.	$2 \times \underline{\hspace{1cm}} + 2 \times \underline{\hspace{1cm}}$
Multiply from left to right.	$\underline{\hspace{1cm}} + 2 \times 1.2$
	$4.8 + \underline{\hspace{1cm}}$
Add.	$\underline{\hspace{1cm}}$

So, the perimeter of the vegetable garden is $\underline{\hspace{1cm}}$ meters.

Math Talk MATHEMATICAL PRACTICES
Describe how evaluating an algebraic expression is different from evaluating a numerical expression.

Name _____

Share and Show

1. Evaluate $5k + 6$ for $k = 4$.

   Write the expression.   _____

   Substitute 4 for k. $5 \times$ _____ $+ 6$

   Multiply.   _____ $+ 6$

   Add.   _____

Evaluate the expression for the given value of the variable.

2. $m - 9$ for $m = 13$

3. $16 - 3b$ for $b = 4$

4. $p^2 + 4$ for $p = 6$

5. The formula $A = \ell w$ gives the area A of a rectangle with length ℓ and width w. What is the area in square feet of a United States flag with a length of 12 feet and a width of 8 feet?

_____

Math Talk   MATHEMATICAL PRACTICES
Tell what information you need to evaluate an algebraic expression.

On Your Own

Practice: Copy and Solve Evaluate the expression for the given value of the variable.

6. $7s + 5$ for $s = 3$

7. $21 - 4d$ for $d = 5$

8. $(t - 6)^2$ for $t = 11$

9. $6 \times (2v - 3)$ for $v = 5$

10. $2 \times (k^2 - 2)$ for $k = 6$

11. $5 \times (f - 32) \div 9$ for $f = 95$

12. The formula $P = 4s$ gives the perimeter P of a square with side length s. What is the perimeter of a square photograph with a side length of $5\frac{1}{2}$ inches?

_____

© Houghton Mifflin Harcourt Publishing Company

Problem Solving  REAL WORLD

The table shows how much a company charges for skateboard wheels. Each pack of 8 wheels costs $50. Shipping costs $7 for any order. Use the table for 13–15.

13. Complete the table.

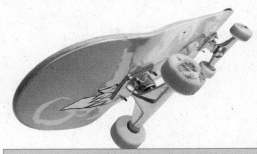

14. A skateboard club has a budget of $200 to spend on new wheels this year. What is the greatest number of packs of wheels the club can order?

_____

15. **H.O.T.** **Pose a Problem** Use the information about skateboard wheels to write a new problem that involves evaluating an expression. Then solve the problem.

_____

_____

_____

_____

Costs for Skateboard Wheels

Packs	50 × n + 7	Cost
1	50 × 1 + 7	$57
2		
3		
4		
5		

· · · · · · · · · **SHOW YOUR WORK** · · · · · · · ·

16. **H.O.T.** **What's the Error?** Bob used these steps to evaluate $3m - 3 \div 3$ for $m = 8$. **Explain** his error.

$$3 \times 8 - 3 \div 3 = 24 - 3 \div 3$$
$$= 21 \div 3$$
$$= 7$$

_____

_____

_____

_____

17. ⭐ **Test Prep** The expression $22g$ gives the distance a car can travel on g gallons of gasoline. How far can the car travel on 8 gallons of gasoline?

Ⓐ 30 miles   Ⓒ 176 miles

Ⓑ 56 miles   Ⓓ 228 miles

✓ Mid-Chapter Checkpoint

▶ Vocabulary

Choose the best term from the box to complete the sentence.

Vocabulary
coefficient
exponent
numerical expression

1. A(n) _____ tells how many times a base is used as a factor. **(p. 249)**

2. The mathematical phrase $5 + 2 \times 18$ is an example of a(n)

_____. **(p. 253)**

▶ Concepts and Skills

Find the value. (CC.6.EE.1)

3. 5^4

4. 21^2

5. 8^3

_____ | _____ | _____

Evaluate the expression. (CC.6.EE.1)

6. $9^2 \times 2 - 4^2$

7. $2 \times (10 - 2) \div 2^2$

8. $30 - (3^3 - 8)$

_____ | _____ | _____

Write an algebraic expression for the word expression. (CC.6.EE.2a)

9. the quotient of c and 8

10. 16 more than the product of 5 and p

11. 9 less than the sum of x and 5

_____ | _____ | _____

Evaluate the expression for the given value of the variable. (CC.6.EE.2c)

12. $5 \times (h + 3)$ for $h = 7$

13. $2 \times (c^2 - 5)$ for $c = 4$

14. $7a - 4a$ for $a = 8$

_____ | _____ | _____

Fill in the bubble to show your answer.

15. The bill with the greatest value ever printed in the United States was worth 10^5 dollars. Which of the following is equal to the value of the bill? (CC.6.EE.1)

Ⓐ $10,000

Ⓑ $50,000

Ⓒ $100,000

Ⓓ $500,000

16. A clothing store is raising the price of all its sweaters by $3.00. Which expression could be used to find the new price of a sweater that originally cost *d* dollars? (CC.6.EE.2a)

Ⓐ $d + 3$ Ⓒ $3 \times d$

Ⓑ $d - 3$ Ⓓ $3 - d$

17. Kendra bought a magazine for $3 and 4 paperback books for $5 each. The expression $3 + 4 \times 5$ represents the total cost in dollars of her purchases. What are the terms in this expression? (CC.6.EE.2b)

Ⓐ 3 and 4

Ⓑ 3 and 4×5

Ⓒ 4 and 5

Ⓓ $3 + 4$ and 5

18. The expression $5c + 7m$ gives the number of passengers who can ride in *c* cars and *m* minivans. What are the coefficients in this expression? (CC.6.EE.2b)

Ⓐ $5c$ and $7m$

Ⓑ $+$ and $\times$

Ⓒ *c* and *m*

Ⓓ 5 and 7

19. The formula $P = a + b + c$ gives the perimeter *P* of a triangle with side lengths *a, b,* and *c*. A triangular field has sides that measure 33 yards, 56 yards, and 65 yards. What is the perimeter of the field? (CC.6.EE.2c)

Ⓐ 89 yards

Ⓑ 121 yards

Ⓒ 154 yards

Ⓓ 166 yards

Name _____

Use Algebraic Expressions

Essential Question How can you use variables and algebraic expressions to solve problems?

COMMON CORE STANDARD CC.6.EE.6
Reason about and solve one-variable equations and inequalities.

Sometimes you are missing a number that you need to solve a problem. You can represent a problem like this by writing an algebraic expression in which a variable represents the unknown number.

🔓 UNLOCK the Problem  REAL WORLD

Rafe's flight from Los Angeles to New York took 5 hours. He wants to know the average speed of the plane in miles per hour.

A **Write an expression to represent the average speed of the plane.**

🔑 **Use a variable to represent the unknown quantity.**

Think: The plane's average speed is equal to the distance traveled divided by the time traveled.

Use a variable to represent the unknown quantity.

Let d represent the _____

traveled in units of _____.

Write an algebraic expression for the average speed.

$$\dfrac{d \text{ mi}}{\boxed{} \text{ hr}}$$

B **Rafe looks up the distance between Los Angeles and New York on the Internet and finds that the distance is 2,460 miles. Use this distance to find the average speed of Rafe's plane.**

🔑 **Evaluate the expression for $d = 2{,}460$.**

Write the expression.

$$\dfrac{d \text{ mi}}{5 \text{ hr}}$$

Substitute 2,460 for d.

$$\dfrac{\boxed{} \text{ mi}}{5 \text{ hr}}$$

Divide to find the unit rate.

$$\dfrac{2{,}460 \text{ mi} \div \boxed{}}{5 \text{ hr} \div 5} = \dfrac{\boxed{} \text{ mi}}{1 \text{ hr}}$$

So, the plane's average speed was _____ miles per hour.

Math Talk

MATHEMATICAL PRACTICES

Explain how you could check whether you found the plane's average speed correctly.

In the problem on the previous page, the variable represented a single value—the distance in miles between Los Angeles and New York. In other situations, a variable may represent any number in a particular set of numbers, such as the set of positive numbers.

🔑 Example Joanna makes and sells candles online. She charges $7 per candle, and shipping is $5 per order.

A Write an expression that Joanna can use to find the total cost for any candle order.

Think: The number of candles a customer buys will vary from order to order.

Let *n* represent the number of _____ a customer buys, where *n* is a whole number greater than 0.

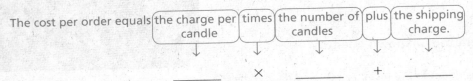

The cost per order equals the charge per candle | times | the number of candles | plus | the shipping charge.

_____ × _____ + _____

So, an expression for the total cost of a candle order is _____.

B In March, one of Joanna's customers placed an order for 4 candles. In May, the same customer placed an order for 6 candles. What was the total charge for both orders?

STEP 1 Find the charge in dollars for each order.

	March	**May**
Write the expression.	$7n + 5$	$7n + 5$
Substitute the number of candles ordered for *n*.	$7 \times$ _____ $+ 5$	$7 \times$ _____ $+ 5$
Follow the order of operations.	_____ $+ 5$	_____ $+ 5$
	_____	_____

STEP 2 Find the charge in dollars for both orders.

Add the charge in dollars for March to the charge in dollars for May.

_____ + _____ = _____

So, the total charge for both orders was _____.

Math Talk MATHEMATICAL PRACTICES
Explain why the value of the variable *n* in the Example is restricted to the set of whole numbers greater than 0.

Name _____

Share and Show MATH BOARD

Louisa read that the highest elevation of Mount Everest is 8,848 meters. She wants to know how much higher Mount Everest is than Mount Rainier. Use this information for 1–2.

✓ 1. Write an expression to represent the difference in heights of the two mountains. Tell what the variable in your expression represents.

_____

_____

✓ 2. Louisa researches the highest elevation of Mount Rainier and finds that it is 4,392 meters. Use your expression to find the difference in the mountains' heights.

_____

Math Talk MATHEMATICAL PRACTICES
Explain whether the variable in Exercise 1 represents a single unknown number or any number in a particular set.

On Your Own

A muffin recipe calls for 3 times as much flour as sugar. Use this information for 3–5.

3. Write an expression that can be used to find the amount of flour needed for a given amount of sugar. Tell what the variable in your expression represents.

_____

_____

4. Use your expression to find the amount of flour needed when $\frac{3}{4}$ cup of sugar is used.

_____

5. Is the value of the variable in your expression restricted to a particular set of numbers? Explain.

_____

_____

Practice: Copy and Solve Write an algebraic expression for each word expression. Then evaluate the expression for these values of the variable: $\frac{1}{2}$, 4, and 6.5.

6. the quotient of p and 4

7. 4 less than the sum of x and 5

Problem Solving · REAL WORLD

Use the graph for 8–11.

8. Write expressions for the distance in feet that each animal could run at top speed in a given amount of time. Tell what the variable in your expressions represents.

_____

_____

_____

9. How far could a giraffe run at top speed in 15 seconds?

_____

10. **H.O.T.** How much farther could a cheetah run in 20 seconds at top speed than a hippopotamus could?

_____

11. **Write Math** ►**Explain** whether the variable you used in Exercise 8 represents a single unknown number or any number in a particular set.

_____

_____

_____

12. ⭐ **Test Prep** A cell phone company charges $5.00 per month for the first 200 texts plus $0.10 for every text over 200. Which expression could be used to find a customer's text charges in dollars for a month in which he or she sent *t* texts over 200?

Ⓐ $0.10 + 5.00t$

Ⓑ $5.00 + 0.10t$

Ⓒ $0.10 \times (5.00 + t)$

Ⓓ $5.00 \times (0.10 + t)$

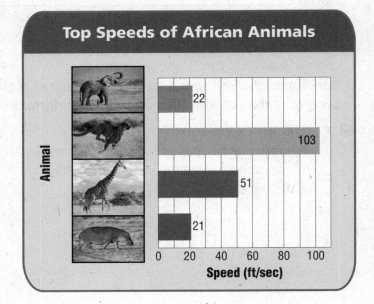

Top Speeds of African Animals

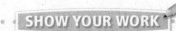

Animal

22

103

51

21

0   20   40   60   80   100

Speed (ft/sec)

····· **SHOW YOUR WORK** ·····

Name _____

Problem Solving • Combine Like Terms

Essential Question How can you use the strategy *use a model* to combine like terms?

Like terms are terms that have the same variables with the same exponents. Numerical terms are also like terms.

COMMON CORE STANDARD **CC.6.EE.3**
Apply and extend previous understandings of arithmetic to algebraic expressions.

Algebraic Expression	Terms	Like Terms
$5x + 3y - 2x$	$5x$, $3y$, and $2x$	$5x$ and $2x$
$8z^2 + 4z + 12z^2$	$8z^2$, $4z$, and $12z^2$	$8z^2$ and $12z^2$
$15 - 3x + 5$	15, $3x$, and 5	15 and 5

🔑 UNLOCK the Problem REAL WORLD

Baseball caps cost \$9, and logo patches cost \$4. Shipping is \$8 per order. The expression $9n + 4n + 8$ gives the cost in dollars of buying caps with logos for n players. Simplify the expression $9n + 4n + 8$ by combining like terms.

Use the graphic organizer to help you solve the problem.

Read the Problem

What do I need to find?	**What information do I need to use?**	**How will I use the information?**
I need to simplify the expression _____.	I need to use the like terms $9n$ and _____.	I can use a bar model to find the sum of the _____ terms.

Solve the Problem

Draw a bar model to add _____ and _____. Each square represents n, or $1n$.

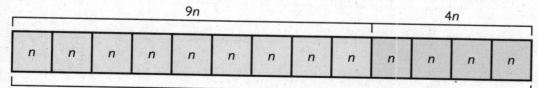

9n   4n

_____ n

The model shows that $9n + 4n =$ _____. $9n + 4n + 8 =$ _____ $+ 8$

So, a simplified expression for the cost in dollars is _____.

Math Talk **Explain** how the bar model shows that your answer is correct.

© Houghton Mifflin Harcourt Publishing Company

🔑 Try Another Problem

Paintbrushes normally cost $5 each, but they are on sale for $1 off. A paintbrush case costs $12. The expression $5p - p + 12$ can be used to find the cost in dollars of buying p paintbrushes on sale plus a case for them. Simplify the expression $5p - p + 12$ by combining like terms.

Use the graphic organizer to help you solve the problem.

Read the Problem

What do I need to find?	What information do I need to use?	How will I use the information?

Solve the Problem

So, a simplified expression for the cost in dollars is _____.

1. Explain how the bar model shows that your answer is correct.

_____

_____

_____

2. Explain how you could combine like terms without using a model.

_____

_____

_____

Name _____

Share and Show

🔓 UNLOCK the Problem Tips

✓ Read the entire problem carefully before you begin to solve it.

✓ Check your answer by using a different method.

1. Museum tickets cost $7, and tickets to the mammoth exhibit cost $5. The expression $7p + 5p$ represents the cost in dollars for p people to visit the museum and attend the exhibit. Simplify the expression by combining like terms.

   First, draw a bar model to combine the like terms.

   Next, use the bar model to simplify the expression.

   _____

   So, a simplified expression for the cost in dollars is _____.

2. 🔶 **H.O.T.** **What if** the cost of tickets to the exhibit were reduced to $3? Write an expression for the new cost in dollars for p people to visit the museum and attend the exhibit. Then simplify the expression by combining like terms.

   _____

3. A store receives tomatoes in boxes of 40 tomatoes each. About 4 tomatoes per box cannot be sold due to damage. The expression $40b - 4b$ gives the number of tomatoes that the store can sell from a shipment of b boxes. Simplify the expression by combining like terms.

   _____

4. Each cheerleading uniform consists of a top and a skirt. Tops cost $12 each, and skirts cost $18 each. The expression $12u + 18u$ represents the cost in dollars of buying u uniforms. Simplify the expression by combining like terms.

   _____

5. A shop sells vases holding 9 red roses and 6 white roses. The expression $9v + 6v$ represents the total number of roses needed for v vases. Simplify the expression by combining like terms.

   _____

SHOW YOUR WORK

© Houghton Mifflin Harcourt Publishing Company

On Your Own . . . .

6. Marco received a gift card. He used it to buy 2 bike lights for $10.50 each. Then he bought a handlebar bag for $18.25. After these purchases, he had $0.75 left on the card. How much money was on the gift card when Marco received it?

_____

Sea snail shells

7. Lydia collects shells. She has 24 sea snail shells, 16 conch shells, and 32 scallop shells. She wants to display the shells in equal rows, with only one type of shell in each row. What is the greatest number of shells Lydia can put in each row?

_____

Scallop shell

8. ⚡ **H.O.T.** The three sides of a triangle measure $3x + 6$ inches, $5x$ inches, and $6x$ inches. Write an expression for the perimeter of the triangle in inches. Then simplify the expression by combining like terms.

_____

Conch shell

9. **Sense or Nonsense?** Karina states that you can simplify the expression $20x + 4$ by combining like terms to get $24x$. Is Karina's statement sense or nonsense? **Explain.**

_____

_____

_____

SHOW YOUR WORK

10. ⭐ **Test Prep** Each student needs 6 test tubes for the first part of an experiment and 8 additional test tubes for the second part of the experiment. Which expression represents the total number of test tubes needed for a class of s students?

Ⓐ $14 + s$

Ⓑ $14s$

Ⓒ $48 + s$

Ⓓ $48s$

FOR MORE PRACTICE:
Standards Practice Book, pp. P135–P136

Generate Equivalent Expressions

Essential Question How can you use properties of operations to write equivalent algebraic expressions?

COMMON CORE STANDARD CC.6.EE.3
Apply and extend previous understandings of arithmetic to algebraic expressions.

Equivalent expressions are equal to each other for any values of their variables. For example, $x + 3$ and $3 + x$ are equivalent. You can use properties of operations to write equivalent expressions.

$$x + 3 \qquad 3 + x$$
$$4 + 3 \qquad 3 + 4$$
$$7 \qquad\qquad 7$$

Properties of Addition

Commutative Property of Addition

If the order of terms changes, the sum stays the same.

$$12 + a = a + 12$$

Associative Property of Addition

When the grouping of terms changes, the sum stays the same.

$$5 + (8 + b) = (5 + 8) + b$$

Identity Property of Addition

The sum of 0 and any number is that number.

$$0 + c = c$$

Properties of Multiplication

Commutative Property of Multiplication

If the order of factors changes, the product stays the same.

$$d \times 9 = 9 \times d$$

Associative Property of Multiplication

When the grouping of factors changes, the product stays the same.

$$11 \times (3 \times e) = (11 \times 3) \times e$$

Identity Property of Multiplication

The product of 1 and any number is that number.

$$1 \times f = f$$

UNLOCK the Problem REAL WORLD

Nelson ran 2 miles, 3 laps, and 5 miles. The expression $2 + 3\ell + 5$ represents the total distance in miles Nelson ran, where ℓ is the length in miles of one lap. Write an equivalent expression with only two terms.

 Rewrite the expression $2 + 3\ell + 5$ with only two terms.

The like terms are 2 and _____. Use the

$$2 + 3\ell + 5 = 3\ell + \text{_____} + 5$$

_____ Property to reorder the terms.

Use the _____ Property to regroup the terms.

$$= 3\ell + (\text{_____} + \text{_____})$$

Add within the parentheses.

$$= 3\ell + \text{_____}$$

So, an equivalent expression for the total distance in miles is _____.

Distributive Property

Multiplying a sum by a number is the same as multiplying each term by the number and then adding the products.

$5 \times (g + 9) = (5 \times g) + (5 \times 9)$

The Distributive Property can also be used with multiplication and subtraction. For example, $2 \times (10 - h) = (2 \times 10) - (2 \times h)$.

🔑 Example 1 Use properties of operations to write an expression equivalent to $5a + 8a - 16$ by combining like terms.

Use the Commutative Property of Multiplication to rewrite the like terms $5a$ and $8a$.

$5a + 8a - 16 = a \times \underline{\hspace{1cm}} + a \times \underline{\hspace{1cm}} - 16$

Use the Distributive Property to rewrite $a \times 5 + a \times 8$.

$= \underline{\hspace{1cm}} \times (5 + 8) - 16$

Add within the parentheses.

$= a \times \underline{\hspace{1cm}} - 16$

Use the Commutative Property of Multiplication to rewrite $a \times 13$.

$= \underline{\hspace{1cm}} - 16$

So, the expression _____ is equivalent to $5a + 8a - 16$.

🔑 Example 2 Use the Distributive Property to write an equivalent expression.

A $6(y + 7)$

Use the Distributive Property. $6(y + 7) = (6 \times \underline{\hspace{1cm}}) + (6 \times \underline{\hspace{1cm}})$

Multiply within the parentheses. $= 6y + \underline{\hspace{1cm}}$

So, the expression _____ is equivalent to $6(y + 7)$.

> **Math Idea**
>
> When one factor in a product is in parentheses, you can leave out the multiplication sign. So, $6 \times (y + 7)$ can be written as $6(y + 7)$.

B $12a + 8b$

Find the greatest common factor (GCF) of the coefficients of the terms.

The GCF of 12 and 8 is _____.

Write the first term, $12a$, as the product of the GCF and another factor.

$12a + 8b = 4 \times 3a + 8b$

Write the second term, $8b$, as the product of the GCF and another factor.

$= 4 \times 3a + 4 \times \underline{\hspace{1cm}}$

Use the Distributive Property.

$= 4 \times (\underline{\hspace{1cm}} + 2b)$

So, the expression _____ is equivalent to $12a + 8b$.

> **MATHEMATICAL PRACTICES**
>
> **Math Talk** Give a different expression that is equivalent to $12a + 8b$. Explain what property you used.

Name _____

Share and Show MATH BOARD

Use properties of operations to write an equivalent expression by combining like terms.

1. $12 + 3x + 7$

Use the Commutative and Associative Properties of Addition.

$$12 + 3x + 7 = 3x + (\underline{\hspace{1cm}} + 7)$$

Add within the parentheses.

$$= 3x + \underline{\hspace{1cm}}$$

2. $3.7r - 1.5r$

☑3. $20a + 18 + 16a$

4. $7s + 8t + 10s + 12t$

_____

_____

_____

Use the Distributive Property to write an equivalent expression.

☑ 5. $8(h + 1.5)$

6. $4m + 4p$

7. $3a + 9b$

_____

_____

_____

Math Talk MATHEMATICAL PRACTICES
List three expressions with two terms that are equivalent to $5x$. Compare and discuss your list with a partner's.

On Your Own

Use properties of operations to write an equivalent expression by combining like terms.

8. $b + b + b$

9. $25 + 9g + 14$

10. $14h + 30k - 12h$

_____

_____

_____

Practice: Copy and Solve Use the Distributive Property to write an equivalent expression.

11. $3.5(w + 7)$

12. $\frac{1}{2}(f + 10)$

13. $4(3z + 2)$

14. $20b + 16c$

15. $30d + 18$

16. $24g - 8h$

Problem Solving REAL WORLD

H.O.T. Sense or Nonsense?

17. Brooks and Jade are using what they know about properties to write an expression equivalent to $2 \times (n + 6) + 3$. Whose answer makes sense? Whose answer is nonsense? **Explain** your reasoning.

I can start with the Associative Property of Addition.

I can start with the Distributive Property.

Brooks's Work

Expression:	$2 \times (n + 6) + 3$
Associative Property of Addition:	$2 \times n + (6 + 3)$
Add within parentheses:	$2 \times n + 9$
Multiply:	$2n + 9$

Jade's Work

Expression:	$2 \times (n + 6) + 3$
Distributive Property:	$(2 \times n) + (2 \times 6) + 3$
Multiply within parentheses:	$2n + 12 + 3$
Associative Property of Addition:	$2n + (12 + 3)$
Add within parentheses:	$2n + 15$

For the answer that is nonsense, correct the statement.

_____

_____

FOR MORE PRACTICE:
Standards Practice Book, pp. P137–P138

Name _____

Identify Equivalent Expressions

Essential Question How can you identify equivalent algebraic expressions?

COMMON CORE STANDARD **CC.6.EE.4**
Apply and extend previous understandings of arithmetic to algebraic expressions.

UNLOCK the Problem REAL WORLD

Each train on a roller coaster has 10 cars, and each car can hold 4 riders. The expression $10t \times 4$ can be used to find the greatest number of riders when there are t trains on the track. Is this expression equivalent to $14t$? Use properties of operations to support your answer.

> • What is one property of operations that you could use to write an expression equivalent to $10t \times 4$?
>
> _____
>
> _____

 Determine whether $10t \times 4$ is equivalent to $14t$.

The expression $14t$ is the product of a number and a variable, so rewrite $10t \times 4$ as a product of a number and a variable.

Use the Commutative Property of Multiplication. $10t \times 4 = 4 \times$ _____

Use the _____ $= (4 \times$ _____$) \times t$
Property of Multiplication.

Multiply within the parentheses. $=$ _____

Compare the expressions $40t$ and $14t$.

Think: 40 times a number is not equal to 14 times the number, except when the number is 0.

Check by choosing a value for t and evaluating $40t$ and $14t$.

Write the expressions.	$40t$	$14t$
Use 2 as a value for t.	$40 \times$ _____	$14 \times$ _____
Multiply. The expressions have different values.	_____	_____

So, the expressions $10t \times 4$ and $14t$ are _____.

Math Talk MATHEMATICAL PRACTICES
Explain why the expressions $7a$ and $9a$ are not equivalent, even though they have the same value when $a = 0$.

🔑 Example Use properties of operations to determine whether the expressions are equivalent.

Ⓐ $7y + (x + 3y)$ and $10y + x$

The expression $10y + x$ is a sum of two terms, so rewrite $7y + (x + 3y)$ as a sum of two terms.

Use the Commutative Property of Addition to rewrite $x + 3y$.

$$7y + (x + 3y) = 7y + (\text{_____} + \text{_____})$$

Use the _____ Property of Addition to group like terms.

$$= (\text{_____} + 3y) + x$$

Combine like terms.

$$= \text{_____} + x$$

Compare the expressions $10y + x$ and $10y + x$: They are the same.

So, the expressions $7y + (x + 3y)$ and $10y + x$

are _____.

> **Math Talk** MATHEMATICAL PRACTICES
>
> **Explain** how you can decide whether two algebraic expressions are equivalent.

Ⓑ $10(m + n)$ and $10m + n$

The expression $10m + n$ is a sum of two terms, so rewrite $10(m + n)$ as a sum of two terms.

Use the Distributive Property.

$$10(m + n) = (10 \times \text{_____}) + (10 \times \text{_____})$$

Multiply within the parentheses.

$$= 10m + \text{_____}$$

Compare the expressions $10m + 10n$ and $10m + n$.

Think: The first terms of both expressions are _____, but the second terms are different.

Check by choosing values for m and n and evaluating $10m + 10n$ and $10m + n$.

Write the expressions.	$10m + 10n$	$10m + n$
Use 2 as a value for m and 4 as a value for n.	$10 \times \text{_____} + 10 \times \text{_____}$	$10 \times \text{_____} + \text{_____}$
Multiply.	$\text{_____} + \text{_____}$	$\text{_____} + \text{_____}$
Add. The expressions have different values.	_____	_____

So, the expressions $10(m + n)$ and $10m + n$ are _____.

> **Math Talk** MATHEMATICAL PRACTICES
>
> **Explain** how you know that the terms $10n$ and n from Part B are not equivalent.

Name _____

Share and Show

Use properties of operations to determine whether the expressions are equivalent.

1. $7k + 4 + 2k$ and $4 + 9k$

   Rewrite $7k + 4 + 2k$. Use the Commutative Property of Addition.

   $7k + 4 + 2k = 4 + $ _____ $ + 2k$

   Use the Associative Property of Addition.

   $= 4 + ($ _____ $+$ _____ $)$

   Add like terms.

   $= 4 + $ _____

   The expressions $7k + 4 + 2k$ and $4 + 9k$ are _____.

2. $9a \times 3$ and $12a$

3. $8p + 0$ and $8p \times 0$

4. $5(a + b)$ and $(5a + 2b) + 3b$

_____ | _____ | _____

Math Talk
Explain how you can use logical reasoning to show that $x + 5$ is not equivalent to $x + 8$

On Your Own

Use properties of operations to determine whether the expressions are equivalent.

5. $3(v + 2) + 7v$ and $16v$

6. $14h + (17 + 11h)$ and $25h + 17$

7. $4b \times 7$ and $28b$

_____ | _____ | _____

8. $3a + (7a \times 0)$ and $10a$

9. $6(w + 5w)$ and $36w$

10. $4a - a + 3$ and $3a + 3$

_____ | _____ | _____

Problem Solving · REAL WORLD

Use the table for 11–15.

Collectible Cards	
Type	**Number per Packet**
Baseball	b
Cartoon	c
Movie	m
Animal	a

11. Zeke bought 4 packets of baseball cards and 4 packets of animal cards. Write an algebraic expression for the total number of cards Zeke bought.

_____

12. **H.O.T.** **Write Math** ▸ Is the expression for the number of cards Zeke bought equivalent to $4(a + b)$? **Justify** your answer.

_____

_____

_____

_____

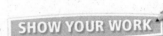

SHOW YOUR WORK

13. Jessica buys 6 packets of movie cards and adds these to the 15 cards she already had. Write an algebraic expression for the total number of cards Jessica has.

_____

14. **H.O.T.** **Write Math** ▸ Is the expression for the number of cards Jessica has equivalent to $6(m + 9)$? **Justify** your answer.

_____

_____

_____

_____

15. ⭐ **Test Prep** Laura bought 4 packets of movie cards. She gave 4 of the cards away. Which expression gives the number of cards she has left?

  (A) $4(m - 1)$ (C) $4 - 4m$

  (B) $m(4 - 1)$ (D) $4m - m$

✓ Chapter 7 Review/Test

▶ Vocabulary

Choose the best term from the box to complete the sentence.

<table>
<tr><td colspan="2">Vocabulary</td></tr>
<tr><td>equivalent expressions</td></tr>
<tr><td>like terms</td></tr>
<tr><td>variables</td></tr>
</table>

1. In the expression $2x + 4x + 5$, the _____ are $2x$ and $4x$. (p. 275)

2. $4y$ and $y \times 4$ are _____ because they are equal to each other for any value of y. (p. 279)

▶ Concepts and Skills

Use one or more exponents to write the expression. (CC.6.EE.1)

3. $4 \times 4 \times 4 \times 4 \times 4$

4. $8 \times 8 \times 8 \times 9 \times 9$

_____

_____

Evaluate the expression for the given value of the variable. (CC.6.EE.2c)

5. $(b - 2)^2 + 10$ for $b = 7$

6. $5f + 70$ for $f = 4$

_____

_____

Use properties of operations to determine whether the expressions are equivalent. (CC.6.EE.4)

7. $2 \times (m + 5)$ and $10 + 2m$

8. $5a + 3a + 0$ and $15a$

_____

_____

GO Online Assessment Options **Chapter Test**

9. Rochelle is decorating a table by gluing small glass tiles to its top. She needs a total of $13^2 + 52$ tiles. How many tiles does Rochelle need? (CC.6.EE.1)

- (A) 78
- (B) 130
- (C) 221
- (D) 324

10. The expression $0.25q + 0.10d$ gives the value in dollars of q quarters and d dimes. What are the terms of this expression?

(CC.6.EE.2b)

- (A) q and d
- (B) q and 0.10
- (C) 0.25 and 0.10
- (D) $0.25q$ and $0.10d$

11. Hugh wants to hike 85 miles during a weeklong hiking trip. He plans to hike m miles per day for 6 days. The expression $85 - 6m$ gives the number of miles that he will need to hike on the seventh day. Which best describes this expression? (CC.6.EE.2b)

- (A) the difference of 85 and the product of 6 and m
- (B) m multiplied by the difference of 85 and 6
- (C) 85 minus the difference of 6 and m
- (D) 85 less than 6 multiplied by m

12. The table shows the cost of several items at a taco stand. The expression $3.00n + 1.00n - 3.50n$ gives the amount of money in dollars a customer would save by buying n value meals instead of n tacos and n drinks. Which is another way to write this expression? (CC.6.EE.3)

Menu	
Item	**Price**
Taco	$3.00
Drink	$1.00
Value meal	$3.50

- (A) $0.50n$
- (B) $0.50 + n$
- (C) $1.50n$
- (D) $1.50 + n$

Fill in the bubble to show your answer.

13. The formula $P = 2(\ell + w)$ gives the perimeter of a rectangle with length ℓ and width w. What is the perimeter of a rectangular soccer field with a length of 120 yards and a width of 75 yards? (CC.6.EE.2c)

Ⓐ 195 yards   Ⓒ 390 yards

Ⓑ 315 yards   Ⓓ 630 yards

14. The expression $2.85 + 2.70m$ gives the taxi fare in dollars for a trip of m miles. On Thursday, Ms. Hurst took a taxi for 6 miles. On Friday, she took a taxi for 4 miles. What was the total fare for the two trips? (CC.6.EE.6)

Ⓐ $55.50

Ⓑ $32.70

Ⓒ $29.85

Ⓓ $19.05

15. There are 12 months in one year. Which expression gives the number of months in y years? (CC.6.EE.2a)

Ⓐ $12 + y$

Ⓑ $y - 12$

Ⓒ $12y$

Ⓓ $y \div 12$

16. A department store is having a sale on coats. The sales clerks use the expression $2 \times (c - 10) \div 3$ to find the sale price of a coat that regularly costs c dollars. What is the sale price of a coat that regularly costs $82? (CC.6.EE.2c)

Ⓐ $35   Ⓒ $51

Ⓑ $48   Ⓓ $55

17. Posters cost $15. Frames cost $12. The expression $15n + 12n$ gives the total cost for n posters and frames. Which is another way to write this expression? (CC.6.EE.3)

Ⓐ $27n$

Ⓑ $27 + n$

Ⓒ $180n$

Ⓓ $180 + n$

► Constructed Response

18. Use the Distributive Property to write an expression equivalent to $14x + 21y$. Show your work. (CC.6.EE.3)

_____

_____

_____

19. Use properties of operations to write two expressions that are equivalent to $2 \times (a + 5)$. Tell which properties you used. (CC.6.EE.3)

_____

_____

_____

► Performance Task (CC.6.EE.2a, CC.6.EE.2c, CC.6.EE.6)

20. It costs $10 per month for membership at a gym. Yoga classes at the gym cost an extra $4 per class.

A Write an expression for the monthly cost in dollars, including the membership fee, for a person who takes _y_ yoga classes at the gym.

_____

B Use your expression from Part A to complete the table.

Monthly Gym Costs	
Yoga Classes Taken	Total Cost
1	
2	
3	
4	

C Ms. Vincent has budgeted $35 per month for the gym. Will she be able to take 7 yoga classes per month and stay within her budget? Explain how you determined your answer.

_____

_____

_____

Algebra: Equations and Inequalities

Show What You Know

Check your understanding of important skills.

Name _____

▶ **Multiplication Properties** Find the unknown number. Write which multiplication property you used.

1. $42 \times$ _____ $= 42$

_____

2. $9 \times 6 =$ _____ $\times 9$

_____

▶ **Evaluate Algebraic Expressions** Evaluate the expression.

3. $4a - 2b$ for $a = 5$ and $b = 3$

_____

4. $7x + 9y$ for $x = 7$ and $y = 1$

_____

5. $8c \times d - 6$ for $c = 10$ and $d = 2$

_____

6. $4s \div t + 10$ for $s = 9$ and $t = 3$

_____

▶ **Add Fractions and Decimals** Find the sum. Write the sum in simplest form.

7. $35.68 + 17.84 =$ _____

8. $24.38 + 25.3 =$ _____

9. $\frac{3}{4} + \frac{1}{8} =$ _____

10. $\frac{2}{5} + \frac{1}{4} =$ _____

MATH DETECTIVE WITH CARMEN SANDIEGO™

The equation $m = 19.32v$ can be used to find the mass m in grams of a pure gold coin with volume v in cubic centimeters. Carl has a coin with a mass of 37.8 grams and a volume of 2.1 cubic centimeters. Be a Math Detective and determine whether Carl's coin could be pure gold. Explain your reasoning.

Vocabulary Builder

Review Words

algebraic expressions

numbers

numerical expressions

operations

variables

Preview Words

Addition Property of
   Equality

equation

inequality

inverse operations

solution of an equation

Subtraction Property
   of Equality

▶ **Visualize It** ·

**Use the review words to complete the tree diagram.
You may use some words more than once.**

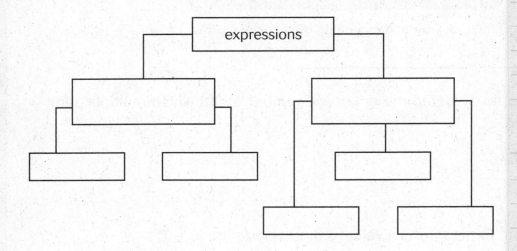

▶ **Understand Vocabulary** ·

Draw a line to match the preview word with its definition.

Preview Words	**Definitions**
1. Addition Property of Equality	• operations that undo each other
2. inequality	• a value of a variable that makes an equation true
3. inverse operations	• property that states that if you add the same number to both sides of an equation, the two sides will remain equal
4. equation	
5. solution of an equation	• a mathematical statement that compares two expressions by using the symbol $<$, $>$, $\leq$, $\geq$, or $\neq$
6. Subtraction Property of Equality	• property that states that if you subtract the same number from both sides of an equation, the two sides will remain equal
	• a statement that two mathematical expressions are equal

GO Online • eStudent Edition • Multimedia eGlossary

Solutions of Equations

Essential Question How do you determine whether a number is a solution of an equation?

COMMON CORE STANDARD CC.6.EE.5
Reason about and solve one-variable equations and inequalities.

An **equation** is a statement that two mathematical expressions are equal. These are examples of equations:

$8 + 12 = 20$ $14 = a - 3$ $2d = 14$

A **solution of an equation** is a value of a variable that makes an equation true.

$x + 3 = 5$ $x = 2$ is the solution of the equation because $2 + 3 = 5$.

 UNLOCK the Problem REAL WORLD

In the 2009–2010 season, the women's basketball team of Duke University lost 5 of their 29 games. The equation $w + 5 = 29$ can be used to find the team's number of wins w. Determine whether $w = 14$ or $w = 24$ is a solution of the equation, and tell what the solution means.

🔑 **Use substitution to determine the solution.**

STEP 1 Check whether $w = 14$ is a solution.

Write the equation.	$w + 5 = 29$
Substitute 14 for w.	_____ $+ 5 \stackrel{?}{=} 29$
Add.	_____ $\neq 29$

The equation is not true when $w = 14$, so $w = 14$ is not a solution.

Math Idea

The symbol $\neq$ means "is not equal to."

STEP 2 Check whether $w = 24$ is a solution.

Write the equation.	$w + 5 = 29$
Substitute 24 for w.	_____ $+ 5 \stackrel{?}{=} 29$
Add.	_____ $= 29$

The equation is true when $w = 24$, so $w = 24$ is a solution.

So, the solution of the equation $w + 5 = 29$ is $w =$ _____,

which means that the team won _____ games.

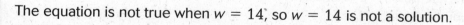

Math Talk MATHEMATICAL PRACTICES
Describe how an algebraic equation, such as $x + 1 = 4$, is different from a numerical equation, such as $3 + 1 = 4$.

🔑 Example 1 Determine whether the given value of the variable is a solution of the equation.

A $x - 0.7 = 4.3$; $x = 3.6$

Write the equation.

$$x - 0.7 = 4.3$$

Substitute the given value for the variable.

$$\underline{\hspace{1.5cm}} - 0.7 \overset{?}{=} 4.3$$

Subtract. Write = or ≠.

$$\underline{\hspace{1.5cm}} \bigcirc 4.3$$

The equation _____ true when $x = 3.6$, so $x = 3.6$

_____ a solution.

B $\frac{1}{3}a = \frac{1}{4}$; $a = \frac{3}{4}$

Write the equation.

$$\frac{1}{3}a = \frac{1}{4}$$

Substitute the given value for the variable.

 $\frac{1}{3} \times \underline{\hspace{1cm}} \overset{?}{=} \frac{1}{4}$

Simplify factors and multiply. Write = or ≠ .

$$\underline{\hspace{1cm}} \bigcirc \frac{1}{4}$$

The equation _____ true when $a = \frac{3}{4}$, so $a = \frac{3}{4}$

_____ a solution.

🔑 Example 2 The sixth-grade class president serves a term of 8 months.
Janice has already served 5 months of her term as class president. The equation $m + 5 = 8$ can be used to determine the number of months m Janice has left. Use mental math to find the solution of the equation.

Think: What number plus 5 is equal to 8? _____ plus 5 is equal to 8.

Use substitution to check whether $m = 3$ is a solution.

Write the equation.

$$m + 5 = 8$$

Substitute 3 for m.

$$\underline{\hspace{1.5cm}} + 5 \overset{?}{=} 8$$

Add. Write = or ≠.

 $\underline{\hspace{1cm}} \bigcirc 8$

So, $m = $ _____ is the solution of the equation, and

_____ months of Janice's term remain.

Math Talk

Give an example of an equation whose solution is $y = 7$. **Explain** how you know that the equation has this solution.

Name _____

Share and Show

Determine whether the given value of the variable is a solution of the equation.

1. $x + 12 = 29; x = 7$

_____ $+ 12 \overset{?}{=} 29$

_____ ◯ 29

_____

2. $n - 13 = 2; n = 15$

_____

✅ **3.** $\frac{1}{2}c = 14; c = 28$

_____

✅ **4.** $m + 2.5 = 4.6; m = 2.9$

_____

5. $d - 8.7 = 6; d = 14.7$

_____

6. $k - \frac{3}{5} = \frac{1}{10}; k = \frac{7}{10}$

_____

Math Talk MATHEMATICAL PRACTICES
Explain why $2x - 6$ is not an equation.

On Your Own

Determine whether the given value of the variable is a solution of the equation.

7. $17.9 + v = 35.8; v = 17.9$

_____

8. $c + 35 = 57; c = 32$

_____

9. $18 = \frac{2}{3}h; h = 12$

_____

Practice: Copy and Solve Use mental math to find the solution of the equation. Use substitution to check your answer.

10. $x + 5 = 12$

11. $t - 3 = 6$

12. $8z = 40$

13. Renee pays for a cat toy with a $10 bill and receives $4.35 in change. The equation $10 - c = 4.35$ gives the cost in dollars of the cat toy. Determine whether $c = 5.35$, $c = 5.65$, or $c = 6.35$ is a solution of the equation, and tell what the solution means.

_____

Problem Solving REAL WORLD

Use the table for 14–16.

14. The length of a day on Saturn is 14 hours less than a day on Mars. The equation $24.7 - s = 14$ gives the length s in hours of a day on Saturn. Determine whether $s = 9.3$ or $s = 10.7$ is a solution of the equation, and tell what the solution means.

_____

15. A day on Pluto is 143.4 hours longer than a day on one of the planets listed in the table. The equation $153.3 - p = 143.4$ gives the length in hours p of a day on the planet. Is the planet Earth, Mars, or Jupiter? **Explain.**

_____

_____

Length of Day

Planet	Length of Day (hours)
Earth	24.0
Mars	24.7
Jupiter	9.9

16. A storm on one of the planets listed in the table lasted for 60 hours, or 2.5 of the planet's days. The equation $2.5h = 60$ gives the length in hours h of a day on the planet. Is the planet Earth, Mars, or Jupiter? **Explain.**

_____

_____

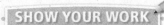

SHOW YOUR WORK

17. **H.O.T.** **What's the Error?** Jason said that the solution of the equation $2m = 4$ is $m = 8$. Describe Jason's error, and give the correct solution.

_____

_____

_____

18. ⭐ **Test Prep** In 30 minutes, a television station plays 8.5 minutes of commercials. The equation $m + 8.5 = 30$ gives the length m in minutes of the cooking show aired during this 30-minute period. Which of the following is a solution of the equation?

Ⓐ $m = 21.5$ Ⓒ $m = 28.5$

Ⓑ $m = 22.5$ Ⓓ $m = 38.5$

FOR MORE PRACTICE:
Standards Practice Book, pp. P145–P146

Name _____

Write Equations

Essential Question How do you write an equation to represent a situation?

COMMON CORE STANDARD CC.6.EE.7
Reason about and solve one-variable equations and inequalities.

CONNECT You can use what you know about writing algebraic expressions to help you write algebraic equations.

 UNLOCK the Problem REAL WORLD

A circus recently spent $1,650 on new trapezes. The trapezes cost $275 each. Write an equation that could be used to find the number of trapezes *t* that the circus bought.

- Circle the information that you need to write the equation.
- What expression could you use to represent the cost of *t* trapezes?

_____

🔒 **Write an equation for the situation.**

Think:

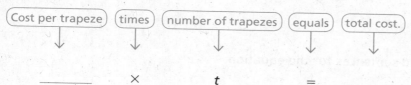
| (Cost per trapeze) | (times) | (number of trapezes) | (equals) | (total cost.) |

_____ × *t* = _____

So, an equation that could be used to find the number of

trapezes *t* is _____.

Try This! Ben is making a recipe for salsa that calls for $3\frac{1}{2}$ cups of tomatoes. He chops 4 tomatoes, which fill $2\frac{1}{4}$ cups. Write an equation that could be used to find how many more cups *c* that Ben needs.

Think: (Cups filled) (plus) (cups needed) (equals) (total cups for recipe.)

_____ + _____ = _____

So, an equation that could be used to find the number of additional

cups *c* is _____.

Math Talk MATHEMATICAL PRACTICES
Describe another equation you could use to model the problem.

Chapter 8 297

🔒 Example 1 Write an equation for the word sentence.

Ⓐ **Six fewer than a number is 46.33.**

Think: Let n represent the unknown number. The phrase "fewer than" indicates

_____.

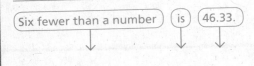

Six fewer than a number) (is) (46.33.)
↓   ↓   ↓

_____ − _____   = _____

> **! ERROR Alert**
>
> The expression $n - 6$ means "6 fewer than n." The expression $6 - n$ means "n fewer than 6."

Ⓑ **Two-thirds of the cost of the sweater is $18.**

Think: Let c represent the _____ of the sweater in dollars. The word "of"

indicates _____.

(Two-thirds) (of) (the cost of the sweater) (is) (18.)
↓   ↓   ↓   ↓   ↓

_____ × _____   = _____

🔒 Example 2 Write two word sentences for the equation.

Ⓐ $a + 15 = 24$

- The _____ of a and 15 _____ 24.

- 15 _____ than a _____ 24.

Ⓑ $r \div 0.2 = 40$

- The _____ of r and 0.2 _____ 40.

- r _____ by 0.2 _____ 40.

---

1. **Explain** how you can rewrite the equation $n + 8 = 24$ so that it involves subtraction rather than addition.

   _____

   _____

2. One student wrote $18 \times d = 54$ for the sentence "The product of 18 and d equals 54." Another student wrote $d \times 18 = 54$ for the same sentence. Are both students correct? **Justify** your answer.

   _____

   _____

Name _____

Share and Show

1. Write an equation for the word sentence "25 is 13 more than a number."

   What operation does the phrase "more than" indicate? _____

   The equation is _____ = _____ + _____.

Write an equation for the word sentence.

2. The difference of a number and 2 is $3\frac{1}{3}$.

   _____

3. Ten times the number of balloons is 120.

   _____

Write a word sentence for the equation.

4. $x - 0.3 = 1.7$

   _____

5. $25 = \frac{1}{4}n$

   _____

Math Talk MATHEMATICAL PRACTICES
Describe how an equation differs from an expression.

On Your Own

Write an equation for the word sentence.

6. The quotient of a number and 20.7 is 9.

   _____

7. 24 less than the number of snakes is 35.

   _____

8. 75 is $18\frac{1}{2}$ more than a number.

   _____

9. d degrees warmer than 50 degrees is 78 degrees.

   _____

Write a word sentence for the equation.

10. $15g = 135$

    _____

11. $w \div 3.3 = 0.6$

    _____

© Houghton Mifflin Harcourt Publishing Company

Problem Solving • REAL WORLD

The distance in miles a car can travel on a certain amount of gas can be found by multiplying the car's fuel efficiency in miles per gallon by the gas used in gallons. Use this information and the table for 12–13.

12. Write an equation that could be used to find how many miles a hybrid SUV can travel in the city on 20 gallons of gas.

_____

Fuel Efficiency		
Vehicle	Miles per gallon, city	Miles per gallon, highway
Hybrid SUV	36	31
Minivan	19	26
Sedan	20	28
SUV	22	26

13. A sedan traveled 504 miles on the highway on a full tank of gas. Write an equation that could be used to find the number of gallons the tank holds.

_____

SHOW YOUR WORK

14. George Washington was born in 1732. Thomas Jefferson was born 11 years after George Washington. Write an equation that could be used to find the year in which Thomas Jefferson was born.

_____

15. H.O.T. A magazine has 110 pages. There are 23 full-page ads and 14 half-page ads. The rest of the magazine consists of articles. Write an equation that can be used to find the number of pages of articles in the magazine.

_____

16. **What's the Error?** Tony is traveling 560 miles to visit his cousins. He travels 313 miles the first day. He says that he can use the equation $m - 313 = 560$ to find the number of miles he has left on his trip. Describe Tony's error.

_____

17. ⭐ **Test Prep** The Vikings scored 7 more points than the Ravens. The Vikings scored 34 points. Which equation could be used to find the number of points p that the Ravens scored?

Ⓐ $p - 7 = 34$ Ⓒ $p + 7 = 34$

Ⓑ $p - 34 = 7$ Ⓓ $p + 34 = 7$

Model and Solve Addition Equations

Essential Question How can you use models to solve addition equations?

COMMON CORE STANDARD CC.6.EE.7
Reason about and solve one-variable equations and inequalities.

You can use algebra tiles to help you find solutions of equations.

Algebra Tiles

x tile   1 tile

Investigate

Materials ■ MathBoard, algebra tiles

Thomas has $2. He wants to buy a poster that costs $7. Model and solve the equation $x + 2 = 7$ to find the amount x in dollars that Thomas needs to save in order to buy the poster.

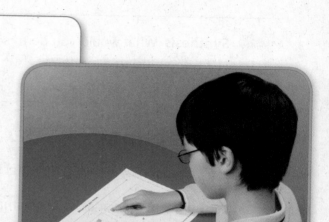

A. Draw 2 rectangles on your MathBoard to represent the two sides of the equation.

B. Use algebra tiles to model the equation. Model $x + 2$ in the left rectangle, and model 7 in the right rectangle.

- What type of tiles and number of tiles did you use to model $x + 2$?

  _____

C. To solve the equation, get the *x* tile by itself on one side. If you remove a tile from one side, you can keep the two sides equal by removing the same type of tile from the other side.

- How many 1 tiles do need to remove from each side to get the *x* tile by itself on the left side? _____

- When the *x* tile is by itself on the left side, how many 1 tiles are on the right side? _____

D. Write the solution of the equation: $x =$ _____.

So, Thomas needs to save $ _____ in order to buy the poster.

Math Talk MATHEMATICAL PRACTICES
Tell what operation you modeled when you removed tiles.

Draw Conclusions

1. **Describe** how you could use your model to check your solution.

   _____

   _____

   _____

2. Tell how you could use algebra tiles to model the equation $x + 4 = 8$.

   _____

   _____

3. **H.O.T.** **Synthesis** What would you do to solve the equation $x + 9 = 12$ without using a model?

   _____

Make Connections

You can solve an equation by drawing a model to represent algebra tiles.

Let a rectangle represent the variable. Let a small square represent 1.

Solve the equation $x + 3 = 7$.

STEP 1

Draw a model of the equation.

STEP 2

Get the variable by itself on one side of the model by doing the same thing to both sides.

Cross out _____ squares on the left side and

_____ squares on the right side.

STEP 3

Draw a model of the solution.

There is 1 rectangle on the left side. There are

_____ squares on the right side.

So, the solution of the equation $x + 3 = 7$ is $x =$ _____.

MATHEMATICAL PRACTICES

Math Talk Discuss which approach you prefer to solve equations, using algebra tiles or drawing a model.

Name _____

Share and Show

Model and solve the equation by using algebra tiles.

1. $x + 5 = 7$ _____

2. $8 = x + 1$ _____

3. $x + 2 = 5$ _____

4. $x + 6 = 8$ _____

5. $5 + x = 9$ _____

6. $5 = 4 + x$ _____

Solve the equation by drawing a model.

7. $x + 1 = 5$ _____

8. $3 + x = 4$ _____

9. $6 = x + 4$ _____

10. $8 = 2 + x$ _____

11. **Write Math** ▶ Describe how you would draw a model to solve the equation $x + 5 = 10$.

_____

_____

_____

_____

Problem Solving  REAL WORLD

12. A movie ticket in the evening costs $9, which is $3 more than in the afternoon. The equation $9 = 3 + c$ can be used to find the cost c in dollars of an afternoon movie ticket. Solve the equation. Then tell what the solution means.

_____

_____

13. The table shows how long several animals have been at a zoo. The giraffe has been at the zoo 4 years longer than the mountain lion. Write and solve an addition equation to find how long the mountain lion has been at the zoo.

_____

Zoo Animals

Animal	Time at zoo (years)
Giraffe	5
Hippopotamus	6
Kangaroo	2
Zebra	9

SHOW YOUR WORK

14. A standard guitar has 6 strings, which is 2 more strings than a violin has. Write and solve an addition equation to find the number of strings a violin has.

_____

15. The Maple Leafs beat the Blue Jackets by 3 goals. The Maple Leafs scored 6 goals. Write and solve an addition equation to find the Blue Jackets' score.

_____

16. **H.O.T.** **Sense or Nonsense?** Gabriela is solving the equation $x + 1 = 6$. She says that the solution must be less than 6. Is Gabriela's statement sense or nonsense? Explain.

_____

_____

17. ⭐ **Test Prep** The length of a photo is 14 inches, which is 3 inches longer than its width. The equation $14 = 3 + w$ can be used to find the photo's width w in inches. What is the width of the photo?

(A) 8 inches   (C) 17 inches

(B) 11 inches   (D) 20 inches

FOR MORE PRACTICE:
Standards Practice Book, pp. P149–P150

Solve Addition and Subtraction Equations

Essential Question How do you solve addition and subtraction equations?

COMMON CORE STANDARD CC.6.EE.7
Reason about and solve one-variable equations and inequalities.

CONNECT To solve an equation, you must get the variable on one side of the equal sign by itself. You have solved equations by using models. You can also solve equations by using Properties of Equality.

Subtraction Property of Equality	
If you subtract the same number from both sides of an equation, the two sides will remain equal.	$3 + 4 = 7$ $3 + 4 - 4 = 7 - 4$ $3 + 0 = 3$ $3 = 3$

🔑 UNLOCK the Problem REAL WORLD

The longest distance jumped on a pogo stick is 23 miles. Emilio has jumped 5 miles on a pogo stick. The equation $d + 5 = 23$ can be used to find the remaining distance d in miles he must jump to match the record. Solve the equation, and explain what the solution means.

🔒 **Solve the addition equation.**

To get d by itself, you must undo the addition by 5. Operations that undo each other are called **inverse operations**. Subtracting 5 is the inverse operation of adding 5.

Write the equation.	$d + 5 = 23$
Use the Subtraction Property of Equality.	$d + 5 - 5 = 23 - \underline{\hspace{1cm}}$
Subtract.	$d + 0 = \underline{\hspace{1cm}}$
Use the Identity Property of Addition.	$\underline{\hspace{1cm}} = 18$

Check the solution.

Write the equation.	$d + 5 = 23$
Substitute _____ for d.	$\underline{\hspace{1cm}} + 5 = 23$
The solution checks.	$\underline{\hspace{1cm}} = 23$

So, the solution means that Emilio must jump _____ more miles.

Math Talk MATHEMATICAL PRACTICES
Explain how you know what number to subtract from both sides of the equation.

When you solve an equation that involves subtraction, you can use addition to get the variable on one side of the equal sign by itself.

Addition Property of Equality	
If you add the same number to both sides of an equation, the two sides will remain equal.	$7 - 4 = 3$ $7 - 4 + 4 = 3 + 4$ $7 + 0 = 7$ $7 = 7$

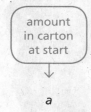 Example

While cooking dinner, Carla pours $\frac{5}{8}$ cup of milk from a carton. This leaves $\frac{7}{8}$ cup of milk in the carton. Write and solve an equation to find how much milk was in the carton when Carla started cooking.

STEP 1 Write an equation.

Let a represent the amount of milk in cups in the carton when Carla started cooking.

amount in carton at start	minus	amount poured out	equals	amount in carton at end
↓	↓	↓	↓	↓
a	$-$	____	$=$	____

STEP 2 Solve the equation.

Think: $\frac{5}{8}$ is subtracted from a, so add $\frac{5}{8}$ to both sides to undo the subtraction.

Write the equation.
$$a - \frac{5}{8} = \frac{7}{8}$$

Use the Addition Property of Equality.
$$a - \frac{5}{8} + \underline{\quad} = \frac{7}{8} + \underline{\quad}$$

Add.
$$a = \underline{\quad}$$

Write the fraction greater than 1 as a mixed number, and simplify.
$$a = \underline{\quad}$$

So, there were _____ cups of milk in the carton when Carla started cooking.

Math Talk MATHEMATICAL PRACTICES
Explain how you can check the solution of the equation.

Name _____

Share and Show

1. Solve the equation $n + 35 = 80$.

$$n + 35 = 80$$

$$n + 35 - 35 = 80 - \text{_____}$$ Use the _____ Property of Equality.

$$n = \text{_____}$$ Subtract.

Solve the equation, and check the solution.

2. $16 + x = 42$

✓ 3. $y + 6.2 = 9.1$

4. $m + \frac{3}{10} = \frac{7}{10}$

5. $z - \frac{1}{3} = 1\frac{2}{3}$

✓ 6. $12 = x - 24$

7. $25.3 = w - 14.9$

Math Talk **MATHEMATICAL PRACTICES**
Explain how to get the variable by itself on one side of a subtraction equation.

On Your Own

Practice: Copy and Solve Solve the equation, and check the solution.

8. $y - \frac{3}{4} = \frac{1}{2}$

9. $75 = n + 12$

10. $m + 16.8 = 40$

11. $w - 36 = 56$

12. $8\frac{2}{5} = d + 2\frac{2}{5}$

13. $8.7 = r - 1.4$

14. The temperature dropped 8 degrees between 6:00 P.M. and midnight. The temperature at midnight was 26°F. Write and solve an equation to find the temperature at 6:00 P.M.

_____

15. **H.O.T.** Write an addition equation that has the solution $x = 9$.

_____

UNLOCK the Problem   REAL WORLD

Bank Statement:
Kimberly Gilson

Deposits	
July 12	$45.50
July 25	$43.24
Withdrawals	
None	

16. In July, Kimberly made two deposits into her bank account. She made no withdrawals. At the end of July, her account balance was $120.62. Write and solve an equation to find Kimberly's balance at the beginning of July.

a. What do you need to find?

_____

_____

b. What information do you need from the bank statement?

_____

_____

c. Write an equation you can use to solve the problem. Explain what the variable represents.

_____

_____

_____

d. Solve the equation. Show your work and describe each step.

e. Write Kimberly's balance at the beginning of July.

_____

---

17. ⭐ **Test Prep** The equation $h - 120 = 80$ may be used to find the original height h in feet of an elevator before it descended. What was the original height of the elevator?

Ⓐ 40 feet

Ⓑ 100 feet

Ⓒ 160 feet

Ⓓ 200 feet

18. ⭐ **Test Prep** Colin adds $2\frac{3}{4}$ quarts of orange juice to some apple juice to make $4\frac{1}{4}$ quarts of fruit punch. He solves the equation $a + 2\frac{3}{4} = 4\frac{1}{4}$ to find the amount a of apple juice in quarts in the punch. What is the solution of the equation?

Ⓐ $a = \frac{1}{2}$ Ⓒ $a = 2\frac{1}{2}$

Ⓑ $a = 1\frac{1}{2}$ Ⓓ $a = 7$

Model and Solve Multiplication Equations

Essential Question How can you use models to solve multiplication equations?

COMMON CORE STANDARD CC.6.EE.7
Reason about and solve one-variable equations and inequalities.

You can use algebra tiles to model and solve equations that involve multiplication.

Algebra Tiles

x tile   1 tile

To model an expression involving multiplication of a variable, you can use more than one x tile. For example, to model the expression $4x$, you can use four x tiles.

$4x$

Investigate

Materials ■ MathBoard, algebra tiles

Tennis balls are sold in cans of 3 tennis balls each. Daniel needs 15 tennis balls for a tournament. Model and solve the equation $3x = 15$ to find the number of cans x that Daniel should buy.

A. Draw 2 rectangles on your MathBoard to represent the two sides of the equation.

B. Use algebra tiles to model the equation. Model $3x$ in the left rectangle, and model 15 in the right rectangle.

C. There are three x tiles on the left side of your model. To solve the equation by using the model, you need to find the value of one x tile. To do this, divide each side of your model into 3 equal groups.

- When the tiles on each side have been divided into 3 equal groups, how many 1 tiles are in each group on

  the right side? _____

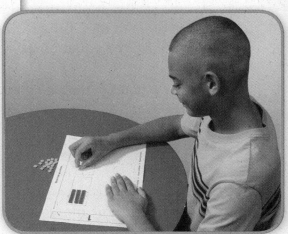

D. Write the solution of the equation: $x =$ _____.

So, Daniel should buy _____ cans of tennis balls.

Math Talk MATHEMATICAL PRACTICES
Tell what operation you modeled in Step C.

Draw Conclusions

1. **Explain** how you could use your model to check your solution.

_____

_____

_____

2. **Describe** how you could use algebra tiles to model the equation $6x = 12$.

_____

3. **H.O.T. Synthesis** What would you do to solve the equation $5x = 35$ without using a model?

_____

Make Connections

You can also solve multiplication equations by drawing a model to represent algebra tiles. Let a rectangle represent x. Let a square represent 1. Solve the equation $2x = 6$.

STEP 1 Draw a model of the equation.

STEP 2 Find the value of one rectangle.

Divide each side of the model into _____ equal groups.

STEP 3 Draw a model of the solution.

There is 1 rectangle on the left side. There are _____ squares on the right side.

So, the solution of the equation $2x = 6$ is $x =$ _____.

Math Talk

Explain why you divided each side of the model into 2 equal groups.

Name _____

Share and Show ·

Model and solve the equation by using algebra tiles.

1. $4x = 16$

_____

2. $3x = 12$

_____

3. $4 = 4x$

_____

4. $3x = 9$

_____

5. $2x = 10$

_____

6. $15 = 5x$

_____

Solve the equation by drawing a model.

7. $4x = 8$ _____

8. $3x = 18$ _____

9. $12 = 2x$ _____

10. $2x = 16$ _____

11. **Write Math** ▶ **Explain** the steps you use to solve a multiplication equation with algebra tiles.

_____

_____

_____

_____

Problem Solving REAL WORLD

The bar graph shows the number of countries that competed in the first four modern Olympic Games. Use the bar graph for 12–13.

12. Naomi is doing a report about the 1900 Olympic Games. Each page will contain information about 4 of the countries that competed. Write and solve an equation to find the number of pages Naomi will need.

_____

13. **H.O.T. Pose a Problem** Use the information in the bar graph to write and solve a problem involving a multiplication equation.

_____

_____

_____

_____

Olympic Games

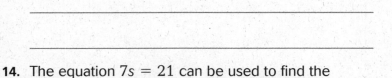

14. The equation $7s = 21$ can be used to find the number of snakes s in each cage at a zoo. Solve the equation. Then tell what the solution means.

_____

15. **Write Math** ► **Explain** how solving an addition equation is similar to solving a multiplication equation.

_____

_____

_____

_____

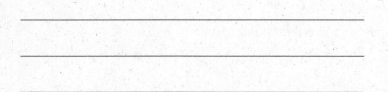

16. **Test Prep** What is the solution of the equation $2x = 8$?

(**A**) $x = 2$ (**C**) $x = 8$

(**B**) $x = 4$ (**D**) $x = 16$

FOR MORE PRACTICE:
Standards Practice Book, pp. P153–P154

Solve Multiplication and Division Equations

Essential Question How do you solve multiplication and division equations?

COMMON CORE STANDARD CC.6.EE.7
Reason about and solve one-variable equations and inequalities.

CONNECT You can use Properties of Equality and inverse operations to solve multiplication and division equations.

Division Property of Equality

If you divide both sides of an equation by the same nonzero number, the two sides will remain equal.

$2 \times 6 = 12$

$\dfrac{2 \times 6}{2} = \dfrac{12}{2}$

$1 \times 6 = 6$

$6 = 6$

UNLOCK the Problem REAL WORLD

Mei ran 14 laps around a track for a total of 4,200 meters. The equation $14d = 4,200$ can be used to find the distance d in meters she ran in each lap. Solve the equation, and explain what the solution means.

• What operation is indicated by $14d$?

_____

 Solve a multiplication equation.

To get d by itself, you must undo the multiplication by 14. Dividing by 14 is the inverse operation of multiplying by 14.

Write the equation.

$$14d = 4,200$$

Use the Division Property of Equality.

$$\frac{14d}{} = \frac{4,200}{}$$

Divide.

$$1 \times d = \underline{}$$

Use the Identity Property of Multiplication.

$$\underline{} = 300$$

Check the solution.

Write the equation.

$$14d = 4,200$$

Substitute _____ for d.

$$14 \times \underline{} = 4,200$$

The solution checks.

$$\underline{} = 4,200$$

So, the solution means that Mei ran _____ meters in each lap.

Math Talk

MATHEMATICAL PRACTICES

Explain how you know what number to divide both sides of the equation by.

🔑 Example 1 Solve the equation $\frac{2}{3}n = \frac{1}{4}$.

Think: n is multiplied by $\frac{2}{3}$, so divide both sides by $\frac{2}{3}$ to undo the division.

Write the equation.

$$\frac{2}{3}n = \frac{1}{4}$$

Use the _____ Property of Equality.

$$\frac{2}{3}n \div \frac{2}{3} = \frac{1}{4} \div \frac{}{}$$

To divide by $\frac{2}{3}$, multiply by its reciprocal.

$$\frac{2}{3}n \times \frac{3}{2} = \frac{1}{4} \times \frac{}{}$$

Multiply.

$$n = \frac{}{}$$

Multiplication Property of Equality

If you multiply both sides of an equation by the same number, the two sides will remain equal.

$$\frac{12}{4} = 3$$
$$4 \times \frac{12}{4} = 4 \times 3$$
$$1 \times 12 = 12$$
$$12 = 12$$

🔑 Example 2

A biologist divides a water sample equally among 8 test tubes. Each test tube contains 24.5 milliliters of water. Write and solve an equation to find the total volume of the water sample.

STEP 1 Write an equation. Let v represent the total volume in milliliters.

Think: The total volume divided by 8 equals the volume in each test tube.

$$\frac{v}{} = \underline{\hspace{2cm}}$$

STEP 2 Solve the equation. v is divided by 8, so multiply both sides by 8 to undo the division.

Write the equation.

$$\frac{v}{8} = 24.5$$

Use the _____ Property of Equality.

$$\underline{\hspace{1cm}} \times \frac{v}{8} = \underline{\hspace{1cm}} \times 24.5$$

Multiply.

$$v = \underline{\hspace{2cm}}$$

So, the total volume of the water sample is _____ milliliters.

Math Talk

MATHEMATICAL PRACTICES

Explain how you can use the Multiplication Property of Equality to solve Example 1.

Name _____

Share and Show

1. Solve the equation $2.5m = 10$.

$$2.5m = 10$$

$$\frac{2.5m}{2.5} = \frac{10}{\boxed{}}$$

Use the _____ Property of Equality.

$$m = \underline{}$$ Divide.

Solve the equation, and check the solution.

2. $3x = 210$

3. $2.8 = 4t$

✓ 4. $\frac{1}{3}n = 15$

5. $\frac{1}{2}y = \frac{1}{10}$

✓ 6. $25 = \frac{a}{5}$

7. $1.3 = \frac{c}{4}$

Math Talk MATHEMATICAL PRACTICES **Explain** how to get the variable by itself on one side of a division equation.

On Your Own

Practice: Copy and Solve Solve the equation, and check the solution.

8. $150 = 6m$

9. $\frac{4}{5}n = 8$

10. $4 = \frac{p}{15}$

11. $14.7 = \frac{b}{7}$

12. $2t = 18.6$

13. $\frac{1}{4} = \frac{3}{5}s$

14. In a serving of 8 fluid ounces of pomegranate juice, there are 32.8 grams of carbohydrates. Write and solve an equation to find the amount of carbohydrates in each fluid ounce of the juice.

_____

15. **H.O.T.** Write a division equation that has the solution $x = 16$.

_____

Problem Solving REAL WORLD

What's the Error?

16. Melinda has a block of clay that weighs 14.4 ounces. She divides the clay into 6 equal pieces. To find the weight w in ounces of each piece, Melinda solved the equation $6w = 14.4$.

Look at how Melinda solved the equation. Find her error.

Correct the error. Solve the equation, and explain your steps.

This is how Melinda solved the equation:

$$6w = 14.4$$
$$\frac{6w}{6} = 6 \times 14.4$$
$$w = 86.4$$

Melinda concludes that each piece of clay weighs 86.4 ounces.

So, $w =$ _____.

This means each piece of clay weighs _____.

- **Describe** the error that Melinda made.

_____

_____

- **Explain** how Melinda could have recognized that her answer was not reasonable.

_____

_____

_____

- **Explain** how you know that your solution is correct.

_____

_____

FOR MORE PRACTICE:
Standards Practice Book, pp. P155–P156

Name _____

Problem Solving • Equations with Fractions

Essential Question How can you use the strategy *solve a simpler problem* to solve equations involving fractions?

COMMON CORE STANDARDS CC.6.EE.7
Reason about and solve one-variable equations and inequalities.

You can change an equation involving a fraction to an equation involving only whole numbers. To do so, multiply both sides of the equation by the denominator of the fraction.

🔑 UNLOCK the Problem › REAL WORLD

On canoe trips, people sometimes carry their canoes between bodies of water. Maps for canoeing use a unit of length called a *rod* to show distances. Victoria and Mick carry their canoe 40 rods. The equation $40 = \frac{2}{11}d$ gives the distance d in yards that they carried the canoe. How many yards did they carry the canoe?

Use the graphic organizer to help you solve the problem.

Read the Problem	Solve the Problem
What do I need to find? I need to find _____ _____.	• Write a simpler equation. Write the equation. $\qquad 40 = \frac{2}{11}d$ Multiply both sides by $\quad 11 \times 40 = $ _____ $\times \frac{2}{11}d$ the denominator. Multiply. $\qquad$ _____ $= 2d$
What information do I need to use? I need to use _____.	• Solve the simpler equation. Write the equation. $\qquad 440 = 2d$
How will I use the information? I can solve a simpler problem by changing the equation to an equation involving only whole numbers. Then I can solve the simpler equation.	Use the Division Property of Equality. $\quad \dfrac{440}{\rule{1cm}{0.4pt}} = \dfrac{2d}{\rule{1cm}{0.4pt}}$ Divide. $\qquad$ _____ $= d$

So, Victoria and Mick carried their canoe _____ yards.

Math Talk MATHEMATICAL PRACTICES
Explain how you can check that your answer to the problem is correct.

If an equation contains more than one fraction, you can change it to an equation involving only whole numbers by multiplying both sides of the equation by the product of the denominators of the fractions.

🔑 Try Another Problem

Trevor is making $\frac{2}{3}$ of a recipe for chicken noodle soup. He adds $\frac{1}{2}$ cup of chopped celery. The equation $\frac{2}{3}c = \frac{1}{2}$ can be used to find the number of cups c of chopped celery in the original recipe. How many cups of chopped celery does the original recipe call for?

Use the graphic organizer to help you solve the problem.

Read the Problem	Solve the Problem
What do I need to find?	
What information do I need to use?	
How will I use the information?	

So, the original recipe calls for _____ cup of chopped celery.

• **Describe** another method that you could use to solve the problem.

_____

_____

© Houghton Mifflin Harcourt Publishing Company

Math Talk MATHEMATICAL PRACTICES
Explain how you know that your answer is reasonable.

Name _____

Share and Show

↑ UNLOCK the Problem Tips

✓ Circle the important information.

✓ Use the Properties of Equality when you solve equations.

✓ Check your solution by substituting it into the original equation.

1. Connor ran 3 kilometers in a relay race. His distance represents $\frac{3}{10}$ of the total distance of the race. The equation $\frac{3}{10}d = 3$ can be used to find the total distance d of the race in kilometers. What was the total distance of the race?

    First, write a simpler equation by multiplying both sides by the denominator of the fraction.

    _____

    Next, solve the simpler equation.

    _____

    So, the race is _____ long.

SHOW YOUR WORK

2. **H.O.T.** **What if** Connor's distance of 3 kilometers represented only $\frac{2}{10}$ of the total distance of the race. What would the total distance of the race have been?

    _____

3. The lightest puppy in a litter weighs 9 ounces, which is $\frac{3}{4}$ of the weight of the heaviest puppy. The equation $\frac{3}{4}w = 9$ can be used to find the weight w in ounces of the heaviest puppy. How much does the heaviest puppy weigh?

    _____

4. Sophia took home $\frac{2}{5}$ of the pizza that was left over from a party. The amount she took represents $\frac{1}{2}$ of a whole pizza. The equation $\frac{2}{5}p = \frac{1}{2}$ can be used to find the number of pizzas p left over from the party. How many pizzas were left over?

    _____

5. A city received $\frac{3}{4}$ inch of rain on July 31. This represents $\frac{3}{10}$ of the total amount of rain the city received in July. The equation $\frac{3}{10}r = \frac{3}{4}$ can be used to find the amount of rain r in inches the city received in July. How much rain did the city receive in July?

    _____

On Your Own.....

Choose a
STRATEGY

Use a Model
Draw a Diagram
Find a Pattern
Solve a Simpler Problem
Work Backward
Use a Formula

6. Nathan has 80 U.S. stamps, 64 Canadian stamps, and 32 Mexican stamps. He wants to put the same number of stamps on each page of his stamp album. Each page will have stamps from only one country. What is the greatest number of stamps that Nathan can put on each page?

_____

7. **H.O.T.** A dog sled race is 25 miles long. The equation $\frac{5}{8}k = 25$ can be used to estimate the race's length k in kilometers. Approximately how many hours will it take a dog sled team to finish the race if it travels at an average speed of 30 kilometers per hour?

_____

8. Gina drove 36 miles in $\frac{3}{4}$ hour. The equation $36 = \frac{3}{4}r$ can be used to find her average rate of speed r in miles per hour. What was Gina's average rate of speed?

_____

SHOW YOUR WORK

9. **Write About It** Explain how you could use the strategy *solve a simpler problem* to solve the equation $\frac{3}{4}x = \frac{3}{10}$.

_____

_____

_____

_____

_____

10. ⭐ **Test Prep** Three-fifths of the animals on a family farm are pigs, and there are 12 pigs on the farm. The equation $\frac{3}{5}a = 12$ can be used to find the total number of animals a on the farm. How many animals are on the farm?

  (A) 8 animals   (C) 60 animals

  (B) 20 animals   (D) 180 animals

© Houghton Mifflin Harcourt Publishing Company

✓ Mid-Chapter Checkpoint

▶ **Vocabulary**

Choose the best term from the box to complete the sentence.

Vocabulary
equation
inverse operations
solution of an equation

1. A(n) _____ is a statement that two mathematical expressions are equal. (p. 293)

2. Adding 5 and subtracting 5 are _____. (p. 305)

▶ **Concepts and Skills**

Write an equation for the word sentence. (CC.6.EE.7)

3. The sum of a number and 4.5 is 8.2.

4. Three times the cost is $24.

Determine whether the given value of the variable is a solution of the equation. (CC.6.EE.5)

5. $x - 24 = 58;\ x = 82$

6. $\frac{1}{3}c = \frac{3}{8};\ c = \frac{3}{4}$

Solve the equation, and check the solution. (CC.6.EE.7)

7. $a + 2.4 = 7.8$

8. $b - \frac{1}{4} = 3\frac{1}{2}$

9. $3x = 27$

10. $\frac{1}{3}s = \frac{1}{5}$

11. $\frac{t}{4} = 16$

12. $\frac{w}{7} = 0.3$

13. A stadium has a total of 18,000 seats. Of these, 7,500 are field seats, and the rest are grandstand seats. Which equation could be used to find the number of grandstand seats s? (CC.6.EE.7)

Ⓐ $s + 7{,}500 = 18{,}000$

Ⓑ $s - 7{,}500 = 18{,}000$

Ⓒ $s + 18{,}000 = 7{,}500$

Ⓓ $s - 18{,}000 = 7{,}500$

14. Aaron wants to buy a bicycle that costs $128. So far, he has saved $56. The equation $a + 56 = 128$ can be used to find the amount a in dollars that Aaron still needs to save. What is the solution of the equation? (CC.6.EE.7)

Ⓐ $a = 64$

Ⓑ $a = 72$

Ⓒ $a = 132$

Ⓓ $a = 184$

15. Ms. McNeil buys 2.4 gallons of gasoline. The total cost is $7.56. The equation $2.4p = 7.56$ can be used to find the price p in dollars of one gallon of gasoline. What is the price of one gallon of gasoline?

(CC.6.EE.7)

Ⓐ $1.81

Ⓑ $2.40

Ⓒ $3.15

Ⓓ $5.16

16. Crystal is picking blueberries. So far, she has filled $\frac{2}{3}$ of her basket, and the blueberries weigh $\frac{3}{4}$ pound. The equation $\frac{2}{3}w = \frac{3}{4}$ can be used to estimate the weight w in pounds of the blueberries when the basket is full. About how much will the blueberries in Crystal's basket weigh when it is full? (CC.6.EE.7)

Ⓐ $\frac{3}{8}$ pound

Ⓑ $\frac{1}{2}$ pound

Ⓒ $1\frac{1}{8}$ pounds

Ⓓ $2\frac{1}{4}$ pounds

Name _____

Solutions of Inequalities

Essential Question How do you determine whether a number is a solution of an inequality?

COMMON CORE STANDARD CC.6.EE.5
Reason about and solve one-variable equations and inequalities.

An **inequality** is a mathematical sentence that compares two expressions using the symbol $<$, $>$, $\leq$, $\geq$, or $\neq$. These are examples of inequalities:

$$8 < 11 \qquad 9 > {}^-4 \qquad a \leq 50 \qquad x \geq 3.2$$

A **solution of an inequality** is a value of a variable that makes the inequality true. Inequalities can have more than one solution.

> ### Math Idea
> - The symbol $\leq$ means "is less than or equal to."
> - The symbol $\geq$ means "is greater than or equal to."

🔑 UNLOCK the Problem REAL WORLD

The books from the Middle Ages in a library are all more than 650 years old. The inequality $a > 650$ represents the possible ages a in years of the books. Determine whether $a = 678$ or $a = 634$ is a solution of the inequality, and tell what the solution means.

 Use substitution to determine the solution.

STEP 1 Check whether $a = 678$ is a solution.

Write the inequality. $a > 650$

Substitute 678 for a.   _____ $\overset{?}{>}$ 650

Compare the values.   678 is _____ than 650.

The inequality is true when $a = 678$, so $a = 678$ is a solution.

STEP 2 Check whether $a = 634$ is a solution.

Write the inequality. $a > 650$

Substitute 634 for a.   _____ $\overset{?}{>}$ 650

Compare the values.   634 _____ greater than 650.

The inequality _____ true when $a = 634$, so $a = 634$ _____ a solution.

The solution $a = 678$ means that a book in the library from the

Middle Ages could be _____ years old.

> **Math Talk** MATHEMATICAL PRACTICES
> Give another solution of the inequality $a > 650$. Explain how you determined the solution.

🔑 Example 1 Determine whether the given value of the variable is a solution of the inequality.

A $b < 0.3$; $b = {}^-0.2$

Write the inequality. $\qquad\qquad\qquad\qquad\qquad b < 0.3$

Substitute the given value for the variable. $\qquad\qquad \underline{\hspace{3cm}} \overset{?}{<} 0.3$

Compare the values. $\qquad\qquad {}^-0.2$ is $\underline{\hspace{3cm}}$ than 0.3.

The inequality $\underline{\hspace{2cm}}$ true when $b = {}^-0.2$, so $b = {}^-0.2$ $\underline{\hspace{2cm}}$ a solution.

B $m \geq \frac{2}{3}$; $m = \frac{3}{5}$

Write the inequality. $\qquad\qquad\qquad\qquad\qquad m \geq \frac{2}{3}$

Substitute the given value for the variable. $\qquad\qquad \underline{\hspace{1.5cm}} \overset{?}{\geq} \frac{2}{3}$

Rewrite the fractions with a common denominator. $\qquad\qquad \dfrac{}{15} \overset{?}{\geq} \dfrac{}{15}$

Compare the values. $\qquad\qquad \dfrac{9}{15} \underline{\hspace{2cm}}$ greater than or equal to $\dfrac{10}{15}$.

The inequality $\underline{\hspace{3cm}}$ true when $m = \frac{3}{5}$, so $m = \frac{3}{5}$ $\underline{\hspace{3cm}}$ a solution.

🔑 Example 2

An airplane can hold no more than 416 passengers. The inequality $p \leq 416$ represents the possible number of passengers p on the airplane, where p is a whole number. Give two solutions of the inequality, and tell what the solutions mean.

Think: The solutions of the inequality are whole numbers $\underline{\hspace{3cm}}$ than or

$\underline{\hspace{3cm}}$ to 416.

- $p = 200$ is a solution because 200 is $\underline{\hspace{3cm}}$ than $\underline{\hspace{2cm}}$.

- $p = \underline{\hspace{3cm}}$ is a solution because $\underline{\hspace{2cm}}$ is $\underline{\hspace{2cm}}$ than 416.

These solutions mean that the number of passengers on the

plane could be $\underline{\hspace{3cm}}$ or $\underline{\hspace{3cm}}$.

Math Talk
Give an example of a value of p that is not a solution of the inequality. Explain why it is not a solution.

Name _____

Share and Show

Determine whether the given value of the variable is a solution of the inequality.

1. $a \geq {}^-6; a = {}^-3$

$\underline{\hspace{2cm}} \overset{?}{\geq} {}^-6$

_____

2. $y < 7.8; y = 8$

_____

3. $c > \frac{1}{4}; c = \frac{1}{5}$

_____

4. $x \leq 3; x = 3$

_____

5. $d < {}^-0.52; d = {}^-0.51$

_____

6. $t \geq \frac{2}{3}; t = \frac{3}{4}$

_____

Math Talk MATHEMATICAL PRACTICES
Explain how you could use a number line to check your answer to Exercise 5.

On Your Own

Practice: Copy and Solve Determine whether the given value of the variable is a solution of the inequality.

7. $s > {}^-1; s = 0$

8. $v \leq 1\frac{5}{6}; v = 1\frac{3}{4}$

9. $x < 0.43; x = 0.48$

Give two solutions of the inequality.

10. $e < 3$

11. $p > {}^-12$

12. $y \geq 5.8$

_____

_____

_____

13. A person must be at least 18 years old to vote. The inequality $a \geq 18$ represents the possible ages a in years at which a person can vote. Determine whether $a = 18$, $a = 17\frac{1}{2}$, and $a = 91.5$ are solutions of the inequality, and tell what the solutions mean.

_____

_____

Problem Solving · REAL WORLD

The table shows ticket and popcorn prices at five movie theater chains. Use the table for 14–15.

14. The inequality $p < 8.00$ represents the prices p in dollars that Paige is willing to pay for a movie ticket. At how many of the theaters would Paige be willing to buy a ticket? What are the ticket prices at those theaters?

_____

15. **H.O.T.** **Sense or Nonsense?** Edward says that the inequality $d \geq 4.00$ represents the popcorn prices in the table, where d is the price of popcorn in dollars. Is Edward's statement sense or nonsense? Explain.

_____

_____

_____

Movie Theater Prices	
Ticket Price ($)	Popcorn Price ($)
8.00	4.25
8.50	5.00
9.00	4.00
7.50	4.75
7.25	4.50

SHOW YOUR WORK

16. The inequality $m \geq 4.78$ represents the distance m in meters that Olga must jump to make it to the final round of the long jump. Give two distances that Olga could jump to make it to the final round.

_____

_____

17. **Write Math** ▶ **Explain** why the statement $t > 13$ is an inequality.

_____

_____

18. ⭐ **Test Prep** The inequality $w < 475$ represents the weight w in pounds that can be safely carried in the basket of a small hot-air balloon. Which of the following is NOT a solution of the inequality?

Ⓐ $w = 463$ Ⓒ $w = 471$

Ⓑ $w = 479$ Ⓓ $w = 457$

Name _____

Write Inequalities

Essential Question How do you write an inequality to represent a situation?

COMMON CORE STANDARD CC.6.EE.8
Reason about and solve one-variable equations and inequalities.

CONNECT You can use what you know about writing equations to help you write inequalities.

 UNLOCK the Problem REAL WORLD

The highest temperature ever recorded at the South Pole was 8°F. Write an inequality to show that the temperature *t* in degrees Fahrenheit at the South Pole is less than or equal to 8°F.

 Write an inequality for the situation.

- Underline the words that tell you which inequality symbol to use.

- Will you use an equal sign in your inequality? Explain.

_____

_____

Think:

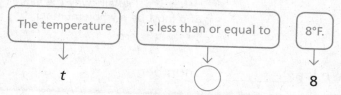

| The temperature | is less than or equal to | 8°F. |

t ○ 8

So, an inequality that describes the temperature *t* in

degrees Fahrenheit at the South Pole is _____.

Try This! The directors of an animal shelter need to raise more than $50,000 during a fundraiser. Write an inequality that represents the amount of money *m* in dollars that the directors need to raise.

Think:

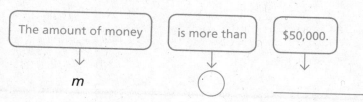

| The amount of money | is more than | $50,000. |

m ○ _____

So, an inequality that describes the amount of money *m* in

dollars is _____.

Math Talk MATHEMATICAL PRACTICES
Explain how you knew which inequality symbol to use in the Try This! problem.

🔑 Example 1 Write an inequality for the word sentence. Tell what type of numbers the variable in the inequality can represent.

A The weight is less than $3\frac{1}{2}$ pounds.

Think: Let w represent the unknown weight in pounds.

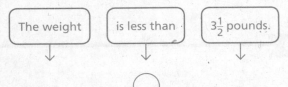

| The weight | is less than | $3\frac{1}{2}$ pounds. |

_____ ⭕ _____ , where w is a positive number

B There must be at least 65 police officers on duty.

Think: Let p represent the number of police officers. The phrase "at least" is

equivalent to "is _____ than or equal to."

| The number of officers | is greater than or equal to | 65. |

_____ ⭕ _____ , where p is a _____ number

> **MATHEMATICAL PRACTICES**
>
> **Math Talk** Explain why the value of p must be a whole number.

🔑 Example 2 Write two word sentences for the inequality.

A $n \le 0.3$

• n is _____ than or _____ to 0.3.

• n is no _____ than 0.3.

B $a > {}^-4$

• a is _____ than ${}^-4$.

• a is _____ than ${}^-4$.

• **H.O.T.** Which inequality symbol would you use to show that the number of people attending a party will be at most 14? Explain.

_____

_____

328

Name _____

Share and Show

1. Write an inequality for the word sentence "The temperature t is less than $^{-}2\,°C$."

   What inequality symbol does the phrase "is less than" indicate? _____

   The inequality is _____ $<$ _____ , where t is the _____ in degrees Celsius.

Write an inequality for the word sentence. Tell what type of numbers the variable in the inequality can represent.

2. The elevation e is greater than or equal to 15 meters.

   _____

3. A passenger's age a must be more than 4 years.

   _____

Write a word sentence for the inequality.

4. $b < \frac{1}{2}$

   _____

5. $m \geq 55$

   _____

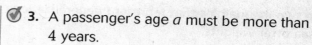

Math Talk | MATHEMATICAL PRACTICES
Explain the difference between $t \leq 4$ and $t < 4$.

On Your Own

Write an inequality for the word sentence. Tell what type of numbers the variable in the inequality can represent.

6. The number of points p scored by a football team is no more than 48.

   _____

7. The cost c of a movie ticket is less than $10.50

   _____

Write a word sentence for the inequality.

8. $t > 62$

   _____

9. $v \leq 4.7$

   _____

Make Generalizations

The reading skill *make generalizations* can help you write inequalities to represent situations. A generalization is a statement that is true about a group of facts.

Sea otters spend almost their entire lives in the ocean. Their thick fur helps them to stay warm in cold water. Sea otters often float together in groups called *rafts*. A team of biologists weighed the female sea otters in one raft off the coast of Alaska. The chart shows their results.

Write two inequalities that represent generalizations about the sea otter weights.

First, list the weights in pounds in order from least to greatest.

50, 51, 54, _____, _____, _____, _____, _____,

_____, _____, _____, _____

Weights of Female Sea Otters	
Otter Number	Weight (pounds)
1	50
2	61
3	62
4	69
5	71
6	54
7	68
8	62
9	58
10	51
11	61
12	66

Next, write an inequality to describe the weights by using the least weight in the list. Let *w* represent the weights of the otters in pounds.

Think: The least weight is _____ pounds, so all of the weights are greater than or equal to 50 pounds.

$w \bigcirc 50$

Now, write an inequality to describe the weights by using the greatest weight in the list.

Think: The greatest weight is _____ pounds, so

all of the weights are _____ than or equal to

_____ pounds.

$w \bigcirc 71$

So, the inequalities _____ and _____ represent generalizations about the weights *w* in pounds of the otters.

10. Use the chart at the right to write two inequalities that represent generalizations about the number of sea otter pups per raft.

_____

_____

Sea Otter Pups per Raft	
Raft Number	Number of Pups
1	7
2	10
3	15
4	23
5	6
6	16
7	20
8	6

Graph Inequalities

Essential Question How do you represent the solutions of an inequality on a number line?

COMMON CORE STANDARD CC.6.EE.8
Reason about and solve one-variable equations and inequalities.

Inequalities can have an infinite number of solutions. The solutions of the inequality $x > 2$, for example, include all numbers greater than 2. You can use a number line to represent all of the solutions of an inequality.

The number line at right shows the solutions of the inequality $x > 2$.

$x > 2$

The empty circle at 2 shows that 2 is not a solution. The shading to the right of 2 shows that values greater than 2 are solutions.

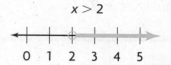 **UNLOCK the Problem** REAL WORLD

Forest fires are most likely to occur when the air temperature is greater than 60°F. The inequality $t > 60$ represents the temperatures t in degrees Fahrenheit for which forest fires are most likely. Graph the solutions of the inequality on a number line.

 Show the solutions of $t > 60$ on a number line.

Think: I need to show all solutions that are greater than 60.

Draw an empty circle at _____ to show that 60 is not a solution.

Shade to the _____ of _____ to show that values greater than 60 are solutions.

```
 +---+---+---+---+---+---+---+---+---+---+--->
 0  10  20  30  40  50  60  70  80  90 100
```

Try This! Graph the solutions of the inequality $y < 5$.

Draw an empty circle at _____ to show that 5 is not a solution.

Shade to the _____ of _____ to show that values less than 5 are solutions.

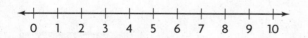
```
<---+---+---+---+---+---+---+---+---+---+---+-->
    0   1   2   3   4   5   6   7   8   9  10
```

- **Explain** why $y = 5$ is not a solution of the inequality $y < 5$.

_____

You can also use a number line to show the solutions of an inequality that includes the symbol ≤ or ≥.

The number line at right shows the solutions of the inequality $x \geq 2$.

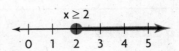
$x \geq 2$

The filled-in circle at 2 shows that 2 is a solution. The shading to the right of 2 shows that values greater than 2 are also solutions.

 Example 1 Graph the solutions of the inequality on a number line.

A $w \leq 0.8$

Draw a filled-in circle at _____ to show that 0.8 is a solution.

Shade to the _____ of _____ to show that values less than 0.8 are also solutions.

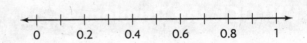

B $n \geq {}^-3$

Draw a filled-in circle at _____ to show that ⁻3 is a solution.

Shade to the _____ of _____ to show that values greater than ⁻3 are also solutions.

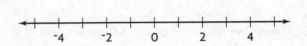

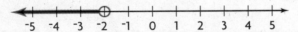 **Example 2** Write the inequality represented by the graph.

Use x (or another letter) for the variable in the inequality.

The _____ circle at _____ shows that ⁻2

_____ a solution.

The shading to the _____ of _____ shows that values

_____ than ⁻2 are solutions.

So, the inequality represented by the graph is _____.

Math Talk

MATHEMATICAL PRACTICES

Explain how you know whether to shade to the right or to the left when graphing an inequality.

Name _____

Share and Show

Graph the inequality.

1. $m < 15$

Draw an empty circle at _____ to show that 15 is

not a solution. Shade to the _____ of _____
to show that values less than 15 are solutions.

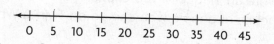

2. $c \geq {}^-1.5$

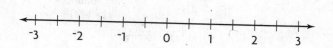

3. $b \leq \frac{5}{8}$

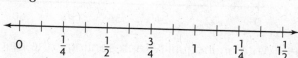

Write the inequality represented by the graph.

4.

_____

5.

_____

Math Talk MATHEMATICAL PRACTICES
Explain why it is easier to graph the solutions of an inequality than it is to list them.

On Your Own

Practice: Copy and Solve Graph the inequality.

6. $a < \frac{2}{3}$

7. $x > {}^-4$

8. $k \geq 0.3$

9. $t \leq 6$

Write the inequality represented by the graph.

10.

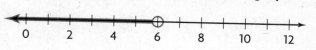

_____

11.

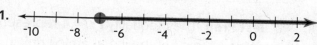

_____

12. The inequality $w \geq 60$ represents the wind
speed w in miles per hour of a tornado.
Graph the solutions of the inequality on the
number line.

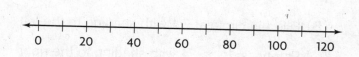

Problem Solving REAL WORLD

The table shows the height requirements for several rides at an amusement park. Use the table for 13–17.

13. Write an inequality representing t, the heights in inches of people who can go on Twirl & Whirl.

_____

14. Graph your inequality from Exercise 13.

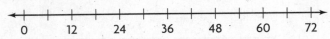

15. Write an inequality representing r, the heights in inches of people who can go on Race Track.

_____

Height Requirements

Ride	Minimum height (in.)
Mighty Mountain	44
Race Track	42
River Rapids	38
Twirl & Whirl	48

16. Graph your inequality from Exercise 15.

```
  +--+--+--+--+--+--+--+--+--+--+--+-->
  0   12   24   36   48   60   72
```

SHOW YOUR WORK

17. **H.O.T.** **Write Math** Write an inequality representing b, the heights in inches of people who can go on *both* River Rapids and Mighty Mountain. Explain how you determined your answer.

_____

_____

_____

_____

18. ⭐ **Test Prep** The inequality $t < {}^-4$ represents the temperatures t of the ice at an ice rink in degrees Celsius. Which best describes a number line showing the graph of the solutions of the inequality?

Ⓐ Empty circle at $^-4$ with shading to the left

Ⓑ Filled-in circle at $^-4$ with shading to the left

Ⓒ Empty circle at $^-4$ with shading to the right

Ⓓ Filled-in circle at $^-4$ with shading to the right

✓ Chapter 8 Review/Test

▶ Vocabulary

Choose the best term from the box to complete the sentence.

1. Dividing by 4 is the _____ of multiplying by 4. (p. 305)

2. The statement $x > 8$ is an example of an _____. (p. 323)

▶ Concepts and Skills

Determine whether the given value of the variable is a solution of the equation. (CC.6.EE.5)

3. $c + 32 = 67; c = 25$

4. $3.5n = 7.35; n = 2.1$

Solve the equation, and check the solution. (CC.6.EE.7)

5. $4 + x = 12$

6. $f - 2.3 = 18.4$

7. $15 + y = 26$

8. $0.8m = 32$

9. $\frac{2}{5}t = 12$

10. $\frac{k}{7} = 14$

Determine whether the given value of the variable is a solution of the inequality. (CC.6.EE.5)

11. $x < 8; x = 0.4$

12. $p \geq \frac{3}{4}; p = \frac{3}{5}$

GO Online Assessment Options
Chapter Test

Fill in the bubble to show your answer.

13. One brand of cheddar cheese sells for $0.29 per ounce. Tanya bought a block of the cheese for $2.61. Which equation could be used to determine the weight w of the cheese in ounces? (CC.6.EE.7)

Ⓐ $\frac{w}{2.61} = 0.29$

Ⓑ $\frac{w}{0.29} = 2.61$

Ⓒ $2.61w = 0.29$

Ⓓ $0.29w = 2.61$

14. A helicopter descends 82 meters to an altitude of 45 meters. The equation $a - 82 = 45$ can be used to find the helicopter's starting altitude a in meters. What is the starting altitude of the helicopter? (CC.6.EE.7)

Ⓐ 37 meters

Ⓑ 43 meters

Ⓒ 127 meters

Ⓓ 161 meters

15. Alana uses algebra tiles to model the equation $3x = 12$. What should she do next to solve the equation? (CC.6.EE.7)

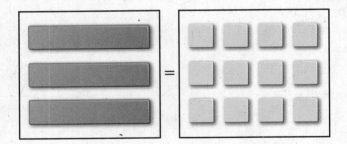

Ⓐ Divide each side into 3 equal groups.

Ⓑ Divide each side into 12 equal groups.

Ⓒ Add 9 more rectangular tiles on the left side.

Ⓓ Remove 9 square tiles from the right side.

16. A chef has a pot of chicken broth. She pours $\frac{2}{3}$ of the broth, or 36 fluid ounces, into a large bowl. The equation $\frac{2}{3}v = 36$ can be used to find the volume v in fluid ounces of the chicken broth originally in the pot. What is the solution of the equation? (CC.6.EE.7)

Ⓐ $v = 24$ Ⓒ $v = 72$

Ⓑ $v = 54$ Ⓓ $v = 108$

Fill in the bubble to show your answer.

17. A bicycle manufacturer is reducing the number of spokes on each bicycle wheel by 4. A wheel on one of the company's new cross-country bikes has 32 spokes. Which equation could be used to determine the number of spokes s that a wheel on a cross-country bike used to have? (CC.6.EE.7)

Ⓐ $s + 32 = 4$

Ⓑ $s + 4 = 32$

Ⓒ $s - 32 = 4$

Ⓓ $s - 4 = 32$

18. Donna purchased fabric to make a purse. She used $\frac{3}{4}$ yard of fabric, which was $\frac{2}{3}$ of the total fabric she bought. The equation $\frac{2}{3}\ell = \frac{3}{4}$ represents the length ℓ in yards of the fabric that Donna bought. How much fabric did Donna buy? (CC.6.EE.7)

Ⓐ $\frac{3}{8}$ yard

Ⓑ $\frac{1}{2}$ yard

Ⓒ $1\frac{1}{8}$ yards

Ⓓ $2\frac{1}{4}$ yards

19. A student in Ms. Blanc's science class must have a score of at least 90 in order to receive an A on a test. Which inequality best represents the possible scores s of a student who receives an A on the test? (CC.6.EE.8)

Ⓐ $s < 90$ Ⓒ $s \le 90$

Ⓑ $s > 90$ Ⓓ $s \ge 90$

20. The inequality $w \ge 33$ represents the wind speed w in meters per second of a hurricane. Which graph represents the solutions of the inequality? (CC.6.EE.8)

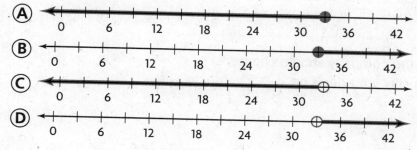

▶ Constructed Response

21. The sale price of a dress is $\frac{7}{10}$ of its regular price. The sale price of a dress is $44.80. The equation $\frac{7}{10}r = 44.80$ can be used to find the regular price r in dollars of the dress. Determine whether $r = 31$, $r = 52$, or $r = 64$ is the solution of the equation, and tell what the solution means. (CC.6.EE.5)

_____

_____

22. The temperature inside a freezer is always less than 6°F. Write an inequality for the temperature t in degrees Fahrenheit inside the freezer. Then graph the inequality. (CC.6.EE.8)

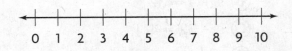

_____

▶ Performance Task (CC.6.EE.7)

23. A company plans to publish a new travel magazine. The manager estimates that the company can publish 20,000 copies of the magazine for a total cost of $18,000.

A Write an equation that can be used to determine the cost of publishing each copy of the magazine. Tell what the variable you use represents.

_____

_____

B Solve your equation, and describe your steps. Then tell what the solution means.

_____

_____

_____

_____

C Decide on a reasonable price that the company should charge customers for the magazine, and justify your decision.

_____

_____

Algebra: Relationships Between Variables

Show What You Know

Check your understanding of important skills.

Name _____

▶ **Number Patterns** Write a rule to explain the pattern. Use the rule to find the missing numbers.

1. 127, 123, 119, ▦, 111, ▦

   _____

2. 5,832, ▦, 648, 216, 72, ▦, 8

   _____

▶ **Identify Points on a Coordinate Grid** Use the ordered pair to name the point on the grid.

3. (4, 6) _____

4. (8, 4) _____

5. (2, 8) _____

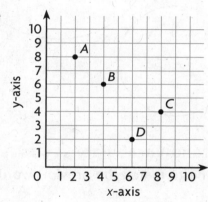

▶ **Evaluate Expressions** Evaluate the expression.

6. $18 + 4 - 7$

   _____

7. $59 - 20 + 5$

   _____

8. $(40 - 15) + 30$

   _____

9. $77 - (59 - 18)$

   _____

Terrell plotted points on the coordinate plane as shown. He noticed that the points lie on a straight line. Be a Math Detective and help him write an equation that shows the relationship between the *x*- and *y*-coordinate of each point he plotted. Then use the equation to find the *y*-coordinate of a point on the line with an *x*-coordinate of 20.

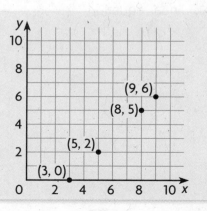

GO Online Assessment Options: **Soar to Success Math**

Vocabulary Builder

► **Visualize It** ∙∙

Use the review words to complete the bubble map.

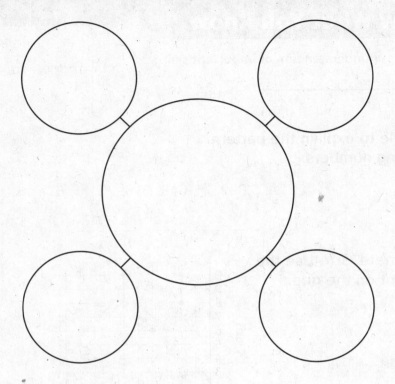

Review Words

coordinate plane

ordered pair

quadrants

x-coordinate

y-coordinate

Preview Words

dependent variable

independent variable

linear equation

► **Understand Vocabulary** ∙∙

Draw a line to match the preview word with its definition.

Preview Words

1. dependent variable

2. independent variable

3. linear equation

Definitions

• has a value that determines the value of another quantity

• names the point where the axes in the coordinate plane intersect

• has a value that depends on the value of another quantity

• forms a straight line when graphed

Independent and Dependent Variables

Essential Question How can you write an equation to represent the relationship between an independent variable and a dependent variable?

COMMON CORE STANDARD CC.6.EE.9
Represent and analyze quantitative relationships between dependent and independent variables.

You can use an equation with two variables to represent a relationship between two quantities. One variable is called the *independent variable*, and the other is called the *dependent variable*. The value of the **independent variable** determines the value of the **dependent variable**.

🔑 UNLOCK the Problem REAL WORLD

Jeri burns 5.8 calories for every minute she jogs. Identify the independent and dependent variables in this situation. Then write an equation to represent the relationship between the number of minutes Jeri jogs and the total number of calories she burns.

- Why do you need to use a variable?

_____

- How many variables are needed to write the equation for this problem?

_____

🔒 **Identify the independent and dependent variables. Then use the variables to write an equation.**

Let *c* represent the total number of _____ Jeri burns.

Let *m* represent the number of _____ Jeri jogs.

Think: The total number of calories Jeri burns **depends** on the number of minutes she jogs.

_____ is the dependent variable.

_____ is the independent variable.

Math Talk MATHEMATICAL PRACTICES
Explain how you know that the value of *c* is dependent on the value of *m*.

Write an equation to represent the situation.

Think: The total calories burned │ is equal to │ 5.8 │ times │ the number of minutes jogged.
↓ ↓ ↓ ↓ ↓

_____ = 5.8 × _____

So, the equation _____ represents the number of calories

c Jeri burns if she jogs *m* minutes, where _____ is the dependent

variable and _____ is the independent variable.

🔑 Example

Lorelei is spending the afternoon bowling with her friends. Each game she plays costs $3.25, and there is a one-time shoe-rental fee of $2.50.

Ⓐ Identify the independent and dependent variables in this situation. Then write an equation to represent the relationship between the number of games and the total cost.

Think: The total cost in dollars *c* depends on the number of games *g* Lorelei plays.

_____ is the dependent variable.

_____ is the independent variable.

Think:

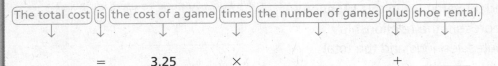

The total cost	is	the cost of a game	times	the number of games	plus	shoe rental.
↓	↓	↓	↓	↓	↓	↓
_____	=	3.25	×	_____	+	_____

> **⚠ ERROR Alert**
> Note that the fee for the shoes, $2.50, is a one-time fee, and therefore is not multiplied by the number of games.

So, the equation _____ represents the total cost in

dollars *c* that Lorelei spends if she bowls *g* games, where _____ is

the dependent variable and _____ is the independent variable.

Ⓑ Use your equation to find the total cost for Lorelei to play 3 games.

Think: Find the value of *c* when *g* = 3.

Write the equation. $c = 3.25g + 2.50$

Substitute 3 for *g*. $c = 3.25(\text{_____}) + 2.50$

Follow the order of operations to solve for *c*. $b = \text{_____} + 2.50 = \text{_____}$

So, it will cost Lorelei _____ to play 3 games.

---

1. **🔥 H.O.T.** What if there were no fee for shoe rentals? How would the equation be different?

   _____

2. How can you use estimation to check that your answer is reasonable?

   _____

   _____

   _____

Share and Show

Identify the independent and dependent variables. Then write an equation to represent the relationship between them.

1. An online store lets customers have their name printed on any item they buy. The total cost c in dollars is the price of the item p in dollars plus \$3.99 for the name.

   The _____ depends on the _____.

   dependent variable: _____

   independent variable: _____

   equation: _____ = _____

2. A raft travels downriver at a rate of 6 miles per hour. The total distance d in miles that the raft travels is equal to the rate times the number of hours h.

   dependent variable: _____

   independent variable: _____

   equation: _____

3. Apples are on sale for \$1.99 a pound. Sheila buys p pounds of apples for a total cost of c dollars.

   dependent variable: _____

   independent variable: _____

   equation: _____

On Your Own

Identify the independent and dependent variables. Then write an equation to represent the relationship between them.

Math Talk MATHEMATICAL PRACTICES

Explain how you know which variable in a relationship is dependent and which is independent.

4. Sean can make 8 origami birds in an hour. The total number of birds b is equal to the number of birds he makes per hour times the number of hours h.

   dependent variable: _____

   independent variable: _____

   equation: _____

5. Billy has \$25. His father is going to give him more money. The total amount t Billy will have is equal to the amount m his father gives him plus the \$25 Billy already has.

   dependent variable: _____

   independent variable: _____

   equation: _____

6. Edeny earns \$8.50 per hour for babysitting. The total amount t she makes in dollars is equal to the amount earned per hour times the number of hours h.

   dependent variable: _____

   independent variable: _____

   equation: _____

7. Belinda pays \$4.25 for each glass she buys. The total cost c is equal to the price per glass times the number of glasses n plus \$9.95 for shipping and handling.

   dependent variable: _____

   independent variable: _____

   equation: _____

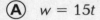 UNLOCK the Problem

8. Benji decides to save $15 per week to buy a computer program. Which equation models the total amount t in dollars Benji will have saved in w weeks?

Ⓐ $w = 15t$

Ⓑ $t = 15w$

Ⓒ $w = 15 + t$

Ⓓ $t = 15 + w$

a. What does the variable t represent?

_____

b. Which is the dependent variable? Which is the independent variable? How do you know?

_____

_____

_____

_____

c. How can you find the total amount saved in w weeks?

_____

_____

d. How do you know that A is not the correct answer?

_____

_____

_____

_____

e. Write an equation for the total amount that Benji will save.

_____

f. Fill in the bubble for the correct answer choice above.

---

9. There are 45 pairs of boots on a shelf at a shoe store. Philip puts more pairs of boots on the shelf. Which equation models the total number of pairs n on the shelf after Philip puts b more pairs on the shelf?

Ⓐ $b = 45 + n$

Ⓑ $b = 45 - n$

Ⓒ $n = 45 + b$

Ⓓ $n = 45 - b$

10. Zubia is cutting a length of rope into equal pieces. The rope is 3 feet long. Which equation models the length l in feet of each piece of rope if Zubia cuts it into p pieces?

Ⓐ $l = 3 \div p$

Ⓑ $l = 3p$

Ⓒ $p = 3 + l$

Ⓓ $p = 3 - l$

Name _____

Equations and Tables

Essential Question How can you translate between equations and tables?

COMMON CORE STANDARD CC.6.EE.9
Represent and analyze quantitative relationships between dependent and independent variables.

When an equation describes the relationship between two quantities, the variable x often represents the independent variable, and y often represents the dependent variable.

A value of the independent variable is called the *input* value, and a value of the dependent variable is called the *output* value.

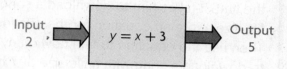

Input 2 → $y = x + 3$ → Output 5

Input 4 → $y = x + 3$ → Output 7

🔑 UNLOCK the Problem REAL WORLD

A skating rink charges $3.00 for each hour of skating, plus $1.75 to rent skates. Write an equation for the relationship that gives the total cost y in dollars for skating x hours. Then make a table that shows the cost of skating for 1, 2, 3, and 4 hours.

🔑 **Write an equation for the relationship, and use the equation to make a table.**

STEP 1 Write an equation.

Think:

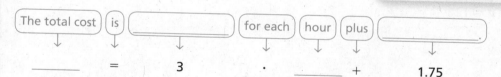

The total cost | is | _____ | for each | hour | plus | _____

_____ = 3 · _____ + 1.75

So, the equation for the relationship is _____.

STEP 2 Make a table.

Input	Rule	Output
Time (hr), x	$3x + 1.75$	Cost ($), y
1	$3 \cdot 1 + 1.75$	4.75
2		
3		
4		

• What is the independent variable? What is the dependent variable?

_____

_____

Replace x with each input value, and then evaluate the rule to find each output value.

MATHEMATICAL PRACTICES

Math Talk Explain how you could use the equation to find the total cost of skating for 6 hours.

🔑 Example

Jamal downloads songs on his MP3 player. The table shows how the time it takes him to download a song depends on the song's file size. Write an equation for the relationship shown in the table. Then use the equation to find how many seconds it takes Jamal to download a song with a file size of 7 megabytes (MB).

Download Times	
File Size (MB), x	Time (s), y
4	48
5	60
6	72
7	?
8	96

STEP 1 Write an equation.

Look for a pattern between the file sizes and the download times.

File Size (MB), x	4	5	6	8
Time (s), y	48	60	72	96

12 · **4**   12 · **5**   12 · _____   12 · _____

Think: You can find each download time by multiplying

the file size by _____.

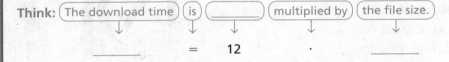

Think: (The download time) (is) (_____) (multiplied by) (the file size.)

_____ = 12 · _____

So, the equation for the relationship is _____.

STEP 2 Use the equation to find the download time for a file size of 7 megabytes.

Write the equation. $y = 12x$

Replace x with 7. $y = 12 \cdot$ _____

Solve for y. $y =$ _____

So, it takes Jamal _____ seconds to download a 7-megabyte song.

1. **Explain** how you can check that your equation for the relationship is correct.

_____

_____

2. **Describe** a situation in which it would be more useful to represent a relationship between two quantities with an equation than with a table of values.

_____

_____

Name _____

Share and Show

Use the equation to complete the table.

1. $y = x + 3$

Input	Rule	Output
x	x + 3	y
6	6 + 3	
8	8 + 3	
10		

 2. $y = 2x + 1$

Input	Output
x	y
4	
7	
10	

Write an equation for the relationship shown in the table. Then find the unknown value in the table.

3.

x	1	2	3	4
y	6	12	?	24

_____

4.

x	9	11	13	15
y	4	6	8	?

_____

> **Math Talk** MATHEMATICAL PRACTICES
> Explain how to write an equation for a relationship between two quantities shown by a table of values.

On Your Own

5. It costs $6 to join an online DVD club and $2.50 to rent each DVD. Write an equation for the relationship that gives the total cost y in dollars for renting x DVDs. Then complete the table.

DVD Club Costs	
DVDs rented, x	Total cost ($), y
3	
4	
5	

_____

Write an equation for the relationship shown in the table. Then find the unknown value in the table.

6.

x	8	9	10	11
y	16	18	?	22

_____

7.

x	10	20	30	40
y	5	10	15	?

_____

Cause and Effect

The reading skill *cause and effect* can help you understand how a change in one variable may cause a change in another variable.

In karate, a person's skill level is often indicated by the color of his or her belt. At Sara's karate school, students must pass a test to move from one belt level to the next. Each test costs $23. Sara hopes to move up 3 belt levels this year. What effect will this plan have on her karate expenses?

Cause:	Effect:
Sara moves to higher belt levels.	Sara's karate expenses go up.

Write an equation for the relationship that relates the cause and effect. Then use the equation to solve the problem.

Let *x* represent the number of belt levels Sara moves up, and let *y* represent the increase in dollars in her karate expenses.

Write the equation. $y = \underline{\hspace{1cm}} \cdot x$

Sara plans to move up 3 levels, so replace *x* with _____. $y = 23 \cdot \underline{\hspace{1cm}}$

Solve for *y*. $y = \underline{\hspace{1cm}}$

So, if Sara moves up 3 belt levels this year, her karate expenses will

increase by $_____.

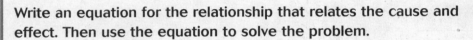

H.O.T. **Write an equation for the relationship that relates the cause and effect. Then use the equation to solve the problem.**

8. Classes at Tony's karate school cost $29.50 per month. This year he plans to take 2 more months of classes than he did last year. What effect will this change have on Tony's karate expenses?

   _____

   _____

   _____

9. A sporting goods store regularly sells karate uniforms for $35.90 each. The store is putting karate uniforms on sale for 10% off. What effect will the sale have on the price of a karate uniform?

   _____

   _____

   _____

Problem Solving • Analyze Relationships

Essential Question How can you use the strategy *find a pattern* to solve problems involving relationships between quantities?

COMMON CORE STANDARD CC.6.EE.9
Represent and analyze quantitative relationships between dependent and independent variables.

🔑 UNLOCK the Problem REAL WORLD

The table shows the amount of water pumped through a fire hose over time. If the pattern in the table continues, how long will it take a firefighter to spray 3,000 gallons of water on a fire using this hose?

Fire Hose Flow Rate

Time (min)	1	2	3	4
Amount of water (gal)	150	300	450	600

Use the graphic organizer to help you solve the problem.

Read the Problem

What do I need to find?

I need to find _____

_____ .

What information do I need to use?

I need to use the relationship between

_____ and _____ .

How will I use the information?

I will find a _____ in the table and write an

_____ .

Solve the Problem

Use the table above to find the relationship between the time and the amount of water.

Think: Let t represent the time in minutes, and w represent the amount of water in gallons. The amount of water in gallons is _____ multiplied by the time in minutes.

$$\text{_____} = 150 \cdot \text{_____}$$

Use the equation to find how long it will take to spray 3,000 gallons.

Write the equation. $w = 150t$

Substitute 3,000 for w. $3{,}000 = 150t$

Solve for t. Divide both sides by 150. $\dfrac{3{,}000}{\rule{1cm}{0.4pt}} = \dfrac{150t}{\rule{1cm}{0.4pt}}$

$$\text{_____} = t$$

So, it will take _____ minutes to spray 3,000 gallons of water.

Math Talk MATHEMATICAL PRACTICES
Explain how you can check that your answer is correct.

Try Another Problem

Dairy cows provide 90% of the world's milk supply. The table shows the amount of milk produced by a cow over time. If the pattern in the table continues, how much milk can a farmer get from a cow in 1 year (365 days)?

Cow Milk Production

Time (days), x	2	7	10	30
Amount of milk (gal), y	50	175	250	750

Read the Problem

What do I need to find?	What information do I need to use?	How will I use the information?

Solve the Problem

Math Talk **Explain** how you wrote an equation to represent the pattern in the table.

So, in 365 days, the farmer can get _____ gallons of milk from the cow.

- **Explain** how you could find the number of days it would take the cow to produce 500 gallons of milk.

_____

_____

_____

Name _____

Share and Show MATH BOARD

♀ UNLOCK the Problem **Tips**
√ Find a pattern in the table.
√ Write an equation to represent the pattern.
√ Check your answer.

1. A soccer coach is ordering shirts for the players. The table shows the total cost based on the number of shirts ordered. How much will it cost the coach to order 18 shirts?

   First, find a pattern and write an equation.

   The cost is _____ multiplied by _____.

   _____ = _____ • _____

   Next, use the equation to find the cost of 18 shirts.

   So, the cost of 18 shirts is _____.

2. **H.O.T.** **What if** the coach spent $375 to purchase a number of shirts? Could you use the same equation to find how many shirts the coach bought? Explain.

   _____

   _____

Soccer Shirts

Number of Shirts, n	2	3	5	6
Cost ($), c	30	45	75	90

3. The table shows the number of miles the Carter family drove over time. If the pattern continues, will the Carter family have driven more than 400 miles in 8 hours? **Explain.**

   _____

   _____

   _____

4. The Carter family drove a total of 564 miles. Describe how to use the pattern in the table to find the number of hours they spent driving.

   _____

   _____

   _____

Carter Family Trip

Time (hr), x	Distance (mi), y
1	47
3	141
5	235
6	282

On Your Own.............

Choose a
STRATEGY

Use a Model
Draw a Diagram
Find a Pattern
Solve a Simpler Problem
Work Backward
Use a Formula

5. A dance troupe practiced for 4 hours in March, 8 hours in April, 12 hours in May, and 16 hours in June. If the pattern continues, how many hours will they practice in November?

_____

6. The table shows the number of hours Jacob worked and the amount he earned each day.

Jacob's Earnings					
Time (hr), h	5	7	6	8	4
Amount earned ($), d	60	84	72	96	48

At the end of the week, he used his earnings to buy a new pair of skis. He had $218 left over. How much did the skis cost?

_____

SHOW YOUR WORK

7. H.O.T. **Pose a Problem** Look back at Problem 6. Use the data in the table to write a new problem in which you could use the strategy *find a pattern*. Then solve the problem.

_____

_____

8. **Write Math** ▶ Marlon rode his bicycle 9 miles the first week, 18 miles the second week, and 27 miles the third week. If the pattern continues, will Marlon ride exactly 100 miles in a week at some point? **Explain** how you determined your answer.

_____

_____

9. ⭐ **Test Prep** The table shows the total cost y for groups of x people to attend a movie.

Movie Tickets				
Group size, x	5	6	7	10
Cost ($), y	45	54	63	90

Which equation describes the pattern in the table?

(A) $y = 9 + x$ (C) $y = \frac{45}{x}$

(B) $y = 9x$ (D) $y = \frac{x}{9}$

FOR MORE PRACTICE:
Standards Practice Book, pp. P173–P174

✓ Mid-Chapter Checkpoint

▶ Vocabulary

Choose the best term from the box to complete the sentence.

1. A(n) _____ has a value that determines the value of another quantity. (p. 341)

2. A variable whose value is determined by the value of another quantity is called a(n) _____. (p. 341)

▶ Concepts and Skills

Identify the independent and dependent variables. (CC.6.EE.9)

3. Marco spends a total of d dollars on postage to mail party invitations to each of g guests.

   dependent variable: _____

   independent variable: _____

4. Sophie has a doll collection with 36 dolls. She decides to sell s dolls to a museum and has r dolls remaining.

   dependent variable: _____

   independent variable: _____

Write an equation for the relationship shown in the table. Then find the unknown value in the table. (CC.6.EE.9)

5.

x	6	7	8	9
y	42	?	56	63

_____

6.

x	20	40	60	80
y	4	8	?	16

_____

Write an equation that describes the pattern shown in the table. (CC.6.EE.9)

7. The table shows how the number of pepperoni slices used depends on the number of pizzas made.

Pepperonis Used				
Pizzas, x	2	3	5	9
Pepperoni slices, y	34	51	85	153

_____

8. Brayden is training for a marathon. The table shows how the number of miles he runs depends on which week of training he is in.

Miles Run During Training				
Week, w	3	5	8	12
Miles, m	8	10	13	17

_____

9. The band has a total of 152 members. Some of the members are in the marching band, and the rest are in the concert band. Which equation models how many marching band members *m* there are if there are *c* concert band members? (CC.6.EE.9)

(A) $m = 152 - c$

(B) $m = 152 + c$

(C) $m = 152 \times c$

(D) $m = 152 \div c$

10. A coach is ordering baseball jerseys from a website. The jerseys cost $15 each, and shipping is $8 per order. Which equation can be used to determine the total cost *y*, in dollars, for *x* jerseys? (CC.6.EE.9)

(A) $y = 8x + 15$

(B) $y = 15x + 8$

(C) $x = 8y + 15$

(D) $x = 15y + 8$

11. Amy volunteers at an animal shelter. She worked 10 hours in March, 12 hours in April, 14 hours in May, and 16 hours in June. If the pattern continues, how many hours will she work in December?

(CC.6.EE.9)

(A) 22 hours

(B) 24 hours

(C) 26 hours

(D) 28 hours

12. Aaron wants to buy a new snowboard. The table shows the amount that he has saved. If the pattern in the table continues, how much will he have saved after 1 year? (CC.6.EE.9)

(A) $450

(B) $540

(C) $630

(D) $720

Aaron's Savings	
Time (months)	Money saved ($)
3	135
4	180
6	270
7	315

Name _____

Graph Relationships

Essential Question How can you graph the relationship between two quantities?

COMMON CORE STANDARD CC.6.EE.9
Represent and analyze quantitative relationships between dependent and independent variables.

CONNECT You have learned that tables and equations are two ways to represent the relationship between two quantities. You can also represent a relationship between two quantities by using a graph.

 UNLOCK the Problem REAL WORLD

A cafeteria has an automatic pancake-making machine. The table shows the relationship between the time in hours and the number of pancakes the machine can make. Graph the relationship represented by the table.

Pancake Production	
Time (hours)	Pancakes Made
1	200
2	400
3	600
4	800
5	1,000

🔑 **Use the table values to graph the relationship.**

STEP 1 Write ordered pairs.

Let x represent the time in hours and y represent the number of pancakes made. Use each row of the table to write an ordered pair.

(1, 200) (2,_____) (3,_____) (_____ , _____) (_____ , _____)

STEP 2 Choose an appropriate scale for each axis of the graph. Label the axes and give the graph a title.

_____

STEP 3 Graph a point for each ordered pair.

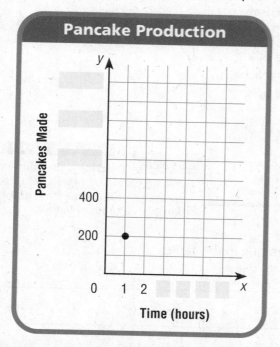

Pancake Production

Math Talk MATHEMATICAL PRACTICES
Describe any patterns you notice in the set of points you graphed.

Example The table shows the relationship between the number of bicycles y Shawn has left to assemble and the number of hours x he has worked. Graph the relationship represented by the table to find the unknown value of y.

Time (hours) x	Bicycles Left to Assemble y
0	10
1	8
2	?
3	4
4	2

STEP 1 Write ordered pairs.

Use each row of the table to write an ordered pair. Skip the row with the unknown y-value.

(0, 10)　(1, _____)　(3, _____)　(_____, _____)

STEP 2 Graph a point for each ordered pair on a coordinate plane.

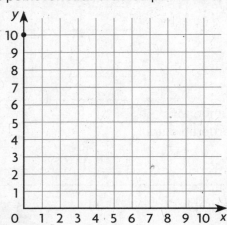

Remember

The first value in an ordered pair represents the independent variable x. The second value represents the dependent variable y.

STEP 3 Find the unknown y-value.

The points on the graph appear to lie on a line. Use a ruler to draw a dashed line through the points.

Use the line to find the y-value that corresponds to an x-value of 2. Start at the origin, and move 2 units right. Move up until you reach the line you drew. Then move left to find the y-value on the y-axis.

When x has a value of 2, y has a value of _____.

So, after 2 hours, Shawn has _____ bicycles left to assemble.

MATHEMATICAL PRACTICES

Math Talk Describe a situation in which it would be more useful to represent a function with a graph than with a table of values.

- **Describe** another way you could find the unknown value of y in the table.

_____

_____

_____

Name _____

Share and Show

Graph the relationship represented by the table.

1.

x	1	2	3	4
y	50	100	150	200

Write ordered pairs.
Then graph.

(1, 50)

(2, _____)

(3, _____)

(_____, _____)

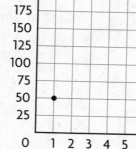

2.

x	20	40	60	80
y	100	200	300	400

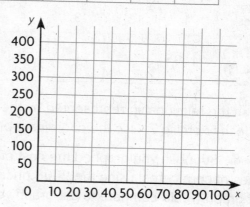

Graph the relationship represented by the table to find the unknown value of y.

3.

x	4	5	6	7	8
y	9	7	5		1

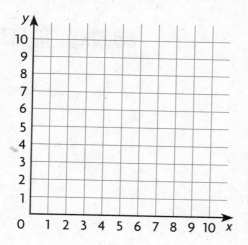

4.

x	1	3	5	7	9
y	3	4	5		7

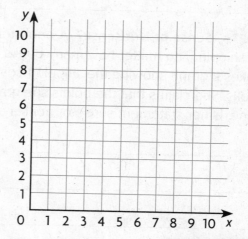

Math Talk MATHEMATICAL PRACTICES Explain how to use a graph to find an unknown y-value in a table.

On Your Own

Practice: Copy and Solve Graph the relationship represented by the table to find the unknown value of y.

5.

x	1	3	5	7	9
y	7	6		4	3

6.

x	1	2	4	6	7
y	2	3	5		8

Problem Solving REAL WORLD

The table at the right shows the typical price of a popular brand of corn cereal over time. Use the table for 7–9.

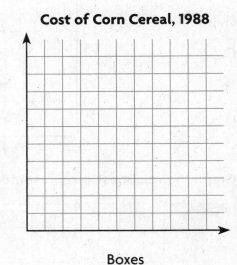

Price of Corn Cereal

Year	Price per box ($)
1968	0.39
1988	1.50
2008	4.50

7. Complete the table below to show the cost of buying 1 to 5 boxes of corn cereal in 1988.

Boxes	1	2	3	4	5
Cost in 1988 ($)	1.50				

8. Graph the relationship represented by the table you made in Exercise 7. Use the coordinate plane at right.

9. **H.O.T.** Suppose you graphed the cost of buying 1 to 5 boxes of corn cereal using the 2008 price. **Explain** how that graph would compare to the graph you made using the 1988 price.

_____

_____

_____

Cost of Corn Cereal, 1988

Cost ($)

Boxes

SHOW YOUR WORK

10. **H.O.T.** **Sense or Nonsense?** A bookstore charges $4 for shipping, no matter how many books you buy. Irena makes a graph showing the shipping cost for 1 to 5 books. She claims that the points she graphed lie on a line. Is her statement sense or nonsense? Explain.

_____

_____

_____

_____

11. ⭐ **Test Prep** DVDs cost $12 each. Jacob graphs the relationship that gives the cost y in dollars of buying x DVDs. Which ordered pair is a point on the graph of the relationship?

Ⓐ (2, 24)   Ⓒ (12, 1)

Ⓑ (3, 4)   Ⓓ (12, 12)

Name _____

Equations and Graphs

Essential Question How can you translate between equations and graphs?

COMMON CORE STANDARD CC.6.EE.9
Represent and analyze quantitative relationships between dependent and independent variables.

The solution of an equation in two variables is an ordered pair that makes the equation true. For example, $(2, 5)$ is a solution of the equation $y = x + 3$ because $5 = 2 + 3$.

A **linear equation** is an equation whose solutions form a straight line on the coordinate plane. Any point on the line is a solution of the equation.

UNLOCK the Problem REAL WORLD

A blue whale is swimming at an average rate of 3 miles per hour. Write a linear equation that gives the distance y in miles that the whale swims in x hours. Then graph the relationship.

- What formula can you use to help you write the equation?

_____

 Write and graph a linear equation.

STEP 1 Write an equation for the relationship.

Think:
Distance	equals	rate	multiplied by	time.
↓	↓	↓	↓	↓
_____	=		·	_____

STEP 2 Find ordered pairs that are solutions of the equation.

Choose several values of x and find the corresponding values of y.

x	$3x$	y	Ordered Pair
1	$3 \cdot 1$	3	(1, 3)
2	$3 \cdot$		(2,)
3	$3 \cdot$		(,)
4	$3 \cdot$		(,)

STEP 3 Graph the relationship.

Graph the ordered pairs. Draw a line through the points to show all the solutions of the linear equation.

Distance Traveled by Blue Whale

(graph with y-axis "Distance (mi)" marked 2, 4, 6, 8, 10, 12, 14, 16, 18, 20 and x-axis "Time (hr)" marked 0 1 2 3 4 5 6 7 8 9 10, with point plotted at (1, 3))

Math Talk MATHEMATICAL PRACTICES Explain why the graph does not show negative values of x or y.

Chapter 9   359

🔑 Example

The graph shows the number of beaded necklaces *y* that Ginger can make in *x* hours. Write the linear equation for the relationship shown by the graph.

STEP 1 Use ordered pairs from the graph to complete the table of values below.

STEP 2 Look for a pattern in the table.

Compare each *y*-value with the corresponding *x*-value.

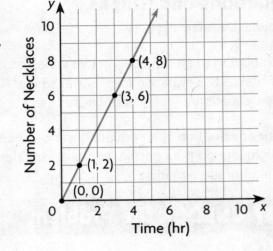

Necklaces Made

x	0	1	3	4
y	0			

↑ 2 · 0   ↑ 2 · 1   ↑ 2 · _____   ↑ 2 · _____

Think: Each *y*-value is _____ times the corresponding *x*-value.

So, the linear equation for the relationship is *y* = _____.

1. **Explain** how to graph a linear equation. _____

_____

_____

2. **Describe** a situation in which it would be more useful to represent a relationship with an equation than with a graph.

_____

_____

Share and Show ·

Graph the linear equation.

1. *y* = *x* − 2

Make a table of values. Then graph.

x	y
2	0
4	
6	
8	

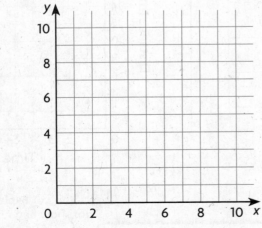

✓ 2. *y* = 3*x*

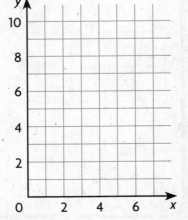

Name _____

Write the linear equation for the relationship shown by the graph.

✓ 3.

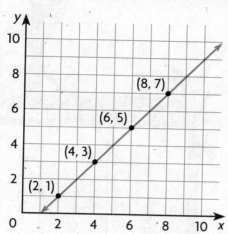

4.

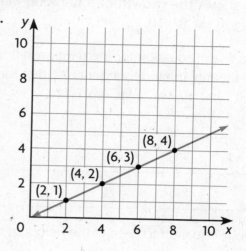

_____

Math Talk MATHEMATICAL PRACTICES
Explain how you can tell whether you have graphed a linear equation correctly.

On Your Own . . . .

Graph the linear equation.

5. $y = x + 1$

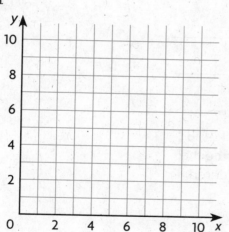

6. $y = 2x - 1$

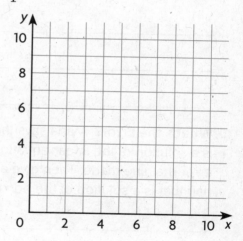

7. The graph shows the number of loaves of bread y that Kareem bakes in x hours. Write the linear equation for the relationship shown by the graph.

_____

Loaves of Bread Baked

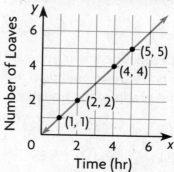

Problem Solving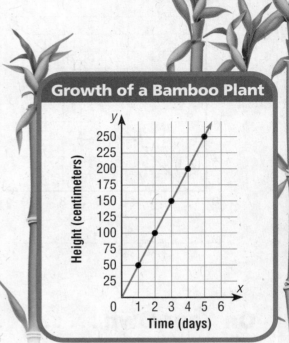

REAL WORLD

The graph shows the growth of a bamboo plant.
Use the graph for 8–10.

8. Write a linear equation for the relationship shown by the graph. Identify the independent and dependent variables, and tell what the variables represent.

_____

_____

_____,

9. Use your equation to predict the height of the bamboo plant after 7 days.

_____

10. **H.O.T.** The height y in centimeters of a second bamboo plant is given by the equation $y = 30x$, where x is the time in days. **Describe** how the graph showing the growth of this plant would compare to the graph showing the growth of the first plant.

_____

_____

_____

Growth of a Bamboo Plant

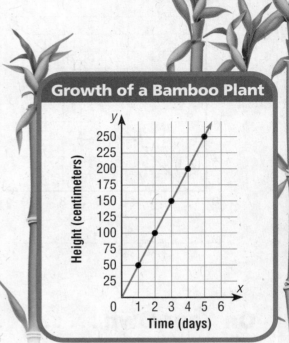

11. **What's the Error?** Maria says that the ordered pair (14, 8) is a solution of the linear equation $y = x + 6$. **Describe** the error that she made. Then give an example of an ordered pair that is a solution of the equation.

_____

_____

_____

12. ⭐ **Test Prep** The linear equation $y = 7x$ represents the cost y in dollars of x pounds of trail mix. Which ordered pair lies on the graph of the equation?

Ⓐ (0, 7)   Ⓒ (4, 11)

Ⓑ (3, 21)   Ⓓ (7, 1)

· · · · · · **SHOW YOUR WORK** · · · · · ·

FOR MORE PRACTICE:
Standards Practice Book, pp. P177–P178

Name _____

 Chapter 9 Review/Test

▶ **Vocabulary**

Choose the best term from the box to complete the sentence.

1. A(n) _____ has a value that is determined by the value of another quantity. (p. 341)

2. The solutions of a(n) _____ form a straight line on the coordinate plane. (p. 359)

▶ **Concepts and Skills**

Identify the independent and dependent variables. (CC.6.EE.9)

3. A shoe store had a profit of d dollars on Monday by selling s pairs of shoes.

    dependent variable: _____

    independent variable: _____

4. Cassidy wants to run 20 miles in one week. Today, she ran m miles and now she has r miles remaining.

    dependent variable: _____

    independent variable: _____

Write an equation for the relationship shown in the table. Then find the unknown value in the table. (CC.6.EE.9)

5.

x	76	77	78	79
y	?	69	70	71

_____

6.

x	3	5	7	9
y	12	20	28	?

_____

Write an equation that describes the pattern shown in the table. (CC.6.EE.9)

7. A lawn care company gains new customers when they distribute flyers. The table shows how the number of customers gained depends on the flyers.

Customers Gained				
Flyers, f	20	60	80	200
Customers, c	1	3	4	10

_____

8. Reina earns points for extra credit assignments. The table shows how the number of points she earns depends on the number of assignments.

Extra Credit Earned				
Assignments, a	3	4	7	9
Points, p	15	20	35	45

_____

GO Online Assessment Options
Chapter Test

Fill in the bubble to show your answer.

9. There are *s* school days in one year. Which equation shows the relationship between *s* and *n*, the number of non-school days in a year? (CC.6.EE.9)

Ⓐ $n = 365 + s$

Ⓑ $n = 365 \times s$

Ⓒ $n = 365 - s$

Ⓓ $n = 365 \div s$

10. A landlord at an apartment building charges $1,500 per month for renting an apartment. He also requires a one-time deposit of $1,000. Which equation can be used to determine the total amount *y* in dollars the landlord collects from someone who rents an apartment from him for *x* months? (CC.6.EE.9)

Ⓐ $y = 1,500x + 1,000$

Ⓑ $y = 1,000x + 1,500$

Ⓒ $x = 1,500y + 1,000$

Ⓓ $x = 1,000y + 1,500$

11. A scuba diver descends to various depths during a dive, as shown in the table. If the pattern in the table continues, how deep will the diver be after 30 minutes? (CC.6.EE.9)

Diving Depth	
Time (min)	Depth (ft)
4	8
5	10
10	20
12	24

Ⓐ 30 feet

Ⓑ 34 feet

Ⓒ 42 feet

Ⓓ 60 feet

12. An author wrote 3 pages during the first week of writing, 6 pages the second week, 9 pages the third week, and 12 pages the fourth week. If this pattern continues, how many pages will she write during her twelfth week of writing? (CC.6.EE.9)

Ⓐ 36 pages

Ⓑ 40 pages

Ⓒ 48 pages

Ⓓ 52 pages

Fill in the bubble to show your answer.

13. The table shows the cost of renting a bicycle. Which set of ordered pairs could be used to graph the relationship shown in the table? (CC.6.EE.9)

Bicycle Rental Costs	
Time (hours), *x*	Cost ($), *y*
2	10
3	15
4	20
5	25

Ⓐ (2, 10), (3, 15), (4, 20), (5, 25)

Ⓑ (2, 3), (4, 5), (10, 15), (20, 25)

Ⓒ (10, 2), (15, 3), (20, 4), (25, 5)

Ⓓ (3, 2), (5, 4), (15, 10), (25, 20)

14. Rajiv pays 19 cents per kilowatt-hour for electricity. His bill shows a graph of the cost *y* in cents of using *x* kilowatt-hours. Which ordered pair is a point on the graph? (CC.6.EE.9)

Ⓐ (19, 1)

Ⓑ (38, 2)

Ⓒ (0, 19)

Ⓓ (3, 57)

15. The linear equation $y = 12x$ represents the cost *y* in dollars for *x* friends to go to the movies. Which ordered pair lies on the graph of this equation? (CC.6.EE.9)

Ⓐ (1, 24)

Ⓑ (4, 48)

Ⓒ (2, 14)

Ⓓ (12, 12)

16. The graph shows the distance an elevator travels over time. Which equation represents the relationship shown in the graph, where *x* is the time in seconds and *y* is the distance traveled in feet? (CC.6.EE.9)

Ⓐ $y = x + 20$

Ⓑ $y = x - 20$

Ⓒ $y = 20x$

Ⓓ $y = \frac{x}{20}$

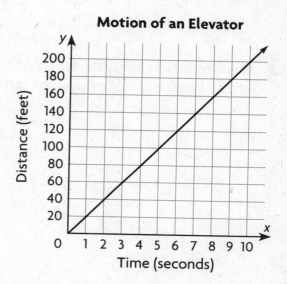

Motion of an Elevator

▶ Constructed Response

17. Nina graphs her cost of gasoline *y* in dollars based on the amount *x* in gallons that she purchases. How will her graph change if the price per gallon of gasoline doubles? Explain. (CC.6.EE.9)

_____

_____

_____

▶ Performance Task

18. The table shows the relationship between the amount Janice earns and the number of hours she babysits. (CC.6.EE.9)

Janice's Earnings	
Time (hours), *x*	Earnings ($), *y*
1	8
2	16
3	24
4	32
5	40

Ⓐ Graph the relationship represented by the table.

Janice's Earnings

Ⓑ Write an equation for the relationship represented by the table.

_____

Ⓒ Janice wants to earn $200 this month. If she babysits for 30 hours, will she be able to make her goal? Explain.

Geometry and Statistics

COMMON CORE

Solve real-world and mathematical problems involving area, surface area, and volume.

CRITICAL AREA Developing understanding of statistical thinking

The Columbus Zoo, in Columbus, Ohio, is home to hundreds of different animals, including the Amur tiger.

Project

This Place is a Zoo!

Planning a zoo is a difficult task. Each animal requires a special environment with different amounts of space and different features.

Get Started

You are helping to design a new section of a zoo. The table lists some of the new attractions planned for the zoo. Each attraction includes notes about the type and the amount of space needed. The zoo owns a rectangle of land that is 100 feet long and 60 feet wide. Find the dimensions of each of the attractions and draw a sketch of the plan for the zoo.

Important Facts

Attraction	Minimum Floor Space (sq ft)	Notes
American Alligators	400	rectangular pen with one side at least 24 feet long
Amur Tigers	750	trapezoid-shaped area with one side at least 40 feet long
Howler Monkeys	450	parallelogram-shaped cage with one side at least 30 feet long
Meerkat Village	250	square pen with glass sides
Red Foxes	350	rectangular pen with length twice as long as width
Tropical Aquarium	200	triangular bottom with base at least 20 feet long

Completed by _____

Show What You Know ✓

Check your understanding of important skills.

Name _____

▶ **Perimeter** Find the perimeter.

1.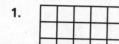

   $P =$ _____ units

2.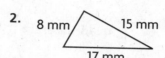

   8 mm   15 mm

   17 mm $P =$ _____ mm

▶ **Identify Polygons** Name each polygon based on the number of sides.

3.

   _____

4.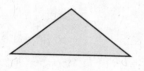

   _____

5.

   _____

▶ **Evaluate Algebraic Expressions** Evaluate the expression.

6. $5x + 2y$ for $x = 7$
   and $y = 9$

   _____

7. $6a \times 3b + 4$ for $a = 2$
   and $b = 8$

   _____

8. $s^2 + t^2 - 2^3$ for $s = 4$
   and $t = 6$

   _____

MATH DETECTIVE

WITH

CARMEN SANDIEGO™

Ross needs to paint the white boundary lines of one end zone on a football field. The area of the end zone is 4,800 square feet, and one side of the end zone measures 30 feet. One can of paint is enough to paint 300 feet of line. Be a Math Detective and find out if one can is enough to line the perimeter of the end zone.

30ft

GO Online   Assessment Options: **Soar to Success Math**

Vocabulary Builder

▶ **Visualize It** •

Complete the bubble map by using the checked words that are types of quadrilaterals.

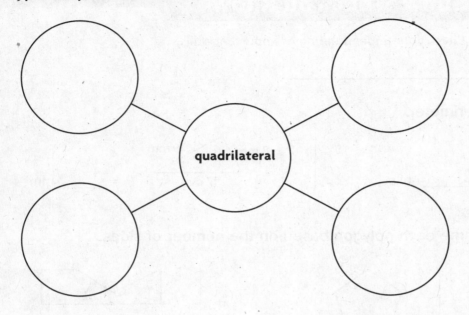

Review Words

acute triangle

base

height

obtuse triangle

✓ polygon

quadrilateral

✓ rectangle

right triangle

✓ square

Preview Words

area

composite figure

congruent

✓ parallelogram

regular polygon

✓ trapezoid

▶ **Understand Vocabulary** •

Complete the sentences using the preview words.

1. The _____ of a figure is the number of square units needed to cover it without any gaps or overlaps.

2. A polygon in which all sides are the same length and all angles have the same measure is called a(n) _____.

3. A(n) _____ is a quadrilateral with exactly one pair of parallel sides.

4. _____ figures have the same size and shape.

5. A quadrilateral with two pairs of parallel sides is called a _____.

6. A(n) _____ is made up of more than one shape.

GO Online • eStudent Edition • Multimedia eGlossary

Area of Parallelograms

Essential Question How can you find the area of parallelograms?

COMMON CORE STANDARDS CC.6.G.1, CC.6.EE.7
Solve real-world and mathematical problems involving area, surface area, and volume.

CONNECT The **area** of a figure is the number of square units needed to cover it without any gaps or overlaps. The area of a rectangle is the product of the length and the width. The rectangle shown has an area of 12 square units. For a rectangle with length l and width w, $A = l \times w$, or $A = lw$.

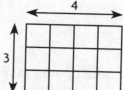

Recall that a rectangle is a special type of parallelogram. A parallelogram is a quadrilateral with two pairs of parallel sides.

🔑 UNLOCK the Problem ▸ REAL WORLD

Lorene is making a quilt. She is using material in the shape of parallelograms to form the pattern. The base of each parallelogram measures 9 cm and the height measures 4 cm. What is the area of each parallelogram?

🔑 Activity Use the area of a rectangle to find the area of the parallelogram.

Materials ■ grid paper ■ scissors

* Draw the parallelogram on grid paper and cut it out.
* Cut along the dashed line to remove a triangle.
* Move the triangle to the right side of the figure to form a rectangle.

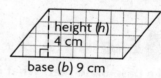

base (b) 9 cm

* What is the area of the rectangle? _____

* What is the area of the parallelogram? _____

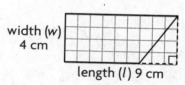

length (l) 9 cm

* base of parallelogram = _____ of rectangle

  height of parallelogram = _____ of rectangle

  area of parallelogram = _____ of rectangle

* For a parallelogram with base b and height h, $A =$ _____

Area of parallelogram = $b \times h$ = 9 cm $\times$ 4 cm = _____ sq cm

So, the area of each parallelogram in the quilt is _____ sq cm.

Math Idea
The height of a parallelogram forms a 90° angle with the base.

Math Talk MATHEMATICAL PRACTICES
Explain how you know that the area of the parallelogram is the same as the area of the rectangle.

🔑 Example 1 Use the formula $A = bh$ to find the area of the parallelogram.

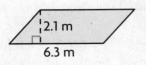
2.1 m
6.3 m

Write the formula. $A = bh$

Replace b and h with their values. $A = 6.3 \times$ _____

Multiply. $A =$ _____

So, the area of the parallelogram is _____ square meters.

A square is a special rectangle in which the length and width are equal.
For a square with side length s, $A = l \times w = s \times s = s^2$, or $A = s^2$.

🔑 Example 2 Find the area of a square with sides measuring 9.5 cm.

9.5 cm

9.5 cm

Write the formula. $A = s^2$

Substitute 9.5 for s. Simplify. $A = ($_____$)^2 =$ _____

So, the area of the square is _____ cm^2.

🔑 Example 3 A parallelogram has an area of 98 square feet and a base of 14 feet. What is the height of the parallelogram?

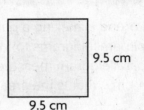
?   Area = 98 ft^2
14 ft

Write the formula. $A = bh$

Replace A and b with their values.   _____ = _____ $\times h$

Use the Division Property of Equality. $\dfrac{98}{} = \dfrac{14h}{}$

Solve for h.   _____ $= h$

So, the height of the parallelogram is _____ feet.

- **Explain** the difference between the height of a rectangle and the height of a parallelogram.

_____

_____

_____

Name _____

Share and Show

Find the area of the figure.

1. $A = bh$

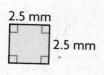

1.2 m
8.3 m

$A = 8.3 \times 1.2$

$A = $ _____ m²

2.

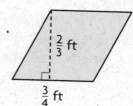

7 ft
12 ft

_____ ft²

3.   2.5 mm

2.5 mm

_____ mm²

4.

$\frac{2}{3}$ ft

$\frac{3}{4}$ ft

_____ ft²

Find the unknown measurement for the figure.

5.   Area = 11 yd²

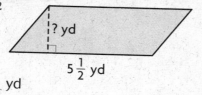

? yd

$5\frac{1}{2}$ yd

_____ yd

6.   Area = 36 yd²

? yd

4 yd

_____ yd

Math Talk   MATHEMATICAL PRACTICES

Explain how the areas of some parallelograms and rectangles are related.

On Your Own

Find the area of the figure.

7.

6.4 m

9.1 m

_____ m²

8.

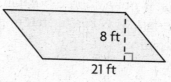

8 ft

21 ft

_____ ft²

Find the unknown measurement for the figure.

9. square

$A = $ _____

$s = 15$ ft

10. parallelogram

$A = 32$ m²

$b = $ _____

$h = 8$ m

11. parallelogram

$A = 51\frac{1}{4}$ in.²

$b = 8\frac{1}{5}$ in.

$h = $ _____

12. parallelogram

$A = 121$ mm²

$b = 11$ mm

$h = $ _____

13. **H.O.T.** The height of a parallelogram is four times the base. The base measures $3\frac{1}{2}$ ft. Find the area of the parallelogram.

_____

Problem Solving REAL WORLD

14. Jane's backyard is shaped like a parallelogram. The base of the parallelogram is 90 feet, and the height, measured from the back of the yard to the front, is 25 feet. What is the area of Jane's backyard?

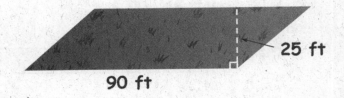
90 ft · 25 ft

_____

15. H.O.T. Jack made a parallelogram by putting together two congruent triangles and a square, like the figures shown at the right. The triangles have the same height as the square. What is the area of Jack's parallelogram?

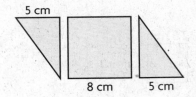
5 cm · 8 cm · 5 cm

_____

16. A playground is in the shape of a parallelogram with a base of 34 meters and a height of 20 meters. What is the area of the playground?

_____

SHOW YOUR WORK

17. The base of a parallelogram is 2 times the parallelogram's height. If the base is 12 inches, what is the area?

_____

18. H.O.T. **Sense or Nonsense?** Li Ping says that a square with 3-inch sides has a greater area than a parallelogram that is not a square but has sides that have the same length. Is Li Ping's statement sense or nonsense? **Explain.**

_____

_____

_____

_____

19. ⭐ **Test Prep** What is the area of a parallelogram with a base of 22 inches and a height of 48 inches?

Ⓐ 70 square inches Ⓒ 956 square inches

Ⓑ 156 square inches Ⓓ 1,056 square inches

Explore Area of Triangles

Essential Question What is the relationship among the areas of triangles, rectangles, and parallelograms?

COMMON CORE STANDARD CC.6.G.1
Solve real-world and mathematical problems involving area, surface area, and volume.

Investigate

Materials ■ tracing paper ■ ruler ■ scissors

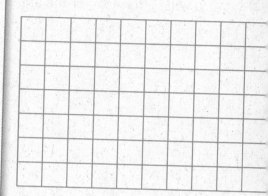

A. On the grid, draw a rectangle with a base of 6 units and a height of 5 units.

- What is the area of the rectangle?

  _____

B. Trace the rectangle onto tracing paper. Draw a diagonal from the top-left corner to the lower-right corner.

- A diagonal is a line segment that connects two nonadjacent vertices of a polygon.

C. Cut out the rectangle. Then cut along the diagonal to divide the rectangle into two right triangles. Compare the two triangles.

- **Congruent** figures are the same shape and size. Are the two right triangles congruent?

  _____

  _____

- How is the area of each right triangle related to the area of the rectangle?

  _____

  _____

- What is the area of each right triangle?

  _____

Draw Conclusions

1. **Explain** how finding the area of a rectangle is like finding the area of a right triangle. How is it different?

_____

_____

2. **Analyze** Because a rectangle is a parallelogram, its area can be found using the formula $A = b \times h$. Use this formula and your results from the Investigate to write a formula for the area of a right triangle with base b and height h.

_____

> **Math Talk** MATHEMATICAL PRACTICES
> Why did the two triangles have to be congruent for the formula to make sense?

Make Connections

The area of any parallelogram, including a rectangle, can be found using the formula $A = b \times h$. You can use a parallelogram to look at more triangles.

A. Trace and cut out two copies of the acute triangle.

B. Arrange the two triangles to make a parallelogram.

- Are the triangles congruent? _____

- If the area of the parallelogram is 10 square centimeters, what is the area of each triangle? **Explain** how you know.

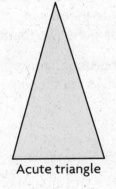

Acute triangle

_____

_____

_____

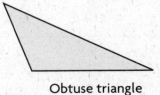

C. Repeat Steps A and B with the obtuse triangle.

Obtuse triangle

3. **Generalize** Can you use the formula $A = \frac{1}{2} \times b \times h$ to find the area of any triangle? Explain.

_____

_____

Name _____

Share and Show

1. Trace the parallelogram, and cut it into two congruent triangles. Find the areas of the parallelogram and one triangle, using square units.

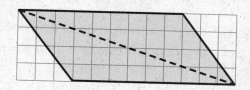

_____

Find the area of each triangle.

2.

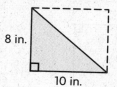

8 in.

10 in.

_____ in.²

✓ **3.**

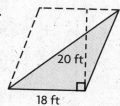

20 ft

18 ft

_____ ft²

✓ **4.**

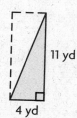

11 yd

4 yd

_____ yd²

5.

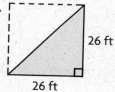

26 ft

26 ft

_____ ft²

6.

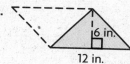

6 in.

12 in.

_____ in.²

7.

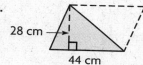

28 cm

44 cm

_____ cm²

8.

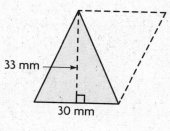

33 mm

30 mm

_____ mm²

9.

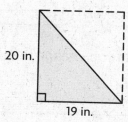

20 in.

19 in.

_____ in.²

10.

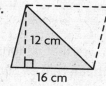

12 cm

16 cm

_____ cm²

11. **Write Math** ▶ Describe how you can use two triangles of the same shape and size to form a parallelogram.

_____

Problem Solving REAL WORLD

H.O.T. Sense or Nonsense?

12. Cyndi and Tyson drew the models below. Each said his or her drawing represents a triangle with an area of 600 square inches. Whose statement makes sense? Whose statement is nonsense? **Explain** your reasoning.

Tyson's Model

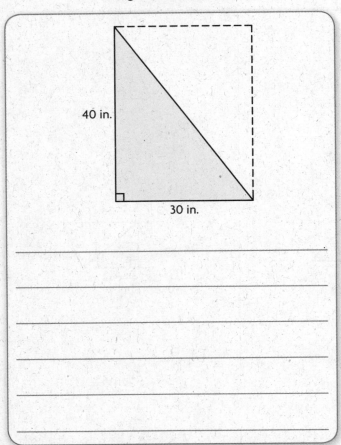

40 in.

30 in.

Cyndi's Model

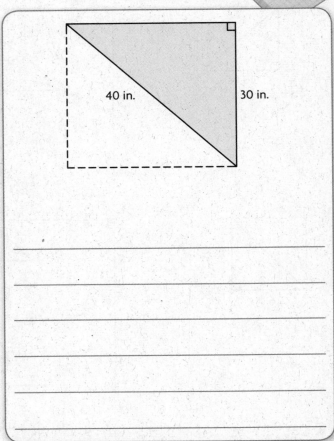

40 in.   30 in.

_____

_____

_____

_____

_____

- For the answer that is nonsense, how could you change the model so that it makes sense?

_____

_____

_____

- What would be the area of Tyson's triangle if the dimensions of both the base and height were divided by 2?

_____

Name _____

Area of Triangles

Essential Question How can you find the area of triangles?

COMMON CORE STANDARD CC.6.G.1
Solve real-world and mathematical problems involving area, surface area, and volume.

Any parallelogram can be divided into two congruent triangles. The area of each triangle is half the area of the parallelogram, so the area of a triangle is half the product of its base and its height.

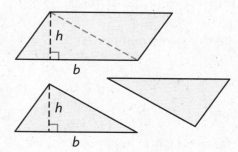

Area of a Triangle

$$A = \frac{1}{2} bh$$

where b is the base and h is the height

 UNLOCK the Problem REAL WORLD

The Flatiron Building in New York is well known for its unusual shape. The building was designed to fit the triangular plot of land formed by 22nd Street, Broadway, and Fifth Avenue. The diagram shows the dimensions of the triangular foundation of the building. What is the area of the triangle?

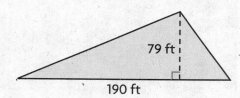

79 ft

190 ft

🔑 **Find the area of the triangle.**

Write the formula. $A = \frac{1}{2} bh$

Substitute 190 for b and 79 for h. $A = \frac{1}{2} \times \underline{\hspace{1cm}} \times \underline{\hspace{1cm}}$

Multiply the base and height. $A = \frac{1}{2} \times \underline{\hspace{1cm}}$

Multiply by $\frac{1}{2}$. $A = \underline{\hspace{1cm}}$

So, the area of the triangle is _____ ft².

• How can you identify the base and the height of the triangle?

_____

_____

_____

_____

Math Talk MATHEMATICAL PRACTICES
Explain how the area of a triangle relates to the area of a rectangle with the same base and height.

🔑 Example 1 Find the area of the triangle.

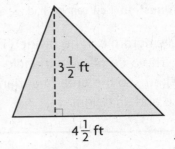

$3\frac{1}{2}$ ft

$4\frac{1}{2}$ ft

Write the formula. 　$A = \frac{1}{2}bh$

Substitute $4\frac{1}{2}$ for b and $3\frac{1}{2}$ for h. 　$A = \frac{1}{2} \times \rule{1.5cm}{0.4pt} \times \rule{1.5cm}{0.4pt}$

Rewrite the mixed numbers as fractions. 　$A = \frac{1}{2} \times \dfrac{\boxed{}}{2} \times \dfrac{\boxed{}}{2}$

Multiply. 　$A = \dfrac{\boxed{}}{8}$

Rewrite the fraction as a mixed number. 　$A = \rule{1.5cm}{0.4pt}$

So, the area of the triangle is \rule{1.5cm}{0.4pt} ft^2.

🔑 Example 2

Daniella is decorating a triangular pennant for her wall. The area of the pennant is 225 in.^{2} and the base measures 30 in. What is the height of the triangular pennant?

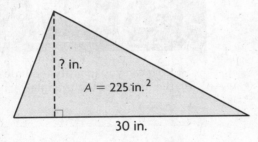

? in.

$A = 225$ in.^{2}

30 in.

Write the formula. 　$A = \frac{1}{2}bh$

Substitute 225 for A and 30 for b. 　$\rule{1.5cm}{0.4pt} = \frac{1}{2} \times \rule{1.5cm}{0.4pt} \times h$

Multiply $\frac{1}{2}$ and 30. 　$225 = \rule{1.5cm}{0.4pt} \times h$

Use the Division Property of Equality. 　$\dfrac{225}{\boxed{}} = \dfrac{\boxed{} \times h}{\boxed{}}$

Simplify. 　$\rule{1.5cm}{0.4pt} = h$

So, the height of the triangular pennant is \rule{1.5cm}{0.4pt} in.

Name _____

Share and Show

· ·

1. Find the area of the triangle.

$A = \frac{1}{2}bh$

$A = \frac{1}{2} \times 14 \times$ _____

$A =$ _____ cm^2

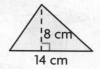

2. The area of the triangle is 132 in.^{2} Find the height of the triangle.

$h =$ _____

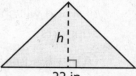

Find the area of the triangle.

3.

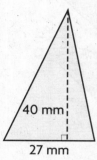

$A =$ _____

4.

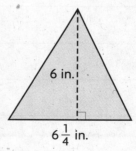

$A =$ _____

Math Talk MATHEMATICAL PRACTICES
Explain how you can identify the height of a triangle.

On Your Own

· ·

Find the area of the triangle.

5.

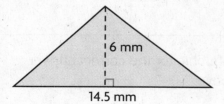

$A =$ _____

6.

6 in.

$6\frac{1}{4}$ in.

$A =$ _____

 H.O.T. **Find the unknown measurement for the figure.**

7. Area = 52.5 in.^{2}

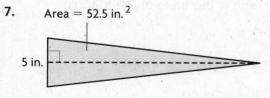

5 in.

$h =$ _____

8.

Area = 14.95 cm^2

h

23 mm

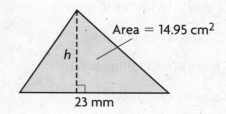

$h =$ _____

© Houghton Mifflin Harcourt Publishing Company

UNLOCK the Problem

9. Sarah is building a set of 4 shelves. Each shelf will have 2 supports in the shape of right isosceles triangles. Each shelf is 14 inches deep. How many square inches of wood will she need to make all of the supports?

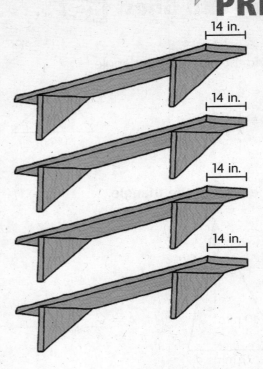

14 in.

14 in.

14 in.

14 in.

Ⓐ 98 square inches

Ⓑ 196 square inches

Ⓒ 392 square inches

Ⓓ 784 square inches

a. What are the base and height of each triangle?

_____

b. What formula can you use to find the area of a triangle?

_____

c. Explain how you can find the area of one triangular support.

_____

_____

_____

_____

d. How many triangular supports are needed to build 4 shelves?

_____

e. How many square inches of wood will Sarah need to make all the supports?

_____

f. Fill in the bubble for the correct answer choice above.

10. Daniel is building a model sailboat with a triangular sail. The base of the sail measures 6 centimeters and the height measures 9 centimeters. What is the area of the sail?

Ⓐ 4.5 square centimeters

Ⓑ 13.5 square centimeters

Ⓒ 27 square centimeters

Ⓓ 54 square centimeters

11. Joni is planting a triangular garden. The area of the garden is 11.5 square meters and the height of the triangle measures 5 meters. How long is the base of the triangle?

Ⓐ 2.3 meters

Ⓑ 4.6 meters

Ⓒ 28.75 meters

Ⓓ 57.5 meters

FOR MORE PRACTICE:
Standards Practice Book, pp. P187–P188

Explore Area of Trapezoids

Essential Question What is the relationship between the areas of trapezoids and parallelograms?

COMMON CORE STANDARD CC.6.G.1
Solve real-world and mathematical problems involving area, surface area, and volume.

CONNECT A **trapezoid** is a quadrilateral with exactly one pair of parallel sides. The parallel sides are the *bases* of the trapezoid. A line segment drawn at a 90° angle to the two bases is the *height* of the trapezoid. You can use what you know about the area of a parallelogram to find the area of a trapezoid.

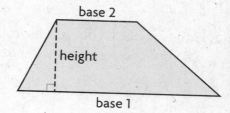

Investigate

Materials ■ grid paper ■ ruler ■ scissors

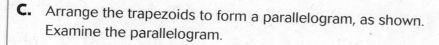

A. Draw two copies of the trapezoid on grid paper.

B. Cut out the trapezoids.

C. Arrange the trapezoids to form a parallelogram, as shown. Examine the parallelogram.

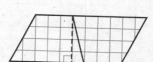

• How can you find the length of the base of the parallelogram?

_____

_____

• The base of the parallelogram is _____ + _____ = _____ units.

• The height of the parallelogram is _____ units.

• The area of the parallelogram is _____ × _____ = _____ square units.

D. Examine the trapezoids.

• How does the area of one trapezoid relate to the area of the parallelogram?

_____

_____

• Find the area of one trapezoid. Explain how you found the area.

_____

_____

Draw Conclusions

1. **Explain** how knowing how to find the area of a parallelogram helped you find the area of the trapezoid.

   _____

2. **Analyze** Use your results from the Investigate to describe how you can find the area of any trapezoid.

   _____

   _____

   _____

3. **Generalize** Can you use the method you described above to find the area of a trapezoid if two copies of the trapezoid can be arranged to form a rectangle? Explain.

   _____

   _____

Make Connections

You can use the formula for the area of a rectangle to find the area of some types of trapezoids.

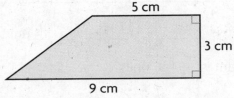

5 cm

3 cm

9 cm

A. Trace and cut out two copies of the trapezoid.

B. Arrange the two trapezoids to form a rectangle. Examine the rectangle.

- The length of the rectangle is _____ + _____ = _____ cm.

- The width of the rectangle is _____ cm.

- The area of the rectangle is _____ × _____ = _____ cm^2.

C. Examine the trapezoids.

- How does the area of each trapezoid relate to the area of the rectangle?

  _____

- The area of the given trapezoid is $\frac{1}{2}$ × _____ = _____ cm^2.

Name _____

Share and Show

1. Trace and cut out two copies of the trapezoid. Arrange the trapezoids to form a parallelogram. Find the areas of the parallelogram and one trapezoid using square units.

_____

Find the area of the trapezoid.

2.
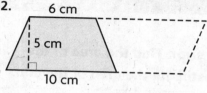
6 cm
5 cm
10 cm

_____ cm²

3.
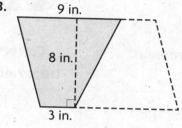
9 in.
8 in.
3 in.

_____ in.²

4.
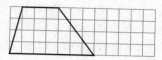
7 m
9 m
12 m

_____ m²

5.
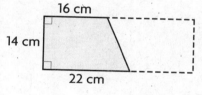
16 cm
14 cm
22 cm

_____ cm²

6.
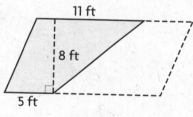
11 ft
8 ft
5 ft

_____ ft²

7.
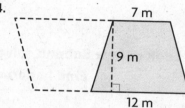
50 in.
12 in.
24 in.

_____ in.²

8.
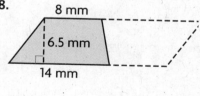
8 mm
6.5 mm
14 mm

_____ mm²

9.
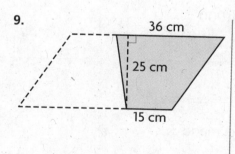
36 cm
25 cm
15 cm

_____ cm²

10.
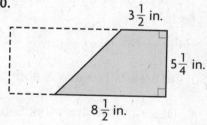
$3\frac{1}{2}$ in.
$5\frac{1}{4}$ in.
$8\frac{1}{2}$ in.

_____ in.²

11. **Write Math** ▸ **Explain** why, in Exercise 1 above, it is important that the trapezoids you use to form the parallelogram be the same shape and size.

_____

_____

Problem Solving  REAL WORLD

H.O.T. What's the Error?

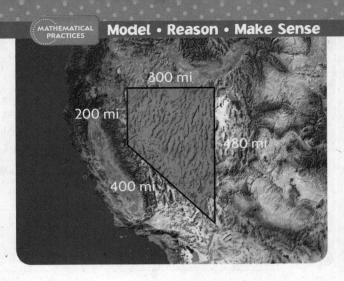

300 mi
200 mi
480 mi
400 mi

12. Except for a small region near its southeast corner, the state of Nevada is shaped like a trapezoid. The map at the right shows the approximate dimensions of the trapezoid. Sabrina used the map to estimate the area of Nevada.

Look at how Sabrina solved the problem. Find her error.

Correct the error. Find the area of the trapezoid to estimate the area of Nevada.

Two copies of the trapezoid can be put together to form a rectangle.

length of rectangle:

$200 + 480 = 680$ mi

width of rectangle: 300 mi

$$A = lw$$

$$= 680 \times 300$$

$$= 204,000$$

The area of Nevada is about 204,000 square miles.

So, the area of Nevada is about _____ mi².

- Describe the error that Sabrina made.

_____

_____

- Explain how you could check that your answer is correct.

_____

_____

FOR MORE PRACTICE:
Standards Practice Book, pp. P189–P190

Area of Trapezoids

Essential Question How can you find the area of trapezoids?

COMMON CORE STANDARD CC.6.G.1
Solve real-world and mathematical problems involving area, surface area, and volume.

Any parallelogram can be divided into two trapezoids with the same shape and size. The bases of the trapezoids, b_1 and b_2, form the base of the parallelogram. The area of each trapezoid is half the area of the parallelogram. So, the area of a trapezoid is half the product of its height and the sum of its bases.

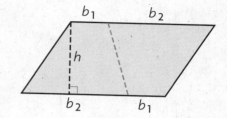

> ### Area of a Trapezoid
>
> $$A = \frac{1}{2}(b_1 + b_2)h$$
>
> where b_1 and b_2 are the two bases and h is the height

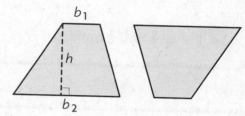

🔑 UNLOCK the Problem REAL WORLD

Mr. Desmond has tables in his office with tops shaped like trapezoids. The diagram shows the dimensions of each tabletop. What is the area of each tabletop?

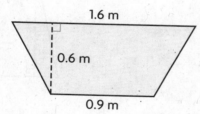

1.6 m
0.6 m
0.9 m

- How can you identify the bases?

_____

_____

- How can you identify the height?

_____

_____

🔒 **Find the area of the trapezoid.**

Write the formula.

$$A = \frac{1}{2}(b_1 + b_2)h$$

Substitute 1.6 for b_1, 0.9 for b_2, and 0.6 for h.

$$A = \frac{1}{2} \times (\underline{\hspace{1cm}} + \underline{\hspace{1cm}}) \times \underline{\hspace{1cm}}$$

Add within the parentheses.

$$A = \frac{1}{2} \times \underline{\hspace{1cm}} \times 0.6$$

Multiply.

$$A = \frac{1}{2} \times \underline{\hspace{1cm}} = \underline{\hspace{1cm}}$$

So, the area of each tabletop is _____ m².

Math Talk

MATHEMATICAL PRACTICES

Describe the relationship between the area of a trapezoid and the area of a parallelogram with the same height and a base equal to the sum of the trapezoid's bases.

🔑 Example 1 Find the area of the trapezoid.

Write the formula.

$$A = \frac{1}{2}(b_1 + b_2)h$$

Substitute 4.6 for b_1, 9.4 for b_2, and 4.5 for h.

$$A = \frac{1}{2} \times (\underline{\hspace{1cm}} + \underline{\hspace{1cm}}) \times 4.5$$

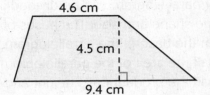

4.6 cm

4.5 cm

9.4 cm

Add.

$$A = \frac{1}{2} \times \underline{\hspace{1cm}} \times 4.5$$

Multiply.

$$A = \underline{\hspace{1cm}} \times 4.5 = \underline{\hspace{1cm}}$$

So, the area of the trapezoid is _____ cm².

🔑 Example 2 The area of the trapezoid is 702 in.² Find the height of the trapezoid.

Write the formula.

$$A = \frac{1}{2}(b_1 + b_2)h$$

Substitute 702 for A, 20 for b_1, and 34 for b_2.

$$702 = \frac{1}{2} \times (20 + \underline{\hspace{1cm}}) \times h$$

Add within the parentheses.

$$702 = \frac{1}{2} \times \underline{\hspace{1cm}} \times h$$

Multiply $\frac{1}{2}$ and 54.

$$702 = \underline{\hspace{1cm}} \times h$$

Use the Division Property of Equality.

$$\frac{702}{\underline{\hphantom{x}}} = \frac{\underline{\hphantom{x}} \times h}{\underline{\hphantom{x}}}$$

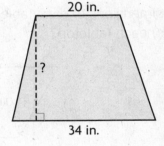

20 in.

?

34 in.

Simplify.

$$\underline{\hspace{1cm}} = h$$

So, the height of the trapezoid is _____ in.

Math Talk

MATHEMATICAL PRACTICES

Explain how to find the height of a trapezoid if you know the area and the lengths of both bases.

- **Explain** why the formula for the area of a trapezoid contains the expression $b_1 + b_2$.

_____

_____

_____

_____

Name _____

Share and Show

1. Find the area of the trapezoid.

$A = \frac{1}{2}(b_1 + b_2)h$

$A = \frac{1}{2} \times (\underline{\hspace{1cm}} + \underline{\hspace{1cm}}) \times 4$

$A = \frac{1}{2} \times \underline{\hspace{1cm}} \times 4$

$A = \underline{\hspace{1cm}} \text{ cm}^2$

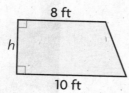

2. The area of the trapezoid is 45 ft². Find the height of the trapezoid.

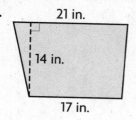

$h = \underline{\hspace{2cm}}$

3. Find the area of the trapezoid.

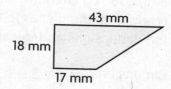

$A = \underline{\hspace{2cm}}$

Math Talk Two trapezoids have the same bases and the same height. Are the areas equal? Must the trapezoids have the same shape? **Explain.**

On Your Own

Find the area of the trapezoid.

4.

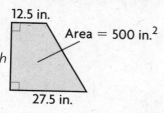

$A = \underline{\hspace{2cm}}$

5.

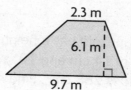

$A = \underline{\hspace{2cm}}$

Find the height of the trapezoid.

6.

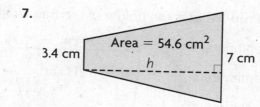

$h = \underline{\hspace{2cm}}$

7.

$h = \underline{\hspace{2cm}}$

Problem Solving REAL WORLD

Home Plate

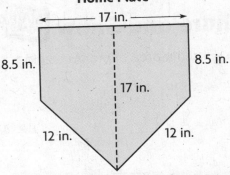

Use the diagram for 8–9.

8. A baseball home plate can be divided into two trapezoids with the dimensions shown in the drawing. Find the area of each trapezoid and the area of home plate.

   trapezoid: _____ in.²

   home plate: _____ in.²

9. Suppose you cut home plate along the dotted line and rearranged the pieces to form a rectangle. What would the dimensions and the area of the rectangle be?

   dimensions: _____

   area: _____

10. **H.O.T.** A pattern used for tile floors is shown. A side of the inner square measures 10 cm, and a side of the outer square measures 30 cm. What is the area of one of the yellow trapezoid tiles?

_____

11. **What's the Error?** A trapezoid has a height of 12 cm and bases with lengths of 14 cm and 10 cm. Tina says the area of the trapezoid is 288 cm². Find her error, and correct the error.

_____

_____

12. ⭐ **Test Prep** What is the height of the trapezoid?

   (A) 5 centimeters

   (B) 6 centimeters

   (C) 12 centimeters

   (D) 24 centimeters

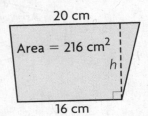

20 cm

Area = 216 cm²

h

16 cm

Name _____

☑ Mid-Chapter Checkpoint

▶ Vocabulary

Choose the best term from the box to complete the sentence.

Vocabulary
area
congruent
parallelogram
trapezoid

1. A _____ is a quadrilateral with two pairs of parallel sides. (p. 371)

2. The number of square units needed to cover a surface without any gaps or overlaps is called the _____. (p. 371)

3. Figures with the same size and shape are _____. (p. 375)

▶ Concepts and Skills

Find the area. (CC.6.G.1, CC.6.EE.2c)

4.

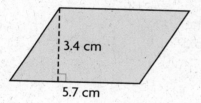

3.4 cm

5.7 cm

_____

5.

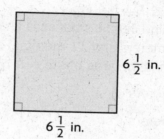

$6\frac{1}{2}$ in.

$6\frac{1}{2}$ in.

_____

6.

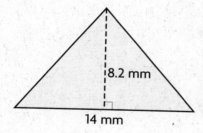

8.2 mm

14 mm

_____

7.

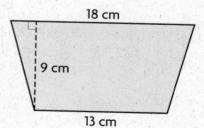

18 cm

9 cm

13 cm

_____

8. A parallelogram has an area of 276 square meters and a base measuring 12 meters. What is the height of the parallelogram?

9. The base of a triangle measures 8 inches and the area is 136 square inches. What is the height of the triangle?

_____   _____

© Houghton Mifflin Harcourt Publishing Company

Chapter 10   **391**

10. The height of a parallelogram is 3 times the base. The base measures 4.5 cm. What is the area of the parallelogram? (CC.6.G.1)

Ⓐ   13.5 square centimeters

Ⓑ   30.375 square centimeters

Ⓒ   60.75 square centimeters

Ⓓ 121.5 square centimeters

11. A triangular window pane has a base of 30 inches and a height of 24 inches. What is the area of the window pane? (CC.6.G.1)

Ⓐ 720 square inches

Ⓑ 360 square inches

Ⓒ 180 square inches

Ⓓ   54 square inches

12. The courtyard behind Jennie's house is shaped like a trapezoid. The bases measure 8 meters and 11 meters. The height of the trapezoid is 12 meters. What is the area of the courtyard? (CC.6.G.1)

Ⓐ   31 square meters

Ⓑ 114 square meters

Ⓒ 228 square meters

Ⓓ 528 square meters

13. Rugs sell for $8 per square foot. Beth bought a 9-foot-long rectangular rug for $432. How wide was the rug? (CC.6.G.1, CC.6.EE.2c)

Ⓐ   6 feet

Ⓑ 48 feet

Ⓒ 54 feet

Ⓓ 72 feet

14. A square painting has a side length of 18 inches. What is the area of the painting? (CC.6.G.1, CC.6.EE.2c)

Ⓐ   36 square inches

Ⓑ   72 square inches

Ⓒ 288 square inches

Ⓓ 324 square inches

Area of Regular Polygons

Essential Question How can you find the area of regular polygons?

COMMON CORE STANDARD CC.6.G.1
Solve real-world and mathematical problems
involving area, surface area, and volume.

🔑 UNLOCK the Problem ⟩ REAL WORLD

Emory is making a cover for a soccer ball. The material pieces he is using are regular polygons. A **regular polygon** is a polygon in which all sides have the same length and all angles have the same measure. Emory needs to find the area of a piece of material shaped like a regular pentagon.

🔑 Activity

You can find the area of a regular polygon by dividing the polygon into congruent triangles.

- Draw line segments from each vertex to the center of the pentagon to divide it into five congruent triangles.

- You can find the area of one of the triangles if you know the side length of the polygon and the height of the triangle.

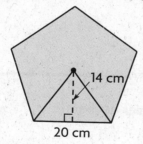

14 cm

20 cm

> **Math Talk** **MATHEMATICAL PRACTICES**
> **Explain** how to determine the number of congruent triangles a regular polygon should be divided into in order to find the area.

- Find the area of one triangle.

Write the formula. $\qquad$ $A = \dfrac{1}{2} bh$

Substitute 20 for b and 14 for h. $\qquad$ $A = \dfrac{1}{2} \times$ _____ $\times$ _____

Simplify. $\qquad$ $A =$ _____ cm^2

- Find the area of the regular polygon by multiplying the number of triangles by the area of one triangle.

$A =$ _____ $\times$ _____ $=$ _____ cm^2

So, the area of the pentagon-shaped piece is _____.

🔑 Example   Find the area of the regular polygon.

STEP 1 Draw line segments from each vertex to the
center of the hexagon.

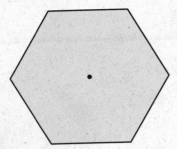

Into how many congruent triangles did you divide the figure? _____

STEP 2 Find the area of one triangle.

Write the formula.

$$A = \frac{1}{2} bh$$

Substitute 4.2 for *b* and 3.6 for *h*.

$$A = \frac{1}{2} \times \underline{\hspace{1cm}} \times \underline{\hspace{1cm}}$$

Simplify.

$$A = \underline{\hspace{1cm}} \ m^2$$

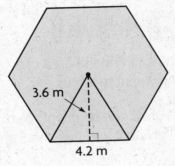

STEP 3 Find the area of the hexagon.

$$A = \underline{\hspace{1cm}} \times \underline{\hspace{1cm}} = \underline{\hspace{2cm}} \ m^2$$

So, the area of the hexagon is _____ m²

---

1. Into how many congruent triangles can you divide a regular decagon
   by drawing line segments from each vertex to the center of the
   decagon? **Explain.**

   _____

   _____

2. ☀H.O.T.☀   In an *irregular polygon*, the sides do not all have the same
   length and the angles do not all have the same measure. Could you
   find the area of an irregular polygon using the method you used in
   this lesson? **Explain** your reasoning.

   _____

   _____

Name _____

Share and Show

Find the area of the regular polygon.

1. number of congruent triangles inside the figure: _____

   area of each triangle: $\frac{1}{2} \times$ _____ $\times$ _____ $=$ _____ cm^2

   area of octagon: _____ $\times$ _____ $=$ _____ cm^2

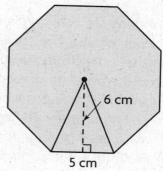

2.
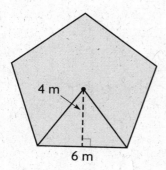

3.
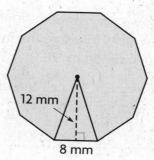

_____

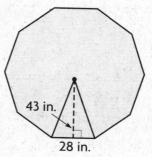

Math Talk MATHEMATICAL PRACTICES
Describe the information you must have about a regular polygon in order to find its area.

On Your Own

Find the area of the regular polygon.

4.
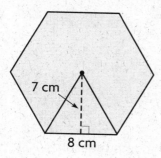

5.

6. A regular pentagon is divided into congruent triangles by drawing a line segment from each vertex to the center. Each triangle has an area of 24 cm^2. What is the area of the pentagon?

_____

Regular Polygons in Nature

Regular polygons are common in nature. Some starfish are shaped like pentagons, rock crystals may form rhombuses, and volcanic lava may form hexagonal columns when it cools. One of the best-known examples of regular polygons in nature is the small hexagonal cells in honeycombs constructed by honeybees. The cells are where bee larvae grow and where bees store honey and pollen. Scientists can gauge the health of a bee population by the size of the cells.

7. Cells in a honeycomb vary in width. To find the average width of a cell, scientists measure the combined width of 10 cells, and then divide by 10.

   The figure shows a typical 10-cell line of worker bee cells. What is the width of each cell?

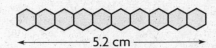

   5.2 cm

   _____

8. A regular hexagonal cell can be divided into triangles. One of them is outlined on the hexagon at the right. Use your answer to Exercise 7 to find h, the height of the triangle.

   _____

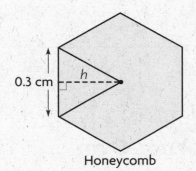

   0.3 cm h

   Honeycomb

9. The base of the triangle measures 0.3 cm. What is the area of the triangle? Explain how you found the area.

   _____

   _____

   _____

   _____

10. Each hexagonal cell is made up of _____ congruent triangles. What is the area of a cell?

    _____ cm^2

11. A rectangular honeycomb measures 35.1 cm by 32.4 cm. Approximately how many cells does it contain?

    _____

Composite Figures

Essential Question How can you find the area of composite figures?

COMMON CORE STANDARD CC.6.G.1
Solve real-world and mathematical problems involving area, surface area, and volume.

A **composite figure** is made up of two or more simpler figures, such as triangles and quadrilaterals.

🔑 UNLOCK the Problem REAL WORLD

The new entryway to the fun house at Happy World Amusement Park is made from the shapes shown in the diagram. It will be painted bright green. Juanita needs to know the area of the entryway to determine how much paint to buy. What is the area of the entryway?

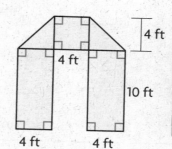

🔒 **Find the area of the entryway.**

STEP 1 Find the area of the rectangles.

Write the formula. $A = lw$

Substitute the values for l and w and evaluate. $A = 10 \times$ _____ = _____

Find the total area of two rectangles. $2 \times$ _____ = _____ ft^2

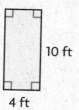

STEP 2 Find the area of the triangles.

Write the formula. $A = \frac{1}{2}bh$

Substitute the values for b and h and evaluate. $A = \frac{1}{2} \times 4 \times$ _____ = _____

Find the total area of two triangles. $2 \times$ _____ = _____ ft^2

STEP 3 Find the area of the square.

Write the formula. $A = s^2$

Substitute the value for s. $A = ($ _____ $)^2 =$ _____ ft^2

STEP 4 Find the total area of the composite figure.

Add the areas. $A = 80\ ft^2 +$ _____ $ft^2 +$ _____ $ft^2 =$ _____ ft^2

So, Juanita needs to buy enough paint to cover _____ ft^2.

Math Talk MATHEMATICAL PRACTICES
Discuss other ways you could divide up the composite figure.

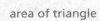 Example 1   Find the area of the composite figure shown.

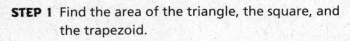

STEP 1 Find the area of the triangle, the square, and
the trapezoid.

area of triangle $A = \frac{1}{2}bh = \frac{1}{2} \times 16 \times$ _____

$=$ _____ cm²

area of square $A = s^2 = ($_____$)^2$

$=$ _____ cm²

area of trapezoid $A = \frac{1}{2}(b_1 + b_2)h = \frac{1}{2} \times ($ _____ $+$ _____ $) \times$ _____

$= \frac{1}{2} \times$ _____ $\times 6$

$=$ _____ cm²

STEP 2 Find the total area of the figure.

total area $A =$ _____ cm² $+$ _____ cm² $+$ _____ cm²

$=$ _____ cm²

So, the area of the figure is _____ cm².

Example 2   Find the area of the shaded region.

STEP 1 Find the area of the rectangle and the square.

area of rectangle
(1 ft = 12 in.) $A = lw =$ _____ $\times$ _____

$A =$ _____ in.²

area of square $A = s^2 = ($_____$)^2$

$A =$ _____ in.²

STEP 2 Subtract the area of the square from the area of the rectangle.

area of shaded
region $A =$ _____ in.² $-$ _____ in.²

$A =$ _____ in.²

So, the area of the shaded region is _____ in.²

Name _____

Share and Show

1. Find the area of the figure.

area of one rectangle $A = lw$

$A =$ _____ × _____ = _____ ft²

area of two rectangles $A = 2 ×$ _____ = _____ ft²

length of base of triangle $b =$ _____ ft + _____ ft + _____ ft

$=$ _____ ft

area of triangle $A = \frac{1}{2}bh$

$A = \frac{1}{2} ×$ _____ × _____ = _____ ft²

area of composite figure $A =$ _____ ft² + _____ ft² = _____ ft²

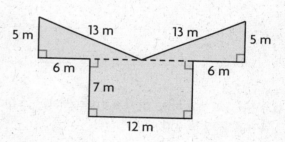

Find the area of the figure.

 2.

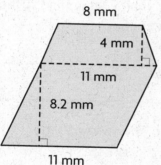

_____

 3.

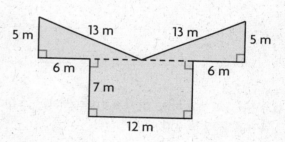

_____

Math Talk **MATHEMATICAL PRACTICES**
Explain how to find the area of a composite figure.

On Your Own

4. Find the area of the figure.

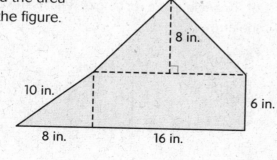

_____

5. **H.O.T.** Find the area of the shaded region.

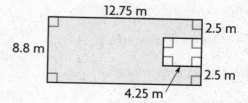

_____

UNLOCK the Problem

6. The flag of the nation of Guyana is shown. What is the area of the yellow shape?

(A) 360 square inches

(B) 540 square inches

(C) 720 square inches

(D) 1,080 square inches

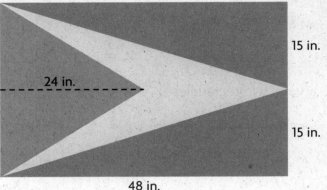

15 in.

24 in.

15 in.

48 in.

a. Explain how you could find the area of the yellow shape if you knew the areas of the green and red shapes and the area of the entire flag.

_____

_____

_____

b. What is the area of the entire flag? Explain how you found it.

_____

_____

_____

c. What is the area of the red shape? What is the area of each green shape?

_____

d. What equation can you write to find *A*, the area of the yellow shape?

_____

_____

e. What is the area of the yellow shape?

_____

f. Fill in the bubble for the correct answer choice above.

7. Four photographs each measuring 8 inches by 10 inches are pinned on a rectangular bulletin board measuring 20 inches by 24 inches. How much of the bulletin board is not covered by photos?

(A) 80 square inches

(B) 160 square inches

(C) 320 square inches

(D) 400 square inches

8. The figure shows an arrow on a road sign with the given dimensions. The arrow is composed of a triangle and a rectangle. What is the area of the arrow?

(A) 168 in.²

(B) 196 in.²

(C) 224 in.²

(D) 336 in.²

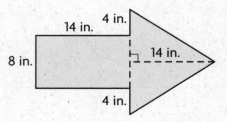

14 in.   4 in.

8 in.   14 in.

4 in.

Name _____

Problem Solving • Changing Dimensions

Essential Question How can you use the strategy *find a pattern* to show how changing dimensions affects area?

COMMON CORE STANDARD CC.6.G.1
Solve real-world and mathematical problems involving area, surface area, and volume.

🔑 UNLOCK the Problem · REAL WORLD

Jason has created a 3-in. by 4-in. rectangular design to be made into mouse pads. To manufacture the pads, the dimensions will be multiplied by 2 or 3. How will the area of the design be affected?

Use the graphic organizer to help you solve the problem.

3 in.
4 in.

Read the Problem

What do I need to find?	**What information do I need to use?**	**How will I use the information?**
I need to find how _____ will be affected by changing the _____.	I need to use _____ of the original design and _____ _____ _____.	I can draw a sketch of each rectangle and calculate _____ of each. Then I can look for _____ in my results.

Solve the Problem

Sketch	Dimensions	Multiplier	Area
	3 in. by 4 in.	none	$A = 3 \times 4 = 12$ in.^{2}
6 in. / 8 in.	6 in. by 8 in.	2	$A = \underline{\quad} \times \underline{\quad} = \underline{\quad}$ in.^{2}
9 in. / 12 in.			

So, when the dimensions are multiplied by 2, the area is

multiplied by _____. When the dimensions are multiplied

by 3, the area is multiplied by _____.

MATHEMATICAL PRACTICES

Math Talk **Predict** what would happen to the area of a rectangle if the dimensions were multiplied by 4.

🔑 Try Another Problem

A stained-glass designer is reducing the dimensions of an earlier design. The dimensions of the triangle shown will be multiplied by $\frac{1}{2}$ or $\frac{1}{4}$. How will the area of the design be affected? Use the graphic organizer to help you solve the problem.

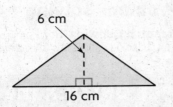

6 cm

16 cm

Read the Problem

What do I need to find?	What information do I need to use?	How will I use the information?

Solve the Problem

Sketch	Multiplier	Area
	none	$A = \frac{1}{2} \times 16 \times$ _____ = _____ cm^2
3 cm 8 cm	$\frac{1}{2}$	

So, when the dimensions are multiplied by $\frac{1}{2}$, the area is multiplied by

_____. When the dimensions are multiplied by _____, the area is

multiplied by _____.

Math Talk MATHEMATICAL PRACTICES
Explain what happens to the area of a triangle when the dimensions are multiplied by a number n.

Name _____

Share and Show ![MATH BOARD]

UNLOCK the Problem Tips
√ Plan your solution by deciding on the steps you will use.
√ Find the original area and the new area, and then compare the two.
√ Look for patterns in your results.

1. The dimensions of a 2-cm by 6-cm rectangle are multiplied by 5. How is the area of the rectangle affected?

    First, find the original area:

    _____

    Next, find the new area:

    _____

    So, the area is multiplied by _____.

2. H.O.T. **What if** the dimensions of the original rectangle in Exercise 1 had been multiplied by $\frac{1}{2}$? How would the area have been affected?

    _____

    _____

    _____

    _____

3. Evan bought two square rugs. The larger one measured 12 ft square. The smaller one had an area equal to $\frac{1}{4}$ the area of the larger one. What fraction of the side lengths of the larger rug were the side lengths of the smaller one?

    _____

4. On Silver Island, a palm tree, a giant rock, and a buried treasure form a triangle with a base of 100 yd and a height of 50 yd. On a map of the island, the three landmarks form a triangle with a base of 2 ft and a height of 1 ft. How many times the area of the triangle on the map is the area of the actual triangle?

    _____

.... SHOW YOUR WORK ....

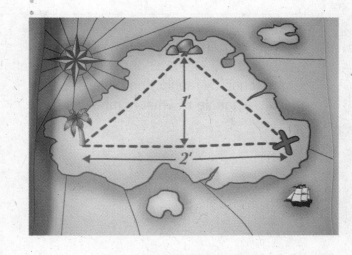

© Houghton Mifflin Harcourt Publishing Company

On Your Own.......

Choose a STRATEGY

Use a Model
Draw a Diagram
Find a Pattern
Solve a Simpler Problem
Work Backward
Use a Formula

5. A square game board is divided into smaller squares, each with sides one-ninth the length of the sides of the board. Into how many squares is the game board divided?

_____

6. **H.O.T.** Flynn County is a rectangle measuring 9 mi by 12 mi. Gibson County is a rectangle with an area 6 times the area of Flynn County and a width of 16 mi. What is the length of Gibson County?

_____

SHOW YOUR WORK

7. Carmen left her house and drove 10 mi north, 15 mi east, 13 mi south, 11 mi west, and 3 mi north. How far was she from home?

_____

8. **Write Math** ▶ Bernie drove from his house to his cousin's house in 6 hours at an average rate of 52 mi per hr. He drove home at an average rate of 60 mi per hr. **Explain** how you could find how long it took him to drive home.

_____

_____

_____

_____

9. ⭐ **Test Prep** The dimensions of a rectangle are multiplied by $\frac{1}{3}$. The area of the smaller rectangle can be found by multiplying the area of the original rectangle by what number?

Ⓐ $\frac{1}{3}$

Ⓑ $\frac{1}{6}$

Ⓒ $\frac{1}{9}$

Ⓓ $\frac{1}{12}$

FOR MORE PRACTICE:
Standards Practice Book, pp. P197–P198

Figures on the Coordinate Plane

Essential Question How can you plot polygons on a coordinate plane and find their side lengths?

COMMON CORE STANDARD CC.6.G.3
Solve real-world and mathematical problems involving area, surface area, and volume.

 UNLOCK the Problem REAL WORLD

The world's largest book is a collection of photographs from the Asian nation of Bhutan. A book collector models the rectangular shape of the open book on a coordinate plane. Each unit of the coordinate plane represents one foot. The collector plots the vertices of the rectangle at $A(9, 3)$, $B(2, 3)$, $C(2, 8)$, and $D(9, 8)$. What are the dimensions of the open book?

- What two dimensions do you need to find?

_____

_____

Plot the vertices and find the dimensions of the rectangle.

STEP 1 Complete the rectangle on the coordinate plane.

Plot points $C(2, 8)$ and $D(9, 8)$.
Connect the points to form a rectangle.

STEP 2 Find the length of the rectangle.

Find the distance between points $A(9, 3)$ and $B(2, 3)$.

The y-coordinates are the same, so the points lie on a _____ line.

Think of the horizontal line passing through A and B as a number line.

Horizontal distance of A from 0: $|9| =$ _____ ft

Horizontal distance of B from 0: $|2| =$ _____ ft

Subtract to find the distance from A to B: _____ − _____ = _____ ft.

STEP 3 Find the width of the rectangle.

Find the distance between points $C(2, 8)$ and $B(2, 3)$.

The x-coordinates are the same, so the points lie on a _____ line.

Think of the vertical line passing through C and B as a number line.

Vertical distance of C from 0: $|8| =$ _____ ft

Vertical distance of B from 0: $|3| =$ _____ ft

Subtract to find the distance from C to B: _____ − _____ = _____ ft.

So, the dimensions of the open book are _____ ft by _____ ft.

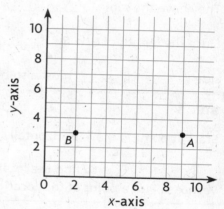

Math Talk MATHEMATICAL PRACTICES **Explain** how you know whether to add or subtract the absolute values to find the distance between the vertices of the rectangle.

CONNECT You can use properties of quadrilaterals to help you find unknown vertices. The properties can also help you graph quadrilaterals on the coordinate plane.

🔒 Example Find the unknown vertex, and then graph.

Three vertices of parallelogram PQRS are P(4, 2), Q(3, ⁻3), and R(⁻3, ⁻3). Give the coordinates of vertex S and graph the parallelogram.

Math Idea

The name of a polygon, such as parallelogram PQRS, gives the vertices in order as you move around the polygon.

STEP 1

Plot the given points on the coordinate plane.

STEP 2

The opposite sides of a parallelogram are _____.

They have the same _____.

Since the length of side $\overline{RQ}$ is _____ units, the length of

side _____ must also be _____ units.

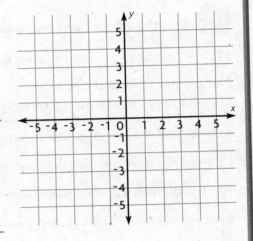

STEP 3

Start at point P. Move horizontally _____ units to the

_____ to find the location of the remaining

vertex, S. Plot a point at this location.

STEP 4

Draw the parallelogram. Check that opposite sides are parallel and congruent.

So, the coordinates of the vertex S are _____.

1. **Explain** why vertex S must be to the left of vertex P rather than to the right of vertex P.

_____

_____

2. **Describe** how you could find the area of parallelogram PQRS in square units.

_____

_____

Name _____

Share and Show ![MATH BOARD]

1. The vertices of triangle *ABC* are *A*(⁻1, 3), *B*(⁻4, ⁻2), and *C*(2, ⁻2). Graph the triangle and find the length of side $\overline{BC}$.

   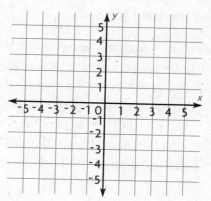

   Horizontal distance of *B* from 0: |⁻4| = _____ units

   Horizontal distance of *C* from 0: |2| = _____ units

   The points are in different quadrants, so add to find the

   distance from *B* to *C*: _____ + _____ = _____ units.

Give the coordinates of the unknown vertex of rectangle *JKLM*, and graph.

2.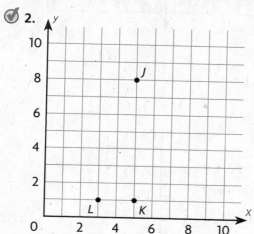

3.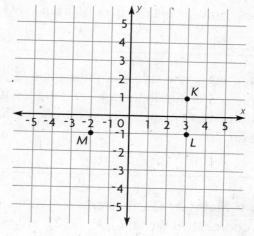

_____

On Your Own

4. Give the coordinates of the unknown vertex of rectangle *PQRS*, and graph.

   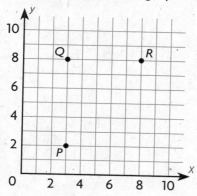

5. The vertices of pentagon *PQRST* are *P*(9, 7), *Q*(9, 3), *R*(3, 3), *S*(3, 7), and *T*(6, 9). Graph the pentagon and find the length of side $\overline{PQ}$.

   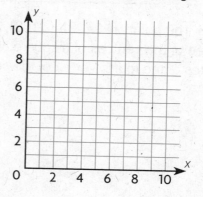

Problem Solving REAL WORLD

The map shows the location of some city landmarks. Use the map for 6–7.

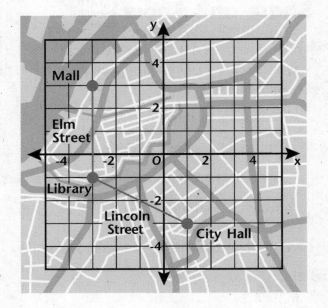

6. A city planner wants to locate a park at the intersection of two new roads. One of the new roads will go to the mall and be parallel to Lincoln Street which is shown in red. The other new road will go to City Hall and be parallel to Elm Street which is also shown in red. Give the coordinates for the location of the park.

_____

7. Each unit of the coordinate plane represents 2 miles. How far will the park be from City Hall?

_____

8. **H.O.T.** $\overline{PQ}$ is one side of right triangle *PQR*. In the triangle, $\angle P$ is the right angle, and the length of side $\overline{PR}$ is 3 units. Give all the possible coordinates for vertex *R*.

_____

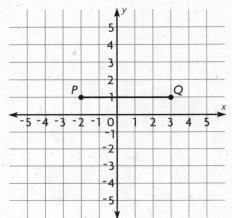

9. **Write Math** ▶ Quadrilateral *WXYZ* has vertices with coordinates $W(^-4, 0)$, $X(^-2, 3)$, $Y(2, 3)$, and $Z(2, 0)$. Classify the quadrilateral using the most exact name possible and explain your answer.

_____

_____

10. ⭐ **Test Prep** The points $(^-1, ^-2)$, $(^-1, 3)$, and $(4, 3)$ are three of the vertices of a square. What are the coordinates of the fourth vertex of the square?

Ⓐ $(^-2, 4)$

Ⓑ $(^-4, ^-2)$

Ⓒ $(4, ^-1)$

Ⓓ $(4, ^-2)$

FOR MORE PRACTICE:
Standards Practice Book, pp. P199–P200

✓ Chapter 10 Review/Test

▶ Vocabulary

Choose the best term from the box to complete the sentence.

Vocabulary
composite figure
parallelogram
regular polygon
trapezoid

1. A _____ is a quadrilateral with exactly one pair of parallel sides. (p. 383)

2. A _____ is made up of more than one shape. (p. 397)

3. A polygon in which all sides have the same length and all angles have the same measure is called a _____. (p. 393)

▶ Concepts and Skills

Find the unknown measure. (CC.6.G.1, CC.6.EE.2c)

4. triangle

$A = 40$ in.^{2}

$b =$ _____

$h = 5$ in.

5. trapezoid

$A = 55$ m^2

$b_1 = 9$ m

$b_2 = 13$ m

$h =$ _____

6. parallelogram

$A = 238$ mm^2

$b =$ _____

$h = 14$ mm

7. Find the area of the shaded region.
(CC.6.G.1, CC.6.EE.2c)

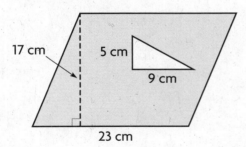

8. Three vertices of parallelogram *PQRS* are $P(2, {}^-2)$, $Q({}^-4, {}^-2)$, and $R({}^-2, 3)$. Give the coordinates of vertex *S* and graph the parallelogram. (CC.6.G.3)

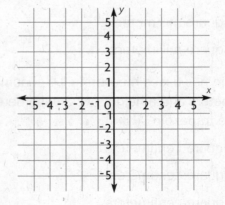

_____

_____

GO Online Assessment Options **Chapter Test**

TEST PREP

9. Samantha made the letter *S* out of fabric to put on a T-shirt. She used three congruent parallelograms. Each parallelogram had a base of 12 centimeters and a height of 3 centimeters. What was the total area of the letter *S* on Samantha's T-shirt? (CC.6.G.1, CC.6.EE.2c)

(A) 18 square centimeters

(B) 36 square centimeters

(C) 54 square centimeters

(D) 108 square centimeters

10. The sail on Mike's sailboat is shaped like a triangle with a base of 12 meters and a height of 20 meters. What is the area of the sail? (CC.6.G.1, CC.6.EE.2c)

(A) 100 square meters

(B) 120 square meters

(C) 200 square meters

(D) 240 square meters

11. A regular pentagon is divided into congruent triangles by drawing a line segment from each vertex to the center. Each triangle has an area of 18 mm². What is the area of the pentagon? (CC.6.G.1)

(A) 3.6 square millimeters

(B) 45 square millimeters

(C) 90 square millimeters

(D) 180 square millimeters

12. A trapezoid has bases measuring 14 centimeters and 18 centimeters and a height of 12 centimeters. What is the area of the trapezoid? (CC.6.G.1, CC.6.EE.2c)

(A) 44 square centimeters

(B) 192 square centimeters

(C) 300 square centimeters

(D) 384 square centimeters

Fill in the bubble to show your answer.

13. The base of a parallelogram measures 4.8 feet and the height measures 7.3 feet. What is the area of the parallelogram? (CC.6.G.1, CC.6.EE.2c)

Ⓐ 12.1 square feet

Ⓑ 17.52 square feet

Ⓒ 19.4 square feet

Ⓓ 35.04 square feet

14. The vertices of quadrilateral *ABCD* are *A*(⁻2, 3), *B*(3, 3), *C*(4, ⁻2), and *D*(⁻4, ⁻2). Classify the quadrilateral using the most exact name possible. (CC.6.G.3)

Ⓐ parallelogram

Ⓑ rectangle

Ⓒ square

Ⓓ trapezoid

15. Find the length of side $\overline{AB}$ in the quadrilateral in Exercise 14. (CC.6.G.3)

Ⓐ 1 unit

Ⓑ 5 units

Ⓒ 6 units

Ⓓ 11 units

16. A wall in Stanley's living room measures 9 feet by 20 feet. There are two windows in the wall, each measuring 4 feet by 4 feet. If he paints the wall, how much area will he have to cover? (CC.6.G.1, CC.6.EE.2c)

Ⓐ 100 square feet

Ⓑ 116 square feet

Ⓒ 148 square feet

Ⓓ 160 square feet

17. The dimensions of a rectangle are multiplied by 9. How is the area of the rectangle affected? (CC.6.G.1)

Ⓐ It is multiplied by 3.

Ⓑ It is multiplied by 9.

Ⓒ It is multiplied by 18.

Ⓓ It is multiplied by 81.

► **Constructed Response**

18. Tell how the formula for the area of a triangle is related to the formula for the area of a parallelogram.

_____

_____

_____

19. Explain how you could find the height of a trapezoid if you knew the length of the two bases and the area of the trapezoid. (CC.6.G.1)

_____

_____

_____

► **Performance Task**

20. Jim is building a gazebo in his backyard. The floor of the gazebo is in the shape of a hexagon. Jim wants to graph the hexagon to find the area.

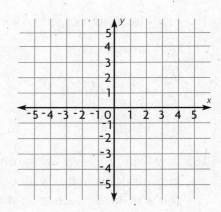

Ⓐ The vertices of hexagon *RSTUVW* are $R(^-3, 2)$, $S(0, 4)$, $T(3, 2)$, $U(3, ^-2)$, $V(0, ^-4)$, and $W(^-3, ^-2)$. Graph the hexagon.

Ⓑ Jim divided the hexagon along the *y*-axis into two congruent trapezoids. If each unit on the graph represents 1 foot, what is the area of one trapezoid? Explain how you determined your answer.

_____

_____

_____

_____

Ⓒ What is the area of the hexagon? Explain how you determined your answer.

_____

_____

_____

Surface Area and Volume

Show What You Know

Check your understanding of important skills.

Name _____

▶ **Estimate and Find Area** **Multiply to find the area.**

1.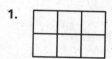

_____

2.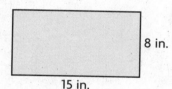

_____

▶ **Area of Squares, Rectangles, and Triangles** **Find the area.**

3.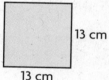

13 cm

13 cm

$A = s^2$

Area = _____

4.

15 in.

8 in.

$A = lw$

Area = _____

5.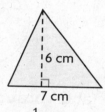

6 cm

7 cm

$A = \frac{1}{2}(b \times h)$

Area = _____

▶ **Evaluate Expressions** **Evaluate the expression.**

6. $3 \times (2 + 4)$

_____

7. $6 + 6 \div 3$

_____

8. $4^2 + 4 \times 5 - 2$

_____

MATH DETECTIVE
WITH CARMEN SANDIEGO™

Jerry is building an indoor beach volleyball court.
He has ordered 14,000 cubic feet of sand.
The dimensions of the court will be 30 feet by 60 feet.
Jerry needs to have a 10-foot boundary around the
court for safety. Be a math detective and determine
how deep the sand will be if Jerry uses all the sand.

GO Online   Assessment Options: **Soar to Success Math**

Vocabulary Builder

▶ Visualize It

Complete the bubble map. Use the review terms
that name solid figures.

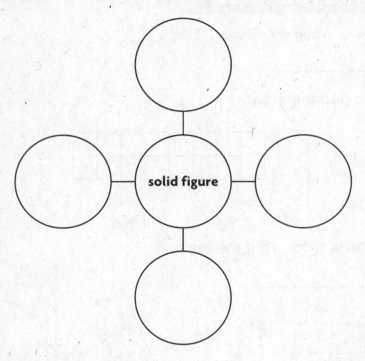

Review Words
base
cube
lateral face
polygon
polyhedron
prism
pyramid
vertex

Preview Words
net
solid figure
surface area
volume

▶ Understand Vocabulary

Complete the sentences using the preview words.

1. A three-dimensional figure having length, width, and height is

   called a(n) _____.

2. A two-dimensional pattern that can be folded into a

   three-dimensional figure is called a(n) _____.

3. _____ is the sum of the areas of all the faces,
   or surfaces, of a solid figure.

4. _____ is the measure of space a solid figure
   occupies.

GO Online • eStudent Edition • Multimedia eGlossary

Three-Dimensional Figures and Nets

Essential Question How do you use nets to represent three-dimensional figures?

COMMON CORE STANDARD CC.6.G.4
Solve real-world and mathematical problems involving area, surface area, and volume.

A **solid figure** is a three-dimensional figure because it has three dimensions—length, width, and height. Solid figures can be identified by the shapes of their bases, the number of bases, and the shapes of their lateral faces.

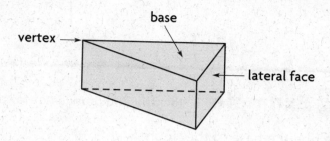

Triangular Prism

🔓 UNLOCK the Problem REAL WORLD

A designer is working on the layout for the cereal box shown. Identify the solid figure and draw a net that the designer can use to show the placement of information and artwork on the box.

• How many bases are there? _____

• Are the bases congruent? _____

• What shape are the bases? _____

🔑 Identify the solid figure.

Recall that a prism is a solid figure with two congruent, parallel bases. Its lateral faces are rectangles. It is named for the shape of its bases.

Is the cereal box a prism? _____

What shape are the bases? _____

So, the box is a _____.

🔑 Draw a net for the figure.

A **net** is a two-dimensional figure that can be folded into a solid figure.

STEP 1

Make a list of the shapes you will use.

top and bottom bases: _____

left and right faces: _____

front and back faces: _____

STEP 2

Draw the net using the shapes you listed in Step 1. One possible net is shown.

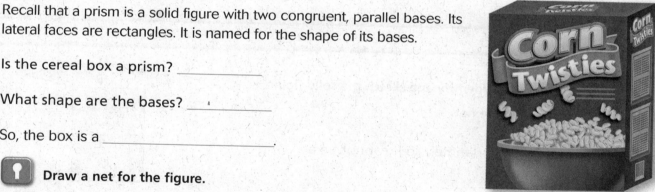

A *pyramid* is a solid figure with a polygon-shaped base and triangles for lateral faces. Like prisms, pyramids are named by the shape of their bases. A pyramid with a rectangle for a base is called a rectangular pyramid.

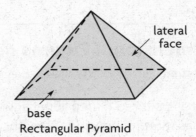

lateral face

base
Rectangular Pyramid

🔑 Example 1 **Identify and draw a net for the solid figure.**

Describe the base of the figure.

_____

Describe the lateral faces.

_____

The figure is a _____.

Shapes to use in the net: Net:

base: _____

lateral faces: _____

🔑 Example 2 **Identify and sketch the solid figure that could be formed by the net.**

The net has only _____ triangles, so it cannot be a

_____.

The triangles must be the _____ for a

_____.

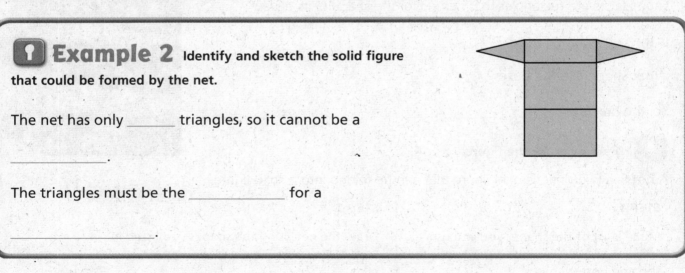

• Compare the bases and lateral faces of prisms and pyramids.

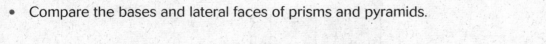

_____

_____

_____

Name _____

Share and Show

Identify and draw a net for the solid figure.

1.   <u>Net:</u>

base: _____

lateral faces: _____

figure: _____

 2.

Identify and sketch the solid figure that could be formed by the net.

 3.

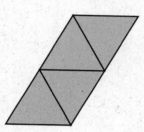

4.

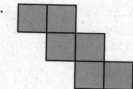

_____   _____

Math Talk   MATHEMATICAL PRACTICES

Describe the characteristics of a solid figure that you need to consider when making its net.

On Your Own

Identify and draw a net for the solid figure.

5.

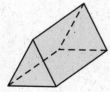

6.

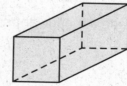

_____   _____

Problem Solving  REAL WORLD

Solve.

7. The lateral faces and bases of crystals of the mineral galena are congruent squares. Identify the shape of a galena crystal.

_____

.... SHOW YOUR WORK ....

8. **H.O.T.** **What's the Error?** Rhiannon draws the net below and labels each square. She says you can fold it up into a cube that displays the letters A through G. Explain Rhiannon's error.

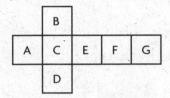

_____

_____

_____

9. **Write Math** ► A crystal of the mineral diamond is shown. Describe the figure in terms of the solid figures you have seen in this lesson.

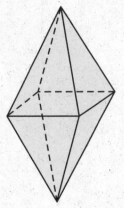

_____

_____

_____

_____

10. ⭐ **Test Prep** Jesse made a triangular prism from paper. What shapes did she use?

   (A) 3 triangles only

   (B) 3 triangles and 2 rectangles

   (C) 4 triangles only

   (D) 2 triangles and 3 rectangles

Explore Surface Area Using Nets

Essential Question What is the relationship between a net and the surface area of a prism?

COMMON CORE STANDARD CC.6.G.4
Solve real-world and mathematical problems involving area, surface area, and volume.

CONNECT The **surface area** of a solid figure is the sum of the areas of all the faces or surfaces of the figure. Surface area is measured in square units. You can use a net to help you find the surface area of a solid figure.

Investigate · REAL WORLD

Materials ■ centimeter grid paper, ruler, scissors

A box shaped like a rectangular prism. The box is 8 cm long, 6 cm wide, and 4 cm high. What is the surface area of the box?

Find the surface area of the rectangular prism.

A. Draw a net of the prism on centimeter grid paper.

B. Cut out the net.

C. Fold the net to confirm that it represents a rectangular prism measuring 8 cm by 6 cm by 4 cm.

D. Count the grid squares on each face of the net.

So, the surface area of the box is _____ cm^2.

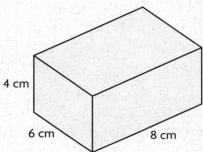

4 cm
6 cm
8 cm

> **!** **ERROR Alert**
>
> Make sure you include all surfaces in the net of a three-dimensional figure, not just the surfaces you can see in the diagram of the figure.

Draw Conclusions ·

1. **Explain** how you used the net to find the surface area of the box.

_____

_____

2. **H.O.T.** **Analysis** Describe how you could find the area of each face of the prism without counting grid squares on the net.

_____

_____

Make Connections

You can also use the formula for the area of a rectangle to find the surface area of the box.

Find the surface area of the box in the Investigate, which measures 8 cm by 6 cm by 4 cm.

STEP 1 Label the rectangles in the net A through F. Then label the dimensions.

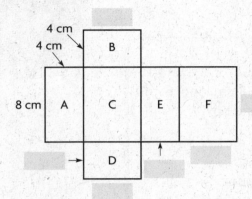

STEP 2 Find the area of each face of the prism.

Think: I can find the area of a rectangle by multiplying the rectangle's _____

times its _____.

Record the areas of the faces below.

Face A: $4 \times 8 = 32$ cm^2 Face B: _____ cm^2 Face C: _____ cm^2

Face D: _____ cm^2 Face E: _____ cm^2 Face F: _____ cm^2

STEP 3 Add the areas to find the surface area of the prism.

The surface area of the prism is _____ cm^2.

3. **Identify** any prism faces that have equal areas. How could you use that fact to simplify the process of finding the surface area of the prism?

_____

_____

_____

4. **Describe** how you could find the surface area of a cube.

_____

> **Math Talk**
> MATHEMATICAL PRACTICES
> Compare the surface area you found by adding the areas of the faces to the surface area you found by counting grid squares. Explain your results.

Name _____

Share and Show

Use the net to find the surface area of the prism.

1.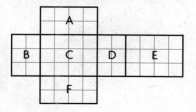

Face A: _____ cm²   Face D: _____ cm²

Face B: _____ cm²   Face E: _____ cm²

Face C: _____ cm²   Face F: _____ cm²

Surface area: _____ cm²

2.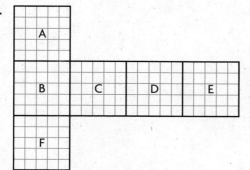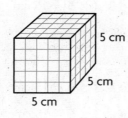

_____

Find the surface area of the rectangular prism.

3.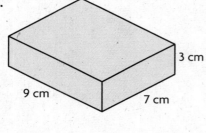

_____

4.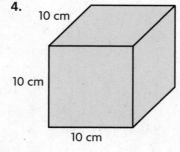

_____

5.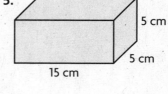

_____

6. Darren is painting a wooden block as part of his art project. The block is a rectangular prism that is 12 cm long by 9 cm wide by 5 cm high. How much surface area does Darren have to paint?

_____

7. **Write Math** ▶ Describe the rectangles that make up the net for the prism in Exercise 6.

_____

_____

Problem Solving 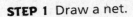 REAL WORLD

What's the Error?

8. Emilio is designing the packaging for a new mp3 player. The box for the mp3 player is 5 cm by 3 cm by 2 cm. Emilio needs to find the surface area of the box.

16-gigabyte MP3 player
Holds up to 4,000 songs

Look at how Emilio solved the problem. Find his error.

STEP 1 Draw a net.

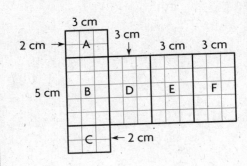

STEP 2 Find the areas of all the faces and add them.

Face A: $3 \times 2 = 6$ cm^2

Face B: $3 \times 5 = 15$ cm^2

Face C: $3 \times 2 = 6$ cm^2

Face D: $3 \times 5 = 15$ cm^2

Face E: $3 \times 5 = 15$ cm^2

Face F: $3 \times 5 = 15$ cm^2

Surface area: 72 cm^2

Correct the error. Find the surface area of the prism.

So, the surface area of the prism is _____.

- Describe the error that Emilio made.

_____

_____

- How could Emilio have checked that he drew his net correctly?

_____

_____

FOR MORE PRACTICE:
Standards Practice Book, pp. P207–P208

Name _____

Surface Area of Prisms

Essential Question How can you find the surface area of a prism?

You can use a net to find the surface area of a solid figure, such as a prism.

COMMON CORE STANDARD CC.6.G.4
Solve real-world and mathematical problems involving area, surface area, and volume.

UNLOCK the Problem REAL WORLD

Alex is designing wooden boxes in which to store his books. Each box measures 15 in. by 12 in. by 10 in. To know how much wood to buy, he needs to find the surface area of each box. What is the surface area of each box?

 Use a net to find the surface area.

- What is the shape of each face?

_____

- What are the dimensions of each face?

_____

_____

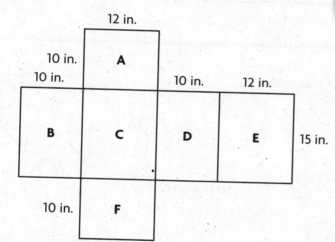

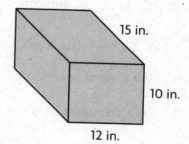

STEP 1 Find the area of each lettered face.

Face A: $12 \times 10 = 120$ in.²   Face B: $15 \times 10 =$ _____ in.²

Face C: _____ × _____ = _____ in.²   Face D: _____ × _____ = _____ in.²

Face E: _____ × _____ = _____ in.²   Face F: _____ × _____ = _____ in.²

STEP 2 Find the sum of the areas of the faces. _____

So, the surface area of each box is _____.

Math Talk
MATHEMATICAL PRACTICES
Describe What do you notice about the opposite faces of the box that could help you find its surface area?

🔑 Example 1 Use a net to find the surface area of the triangular prism.

The surface area equals the sum of the areas of the three rectangular faces and two triangular bases. Note that the bases have the same area.

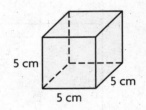

area of bases A and E: $A = \frac{1}{2}bh = \frac{1}{2} \times 12 \times$ _____ = _____

area of face B: $A = lw = 5 \times 10 =$ _____

area of face C: $A = lw =$ _____ × _____ = _____

area of face D: $A = lw =$ _____ × _____ = _____

Surface area: 2 × _____ + _____ + _____ + _____ = _____

So, the surface area of the triangular prism is _____.

Math Talk | MATHEMATICAL PRACTICES
Explain why the area of one triangular base was multiplied by 2.

🔑 Example 2 Find the surface area of the cube.

🔑 One Way Use a net.

STEP 1 Find the area of each face.

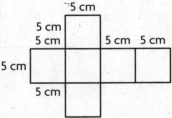

All of the faces are squares with a side length of _____, so the areas of all the squares are the same.

Area of one face: $A =$ _____ × _____ = _____

STEP 2 Find the sum of the areas of all _____ faces.

_____ + _____ + _____ + _____ + _____ + _____ = _____

🔑 Another Way Use a formula.

You can also find the surface area of a cube using the formula $S = 6s^2$, where S is the surface area and s is the side length of the cube.

Write the formula. $S = 6s^2$

Replace s with 5. $S = 6 ($_____$)^2$

Simplify. $S = 6 ($_____$) =$ _____

The surface area of the cube is _____.

Name _____

Share and Show

Use a net to find the surface area.

1.

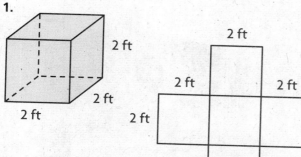

area of each face: _____ × _____ = _____

number of faces: _____

surface area = _____ × _____ = _____ ft²

2.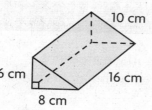

3.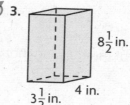

_____

_____

Math Talk MATHEMATICAL PRACTICES
Explain how to find the surface area of a rectangular prism with a length of 8 ft, a width of 2 ft, and a height of 3 ft. Then find the surface area.

On Your Own

Use a net to find the surface area.

4.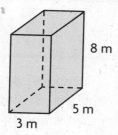

5.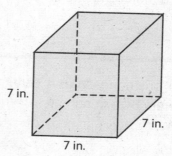

_____

_____

6. Calculate the surface area of the cube in Exercise 5 using the formula $S = 6s^2$. Show your work.

_____

🔑 UNLOCK the Problem

7. The Vehicle Assembly Building at Kennedy Space Center is a rectangular prism. It is 218 m long, 158 m wide, and 160 m tall. There are four 139 m tall doors in the building, averaging 29 m in width. What is the building's outside surface area when the doors are open?

Ⓐ   536 m^2

Ⓑ   138,640 m^2

Ⓒ   154,764 m^2

Ⓓ   5,511,040 m^2

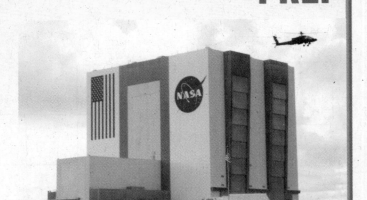

a. 🔥 H.O.T.   Draw each face of the building, not including the floor.

d. Find the building's surface area (not including the floor) when the doors are closed.

_____

e. Find the area of the four doors.

_____

b. What are the dimensions of the 4 walls?

_____

_____

f. Find the building's surface area (not including the floor) when the doors are open.

_____

c. What are the dimensions of the roof?

_____

g. Fill in the bubble for the correct answer choice above.

---

8. A rectangular prism measures 4 centimeters by 5 centimeters by 6 centimeters. What is its surface area?

Ⓐ   74 square centimeters

Ⓑ   120 square centimeters

Ⓒ   148 square centimeters

Ⓓ   240 square centimeters

9. Emma covers the surface of a cube-shaped box with wrapping paper. The side length of the cube is 6 inches. How much wrapping paper will Emma need to cover the cube without any overlap?

Ⓐ 36 in.^{2} Ⓒ 180 in.^{2}

Ⓑ 144 in.^{2} Ⓓ 216 in.^{2}

Name _____

Surface Area of Pyramids

Essential Question How can you find the surface area of a pyramid?

Most people think of Egypt when they think of pyramids, but there are ancient pyramids throughout the world. The Pyramid of the Sun in Mexico was built around 100 C.E. and is one of the largest pyramids in the world.

COMMON CORE STANDARD CC.6.G.4
Solve real-world and mathematical problems involving area, surface area, and volume.

UNLOCK the Problem REAL WORLD

Cara is making a model of the Pyramid of the Sun for a history project. The base is a square with a side length of 12 in. Each triangular face has a height of 7 in. What is the surface area of Cara's model?

 Find the surface area of the square pyramid.

STEP 1

Label the dimensions on the net of the pyramid.

_____

STEP 2

Find the area of the base and each triangular face.

Base:

Write the formula for the area of a square. $A = s^2$

Substitute _____ for s and simplify. $A =$ _____ = _____ in.^{2}

Face:

Write the formula for the area of a triangle. $A = \frac{1}{2}bh$

Substitute _____ for b and _____ for h and simplify. $A = \frac{1}{2}$ (_____)(_____)

= _____ in.^{2}

_____

STEP 3

Add the areas to find the surface area of the pyramid.

$S =$ _____ + 4 × _____ = _____ + _____ = _____ in.^{2}

So, the surface area of Cara's model is _____.

Math Talk
MATHEMATICAL PRACTICES
Explain why you multiplied the area of the triangular face by 4 when finding the surface area.

Sometimes you need to find the total area of the lateral faces of a solid figure, but you don't need to include the area of the base. The **lateral area** L of a solid figure is the sum of the areas of the lateral faces.

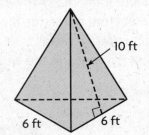

10 ft

6 ft   6 ft

🔑 **Example** Trevor is making a tent in the shape of a triangular pyramid. The three sides of the tent are made of fabric, and the bottom will be left open. The faces have a height of 10 ft and a base of 6 ft. What is the area of the fabric Trevor needs to make the tent?

Find the lateral area of the triangular pyramid.

STEP 1

Draw and label a net for the pyramid. _____

STEP 2

Shade the lateral area of the net. _____

STEP 3

Find the area of one of the lateral faces of the pyramid.

Write the formula for the area of a triangle $A = \frac{1}{2}bh$

Substitute _____ for b and _____ for h. $A = \frac{1}{2}$ (_____)(_____)

Simplify $A =$ _____ ft²

STEP 4

To find the lateral area, find the area of all three lateral faces of the pyramid.

$L = 3 \times$ _____ $=$ _____ ft²

So, the area of fabric Trevor needs is _____.

1. Explain the difference between finding the surface area and the lateral area of a three-dimensional figure.

_____

_____

2. **Explain** how you could find the amount of fabric needed if Trevor decided to make a fabric base for the tent. The height of the triangular base is about 5 ft.

_____

_____

Name _____

Share and Show

1. Use a net to find the surface area of the square pyramid.

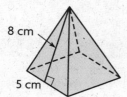

8 cm

5 cm

Base: $A =$ _____ = _____ cm²

Face: $A = \frac{1}{2}$ (_____)(_____) = _____ cm²

Surface area of pyramid: $S =$ _____ $+ 4 \times$ _____

= _____ + _____ = _____ cm²

2. A triangular pyramid has a base with an area of 43 cm² and lateral faces with bases of 10 cm and heights of 8.6 cm. What is the surface area of the pyramid?

_____

3. A square pyramid has a base with a side length of 3 ft and lateral faces with heights of 2 ft. What is the lateral area of the pyramid?

_____

 Math Talk MATHEMATICAL PRACTICES
Explain how to find the surface area of a square pyramid if you know the height of each face and the perimeter of the base.

On Your Own

Use a net to find the surface area of the square pyramid.

4.
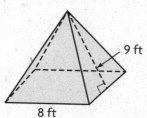
9 ft
8 ft

_____

5.
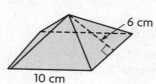
6 cm
10 cm

_____

6.
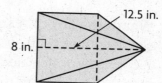
12.5 in.
8 in.

_____

7. The Pyramid Arena is located in Memphis, Tennessee. It is in the shape of a square pyramid, and the lateral faces are made almost entirely of glass. The base has a side length of about 600 ft and the lateral faces have a height of about 440 ft. What is the total area of the glass in the Pyramid Arena?

_____

Problem Solving REAL WORLD

Use the table for 8–9.

8. The Great Pyramids are located near Cairo, Egypt. They are all square pyramids, and their dimensions are shown in the table. What is the lateral area of the Pyramid of Cheops?

_____

9. What is the difference between the surface areas of the Pyramid of Khafre and the Pyramid of Menkaure?

_____

Dimensions of the Great Pyramids (in m)		
Name	Side Length of Base	Height of Lateral Faces
Cheops	230	180
Khafre	215	174
Menkaure	103	83

10. A store sells a lamp with a shade shaped like a triangular pyramid. The lateral faces of the shade are made of fabric, and the base is open. Each face has a base of 11 in. and a height of 13.5 in. What is the area of the fabric?

.... SHOW YOUR WORK ....

_____

11. **H.O.T.** **Algebra** Write an expression for the surface area of the square pyramid shown.

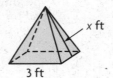

x ft

3 ft

_____

12. **What's the Error?** A square pyramid has a base with a side length of 4 cm and triangular faces with a height of 7 cm. Esther calculated the surface area as $(4 \times 4) + 4(4 \times 7) = 128$ cm^2. Explain Esther's error and find the correct surface area.

_____

_____

_____

13. ⭐ **Test Prep** A square pyramid has a base with a side length of 16 in. and triangular faces with heights of 16 in. What is the surface area of the pyramid?

Ⓐ 384 in.^{2} Ⓒ 768 in.^{2}

Ⓑ 512 in.^{2} Ⓓ 1,280 in.^{2}

 FOR MORE PRACTICE:
Standards Practice Book, pp. P211–P212

Name _____

✓ Mid-Chapter Checkpoint

► Vocabulary

Choose the best term from the box to complete the sentence.

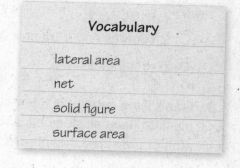

1. _____ is the sum of the areas of all the faces, or surfaces, of a solid figure. (p. 419)

2. A three-dimensional figure having length, width, and height is called a(n) _____. (p. 415)

3. The _____ of a solid figure is the sum of the areas of its lateral faces. (p. 428)

► Concepts and Skills

4. Identify and draw a net for the solid figure. (CC.6.G.4)

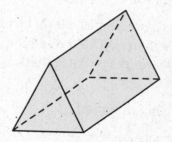

_____

5. Use a net to find the lateral area of the square pyramid. (CC.6.G.4)

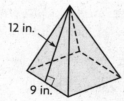

12 in.

9 in.

_____

6. Use a net to find the surface area of the prism. (CC.6.G.4)

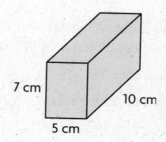

7 cm

10 cm

5 cm

_____

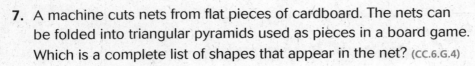

7. A machine cuts nets from flat pieces of cardboard. The nets can be folded into triangular pyramids used as pieces in a board game. Which is a complete list of shapes that appear in the net? (CC.6.G.4)

(A) 4 triangles

(B) 1 square and 3 triangles

(C) 2 squares and 4 triangles

(D) 6 rectangles

8. Fran's filing cabinet is 6 feet tall, $1\frac{1}{3}$ feet wide, and 3 feet deep. She plans to paint all sides except the bottom of the cabinet. Find the area of the sides she intends to paint. (CC.6.G.4)

(A) 26 square feet

(B) 41 square feet

(C) 56 square feet

(D) 71 square feet

9. A triangular pyramid has lateral faces with bases of 6 meters and heights of 9 meters. The area of the base of the pyramid is 15.6 square meters. What is the surface area of the pyramid? (CC.6.G.4)

(A) 62.4 square meters

(B) 81 square meters

(C) 96.6 square meters

(D) 177.6 square meters

10. What is the surface area of a storage box that measures 15 centimeters by 12 centimeters by 10 centimeters? (CC.6.G.4)

(A) 450 square centimeters

(B) 900 square centimeters

(C) 1,350 square centimeters

(D) 1,800 square centimeters

11. A footstool is a cube with a side length of 16 inches. Use the formula $S = 6s^2$ to find the surface area of the cube. (CC.6.EE.2c)

(A) 256 square inches

(B) 1,024 square inches

(C) 1,536 square inches

(D) 4,096 square inches

Name _____

Fractions and Volume

Essential Question What is the relationship between the volume and the edge lengths of a prism with fractional edge lengths?

COMMON CORE STANDARD CC.6.G.2
Solve real-world and mathematical problems involving area, surface area, and volume.

CONNECT **Volume** is the number of cubic units needed to occupy a given space without gaps or overlaps. You can find the volume of a rectangular prism by seeing how many unit cubes it takes to fill the prism. Recall that a unit cube is a cube with a side length of 1.

Investigate REAL WORLD

Materials ■ net of a rectangular prism, cubes, scissors, tape

A jewelry box has a length of $3\frac{1}{2}$ units, a width of $1\frac{1}{2}$ units, and a height of 2 units. What is the volume of the box in cubic units?

A. Each of the cubes in this activity has a side length of $\frac{1}{2}$ unit.

How many cubes with side length $\frac{1}{2}$ does it take to form

a unit cube? _____

So, each smaller cube represents _____ of a unit cube.

B. Cut out the net. Then fold and tape the net into a rectangular prism. Leave one face open so you can pack the prism with cubes.

C. Pack the prism with cubes.

How many cubes with side length $\frac{1}{2}$ does it take to fill the

prism? _____

D. To find the volume of the jewelry box in cubic units, determine how many unit cubes you could make from the smaller cubes you used to pack the prism.

Think: It takes 8 smaller cubes to make 1 unit cube.

Divide the total number of smaller cubes by 8. Write the remainder as a fraction.

_____ ÷ 8 = _____ = _____

So, the volume of the jewelry box is _____ cubic units.

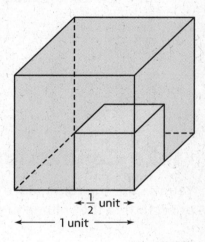

$\frac{1}{2}$ unit
1 unit

Math Talk MATHEMATICAL PRACTICES
Explain how you determined how many cubes with side length $\frac{1}{2}$ it takes to form a unit cube.

Draw Conclusions

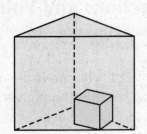

1. **Application** Could you use the method of packing cubes to find the volume of a triangular prism? **Explain.**

   _____

   _____

   _____

   _____

2. 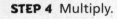 How many cubes with a side length of $\frac{1}{2}$ unit do you need to form 3 unit cubes? **Explain** how you know.

   _____

   _____

   _____

Make Connections

You can use the formula for the volume of a rectangular prism to find the volume of the jewelry box.

STEP 1 Write the formula you will use. $V = l \times w \times h$

STEP 2 Replace the variables using the values you know.

$V = 3\frac{1}{2} \times \boxed{} \times \boxed{}$

STEP 3 Write the mixed numbers as fractions greater than 1.

$V = \dfrac{\boxed{}}{\boxed{}} \times \dfrac{3}{2} \times 2$

STEP 4 Multiply.

$V = \dfrac{\boxed{}}{\boxed{}}$

STEP 5 Write the fraction as a mixed number.

$V = \boxed{}\,\dfrac{2}{4} = \boxed{}$

So, the volume of the jewelry box is _____ cubic units.

> **Remember**
> The volume of a rectangular prism is the product of the length, the width, and the height: $V = l \times w \times h$.

MATHEMATICAL PRACTICES

Math Talk Tell how the volume you found by using the formula compares to the volume you found by packing the prism with cubes.

Share and Show

1. A prism is filled with 38 cubes with a side length of $\frac{1}{2}$ unit. What is the volume of the prism in cubic units?

   $38 \div 8 =$ _____ = _____

   volume = _____ cubic units

2. A prism is filled with 58 cubes with a side length of $\frac{1}{2}$ unit. What is the volume of the prism in cubic units?

   _____

Find the volume of the rectangular prism.

3.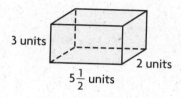

   3 units
   2 units
   $5\frac{1}{2}$ units

   _____

4.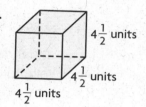

   $4\frac{1}{2}$ units
   $4\frac{1}{2}$ units
   $4\frac{1}{2}$ units

   _____

5. Theodore wants to put three flowering plants in his window planter. The window planter is shaped like a rectangular prism that is 30.5 in. long, 6 in. wide, and 6 in. deep. The three plants need a total of 1,200 in.³ of potting soil to grow well. Is the planter large enough? **Explain.**

   _____

   _____

   _____

6. **Write Math** ▸ **Explain** how use the formula $V = l \times w \times h$ to verify that a cube with a side length of $\frac{1}{2}$ unit has a volume of $\frac{1}{8}$ of a cubic unit.

   _____

   _____

   _____

Problem Solving · REAL WORLD

Use the diagram for 8–11.

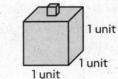

A

$\frac{1}{2}$ unit

1 unit

1 unit

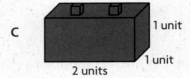

B

1 unit

1 unit

1 unit

C

1 unit

1 unit

2 units

8. Karyn is using a set of building blocks shaped like rectangular prisms to make a model. The three types of blocks she has are shown at right. What is the volume of an A block? (Do not include the pegs on top.)

_____

9. How many A blocks would you need to take up the same amount of space as a C block?

_____

10. Karyn puts a B block, two C blocks, and three A blocks together. What is the total volume of these blocks?

_____

11. **H.O.T.** Karyn uses the blocks to make a prism that is 2 units long, 3 units wide, and $1\frac{1}{2}$ units high. The prism is made of two C blocks, two B blocks, and some A blocks. What is the total volume of A blocks used?

_____

12. **Sense or Nonsense?** Jo says that you can use $V = l \times w \times h$ or $V = h \times w \times l$ to find the volume of a rectangular prism. Is Jo's statement sense or nonsense? **Explain.**

_____

_____

_____

13. ⭐ **Test Prep** A box measures 3 units by 2 units by $1\frac{1}{2}$ units. What is the greatest number of cubes with a side length of $\frac{1}{2}$ unit that can be packed inside the larger box?

(A) 18   (C) 48

(B) 36   (D) 72

SHOW YOUR WORK

Name _____

Volume of Rectangular Prisms

Essential Question How can you find the volume of rectangular prisms with fractional edge lengths?

COMMON CORE STANDARD CC.6.G.2
Solve real-world and mathematical problems involving area, surface area, and volume.

You can use the formula $V = l \times w \times h$ to find the volume of a rectangular prism when you know the length, width, and height of the prism.

🔑 UNLOCK the Problem REAL WORLD

A bento is a single-portion meal that is common in Japan. The meal is usually served in a box. A small bento box is a rectangular prism that is 5 inches long, 4 inches wide, and $2\frac{1}{2}$ inches high. How much food can the box hold?

> • Underline the sentence that tells you what you are trying to find.
> • Circle the numbers you need to use.

 Find the volume of a rectangular prism

You can use the formula $V = l \times w \times h$ to find the volume of a rectangular prism when you know the length, width, and height of the prism.

STEP 1

Sketch the rectangular prism.

$2\frac{1}{2}$ in.   4 in.   5 in.

_____

STEP 2 Identify the value for each variable.

The length l is 5 in.

The width w is _____ in.

The height h is _____ in.

_____

STEP 3 Evaluate the formula.

Write the formula. $V = l \times w \times h$

Replace l with 5, w with $V = $ _____ × _____ × _____

_____, and h with _____. $V = $ _____ in.³

Multiply.

So, the bento box can hold _____ in.³ of food.

© Houghton Mifflin Harcourt Publishing Company

Math Talk MATHEMATICAL PRACTICES
Explain how you know what units to use for the volume of the box.

Chapter 11 437

CONNECT You know that the volume of a rectangular prism is the product of its length, width, and height. Since the product of the length and width is the area of one base, the volume is also the product of the area of one base and the height.

> **Volume of a Prism**
>
> Volume = area of one base × height | $V = Bh$

🔒 Example 1 Find the volume of the prism.

STEP 1 Identify the value for each variable.

The height h is _____ in.

The area of the base B is _____ in.^{2}

STEP 2 Evaluate the formula.

Write the formula.

$$V = Bh$$

Replace B with _____ and h with _____.

$$V = \boxed{} \times \boxed{}$$

Write the mixed number as a fraction greater than 1.

$$V = \boxed{} \times \frac{\boxed{}}{4}$$

Multiply and write the product as a mixed number.

$$V = \boxed{} = \boxed{} \, \frac{1}{4} \, \text{in.}^3$$

So, the volume of the prism is _____.

🔒 Example 2 Find the volume of the cube.

Write the formula. The area of the square base is s^2. The height of a cube is also s, so $V = Bh = s^3$.

$$V = s^3$$

Substitute _____ for s.

$$V = \left(\boxed{}\right)^3$$

Write the mixed number as a fraction greater than 1. Then use repeated multiplication.

$$V = \left(\boxed{}\right)^3 = \left(\boxed{}\right)\left(\boxed{}\right)\left(\boxed{}\right)$$

Simplify.

$$V = \frac{\boxed{}}{8} = 42\frac{\boxed{}}{8} \, \text{ft}^3$$

So, the volume of the cube is _____.

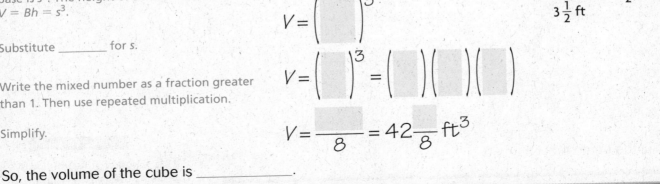

438

Name _____

Share and Show

Find the volume.

1.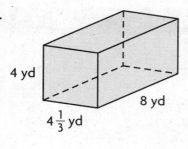

$V = lwh$

$V = $ _____ $\times$ _____ $\times$ _____

$V = $ _____ in.^{3}

2.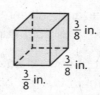

$\frac{3}{8}$ in.
$\frac{3}{8}$ in.
$\frac{3}{8}$ in.

_____

3.

4 yd

8 yd

$4\frac{1}{3}$ yd

_____

4.

$9\frac{1}{2}$ ft

6 ft

$5\frac{1}{4}$ ft

_____

5.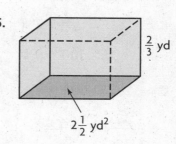

$\frac{2}{3}$ yd

$2\frac{1}{2}$ yd^2

_____

MATHEMATICAL PRACTICES

Math Talk Describe the steps for finding the volume of a cube.

On Your Own

Find the volume of the prism.

6.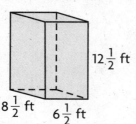

$12\frac{1}{2}$ ft

$8\frac{1}{2}$ ft $6\frac{1}{2}$ ft

_____

7.

$\frac{5}{16}$ in.
$\frac{5}{16}$ in.
$\frac{5}{16}$ in.

_____

8.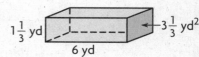

$1\frac{1}{3}$ yd $3\frac{1}{3}$ yd^2

6 yd

_____

9. Wayne's gym locker is a cube with a side length of $14\frac{1}{2}$ inches. What is the volume of the locker? Explain how you found the answer.

_____

Connect to Science | REAL WORLD

Aquariums

Large public aquariums like the Tennessee Aquarium in Chattanooga have a wide variety of freshwater and saltwater fish species from around the world. The fish are kept in aquariums of various sizes.

The table shows information about several aquariums that are rectangular prisms. Use the formula $V = Bh$ or $V = lwh$ to find the missing values in the table.

Find the length of Tank 1.

$$V = lwh$$

$$52,500 = l \times \underline{\hspace{1cm}} \times \underline{\hspace{1cm}}$$

$$52,500 = l \times \underline{\hspace{1.5cm}}$$

$$\frac{52,500}{\underline{\hspace{1cm}}} = l$$

$$\underline{\hspace{1cm}} = l$$

So, the length of Tank 1 is _____.

Solve.

Aquarium Tanks

	Length	Width	Height	Volume
Tank 1		30 cm	35 cm	52,500 cm³
Tank 2	12 m		4 m	384 m³
Tank 3	18 m	12 m		2,160 m³
Tank 4	72 cm	55 cm	40 cm	

10. Find the width of Tank 2.

_____

11. Find the height of Tank 3.

_____

12. **H.O.T.** To keep aquarium fish healthy, there should be the correct ratio of water to fish. One recommended ratio is 9 L of water for every 2 fish. Find the volume of Tank 4. Then use the equivalencies $1 \text{ cm}^3 = 1 \text{ mL}$ and $1,000 \text{ mL} = 1 \text{ L}$ to find how many fish can be safely kept in Tank 4.

_____

13. Give another set of dimensions for an aquarium that would have the same volume as Tank 2. Explain how you found your answer.

_____

_____

FOR MORE PRACTICE:
Standards Practice Book, pp. P215–P216

Name _____

Problem Solving • Geometric Measurements

Essential Question How can you use the strategy *use a formula* to solve problems involving area, surface area, and volume?

COMMON CORE STANDARD CC.6.G.4
Solve real-world and mathematical problems involving area, surface area, and volume.

🔑 UNLOCK the Problem REAL WORLD

Shedd Aquarium in Chicago has one of the country's few full-scale animal hospitals linked to an aquarium. One tank used to hold sick fish is a rectangular prism measuring 75 cm long, 60 cm wide, and 36 cm high along the outside. The glass on the tank is 2 cm thick. How much water can the tank hold? Which measure—area, surface area, or volume—should you use to solve the problem?

Use the graphic organizer to help you solve the problem.

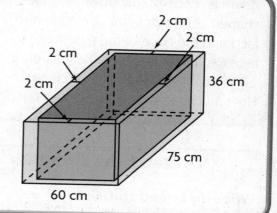

2 cm
2 cm
2 cm
2 cm
36 cm
75 cm
60 cm

Read the Problem

What do I need to find?

I need to find _____ and

_____.

What information do I need to use?

I need to use _____ and

_____.

How will I use the information?

First I will decide _____.

Then I will choose a _____ I can

use to calculate the measure. Finally, I will

substitute the values for the _____,

and I will _____ the formula.

So, the volume of the tank is _____.

Solve the Problem

• Choose the measure that specifies the amount of water that will fill a tank.

_____

• Choose an appropriate formula.

_____

• Subtract the width of the glass twice from the length and width and once from the height to find the inner dimensions.

Find the length.   75 cm − 4 cm = _____ cm

Find the width.   60 cm − 4 cm = _____ cm

Find the height.   36 cm − 2 cm = _____ cm

• Substitute and evaluate.

$V = 71 \times$ _____ $\times$ _____

$=$ _____ cm^3

Math Talk MATHEMATICAL PRACTICES
Explain why volume is the correct measure to use to solve the problem.

Chapter 11   441

Try Another Problem

Alexander Graham Bell, the inventor of the telephone, also invented a kite made out of "cells" shaped like triangular pyramids.

A kite is made of triangular pyramid-shaped cells with fabric covering one face and the base of the pyramid. The face and base both have heights of 17.3 cm and side lengths of 20 cm. How much fabric is needed to make one pyramid cell?

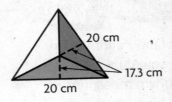

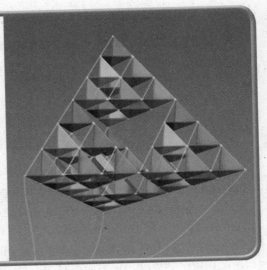

Read the Problem	Solve the Problem
What do I need to find?	
What information do I need to use?	
How will I use the information?	

So, _____ cm² of fabric is needed.

- **Explain** how you knew which units to use for your answer.

_____

Math Talk MATHEMATICAL PRACTICES Explain how the strategy of using a formula helped you solve the problem.

Name _____

Share and Show

UNLOCK the Problem **Tips**

√ Draw a diagram.

√ Identify the measure needed.

√ Choose an appropriate formula.

1. An aquarium tank in the shape of a rectangular prism is 60 cm long, 30 cm wide, and 24 cm high. The top of the tank is open, and the glass used to make the tank is 1 cm thick. How much water can the tank hold?

   First identify the measure and choose an appropriate formula.

   _____

   Next find the inner dimensions and replace the variables with the correct values.

   _____

   Finally, evaluate the formula.

   _____

   So, the tank can hold _____ of water.

2. **H.O.T.** **What if**, to provide greater strength, the glass bottom were increased to a thickness of 4 cm? How much less water would the tank hold?

   _____

3. An aquarium tank in the shape of a rectangular prism is 40 cm long, 26 cm wide, and 24 cm high. If the top of the tank is open, how much tinting is needed to cover the glass on the tank? Identify the measure you used to solve the problem.

   _____

4. The Louvre Museum in Paris, France, has a square pyramid made of glass in its central courtyard. The four triangular faces of the pyramid have bases of 35 meters and heights of 27.8 meters. What is the area of glass used for the four triangular faces of the pyramid?

   _____

The Louvre Museum in Paris, France

SHOW YOUR WORK

On Your Own...........

Choose a STRATEGY

Use a Model
Draw a Diagram
Find a Pattern
Solve a Simpler Problem
Work Backward
Use a Formula

5. A rectangular-prism-shaped block of wood measures 3 m by $1\frac{1}{2}$ m by $1\frac{1}{2}$ m. How much of the block must a sculptor carve away to obtain a prism that measures 2 m by $\frac{1}{2}$ m by $\frac{1}{2}$ m?

_____

6. **H.O.T.** The sculptor (Problem 5) varnished the outside of the smaller piece of wood, all except for the bottom, which measures $\frac{1}{2}$ m by $\frac{1}{2}$ m. Varnish costs $2.00 per square meter. What was the cost of varnishing the wood?

_____

SHOW YOUR WORK

7. A wax candle is in the shape of a cube with a side length of $2\frac{1}{2}$ in. What volume of wax is needed to make the candle?

_____

8. **H.O.T.** **Pose a Problem** A rectangular prism-shaped box measures 6 cm by 5 cm by 4 cm. A cube-shaped box has a side length of 2 cm. Write and solve a problem involving the volumes of the two boxes.

_____

_____

_____

_____

9. ⭐ **Test Prep** The sea otters at the aquarium play in a pool shaped like a rectangular prism that has a length of $10\frac{1}{2}$ ft, a width of 20 feet, and a depth of 6 feet. Find the amount of water needed to fill the pool.

Ⓐ 630 cubic feet

Ⓑ 1,260 cubic feet

Ⓒ 3,266 cubic feet

Ⓓ 5,040 cubic feet

FOR MORE PRACTICE:
Standards Practice Book, pp. P217–P218

Name _____

✓ Chapter 11 Review/Test

▶ **Vocabulary**

Choose the best term from the box to complete the sentence.

Vocabulary
net
solid figure
surface area
volume

1. A three-dimensional figure having length, width, and height is

   called a(n) _____. (p. 415)

2. _____ is the sum of the areas of all the faces, or surfaces, of a solid figure. (p. 419)

3. _____ is the measure of space a solid figure occupies. (p. 433)

4. A two-dimensional pattern that can be folded into a

   three-dimensional figure is called a(n) _____. (p. 415)

▶ **Concepts and Skills**

Use a net to find the surface area. (CC.6.G.4)

5.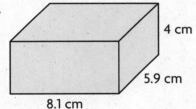
   4 cm
   5.9 cm
   8.1 cm

6.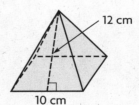
   12 cm
   10 cm

_____

_____

Find the volume. (CC.6.G.2)

7. The water hazard on a miniature golf course is a rectangular prism with a length of 30 inches, a width of $10\frac{1}{2}$ inches, and a depth of $2\frac{1}{2}$ inches. How many cubic inches of water are needed to fill the hazard?

8. The outside of a packing box is 30 cm long, 20 cm wide, and 15 cm high. The cardboard used to make the box is 0.5 cm thick. What is the volume of the inside of the box?

_____

_____

GO Online
Assessment Options
Chapter Test

9. A pyramid on Mexico's Yucatan Peninsula is a square pyramid. How many faces does the pyramid have, not including its base? (CC.6.G.4)

Ⓐ 3 faces

Ⓑ 4 faces

Ⓒ 5 faces

Ⓓ 6 faces

10. A rectangular prism can be exactly filled with 92 cubes with a side length of $\frac{1}{2}$ unit. What is the volume of the prism in cubic units?
(CC.6.G.2)

Ⓐ $11\frac{1}{2}$ cubic units

Ⓑ $22\frac{1}{2}$ cubic units

Ⓒ 46 cubic units

Ⓓ 92 cubic units

11. A jewelry box is a rectangular prism with a length of 9 inches and a height of $5\frac{1}{4}$ inches. The volume of the jewelry box is $283\frac{1}{2}$ cubic inches. What is the width of the jewelry box? (CC.6.G.2)

Ⓐ 3 inches

Ⓑ 6 inches

Ⓒ 12 inches

Ⓓ 45 inches

12. A triangular pyramid has a base with an area of 43.3 square feet. The lateral faces have a base length of 10 feet and a height of 6 feet. What is the surface area of the pyramid? (CC.6.G.2)

Ⓐ 103.3 square feet

Ⓑ 133.3 square feet

Ⓒ 163.3 square feet

Ⓓ 173.2 square feet

13. Which formula could you use to find the surface area of a cube with side length s? (CC.6.EE.2c)

Ⓐ $S = 4s^2$ Ⓒ $S = 6s^2$

Ⓑ $S = 4s^3$ Ⓓ $S = \frac{1}{2}s^2$

14. Paula wants to know how much fruit juice a carton in the shape of a rectangular prism can hold. Which measure should she find? (CC.6.G.2)

(A) The area of the carton

(B) The surface area of the carton

(C) The perimeter of the carton

(D) The volume of the carton

15. A container for mailing posters is in the shape of a rectangular prism. Which of the following is the best estimate for the volume of the figure? (CC.6.G.2)

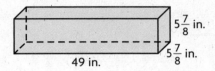

$5\frac{7}{8}$ in.

$5\frac{7}{8}$ in.

49 in.

(A)　300 cubic inches

(B) 1,000 cubic inches

(C) 1,800 cubic inches

(D) 2,400 cubic inches

16. How many squares are there in the net of a triangular pyramid?
(CC.6.G.4)

(A) 0

(B) 1

(C) 4

(D) 6

17. A pool in the shape of a rectangular prism has a length of 12 meters, a width of 6 meters, and a depth of 1.5 meters. Find the volume of water needed to fill the pool. (CC.6.G.2)

(A)　19.5 cubic meters

(B)　39 cubic meters

(C)　54 cubic meters

(D) 108 cubic meters

▶ Constructed Response

18. Give an example of a real-world problem that would require the solver to find the surface area of a prism. (CC.6.G.4)

_____

_____

19. The stones that make up Stonehenge in England are shaped roughly like rectangular prisms. The average stone in the outer circle has a height of 13 feet and a base area of $19\frac{1}{2}$ square feet. Explain how to find the volume of one of the stones and then calculate the volume. (CC.6.G.2)

_____

_____

▶ Performance Task (CC.6.G.2, CC.6.EE.2c)

20. A carton for a basketball is a cube with a side length of $9\frac{1}{2}$ inches. A designer wants to find out how much surface area needs to be decorated.

A Draw and label a net for the cube. What is the surface area of the cube?

_____

B The designer doesn't need to decorate the bottom of the box. Explain how he can find the area of 5 faces if he knows the surface area of the entire box. Then calculate the area.

_____

_____

C The designer also wants to cut a shape out of front of the box so that customers can see the ball inside. Choose a shape for the opening and decide its dimensions. Then write and evaluate an expression to find the amount of the box's surface area that will be decorated.

_____

_____

Chapter 12 Data Displays and Measures of Center

Show What You Know ✓

Check your understanding of important skills

Name _____

▶ **Read a Bar Graph** Use the bar graph to answer the questions.

1. Who has the highest test score?

   _____

2. Who has a score between 70 and 80?

   _____

3. What is the difference between the highest and lowest scores?

   _____

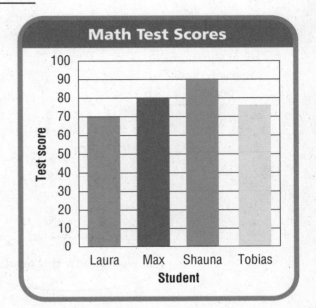

Math Test Scores

▶ **Division** Find the quotient.

4. $35\overline{)980}$

5. $16\overline{)352}$

6. $24\overline{)3,456}$

7. $42\overline{)3,276}$

▶ **Compare Decimals** Compare. Write <, >, or =.

8. $2.48 \bigcirc 2.53$

9. $0.3 \bigcirc 0.04$

10. $4.63 \bigcirc 4.3$

11. $1.7 \bigcirc 1.70$

MATH DETECTIVE WITH CARMEN SANDIEGO™

Kayla scored 110 in the first game she bowled, but she can't remember her score from the second game. The average of the two scores is 116. Be a Math Detective and help her figure out what her second score was.

_____

Vocabulary Builder

▶ **Visualize It** ● ● ● ● ● ● ● ● ● ● ● ● ● ● ● ● ● ●

Sort the review words into the chart.

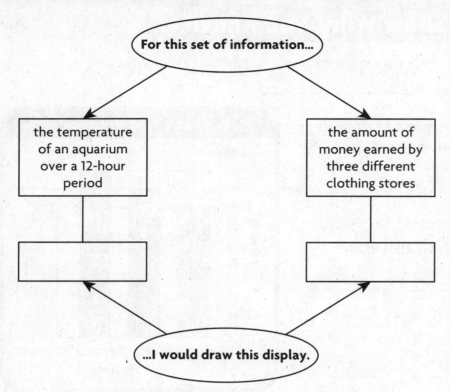

For this set of information...

the temperature of an aquarium over a 12-hour period

the amount of money earned by three different clothing stores

...I would draw this display.

▶ **Understand Vocabulary** ● ● ● ● ● ● ● ● ● ● ● ● ● ● ● ● ● ●

Complete the sentences using the preview words.

1. A(n) _____ is a bar graph that shows the frequency of data in specific intervals.

2. The _____ is the middle value when a data set with an odd number of values is ordered from least to greatest.

3. A(n) _____ is a value that is much less or much greater than the other values in a data set.

4. A(n) _____ is a number line with dots that show

   the _____ of the values in a data set.

5. You can calculate the _____ of a data set by adding the values and then dividing the sum by the number of values.

6. The item(s) that occurs most often in a data set is called the

   _____ of the data.

GO
Online

● eStudent Edition ● Multimedia eGlossary

Name

Recognize Statistical Questions

Essential Question How do you identify a statistical question?

COMMON CORE STANDARD CC.6.SP.1
Develop understanding of statistical variability.

If you measure the heights of your classmates, you are collecting data. A set of **data** is a set of information collected about people or things. A question that asks about a set of data that can vary is called a **statistical question**.

"What are the heights of my classmates on July 1?" is a statistical question because height usually varies in a group of people. "What is Sasha's height on July 1?" is not a statistical question because it asks for only one piece of information at one time.

🔑 UNLOCK the Problem REAL WORLD

The New England Aquarium in Boston is home to over 80 penguins. Which of the following is a statistical question a biologist could ask about the penguins? Explain your reasoning.

A How much does the penguin named Pip weigh this morning?

B How much does the penguin named Pip weigh each morning on 30 different days?

🔑 **Identify the statistical question.**

Question A asks for Pip's weight at _____ time(s),

so it _____ ask about a set of data that varies.

Question A _____ a statistical question.

Question B asks for Pip's weight at _____ time(s), and it is

likely that Pip's weight _____ vary during this period.

Question B asks about a set of data that can vary, so it _____ a statistical question.

• Another biologist asks how old the penguin named Royal Pudding is. Is this a statistical question? Explain your reasoning.

_____

_____

A statistical question can ask about an entire set of data that can vary or a value that describes that set of data. For example, "What is the height of the tallest person in my class?" is a statistical question because it will tell you the greatest value in a set of data that can vary. You will learn other ways to describe a set of data later in this chapter.

🔒 Example

Bongos are a kind of antelope that live in central Africa. Bongos are unusual because both males and females have horns. Write two statistical questions a biologist could ask about a group of bongos.

1. What is the _____ in inches of the horns on the

   bongo that has the _____ horns in the group?

   Different bongos will have different horn lengths. This

   question asks about a value in a set of data that _____

   vary, so it _____ a statistical question.

2. What is the weight of the _____ bongo in the group?

   Different bongos will have different weights. This question asks

   about a value in a set of data that _____ vary, so it _____ a
   statistical question.

Math Talk MATHEMATICAL PRACTICES
Give a different statistical question you could ask about the heights of students in your class.

Try This! Write a statistical question you could ask in the situations described below.

A A researcher knows the amount of electricity used in 20 different homes on a Monday.

_____

_____

_____

_____

_____

B A museum director records the number of students in each tour group that visits the museum during one week.

_____

_____

_____

_____

_____

Name _____

Identify the statistical question. Explain your reasoning.

☑ 1. **A.** What was the low temperature in Chicago each day in March?

    B. What was the low temperature in Chicago on March 7?

    Question A asks for the low temperature at _____ time(s),

    and it is likely the temperature _____.

    Question B asks for the low temperature at _____ time(s).

    Question _____ is a statistical question.

2. **A.** How long did it take you to get to school this morning?

    B. How long did it take you to get to school each morning this week?

    _____

    _____

Write a statistical question you could ask in the situation.

☑ 3. A student recorded the number of pets in the households of 50 sixth-graders.

    _____

> **Math Talk** [MATHEMATICAL PRACTICES]
> **Explain** how to determine whether a question is a statistical question.

On Your Own . . . .

Identify the statistical question. Explain your reasoning.

4. **A.** How many gold medals has Finland won at each of the last 10 Winter Olympics?

    B. How many gold medals did Finland win at the 2008 Winter Olympics?

    _____

    _____

Write a statistical question you could ask in the situation.

5. A wildlife biologist measured the length of time that 17 grizzly bears hibernated.

    _____

6. A doctor recorded the birth weights of 48 babies.

    _____

Problem Solving REAL WORLD

Use the table for 7–9.

7. Give a statistical question that you could ask about the data recorded in the table.

_____

_____

8. **H.O.T.** What statistical question could "92 mi/hr" be the answer to?

_____

_____

9. **Sense or Nonsense?** Rory says that this is a statistical question: How tall is the Varmint? Is Rory's statement sense or nonsense? Explain.

_____

_____

_____

_____

Roller Coaster Data

Name	Height (ft)	Maximum Speed (mi/hr)
Rocket	256	83
Thunder Dolphin	281	87
Varmint	240	81
Screamer	302	92

SHOW YOUR WORK

10. **Write Math** The manager of a video game company wants to determine whether to release a role-playing game or an action game next. He asks his sales staff which of the last 10 released games sold the most copies. Explain why this is a statistical question.

_____

_____

_____

11. ⭐ **Test Prep** Which question is a statistical question?

(A) How far is it from Dallas to Phoenix?

(B) Which candidate received the most votes?

(C) In what year was Abraham Lincoln born?

(D) What team won the 2010 World Series?

Describe Data Collection

Essential Question How can you describe how a data set was collected?

COMMON CORE STANDARDS CC.6.SP.5a, CC.6.SP.5b
Summarize and describe distributions.

UNLOCK the Problem REAL WORLD

One way to describe a set of data is by stating the number of *observations*, or measurements, that were made. Another way is by listing the attributes that were measured. An *attribute* is a property or characteristic of the item being measured, such as its color or length.

Jeffrey's hobby is collecting rocks and minerals. The chart gives data on garnets he found during a recent mineral-hunting trip. Identify:

- The attribute being measured
- The unit of measure
- The likely means by which measurements were made
- The number of observations

Garnet Data			
Garnet	Mass (g)	Garnet	Mass (g)
1	7.2	7	4.6
2	3.5	8	5.6
3	4.0	9	9.0
4	3.9	10	3.6
5	5.2	11	3.8
6	5.8	12	4.3

Describe the data set.

Think: What property or characteristic of the garnets did Jeffrey measure?

- The attribute Jeffrey measured was the _____ of the garnets.

- The unit used to measure the mass of the garnets was _____.

- To measure mass in grams, Jeffrey probably used a _____.

- The number of observations Jeffrey made was _____.

---

1. Would Jeffrey likely have gotten the same data set if he had measured a different group of garnets? Explain.

_____

_____

2. What other attributes of the garnets could Jeffrey have measured?

_____

_____

🔑 Activity Collect a data set.

Materials ▪ ruler

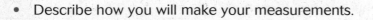

In this activity, you will work with other students to collect data on the length of the students' index fingers in your group. You will present the data in a chart.

- Describe the attribute you will measure. What unit will you use?

  _____

  _____

- Describe how you will make your measurements.

  _____

  _____

  _____

- Describe the data you will record in your chart.

  _____

  _____

- In the space at the right, make a chart of your data.

- How many observations did you make?

  _____

Math Talk MATHEMATICAL PRACTICES

Explain what statistical question your data set in the Activity answers.

3. One of your classmates made 3 observations and another made 10 observations to answer a statistical question. Who do you think arrived at a better answer to the statistical question? **Explain.**

_____

_____

_____

Name _____

Share and Show

Describe the data set by listing the attribute measured, the unit of measure, the likely means of measurement, and the number of observations.

1. Greg's 100-meter race results

attribute: _____

unit of measure: _____

likely means by which measurements were taken: _____

number of observations: _____

100-Meter Run Data			
Race	Time (sec)	Race	Time (sec)
1	12.8	5	13.5
2	12.5	6	13.7
3	12.9	7	12.6
4	13.4		

2. The Andrews family's water use

_____

_____

_____

_____

Daily Water Use (gal)				
153.7	161.8	151.5	153.7	160.1
161.9	155.5	152.3	166.7	158.3
155.8	167.5	150.8	154.6	

MATHEMATICAL PRACTICES

Math Talk Explain why it is important to make more than one observation when attempting to answer a statistical question.

On Your Own

Describe the data set by listing the attribute measured, the unit of measure, the likely means of measurement, and the number of observations.

3. Miami rainfall

_____

_____

_____

_____

Average Monthly Rainfall (in.)				
1.9	2.1	2.6	3.4	5.5
8.5	5.8	8.6	8.4	6.2
3.4	2.2			

4. Practice: Copy and Solve Collect data on one of the topics listed below. You may wish to work with other students. Make a chart of your results. Then describe the data set.

- Weights of cereal boxes, soup cans, or other items
- Numbers of family members
- Lengths of time to multiply two two-digit numbers
- Numbers of pets in families
- Lengths of forearm (elbow to fingertip)
- Numbers of pages in books

Connect to Reading

Summarize

When you *summarize* a reading passage, you restate the most important information in a shortened form. This allows you to understand more easily what you have read. Read the followng passage:

A biologist is studying green anacondas. The green anaconda is the largest snake in the world. Finding the length of any snake is difficult because the snake can curl up or stretch out while being measured. Finding the length of a green anaconda is doubly difficult because of the animal's great size and strength. The standard method for measuring a green anaconda is to calm the snake, lay a piece of string along its entire length, and then measure the length of the string. The table at the right gives data collected by the biologist using the string method.

5. Summarize the passage in your own words.

_____

_____

_____

_____

Green Anaconda Lengths (cm)			
357.2	407.6	494.5	387.0
417.6	305.3	189.4	267.7
441.3	507.5	413.2	469.8
168.9	234.0	366.2	499.1
370.0	488.8	219.2	

Use your summary to answer 6–7.

6. What attribute was the biologist measuring?

_____

7. How did the biologist measure this attribute?

_____

_____

8. Give any other information that is important for describing the data set.

_____

_____

9. **H.O.T.** Find the greatest green anaconda length that the biologist measured. Convert the measurement to feet, and round your answer to the nearest foot. (Hint: 1 foot is equal to about 30 centimeters.)

_____

© Houghton Mifflin Harcourt Publishing Company

FOR MORE PRACTICE:
Standards Practice Book, pp. P225–P226

Dot Plots and Frequency Tables

Essential Question How can you use dot plots and frequency tables to display data?

COMMON CORE STANDARD CC.6.SP.4
Summarize and describe distributions.

A **dot plot** is a number line with marks that show the frequency of data. **Frequency** is the number of times a data value occurs.

 UNLOCK the Problem REAL WORLD

Hannah is training for a walkathon. The table shows the number of miles she walks each day. She has one day left in her training. How many miles is she most likely to walk on the last day?

• What do you need to find?

_____

_____

🔑 **Make a dot plot.**

STEP 1

Draw a number line with an appropriate scale.

Numbers vary from _____ to _____, so use a scale from 0 to 10.

STEP 2

For each piece of data, plot a dot above the number that corresponds to the number of miles Hannah walked.

Complete the dot plot by making the correct number of dots above the numbers 5 through 10.

The number of miles Hannah walked most often is the value with the tallest stack of dots. The tallest stack in this dot plot is for

_____.

So, the number of miles Hannah is most likely to

walk on the last day of her training is _____.

Distance Hannah Walked (mi)				
4	2	9	3	3
5	5	1	6	2
5	2	5	4	5
4	9	3	2	4

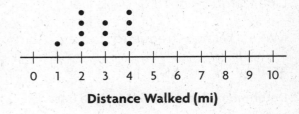

Distance Walked (mi)

Math Idea

A dot plot is sometimes called a line plot.

• **Explain** why a dot plot is useful for solving this problem.

_____

_____

A **frequency table** shows the number of times each data value or range of values occurs. A **relative frequency table** shows the percent of time each piece of data or group of data occurs.

 Example 1

Jill kept a record of her workout times. How many of Jill's workouts lasted exactly 90 minutes?

Make a frequency table.

STEP 1

List the workout times in the first column.

STEP 2

Record the frequency of each time in the Frequency column.

Complete the frequency table.

So, _____ of Jill's workouts lasted exactly 90 minutes.

Jill's Workout Times (minutes)						
30	60	30	90	60	30	60
90	60	120	30	60	90	90
60	120	60	60	60	30	30
120	30	120	60	120	60	120

Jill's Workout Times	
Minutes	**Frequency**
30	7
60	
90	
120	

 Example 2

The table shows the number of laps Ricardo swam each day. What percent of the days did Ricardo swim 18 or more laps?

Make a relative frequency table.

STEP 1

Determine equal intervals for the data. List the intervals in the first column.

STEP 2

Count the number of data values in each interval. Record this in the Frequency column.

STEP 3

Divide each frequency by the total number of data values. Write the result as a percent in the Relative Frequency column.

Complete the relative frequency table.

So, Ricardo swam 18 or more laps on _____ of the days.

Ricardo's Lap Swimming				
10	10	15	5	12
12	5	19	3	19
16	14	17	18	13
6	17	16	11	8

Ricardo's Lap Swimming		
Number of Laps	**Frequency**	**Relative Frequency**
3–7	4	20%
8–12	6	30%
13–17	7	
18–22	3	

There are 20 data values.

$\frac{4}{20} = 0.2 = 20\%$

$\frac{6}{20} = 0.3 = 30\%$

Math Talk

MATHEMATICAL PRACTICES

Explain how you could find the percent of days on which Ricardo swam 13 or more laps.

Name _____

Share and Show

For 1—4, use the data at right.

✓ 1. Complete the dot plot.

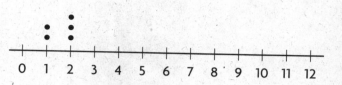

Daily Distance Lionel Biked (km)				
3	5	12	2	1
8	5	8	6	3
11	8	6	4	10
10	9	6	6	6
5	2	1	2	3

2. What was the most common distance Lionel biked? How do you know?

_____

_____

✓ 3. Make a frequency table. Use the intervals 1—3 km, 4—6 km, 7—9 km, and 10—12 km.

4. Make a relative frequency table. Use the same intervals as in Exercise 3.

On Your Own

Practice: Copy and Solve For 5—9, use the table.

5. Make a dot plot of the data.

6. Make a frequency table of the data with three intervals.

7. Make a relative frequency table of the data with three intervals.

8. **Write Math** ▶ **Describe** how you decided on the intervals for the frequency table.

Gloria's Daily Sit-Ups				
13	3	14	13	12
12	13	4	15	12
15	13	14	3	11
13	13	12	14	15
11	14	13	15	11

9. **H.O.T.** Could someone use the information in the frequency table to make a dot plot? **Explain.**

_____

🔑 UNLOCK the Problem

10. The manager of a fitness center asked members to rate the fitness center. The results of the survey are shown in the frequency table. What percent of members in the survey rated the center as excellent or good?

(A) 25%   (C) 33%

(B) 30%   (D) 55%

a. What do you need to find?

_____

_____

b. How can you use relative frequency to help you solve the problem?

_____

_____

Fitness Center Survey

Response	Frequency
Excellent	18
Good	15
Fair	21
Poor	6

c. Show the steps you use to solve the problem.

d. Complete the sentences.

The percent of members who rated the center as excellent is _____.

The percent of members who rated the center as good is _____.

The percent of members who rated the center as excellent or good is _____.

e. Fill in the bubble for the correct answer choice above.

Use the table above for 11–12.

11. What percent of members in the survey rated the fitness center as fair or poor?

(A) 10%   (C) 35%

(B) 27%   (D) 45%

12. Which response was given by $\frac{1}{4}$ of the members in the survey?

(A) Excellent   (C) Fair

(B) Good   (D) Poor

FOR MORE PRACTICE:
Standards Practice Book, pp. P227–P228

Name _____

Histograms

Essential Question How can you use histograms to display data?

COMMON CORE STANDARD CC.6.SP.4
Summarize and describe distributions.

When there is a large number of data values, it is helpful to group the data into intervals. A **histogram** is a bar graph that shows the frequency of data in intervals. Unlike a bar graph, there are no gaps between the bars in a histogram.

 UNLOCK the Problem REAL WORLD

The histogram shows the ages of winners of the Academy Award for Best Actor from 1990 to 2009. How many winners were under 40 years old?

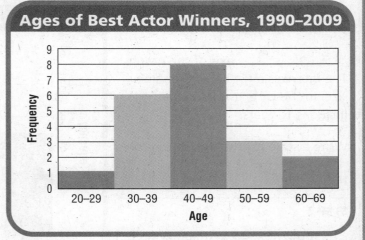

Interpret the histogram.

The height of each bar shows how many data values are in the interval the bar represents.

How many winners were 20–29 years old?

_____

Which other bar represents people under 40?

_____

How many winners were 30–39 years old? _____

To find the total number of winners who were under 40 years old, add the frequencies for the intervals 20–29 and 30–39.

_____ + _____ = _____

So, _____ of the winners were under 40 years old.

1. **Explain** whether it is possible to know from the histogram if any winner was 37 years old.

_____

Example

The table shows the ages of winners of the Academy Award for Best Actress from 1986 to 2009. How many of the winners were under 40 years old?

Make a histogram.

Ages of Best Actress Winners					
45	21	41	26	80	42
29	33	36	45	49	39
34	26	25	33	35	35
28	30	29	61	32	33

STEP 1

Make a frequency table using intervals of 10.

Interval	20–29	30–39	40–49	50–59	60–69	70–79	80–89
Frequency	7			0			1

STEP 2

Set up the intervals along the

_____ axis of the graph. The intervals must be all the same size. In this case, every interval includes 10 years.

Write a scale for the frequencies on

the _____ axis.

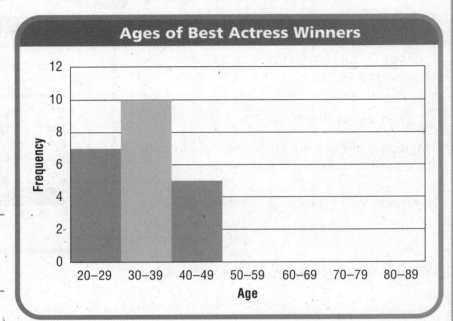

Ages of Best Actress Winners

STEP 3

Graph the number of winners in each interval.

STEP 4

Give the graph a title and label the axes.

Complete the histogram by drawing the bars for the intervals 60–69, 70–79, and 80–89.

To find the number of winners who were under 40 years old, add the frequencies for the intervals 20–29 and 30–39.

_____ + _____ = _____

So, _____ of the winners were under 40 years old.

2. **Explain** how you can tell from the histogram which age group has the most winners.

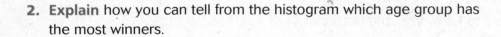

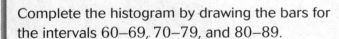

Name _____

Share and Show

For 1–3, use the data at right.

1. Complete the frequency table for the age data in the table at right.

Interval	10–19	20–29	30–39	40–49
Frequency	2			

Ages of People at a Health Club (yr)				
21	25	46	19	33
38	18	22	30	29
26	34	48	22	31

✓ 2. Complete the histogram for the data.

✓ 3. Use your histogram to find the number of people at the health club who are 30 or older.

_____

4. Use your histogram to determine the percent of the people at the health club who are 20–29 years old.

_____

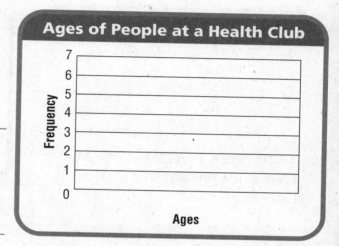

Ages of People at a Health Club

Frequency: 7 6 5 4 3 2 1 0

Ages

Math Talk MATHEMATICAL PRACTICES
Explain whether you could use the histogram to find the number of people who are 25 or older.

On Your Own

Practice: Copy and Solve For 5–7, use the table.

5. Make a histogram of the data using the intervals 10–19, 20–29, and 30–39.

6. Make a histogram of the data using the intervals 10–14, 15–19, 20–24, 25–29, 30–34, and 35–39.

Weights of Dogs (lb)				
16	20	15	24	32
33	26	30	15	21
21	12	19	21	37
10	39	21	17	35

7. Explain how using different intervals changed the appearance of your histogram.

_____

_____

_____

Problem Solving · REAL WORLD

The histogram shows the hourly salaries, to the nearest dollar, of the employees at a small company. Use the histogram to solve 8–11.

8. How many employees make less than $20 per hour?

   _____

9. How many employees work at the company? Explain how you know.

   _____

   _____

10. **H.O.T.** **Pose a Problem** Write and solve a new problem that uses the histogram.

   _____

   _____

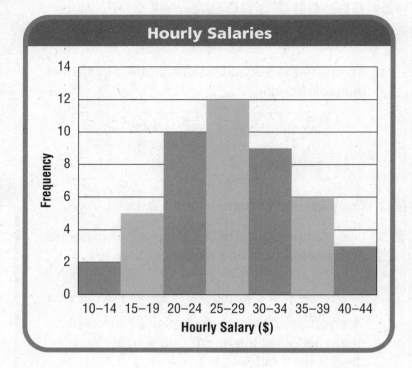

Hourly Salaries

Frequency vs. *Hourly Salary ($)*

10–14, 15–19, 20–24, 25–29, 30–34, 35–39, 40–44

11. **Write Math** ▶ Describe the overall shape of the histogram. What does this tell you about the salaries at the company?

   _____

   _____

12. ⭐ **Test Prep** The histogram shows the height, in inches, of some basketball players. What fraction of the players are less than 70 inches tall?

   (A) $\frac{1}{12}$

   (B) $\frac{1}{6}$

   (C) $\frac{1}{5}$

   (D) $\frac{1}{2}$

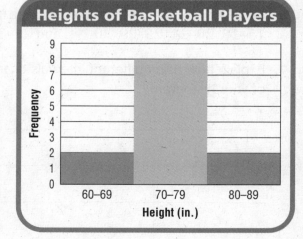

Heights of Basketball Players

Frequency vs. *Height (in.)*

60–69, 70–79, 80–89

FOR MORE PRACTICE:
Standards Practice Book, pp. P229–P230

Name _____

☑ Mid-Chapter Checkpoint

▶ Vocabulary

Choose the best term from the box to complete the sentence.

Vocabulary
dot plot
histogram
statistical question

1. A _____ is a kind of bar graph that shows the frequency of data grouped into intervals. (p. 463)

2. A question that asks about a set of data that varies is called a

   _____ . (p. 451)

▶ Concepts and Skills

3. A sports reporter records the number of touchdowns scored each week during the football season. What statistical question could the reporter ask about the data? (CC.6.SP.1)

   _____

   _____

   _____

4. Liz records her pet hamster's weight once every week for one year. How many observations does she make? (CC.6.SP.5a)

   _____

5. The number of runs scored by a baseball team in 20 games is given below. Draw a dot plot of the data and use it to find the most common number of runs scored in a game. (CC.6.SP.4)

Runs Scored									
3	1	4	3	4	2	1	7	2	3
5	3	2	9	4	3	2	1	1	4

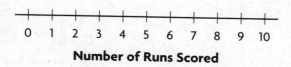

Number of Runs Scored

   _____

Fill in the bubble for the correct answer choice.

6. Which of the following could be a statistical question about a set of data? (CC.6.SP.1)

   (A) How tall is the Empire State Building?

   (B) How many milliliters are in a liter?

   (C) What are the ages of the visitors to an amusement park?

   (D) How many rooms are in the White House?

7. A school principal is trying to decide how long the breaks should be between periods. He plans to time how long it takes several students to get from one classroom to another. What tool could he use to collect the data? (CC.6.SP.5b)

   (A) tape measure

   (B) stopwatch

   (C) balance scale

   (D) compass

8. The U.S. Mint uses very strict standards when making coins. Which of the following is **not** a statistical question the U.S. Mint might ask about the coins? (CC.6.SP.1)

   (A) What are the weights of the quarters?

   (B) What are the thicknesses of the dimes?

   (C) How much copper is in each penny?

   (D) What is the value of a nickel?

9. Terry checks the temperature at dawn and at dusk every day for a week for a science project. How many observations does he make? (CC.6.SP.5a)

   (A) 7

   (B) 14

   (C) 28

   (D) 52

10. The table shows the lengths of the songs played by a radio station during a 90-minute period. Alicia is making a histogram of the data. What frequency should she show for the interval 160–169 seconds? (CC.6.SP.4)

Song Lengths (sec)				
166	157	153	194	207
150	175	168	209	206
151	201	187	162	152
209	194	168	165	156

    (A) 4   (C) 6

    (B) 5   (D) 7

Mean as Fair Share and Balance Point

Essential Question How does the mean represent a fair share and balance point?

COMMON CORE STANDARD CC.6.SP.5c
Summarize and describe distributions.

Investigate

Materials ■ counters

On an archaeological dig, five students found 1, 5, 7, 3, and 4 arrowheads. The students agreed to divide the arrowheads evenly. How many arrowheads should each student get?

A. Use counters to show how many arrowheads each of the five students found. Use one stack of counters for each student.

B. Remove a counter from the tallest stack and move it to the shortest. Keep moving counters from taller stacks to shorter stacks until each stack has the same height.

C. Count the number of counters in each stack.

The number of counters in each stack is the *mean*, or average, of the data. The mean represents the number of arrowheads each student should get if the arrowheads are shared equally.

There are 5 stacks of _____ counters.

So, each student should get _____ arrowheads.

Math Talk MATHEMATICAL PRACTICES
What is the mean of the data set 3, 3, 3, 3, 3? Explain how you know.

Draw Conclusions

1. **Explain** what is "fair" about a fair share of a group of items.

   _____

   _____

   _____

2. **H.O.T. Analysis** How could you find the fair share of arrowheads using the total number of arrowheads and division?

   _____

   _____

Make Connections

The mean can also be seen as a kind of balance point.

Ms. Burnham's class holds a walk-a-thon to help raise money to update the computer lab. Five of the students walked 1, 1, 2, 4, and 7 miles. The mean distance walked is 3 miles.

Complete the dot plot of the data set.

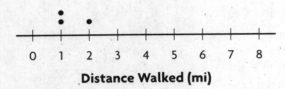

Distance Walked (mi)

Circle the number that represents the mean.

Complete the table to find the distances of the data points from the mean.

	Values Less than the Mean			Values Greater than the Mean	
Data point	1 mi	1 mi	mi	4 mi	mi
Distance from the mean	2 mi	mi	mi	mi	mi

The total distance from the mean for values less than the mean is:

2 miles + 2 miles + 1 mile = _____ miles

The total distance from the mean for values greater than the mean is:

_____ mile + _____ miles = _____ miles

The total distance of the data values less than the mean is _____ the total distance of the data values greater than the mean. The mean represents a balance point for data values less than the mean and greater than the mean.

3. **Explain** how you found the distance of each data value from the mean.

_____

_____

4. **H.O.T. Analysis** Can all of the values in a data set be greater than the mean? Explain why or why not.

_____

_____

Name _____

Share and Show ·

Use counters to find the mean of the data set.

1. On the first day of a school fundraiser, five students sell 1, 1, 2, 2, and 4 gift boxes of candy.

   Make _____ stacks of counters with heights 1, 1, 2, 2, and 4.

   Rearrange the counters so that all _____ stacks have the same height.

   After rearranging, every stack has _____ counters.

   So, the mean of the data set is _____.

✅ 2. Four students live 1, 2, 3, and 6 miles from school.

   _____

Make a dot plot for the data set and use it to check whether the given value is a balance point for the data set.

✅ 3. Rosanna's friends have 0, 1, 1, 2, 2, and 12 pets at home. Rosanna says the mean of the data is 3. Is Rosanna correct?

   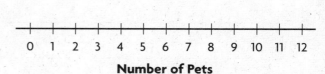

   Number of Pets

   The total distance from 3 for data values less than 3 is _____.

   The total distance from 3 for data values greater than 3 is _____.

   The mean of 3 _____ a balance point.

   So, Rosanna _____ correct.

4. **Write Math** ▶ Four people go to lunch, and the costs of their orders are $6, $9, $10, and $11. They want to split the bill evenly. Describe how they could use stacks of $1 bills to find the fair share. Then find the fair share.

   _____

   _____

   _____

   _____

Math Talk MATHEMATICAL PRACTICES

Every student in a class has 4 notebooks. **Explain** what the mean number of notebooks is using the idea of fair share.

Problem Solving REAL WORLD

Use the table for 5–8.

5. A grocer is preparing fruit baskets to sell as holiday presents. If the grocer rearranges the apples in baskets A, B, and C so that each has the same number, how many apples will be in each basket? Use counters to find the fair share.

_____

6. Draw a dot plot showing the number of apples originally in baskets A, B, and C. Use the plot to explain why your answer to Exercise 5 is a balance point.

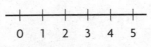

Number of Apples

_____

_____

_____

_____

7. **Write Math** ▶ Can the pears be rearranged so that there is an equal whole number of pears in each basket? **Explain** why or why not.

_____

_____

_____

8. ⭐ **Test Prep** Which is the mean number of oranges in the three baskets?

  Ⓐ 1   Ⓒ 3

  Ⓑ 2   Ⓓ 6

Fruit Baskets

Basket	Apples	Oranges	Pears
A	4	2	2
B	1	2	1
C	4	2	5

SHOW YOUR WORK

Measures of Center

Essential Question How can you describe a set of data using mean, median, and mode?

COMMON CORE STANDARD CC.6.SP.5c
Summarize and describe distributions.

A **measure of center** is a single value used to describe the middle of a data set. A measure of center can be a useful way to summarize a data set, especially when the data set is large.

🔑 UNLOCK the Problem REAL WORLD

Kara is entering a paper airplane in a competition. In one of the categories in the competition, the plane that stays in the air for the longest time wins. The times in seconds for Kara's test flights are 5.8, 2.9, 6.7, 1.6, 2.9, and 4.7. What are the mean, median, and mode of the data?

What unit of time is used in the problem?

_____

How many flight times are given?

_____

 Find the mean, median, and mode.

The **mean** is the sum of the data items divided by the number of data items.

Mean = $\dfrac{5.8 + 2.9 + 6.7 + 1.6 + 2.9 + 4.7}{}$ = _____ = _____

The **median** is the middle value when the data are written in order. If the number of data items is even, the median is the mean of the two middle values.

Order the values from least to greatest.

1.6, 2.9, 2.9, 4.7, 5.8, 6.7

The data set has an _____ number of values, so the median is the mean of the two middle values. Circle the two middle values of the data set.

Now find the mean of the two middle values.

$\dfrac{ + }{}$ = _____ = _____

The **mode** is the data value or values that occur most often.

_____ occurs twice, and all the other values occur once.

_____ is the mode.

Math Talk MATHEMATICAL PRACTICES
Explain how you could use a dot plot and the idea of a balance point to check your answer for the mean.

Try This! In 2009, an engineer named Takuo Toda set a world record for flight time for a paper airplane. His plane flew for 27.9 sec. If Toda's time was included in Kara's set of times, what would the median be?

_____

Example 1

Mrs. O'Donnell's class has a fundraiser for a field trip to a wildlife preservation. Five of the donations are $15, $25, $30, $28, and $27. Find the mean, median, and mode of the donations.

Mean = $\dfrac{\boxed{} + \boxed{} + \boxed{} + \boxed{} + \boxed{}}{\boxed{}}$

$= \dfrac{\boxed{}}{\boxed{}} = \boxed{}$

Order the data from least to greatest to find the median.

_____, _____, _____, _____, _____

Median = _____

If all of the values in a data set occur with equal frequency, then the data set has no mode.

The data set has no repeated values, so there is no _____.

Example 2

Keith surveys his classmates about how many brothers and sisters they have. Six of the responses were 1, 3, 1, 2, 2, and 0. Find the mean, median, and mode of the data.

Mean = $\dfrac{\boxed{} + \boxed{} + \boxed{} + \boxed{} + \boxed{}}{\boxed{}} = \dfrac{\boxed{}}{\boxed{}} = \boxed{}$

Order the data from least to greatest to find the median.

_____, _____, _____, _____, _____, _____

The number of data values is even, so find the mean of the two middle values.

Median = $\dfrac{\boxed{} + \boxed{}}{\boxed{}} = \dfrac{\boxed{}}{\boxed{}} = \boxed{}$

The data values _____ and _____ appear twice in the set. If two or more values appear in the data set the most number of times, then the data set has two or more modes.

Modes = _____ and _____

Name _____

Share and Show

1. Terrence records the number of e-mails he receives per day.
   During one week, he receives 7, 3, 10, 5, 5, 6, and 6 e-mails.
   What are the mean, median, and mode of the data?

   Mean = _____   Median = _____   Mode(s) = _____

2. Julie goes to several grocery stores and researches the price
   of a 12 oz bottle of juice. Find the mean, median, and mode
   of the prices shown.

Juice Prices		
$0.95	$1.09	$0.99
$1.25	$0.99	$1.99

   Mean = _____   Median = _____   Mode(s) = _____

Math Talk MATHEMATICAL PRACTICES
Explain how to find the
median of a set of data with an even
number of values.

On Your Own

3. T.J. is training for the 200-meter dash event for his school's
   track team. Find the mean, median, and mode of the
   times shown in the table.

T.J.'s Times (sec)		
22.3	22.4	23.3
24.5	22.5	

   Mean = _____   Median = _____   Mode(s) = _____

4. **Algebra** The values of a data set can be represented by the
   expressions x, $2x$, $4x$, and $5x$. Write the data set for $x = 3$
   and find the mean.

   _____

5. In the last six months, Sonia's family used 456, 398, 655, 508,
   1,186, and 625 minutes on their cell phone plan. To save money,
   Sonia's family wants to keep their mean cell phone usage below
   600 minutes per month. Did they meet their goal? If not, by how
   many minutes did they go over?

   _____

   _____

Problem Solving REAL WORLD

H.O.T. Sense or Nonsense?

6. Jeremy scored 85, 90, 72, 88, and 92 on five math tests, for a mean of 85.4. On the sixth test he scored a 95. He calculates his mean score for all 6 tests as shown below, but Deronda says he is incorrect. Whose answer makes sense? Whose answer is nonsense? **Explain** your reasoning.

I just need to find the mean of 85.4 and 95.

You should find the mean of all 6 scores.

Jeremy's Work

The mean of my first 5 test scores was 85.4, so to find the mean of all 6 test scores, I just need to find the mean of 85.4 and 95.

$$\text{Mean} = \frac{85.4 + 95}{2} = \frac{180.4}{2} = 90.2$$

So, my mean score for all 6 tests is 90.2.

Deronda's Work

To find the mean of all 6 test scores, you need to add up all 6 scores and divide by 6.

$$\text{Mean} = \frac{85 + 90 + 72 + 88 + 92 + 95}{6}$$

$$= \frac{522}{6} = 87$$

So, Jeremy's mean score for all 6 tests is 87.

- For the answer that is nonsense, how does the mean that the student found compare to the correct mean?

Effects of Outliers

Essential Question How does an outlier affect measures of center?

COMMON CORE STANDARD CC.6.SP.5d
Summarize and describe distributions.

An **outlier** is a value that is much less or much greater than the other values in a data set. An outlier may greatly affect the mean of a data set. This may give a misleading impression of the data.

🔓 UNLOCK the Problem   REAL WORLD

The table gives the number of days that the 24 members of the Garfield Middle School volleyball team were absent from school last year.

Volleyball Team Absences (days)							
4	6	7	4	5	5	3	6
6	7	3	5	8	16	5	4
5	6	5	7	6	4	5	4

Does the data set contain any outliers?

🔒 **Use a dot plot to find the outlier(s).**

STEP 1 Plot the data on the number line.

• Why might a dot plot be helpful in determining if there is an outlier?

_____

_____

_____

_____

_____

_____

```
├─┼─┼─┼─┼─┼─┼─┼─┼─┼─┼─┼─┼─┼─┼─┼─┼─┼─┤
0  1  2  3  4  5  6  7  8  9 10 11 12 13 14 15 16 17 18
```
Team Absences (days)

STEP 2 Find any values that are much greater or much less than the other values.

Most of the data values are between _____ and _____.

The value _____ is much greater than the rest, so _____ is an outlier.

---

1. What effect do you think an outlier greater than the other data would have on the mean of the data set? **Justify** your answer.

_____

_____

🔑 Example. The high temperatures for the week in Foxdale,
in degrees Fahrenheit, were 43, 43, 45, 42, 26, 43, and 45. The
mean of the data is 41°F, and the median is 43°F. Identify the outlier
and describe how the mean and median are affected by it.

STEP 1 Draw a dot plot of the data and identify the outlier.

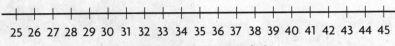

25 26 27 28 29 30 31 32 33 34 35 36 37 38 39 40 41 42 43 44 45

High Temperatures (°F)

The outlier is _____ °F.

STEP 2 Find the mean and median of the temperatures *without* the outlier.

$$\text{Mean} = \frac{43 + \boxed{} + \boxed{} + \boxed{} + \boxed{} + \boxed{}}{\boxed{}}$$

$$= \frac{\boxed{}}{6} = \boxed{} \text{°F}$$

Values ordered least to greatest: 42, _____, _____, _____, _____, _____

$$\text{Median} = \frac{43 + \boxed{}}{2} = \boxed{} \text{°F}$$

The mean with the outlier is _____ °F, and the mean without the outlier is _____ °F.

The outlier made the mean _____.

The median with the outlier is _____ °F, and the median without the outlier is _____ °F.

The outlier _____ affect the median.

2. **Explain** why the mean without the outlier could be a better
   description of the data set than the mean with the outlier.

   _____

   _____

3. If the outlier had been 59°F rather than 26°F, how would the mean
   have been affected by the outlier? **Explain** your reasoning.

   _____

   _____

Name _____

Share and Show

1. Find the outlier by drawing a dot plot of the data.

Foul Shots Made						
2	3	1	3	2	2	1
15	2	1	3	1	3	

0 1 2 3 4 5 6 7 8 9 10 11 12 13 14 15 16 17 18

Foul Shots Made

The outlier is _____.

2. The prices of the X-40 Laser Printer at five different stores are $99, $68, $98, $105, and $90. The mean price is $92, and the median price is $98. Identify the outlier and describe how the mean and median are affected by it.

The outlier is _____.

without the outlier: Mean = $_____

Median = $_____

Math Talk | MATHEMATICAL PRACTICES

The mean of a certain data set is much greater than the median. **Explain** how this can happen.

On Your Own

3. Identify the outlier in the data set of melon weights. Then describe the effect the outlier has on the mean and median.

Melon Weights (oz)					
47	45	48	45	49	47
14	45	51	46	47	

The outlier is _____ oz.

_____

_____

4. In a set of Joanne's test scores, there is an outlier. On the day of one of those tests, Joanne had the flu. Do you think the outlier is greater or less than the rest of her scores? **Explain.**

_____

_____

Problem Solving REAL WORLD

Use the table for 5–7.

Baseball All-Time Stolen Base Leaders	
Player	**Stolen Bases**
Rickey Henderson	1,406
Lou Brock	938
Billy Hamilton	914
Ty Cobb	897
Tim Raines	808

5. Which player's number of stolen bases is an outlier?

_____

6. What effect does the outlier have on the median of the data set?

_____

_____

▲ Ty Cobb steals a base.

7. **H.O.T.** Terence wrote that the mean of the data set is 992.6. Is this the mean with or without the outlier? Explain how you can tell without doing a calculation.

_____

_____

_____

_____

SHOW YOUR WORK

8. **Write Math** **H.O.T.** Does an outlier have any effect on the mode of a data set? **Explain**.

_____

_____

_____

9. ★ **Test Prep** By how much does the median of the data set 2, 3, 5, 5, 5, and 10 change if the outlier is removed?

(A) It decreases by 2.

(B) It decreases by 1.

(C) It is unchanged.

(D) It increases by 1.

Problem Solving • Data Displays

Essential Question How can you use the strategy *draw a diagram* to solve problems involving data?

COMMON CORE STANDARD CC.6.SP.4
Summarize and describe distributions.

UNLOCK the Problem REAL WORLD

The 32 students in the History Club are researching their family histories so they can draw family trees. The data set at the right shows the numbers of aunts and uncles the students have. What is the most common number of aunts and uncles among the students in the club?

Use the graphic organizer to help you solve the problem.

Number of Aunts and Uncles							
4	3	2	4	5	7	0	3
1	4	2	4	6	3	5	1
2	5	0	6	3	2	4	5
4	1	3	0	4	2	8	3

Read the Problem

What do I need to find?

I need to find the

_____ number of aunts and uncles among students in the club.

The most common number in

the data is the _____.

What information do I need to use?

I need to use the number

of _____ each student has from the table.

How will I use the information?

I can draw a diagram that shows

the _____ of each value in the data set. A good way to show the frequency of each value

in a data set is a _____.

Solve the Problem

• Make a dot plot of the data.

   Check: Are there the same number of dots on the plot as there are data values?

• Use the plot to determine the mode. The mode is the data value

   with the _____ dots. The data value with the most dots is _____.

0 1 2 3 4 5 6 7 8 9 10
Number of Aunts and Uncles

Math Talk MATHEMATICAL PRACTICES Explain why displaying the data in a dot plot is a better choice for solving this problem than displaying the data in a histogram.

So, the most common number of aunts and uncles is _____.

🔑 Try Another Problem

The table shows the attendance for the Pittsburgh Pirates' last 25 home games of the 2009 baseball season. What percent of the games were attended by at least 25,000 people?

Attendance at 25 Pittsburgh Pirates Games (in thousands)				
12	13	23	33	21
17	17	24	15	27
19	15	18	11	26
20	24	13	16	16
16	19	36	27	17

Read the Problem

What do I need to find?	What information do I need to use?	How will I use the information?

Solve the Problem

© Houghton Mifflin Harcourt Publishing Company

MATHEMATICAL PRACTICES

Math Talk What other type of display might you have used to solve this problem? **Explain** how you could have used the display.

So, _____ of the last 25 home games were attended by at least 25,000 people.

Name _____

Share and Show

1. The table shows the number of goals scored by the Florida Panthers National Hockey League team in the last 20 games of the 2009 season. What was the most common number of goals the team scored?

Goals Scored									
1	3	3	2	1	1	2	2	2	1
4	5	1	3	3	3	0	2	4	2

First, draw a dot plot of the data.

Next, use the plot to find the mode of the data: The

value _____ appears _____ times.

So, the most common number of goals the Panthers

scored was _____.

2. Draw a histogram of the hockey data. Use it to find the percent of the games in which the Panthers scored more than 3 goals.

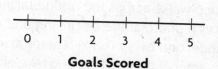

Goals Scored

SHOW YOUR WORK

_____

_____

3. **Write Math** ▸ If you needed to find the mean of a data set, which data display—dot plot or histogram— would you choose? Explain your reasoning.

_____

_____

_____

♀ UNLOCK the Problem **Tips**

√ Read the question carefully to be sure you understand what you need to find.

√ Check that you plot every data value exactly once.

√ Check that you answered the question.

On Your Own......

Choose a
STRATEGY

Use a Model

Draw a Diagram

Find a Pattern

Solve a Simpler Problem

Work Backward

Use a Formula

4. Corey collected data on the ages of the parents of his classmates. Make a data display and use it to find the percent of parents over 40 years old.

42, 36, 35, 49, 52, 43, 41, 32, 45, 39, 50, 38, 37, 39

_____

5. What is the mode of the data in Exercise 4?

_____

6. The Golden Gate Bridge is 2.7 kilometers long. Grace walks across the bridge taking photos. She takes a photo at the beginning and end of the bridge, and every 0.3 kilometer along the way. How many photos does she take altogether?

_____

7. ⭐ **H.O.T.** A recipe for punch calls for apple juice and cranberry juice. The ratio of apple juice to cranberry juice is 3:2. Tyrone wants to make at least 20 cups of punch, but no more than 30 cups of punch. Describe two different ways he can use apple juice and cranberry juice to make the punch.

_____

_____

_____

SHOW YOUR WORK

8. ⭐ **Test Prep** Shawna is making a histogram of the heights of her classmates. The heights range from 49 in. to 64 in. Which of the following could she use for intervals in her histogram?

(A) 49–58, 59–64

(B) 49–52, 53–56, 57–60, 61–62

(C) 49–54, 49–58, 49–64

(D) 49–52, 53–56, 57–60, 61–64

Name _____

✓ Chapter 12 Review/Test

▶ Vocabulary

Choose the best term from the box to complete the sentence.

Vocabulary
mean
median
mode

1. The _____ of a set of data is the sum of all the data values divided by the number of data values. (p. 473)

2. The data value(s) that occur the most often in a data set is

   called the _____. (p. 473)

▶ Concepts and Skills

3. The times for five students to complete a science test were 41, 19, 32, 27, and 24 minutes. What is the median of the data? (CC.6.SP.5c)

   _____

4. The table shows the time, in minutes, that it took 25 students to complete a 3-mile hike. Make a histogram for the data. (CC.6.SP.4)

Time to Complete Hike (min)				
50	74	55	64	65
90	45	68	60	48
65	90	55	47	94
62	69	60	94	62
65	62	72	69	48

Fill in the bubble for the correct answer choice.

5. The prices for a 3-pound bag of apples at 5 different grocery stores are $2.99, $1.99, $3.99, $2.50, and $3.25. What is the median price? (CC.6.SP.5c)

Ⓐ $2.99   Ⓒ $3.25

Ⓑ $3.00   Ⓓ $3.99

6. The numbers of deliveries made per day by a takeout restaurant in one week are 25, 22, 31, 28, 6, 20, and 32. Which data value is an outlier? (CC.6.SP.5d)

Ⓐ 6   Ⓒ 31

Ⓑ 25   Ⓓ 32

7. Julia is weighing several mineral samples for science class. What unit of measure could she use to record her measurements? (CC.6.SP.5b)

Ⓐ inches

Ⓑ milliliters

Ⓒ seconds

Ⓓ ounces

8. Which of the following could you NOT use to find the mean of a data set? (CC.6.SP.5c)

Ⓐ a complete list of the data

Ⓑ a dot plot of the data

Ⓒ the sum of the data and the number of data values

Ⓓ a histogram

9. Luis surveys 10 students about the number of hours they spend doing homework on a typical day. The table shows his data. Which is a true statement about his survey results? (CC.6.SP.5c)

Number of Hours Spent Doing Homework				
1	2	1	2	2
2	1	3	4	3

Ⓐ The mode and the mean are equal.

Ⓑ The mean is greater than the mode.

Ⓒ The median is greater than the mean.

Ⓓ The mode is 4.

10. Four students at a school fair win 3, 5, 6, and 6 prize tickets. They use the mean number of tickets to share the tickets equally. How many tickets does each student get? (CC.6.SP.5c)

    Ⓐ 2

    Ⓑ 4

    Ⓒ 5

    Ⓓ 20

11. Meredith records the race times for a track meet. She records times for 5 groups of 4 students each. How many observations does she make? (CC.6.SP.5a)

    Ⓐ 4   Ⓒ 20

    Ⓑ 5   Ⓓ 40

12. Sasha surveys students from her homeroom about the number of siblings each student has. The results are 1, 0, 2, 2, 3, 0, 1, 1, 4, and 5. What is the mode(s) of the data? (CC.6.SP.5c)

    Ⓐ 1.5   Ⓒ 1

    Ⓑ 0 and 2   Ⓓ 1 and 2

13. Students in Ms. Chu's class rode a roller coaster called the Viper during a class trip to an amusement park. The dot plot shows the number of minutes each student waited in line for the ride. What is the median of the data? (CC.6.SP.5c)

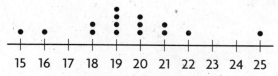

    Number of Minutes

    Ⓐ 10 min   Ⓒ 19 min

    Ⓑ 15 min   Ⓓ 25 min

14. Mr. Schwartz gives his class a challenge problem. Five students take 2, 12, 10, 11, and 15 minutes to solve it. How does the outlier affect the mean of the data? (CC.6.SP.5d)

    Ⓐ It makes the mean less than it would be otherwise.

    Ⓑ It makes the mean greater than it would be otherwise.

    Ⓒ It makes the mean equal to the median.

    Ⓓ It has no effect on the mean.

15. Althea wants to survey 25 students at her school about their music-listening habits. What is a statistical question that she could ask? (CC.6.SP.1)

_____

_____

16. Clara records the time she spent practicing the oboe every day for a week. She practiced for 1, 2, 0, 3, 1, 2, and 2 hours. Make a dot plot of the data. (CC.6.SP.4)

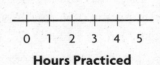

Hours Practiced

▶ **Performance Task** (CC.6.SP.4, CC.6.SP.5c)

17. The table gives the number of frozen yogurts sold each day at a cafeteria.

Number of Frozen Yogurts Sold Each Day				
20	24	13	34	39
38	10	38	13	25
21	35	20	27	42
45	16	38	18	25

A Find the median and mode of the data.

_____

_____

B Make a histogram of the data. Use the intervals 10–19, 20–29, etc.

C Sasha says that the mode of a set of data is always in the interval represented by the highest bar in a histogram of the data. Use your answers from parts a and b to explain Sasha's error.

_____

_____

Chapter 13 Variability and Data Distributions

Show What You Know

Check your understanding of important skills.

Name _____

▶ **Place the First Digit** Tell where to place the first digit. Then divide.

1. 4)872 _____ place

2. 8)256 _____ place

▶ **Order of Operations** Evaluate the expression.

3. $9 + 4 \times 8$

_____

4. $2 \times 7 + 5$

_____

5. $6 \div (3 - 2)$

_____

6. $(12 - 3^2) \times 5$

_____

7. $2^3 \times (22 \div 2)$

_____

8. $(8 - 2)^2 - 9$

_____

9. $(9 - 2^3) + 8$

_____

10. $(27 + 9) \div 3$

_____

▶ **Mean** Find the mean for the set of data.

11. 285, 420, 345, 390 _____

12. 0.2, 0.23, 0.16, 0.21, 0.2 _____

13. $33, $48, $55, $52 _____

14. 8.1, 7.2, 8.4 _____

Raina watched two of her friends play a game of darts. She has to pick one of them to be her partner in a tournament. Be a Math Detective and help her figure out which of her friends is a more consistent dart player.

_____

_____

Dart Scores						
Hector	15	5	7	19	3	19
Marin	12	10	11	11	10	14

Vocabulary Builder

▶ **Visualize It** ●

Sort the review words into the chart.

```
          ┌─────────────────────┐
          │  Measures of Center │
          └─────────────────────┘
         ╱          │          ╲
   ┌────────┐   ┌────────┐   ┌────────┐
   │        │   │        │   │        │
   └────────┘   └────────┘   └────────┘
        │      How Do I Find It?  │
        │           │            │
```

Find the sum of all the data values and divide the sum by the number of data values.	Order the data and find the middle value or the mean of the two middle values if the number of values is even.	Find the data value(s) that occurs most often.

▶ **Understand Vocabulary** ● ● ● ● ● ● ● ● ● ● ● ● ● ● ● ● ● ● ●

Complete the sentences using the preview words.

1. The median of the upper half of a data set is the

   _____ .

2. The _____ is the difference
   between the greatest value and the least value in a data set.

3. A(n) _____ is a graph that shows the median,
   quartiles, least value, and greatest value of a data set.

4. A data set's _____ is the difference between
   its upper and lower quartiles.

5. You can describe how spread out a set of data is using a(n)

   _____ .

GO Online • eStudent Edition • Multimedia eGlossary

Name _____

Patterns in Data

Essential Question How can you describe overall patterns in a data set?

COMMON CORE STANDARD CC.6.SP.5c
Summarize and describe distributions.

CONNECT Seeing data sets in graphs, such as dot plots and histograms, can help you find and understand patterns in the data.

🔑 UNLOCK the Problem REAL WORLD

Many lakes and ponds contain freshwater fish species such as bass, pike, bluegills, and trout. Jacob and his friends went fishing at a nearby lake. The dot plot shows the sizes of the fish that the friends caught. What patterns do you see in the data?

Fish Caught

```
      •           •
   •  •  •     •  •  •
•  •  •  •     •  •  •  •  •
+--+--+--+--+--+--+--+--+--+--+-->
5  6  7  8  9  10 11 12 13 14
```
Length (inches)

- Circle any spaces with no data.
- Place a box around any groups of data.

🔒 Analyze the dot plot.

A *gap* is an interval that contains no data.

Does the dot plot contain any gaps?

If so, where? _____

So, there were no fish from _____ to _____ inches long,

and there were two clusters of fish measuring from _____

to _____ inches long and from _____ to _____ inches long.

A *cluster* is a group of data points that lie within a small interval.

There is a cluster from _____ to _____ and

another cluster from _____ to _____.

Math Talk MATHEMATICAL PRACTICES
What is the mode(s) of the data? **Explain** how you know.

1. Summarize the information shown in the dot plot.

_____

_____

2. What conclusion can you draw about why the data might have this pattern?

_____

_____

You can also analyze patterns in data that are displayed in histograms. Some data sets have symmetry about a peak, while others do not.

 Example Analyze a histogram.

Erica made this histogram to show the weights of the pumpkins grown at her father's farm in October. What patterns do you see in the data?

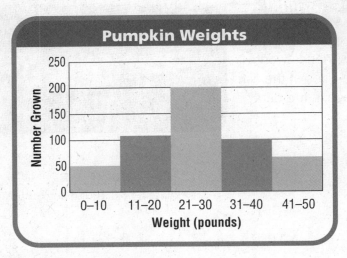

STEP 1 Identify any peaks in the data.

The histogram has _____ peak(s).

The interval representing the greatest number of pumpkins is for

weights between _____ and _____ pounds.

STEP 2 Describe how the data changes across the intervals.

The number of pumpkins increases from 0 to _____ pounds

and _____ from 30 to 50 pounds.

STEP 3 Describe any symmetry the graph has.

If I draw a vertical line through the interval for _____ to

_____ pounds, the left and right parts of the histogram are very

close to being mirror images. The histogram _____ line symmetry.

So, the data values increase to one peak in the interval for _____ to

_____ pounds and then decrease. The data set _____ line symmetry about the peak.

Remember

A geometric figure has line symmetry if you can draw a line through it so that the two parts are mirror images of each other.

Name _____

Share and Show

For 1–3, use the dot plot.

1. The dot plot shows the number of paintings students in the art club displayed at the art show. Does the dot plot contain any gaps?

   If so, where? _____

2. Identify any clusters in the data.

   _____

3. Summarize the information in the dot plot.

   _____

   _____

   _____

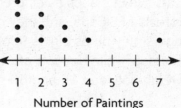

Number of Paintings

Math Talk MATHEMATICAL PRACTICES
Explain how you can tell if a graph has line symmetry.

On Your Own

For 4–7, use the histogram.

4. The histogram shows the ages of visitors to the zoo on Monday. How many peaks does the histogram have? _____

5. Describe how the data values change across the intervals.

   _____

   _____

   _____

   _____

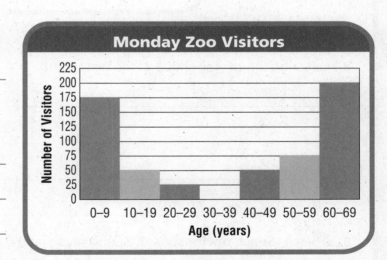

6. Does the graph have line symmetry? **Explain.**

   _____

7. **Write Math** ▶ Give a possible reason why the data might have this pattern.

   _____

© Houghton Mifflin Harcourt Publishing Company

Big Cats

There are 41 species of cats living in the world today. Wild cats live in places as different as deserts and the cold forests of Siberia, and they come in many sizes. Siberian tigers may be as big as 9 feet long and weigh over 2,000 pounds, while bobcats are often just 2 to 3 feet long and weigh between 15 and 30 pounds.

You can find bobcats in many zoos in the United States. The histogram below shows the weights of several bobcats. The weights are rounded to the nearest pound.

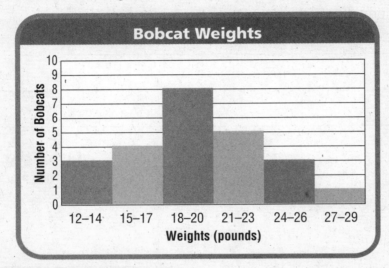

Bobcat Weights

Use the histogram for 8 and 9.

8. Describe the overall shape of the histogram.

_____

_____

_____

_____

9. **H.O.T.** **Sense or Nonsense?** Sunny says that the graph might have a different shape if it was redrawn as a bar graph with one bar for each number of pounds. Is Sunny's statement sense or nonsense? **Explain.**

_____

_____

_____

Box Plots

Essential Question How can you use box plots to display data?

COMMON CORE STANDARD CC.6.SP.4
Summarize and describe distributions.

The median is the middle value, or the mean of the two middle values, when data is written in order. The **lower quartile** is the median of the lower half of a data set, and the **upper quartile** is the median of the upper half of a data set.

🔑 UNLOCK the Problem · REAL WORLD

In 1885, a pair of jeans cost $1.50. Today, the cost of jeans varies greatly. The chart lists the prices of jeans at several different stores. What are the median, lower quartile, and upper quartile of the data?

Prices of Jeans								
$35	$28	$42	$50	$24	$75	$47	$32	$60

🔒 **Find the median, lower quartile, and upper quartile.**

STEP 1 Order the numbers from least to greatest.

$24 $28 $32 $35 $42 $47 $50 $60 $75

STEP 2 Circle the middle number, the median.

The median is $ _____ .

STEP 3 Calculate the upper and lower quartiles.

Find the median of each half of the data set.

Think: If a data set has an even number of values, the median is the mean of the two middle values.

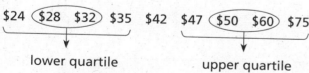

$24 ⟨$28 $32⟩ $35 $42 $47 ⟨$50 $60⟩ $75

      lower quartile   upper quartile

$$\frac{\$28 + \$32}{2} = \frac{\$\quad}{2} = \$\underline{\quad} \qquad \frac{\$\quad + \$\quad}{2} = \frac{\$\quad}{2} = \$\underline{\quad}$$

So, the median is $ _____ , the lower quartile is $ _____ , and the

upper quartile is $ _____ .

> ⚠ **ERROR Alert**
>
> When a data set has an odd number of values, do not include the median when finding the lower and upper quartiles.

A **box plot** is a type of graph that shows how data are distributed by using the least value, the lower quartile, the median, the upper quartile, and the greatest value. Below is a box plot showing the data for jean prices from the previous page.

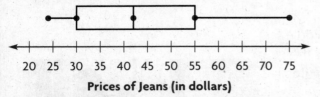

20 25 30 35 40 45 50 55 60 65 70 75

Prices of Jeans (in dollars)

Example   Make a box plot.

The data set below represents the ages of the top ten finishers in a 5K race. Use the data to make a box plot.

Ages of Top 10 Runners (in years)									
33	18	21	23	35	19	38	30	23	25

STEP 1 Order the data from least to greatest. Then find the median and the lower and upper quartiles.

18, _____, _____, _____, _____, _____, _____, _____, _____, _____

Median = $\dfrac{ + }{2}$ = _____ years

Lower quartile = _____ years   The lower quartile is the median of the lower half of the data set, which goes from 18 to 23.

Upper quartile = _____ years   The upper quartile is the median of the upper half of the data set, which goes from 25 to 38.

STEP 2 Draw a number line. Above the number line, plot a point for the least value, the lower quartile, the median, the upper quartile, and the greatest value.

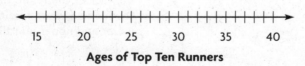

15   20   25   30   35   40

Ages of Top Ten Runners

STEP 3 Draw a box from the lower to upper quartile. Inside the box, draw a vertical line segment through the median. Then draw line segments from the box to the least and greatest values.

Math Talk   MATHEMATICAL PRACTICES
Describe the steps for making a box plot.

- Would the box plot change if the data point for 38 years were replaced with 40 years? **Explain.**

_____

Name _____

Share and Show

Find the median, lower quartile, and upper quartile of the data.

1. the scores of 11 students on a geography quiz:
   87, 72, 80, 95, 86, 80, 78, 92, 88, 76, 90

   Order the data from least to greatest.   72, 76, 78, 80, 80, 86, 87, 88, 90, 92, 95

   median: _____   lower quartile: _____   upper quartile: _____

2. the lengths, in seconds, of 9 videos posted online:
   50, 46, 51, 60, 62, 50, 65, 48, 53

   median: _____   lower quartile: _____   upper quartile: _____

3. Make a box plot to display the data set in Exercise 2.

Lengths of Online Videos (seconds)

Math Talk MATHEMATICAL PRACTICES How are box plots and dot plots similar? How are they different?

On Your Own

Find the median, lower quartile, and upper quartile of the data.

4. 13, 24, 37, 25, 56, 49, 43, 20, 24

   median: _____

   lower quartile: _____

   upper quartile: _____

5. 61, 23, 49, 60, 83, 56, 51, 64, 84, 27

   median: _____

   lower quartile: _____

   upper quartile: _____

6. The chart shows the height of trees in a park. Display the data in a box plot.

Tree Heights (feet)											
8	12	20	30	25	18	18	8	10	28	26	29

7. **What's the Error?** Eric made this box plot to display the data set below. **Explain** his error.

Number of Books Read								
5	13	22	8	31	37	25	24	10

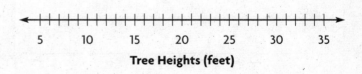

Tree Heights (feet)

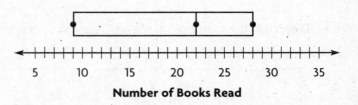

Number of Books Read

Problem Solving REAL WORLD

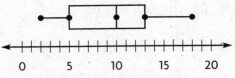 Pose a Problem

8. The box plots show the number of flights delayed per day for two different airlines. Which data set is more spread out?

Flights Delayed: Airline A

Flights Delayed: Airline B

Find the distance between the least and greatest values for each data set.

Airline A: greatest value − least value = _____ − _____ = _____

Airline B: greatest value − least value = _____ − _____ = _____

So, the data for _____ is more spread out.

Write a new problem that can be solved using the data in the box plots.

Pose a Problem

_____

_____

_____

_____

_____

_____

Solve Your Problem

- **Describe** how box plots make it easy to compare two related data sets.

_____

_____

FOR MORE PRACTICE:
Standards Practice Book, pp. P249–P250

Mean Absolute Deviation

Essential Question How do you calculate the mean absolute deviation of a data set?

COMMON CORE STANDARD CC.6.SP.5c
Summarize and describe distributions.

One way to describe a set of data is with the mean. However, two data sets may have the same mean but look very different when graphed. When interpreting data sets, it is important to consider how far away the data values are from the mean.

Investigate

Materials ■ counters, large number line from 0–10

The number of magazine subscriptions sold by two teams of students for a drama club fundraiser is shown below. The mean number of subscriptions for each team is 4.

Team A				
3	3	4	5	5

Team B				
0	1	4	7	8

A. Make a dot plot of each data set using counters for the dots. Draw a vertical line through the mean.

B. Count to find the distance between each counter and the mean. Write the distance underneath each counter.

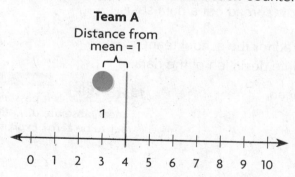

Team A
Distance from
mean = 1

1

0 1 2 3 4 5 6 7 8 9 10

C. Find the mean of the distances for each data set.

Team A

$$\frac{1 + \boxed{} + \boxed{} + \boxed{} + \boxed{}}{5} = \frac{\boxed{}}{5} = \boxed{}$$

Team B

$$\frac{\boxed{} + \boxed{} + \boxed{} + \boxed{} + \boxed{}}{\boxed{}} = \frac{\boxed{}}{\boxed{}} = \boxed{}$$

Draw Conclusions

1. **H.O.T.** Which data set, Team A or B, looks more spread out in your dot plots? Which data set had a greater average distance from the mean? **Explain** how these two facts are connected.

_____

_____

_____

2. **Application** The table shows the average distance from the mean for the heights of players on two basketball teams. Tell which set of heights is more spread out. Explain how you know.

Heights of Players	
Team	**Average Distance from Mean (in.)**
Chargers	2.8
Wolverines	1.5

_____

_____

Make Connections

The mean of the distances of data values from the mean of the data set is called the **mean absolute deviation**. As you learned in the Investigation, mean absolute deviation is a way of describing how spread out a data set is.

The dot plot shows the ages of gymnasts registered for the school team. The mean of the ages is 10. Find the mean absolute deviation of the data.

STEP 1 Label each dot with its distance from the mean.

Age of Gymnasts

Age (years)

> **MATHEMATICAL PRACTICES**
>
> **Math Talk** Is it possible for the mean absolute deviation of a data set to be zero? **Explain.**

STEP 2 Find the mean of the distances.

☐ + ☐ + ☐ + ☐ + ☐ + ☐ + ☐ + ☐ + ☐ + ☐ + ☐ = ___ = ☐

So, the mean absolute deviation of the data is _____ years.

Name _____

Share and Show

Use counters or a dot plot to find the mean absolute deviation of the data.

1. Find the mean absolute deviation for both data sets. Explain which data set is more spread out.

   the number of laps Shawna swam on 5 different days:

   5, 6, 6, 8, 10

   mean = 7

   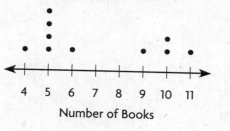

   mean absolute deviation = _____ laps

   the number of laps Lara swam on 5 different days:

   1, 3, 7, 11, 13

   mean = 7

   mean absolute deviation = _____ laps

   The data set of _____ laps is more spread out because the mean

   absolute deviation of her data is _____.

Use the dot plot to find the mean absolute deviation of the data.

2. mean = 7 books

   Books Read Each Semester

   ```
              •
              •
              •
        •     •   •         •   •   •
   ←——+——+——+——+——+——+——+——+——→
        4  5  6  7  8  9  10 11
           Number of Books
   ```

   mean absolute deviation = _____

3. mean = 29 pounds

   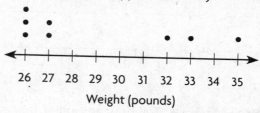

   Packages Shipped on Tuesday

   mean absolute deviation = _____

4. **Write Math** ▸ The mean absolute deviation of the number of daily visits to Scott's website for February is 167.7. In March, the absolute mean deviation is 235.9. In which month did the number of visits to Scott's website vary more? **Explain** how you know.

   _____

5. **Algebra** In April, the data for Scott's website visits are less spread out than they were in February. Use *a* to represent the mean absolute deviation for April to write an inequality to describe the possible values of *a*.

   _____

Problem Solving REAL WORLD

Use a dot plot to solve.

6. Elijah recorded the number of days of precipitation each month.

Days of Precipitation											
Jan	Feb	Mar	Apr	May	Jun	Jul	Aug	Sep	Oct	Nov	Dev
10	12	13	18	10	8	7	6	16	14	8	10

The mean of the data is 11. What is the mean absolute deviation
of the data?

_____

7. Elijah collects precipitation data from a second year and finds
that the mean absolute deviation of the data from the second
year is 1.5 days. For which year are the data more spread out?

_____

_____

SHOW YOUR WORK

8. **H.O.T.** Suppose all of the players on a basketball team had the
same height. Explain how you could use reasoning to find the
mean absolute deviation of the players' heights.

_____

_____

_____

9. **Write Math** ▶ Tell how an outlier that is much greater than
the mean would affect the mean absolute deviation of the data
set. **Explain** your reasoning.

_____

_____

_____

10. ★ **Test Prep** Carlos plays the piano. The hours he practiced
each week for 8 weeks were 2, 4, 4, 6, 6, 8, 9, 9. What is the
mean absolute deviation of the data?

   Ⓐ 8 hours   Ⓒ 6 hours

   Ⓑ 7 hours   Ⓓ 2 hours

Measures of Variability

Essential Question How can you summarize a data set by using range, interquartile range, and mean absolute deviation?

COMMON CORE STANDARD CC.6.SP.5c
Summarize and describe distributions.

CONNECT A **measure of variability** is a single value used to describe how spread out a set of data values are. The mean absolute deviation is a measure of variability.

🔑 UNLOCK the Problem REAL WORLD

In gym class, the students recorded how far they could jump. The data set below gives the distances in inches that Mary jumped. What is the mean absolute deviation of the data set?

Mary's Jumps (in inches)					
54	58	56	59	60	55

 Find the mean absolute deviation.

STEP 1: Find the mean of the data set.

Add the data values and divide the sum by the number of data values.

$54 + \underline{\quad} + \underline{\quad} + \underline{\quad} + \underline{\quad} + \underline{\quad} = \dfrac{\quad}{\quad} = \underline{\quad}$

The mean of the data set is _____ inches.

STEP 2: Find the distance of each data value from the mean.

Subtract the lesser value from the greater value.

Data Value	Subtract (Mean = 57)	Distance between data value and the mean
54	57 − 54 =	3
58	58 − 57 =	
56	57 − 56 =	
59	59 − 57 =	
60	60 − 57 =	
55	57 − 55 =	

Total of distances from the mean:

STEP 3: Add the distances.

STEP 4: Find the mean of the distances.

Divide the sum of the distances by the number of data values.

_____ ÷ 6 = _____

So, the mean absolute deviation of the data is _____ inches.

Math Talk MATHEMATICAL PRACTICES Give an example of a data set that has a small mean absolute deviation. **Explain** how you know that the mean absolute deviation is small without doing any calculations.

Range is the difference between the greatest value and the least value in a data set. **Interquartile range** is the difference between the upper quartile and the lower quartile of a data set. Range and interquartile range are also measures of variability.

🔑 **Example** Use the range and interquartile range to compare the data sets.

The box plots show the price in dollars of the handheld game players at two different electronic stores. Find the range and interquartile range for each data set. Then compare the variability of the prices of the handheld game players at the two stores.

Cost of MP3 Players

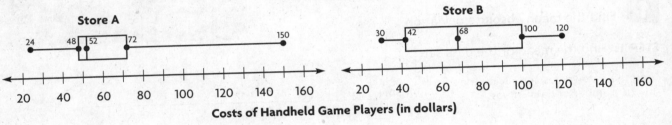

Costs of Handheld Game Players (in dollars)

STORE A	**STORE B**

Calculate the range.

Find the difference between the greatest and least values.

STORE A
150 − 24 = _____

The range for Store A is _____.

STORE B
120 − _____ = _____

The range for Store B is _____.

Calculate the interquartile range.

Find the difference between the upper quartile and lower first quartile.

72 − 48 = _____

The interquartile range for Store A is _____.

100 − _____ = _____

The interquartile range for Store B is _____.

So, Store A has a greater _____, but

Store B has a greater _____.

MATHEMATICAL PRACTICES

Math Talk Explain how range and interquartile range are alike and how they are different.

Name _____

Share and Show . . . .

1. Find the range and interquartile range of the data in the box plot.

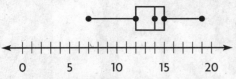

Cost of T-shirts (in dollars)

For the range, find the difference between the greatest and least values.

_____ − _____ = _____

range: $ _____

For the interquartile range, find the difference between the third and first quartiles.

_____ − _____ = _____

interquartile range: $ _____

Practice: Copy and Solve Find the mean absolute deviation for the data set.

2. heights in inches of several tomato plants:

16, 18, 18, 20, 17, 20, 18, 17

mean absolute deviation: _____

3. times in seconds for students to run one lap:

68, 60, 52, 40, 64, 40

mean absolute deviation: _____

> **Math Talk** MATHEMATICAL PRACTICES
> Explain how to find mean absolute deviation of a data set.

On Your Own . . . .

Use the box plot for 4 and 5.

4. What is the range of the data? _____

5. What is the interquartile range of the data?

_____

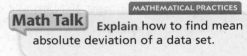

Price of Pottery Sold (in dollars)

Practice: Copy and Solve Find the mean absolute deviation for the data set.

6. times in minutes spent on a history quiz

35, 35, 32, 34, 34, 32, 34, 36

mean absolute deviation: _____

7. number of excused absences for one semester:

1, 2, 1, 10, 9, 9, 10, 6, 1, 1

mean absolute deviation: _____

8. The chart shows the price of different varieties of dog food at a pet store. Find the range, interquartile range, and the mean absolute deviation of the data set.

Cost of Bag of Dog Food ($)									
18	24	20	26	24	20	32	20	16	20

_____

_____

Problem Solving  REAL WORLD

9. Gabriel's family began a walking program. They walked 30, 45, 25, 35, 40, 30, and 40 minutes each day during one week. In the column at right, make a box plot of the data. Then find the interquartile range.

_____

10. Jack recorded the number of minutes his family walked each day for a month. The range of the data is 15. How does this compare to the data for Gabriel's family?

_____

_____

_____

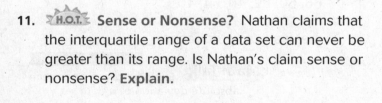

Time Spent Walking (in minutes)

11. 🔆 **H.O.T.** **Sense or Nonsense?** Nathan claims that the interquartile range of a data set can never be greater than its range. Is Nathan's claim sense or nonsense? **Explain.**

_____

_____

_____

_____

- - - - - - - - - - - - ✏️ **SHOW YOUR WORK** - - - - - - - - - - - -

12. ⭐ **Test Prep** The box plot shows the number of roses sold by a flower shop each day for a week.

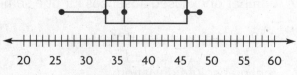

Number of Roses Sold

Which statement about the data is true?

(A) The range is 13.

(B) The interquartile range is 33.

(C) The median is 38.

(D) The lower quartile is 33.

FOR MORE PRACTICE:
Standards Practice Book, pp. P249–P250

✓ Mid-Chapter Checkpoint

▶ Vocabulary

Choose the best term from the box to complete the sentence.

Vocabulary

box plot

interquartile range

mean absolute
deviation

measure of variability

range

1. The _____ is the difference between the median of the upper half and the median of the lower half of a data set. (p. 503)

2. A graph that shows the median, quartiles, and least and greatest values of a data set is called a(n) _____. (p. 496)

3. The difference between the greatest value and the least value in a data set is the _____. (p. 503)

4. The _____ is the mean of the distances between the values of a data set and the mean of the data set. (p. 499)

▶ Concepts and Skills

5. Make a box plot for this data set: 73, 65, 68, 72, 70, 74. (CC.6.SP.4)

Find the mean absolute deviation of the data. (CC.6.SP.5c)

6. 43, 46, 48, 40, 38

7. 26, 20, 25, 21, 24, 27, 26, 23

8. 99, 70, 78, 85, 76, 81

_____

_____

_____

Find the range and interquartile range of the data. (CC.6.SP.5c)

9. 2, 4, 8, 3, 2

10. 84, 82, 86, 87, 88, 83, 84

11. 39, 22, 33, 45, 42, 40, 28

_____

_____

_____

12. Yasmine keeps track of the number of hockey goals scored by her school's team at each game. The dot plot shows her data.

Goals Scored

Where is there a gap in the data? (CC.6.SP.5c)

(A) between 0 and 2

(C) between 2 and 4

(B) between 1 and 3

(D) There are no gaps.

13. What is the interquartile range of the data shown in the dot plot with Question 12? (CC.6.SP.5c)

(A) 1

(C) 3

(B) 2

(D) 4

14. Randall's teacher added up the class scores for the quarter and used a histogram to display the data. Which of the following statements is true? (CC.6.SP.5c)

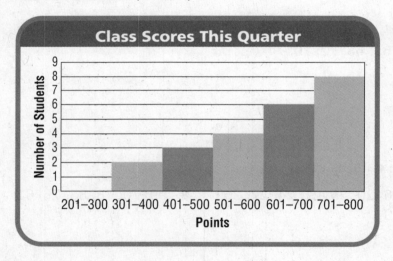

(A) The histogram has line symmetry.

(B) Most students in the class have more than 500 points.

(C) The histogram has two peaks.

(D) The histogram shows exactly how many students have 500 points.

15. In a box plot of the data below, where would the box be drawn? (CC.6.SP.4)

55, 37, 41, 62, 50, 49, 64

(A) from 37 to 64

(C) from 50 to 64

(B) from 41 to 50

(D) from 41 to 62

508

Name _____

Choose Appropriate Measures of Center and Variability

COMMON CORE STANDARD CC.6.SP.5d
Develop understanding of statistical variability.

Essential Question How can you choose appropriate measures of center and variability to describe a data set?

Outliers, gaps, and clusters in a set of data can affect both the measures of center and variability. Some measures of center and variability may describe a particular set of data better than others.

🔑 UNLOCK the Problem · REAL WORLD

Thomas is writing an article for the school newsletter about a paper airplane competition. In the distance category, Kara's airplanes flew 17 ft, 16 ft, 18 ft, 15 ft, and 2 ft. Should Thomas use the mean, median, or mode to best describe Kara's results? Explain your reasoning.

Find the mean, median, and mode and compare them.

Mean = $\dfrac{\boxed{} + \boxed{} + \boxed{} + \boxed{} + \boxed{}}{\boxed{}}$

= $\dfrac{\boxed{}}{}$ = $\boxed{}$

Order the data from least to greatest to find the median.

_____, _____, _____, _____, _____,

Median = _____

The data set has no repeated values so there is no _____.

The mean is _____ than 4 of the 5 values, so it is not a good

description of the center of the data. The _____ is closer to most of the values, so it is the best way to describe Kara's results.

So, Thomas should use the _____ to describe Kara's results.

* Do you need to order the numbers?

_____

_____

_____

_____

Math Idea

The measures of center for some data sets may be very close together. If that is the case, you can list more than one measure as the best way to describe the data.

1. **Explain** why the two modes may be a better description than the mean or median of the data set 2, 2, 2, 2, 7, 7, 7, 7.

_____

_____

Example

Mr. Tobin is buying a book online. He compares prices of the book at several different sites. The table shows his results. Make a box plot of the data. Then use the plot to find the range and interquartile range. Which measure better describes the data? Explain your reasoning.

Prices of Book	
Site	Price ($)
1	15
2	35
3	17
4	18
5	5
6	16
7	17

STEP 1 Make a box plot.

Write the data in order from least to greatest.

_____, _____, _____, _____,

_____, _____, _____

Find the median of the data.

median = _____

Find the first quartile—the median of the lower half of the data.

first quartile = _____

Find the third quartile—the median of the upper half of the data.

third quartile = _____

Make the plot.

3 5 7 9 11 13 15 17 19 21 23 25 27 29 31 33 35 37 39

Prices of Books (in dollars)

Math Talk MATHEMATICAL PRACTICES

Describe a data set for which the range is a better description than the interquartile range.

STEP 2 Use the box plot to find the range and the interquartile range.

range = _____ − _____ = _____

interquartile range = _____ − _____ = _____

_____ of the seven prices are within the _____. The other two prices are much higher or lower.

So, the _____ better describes the data because the

_____ makes it appear that the data values vary more than they actually do.

2. **H.O.T.** How can you tell from the box plot how varied the data are? **Explain.**

_____

_____

Name _____

Share and Show

☑ **1.** The distances in miles students travel to get to school are 7, 1, 6, 8, 9, and 8. Decide which measure(s) of center best describes the data set. Explain your reasoning.

mean = _____

median = _____

mode = _____

The _____ is less than 4 of the 6 data points, and the _____ describes only 2 of

the data points. So, the _____ best describes the data.

☑ **2.** The numbers of different brands of orange juice carried in several stores are 2, 1, 3, 1, 12, 1, 2, 2, and 5. Make a box plot of the data and find the range and interquartile range. Decide which measure better describes the data set and explain your reasoning.

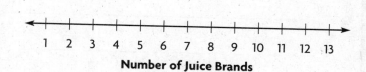

Number of Juice Brands

range = _____

interquartile range = _____

_____

_____

> **Math Talk** MATHEMATICAL PRACTICES
> Explain how an outlier affects the range of a data set.

On Your Own

3. The ages of students in a computer class are 14, 13, 14, 15, 14, 35, 14. Decide which measure of center(s) best describes the data set. Explain your reasoning.

mean = _____

median = _____

mode = _____

_____

_____

4. Find the range and interquartile range of the data in Exercise 1. Decide which best represents the data, and explain your reasoning.

_____

_____

_____

UNLOCK the Problem REAL WORLD

5. Jaime is on the community swim team. The table shows the team's results in the last 8 swim meets. Jaime believes they can place in the top 3 at the next swim meet. Which measure of center should Jaime use to persuade her team that she is correct? Explain.

Swim Team Results	
Meet	**Place**
Meet 1	1
Meet 2	2
Meet 3	3
Meet 4	18
Meet 5	1
Meet 6	2
Meet 7	3
Meet 8	2

a. What do you need to find?

_____

_____

_____

_____

b. What information do you need to solve the problem?

_____

_____

c. What are the measures of center?

_____

d. Which measure of center should Jaime use? Explain.

_____

_____

_____

_____

6.  **Test Prep** Josh scored 98, 85, 84, 80, 81, and 82 on his math tests. Which measure of center best describes Josh's scores?

Ⓐ median

Ⓑ mode

Ⓒ range

Ⓓ mean

7. **Test Prep** The following list shows the points that Shannon scored in several basketball games. Which best describes the variation in the data?

21, 12, 10, 11, 13, 15, 13, 17

Ⓐ lower quartile

Ⓑ interquartile range

Ⓒ range

Ⓓ upper quartile

Name _____

Apply Measures of Center and Variability

COMMON CORE STANDARD CC.6.SP.3
Develop understanding of statistical variability.

Essential Question What do measures of center and variability indicate about a data set?

🔑 UNLOCK the Problem REAL WORLD

Julia is collecting data on her favorite sports teams for a report. The table shows the median and interquartile range of the heights of the players on her favorite baseball and basketball teams. How do the heights of the two teams compare?

Sports Team Data		
	Median	**Interquartile Range**
Baseball Team Heights	70 in.	6 in.
Basketball Team Heights	78 in.	4 in.

 Compare the medians and interquartile ranges of the two teams.

Median

The median of the _____ players' heights is _____ inches

greater than the median of the _____ players' heights.

Interquartile Range

The interquartile range of the baseball team is _____ the interquartile range of the basketball team, so the heights

of the baseball players vary _____ the heights of the basketball team.

So, the players on the _____ team are typically taller than the

players on the _____ team, and the heights of the _____

team vary more than the those of the _____ team.

> **Math Talk** MATHEMATICAL PRACTICES
> What if the mean of the heights of players on the baseball team is 75 in.? **Explain** what this could tell you about the data.

1. Julia randomly picks one player from the basketball team and one player from the baseball team. Given data in the table, can you say that the basketball player will definitely be taller than the baseball player? **Explain** your reasoning.

_____

_____

_____

Example

Kamira and Joey sold T-shirts during lunch to raise money for a charity. The table shows the number of T-shirts each student sold each day for two weeks. Find the mean and range of each data set, and use these measures to compare the data.

T-Shirts Sold	
Kamira	5, 1, 2, 1, 3, 3, 1, 4, 5, 5
Joey	0, 1, 2, 13, 2, 1, 3, 4, 4, 0

STEP 1 Find the mean of each data set.

Kamira:

Mean = \(\dfrac{\square + \square + \square + \square + \square + \square + \square + \square + \square + \square}{\square}\)

\(= \dfrac{\square}{\square} = \square\)

Joey:

Mean = \(\dfrac{\square + \square + \square + \square + \square + \square + \square + \square + \square + \square}{\square}\)

\(= \dfrac{\square}{\square} = \square\)

 ERROR Alert

Make sure you include zeroes when you count the total number of data values.

STEP 2 Find the range of each data set.

Kamira: **Joey:**

Range = $\square$ $-$ $\square$ $=$ $\square$ Range = $\square$ $-$ $\square$ $=$ $\square$

STEP 3 Compare the mean and range.

The mean of Joey's sales is _____ the mean of Kamira's sales

The range of Joey's sales is _____ the range of Kamira's sales.

So, the typical number of shirts Joey sold each day was _____ the typical number of shirts Kamira sold. However, since the range of Joey's

data was _____ than Kamira's, the number of shirts Joey sold

varied _____ from day to day than the number of shirts Kamira sold.

2. Which measure of center would better describe Joey's data set? **Explain.**

_____

_____

Name _____

Share and Show

✓ **1.** Zoe collected data on the number of points her favorite basketball players scored in several games. Use the information in the table to compare the data.

Points Scored		
	Mean	Interquartile Range
Player 1	24	8
Player 2	33	16

The mean of Player 1's points is _____ the mean of Player 2's points.

The interquartile range of Player 1's points is _____ the interquartile range of Player 2's points.

So, Player 2 typically scores _____ points than Player 1, but

Player 2's scores typically vary _____ Player 1's scores.

✓ **2.** Mark collected data on puppy weights at two animal shelters. Find the median and range of each data set, and use these measures to compare the data.

Puppy Weight, in pounds
Shelter A: 7, 10, 5, 12, 15, 7, 7
Shelter B: 4, 11, 5, 11, 15, 5, 13

_____

_____

_____

_____

On Your Own

Brenda analyzed data about the number of hours musicians in her band practice each week. The table shows her results. Use the table for Exercises 3–5.

3. Which two students typically practiced the same amount each week, with about the same variation in practcie times?

_____

4. Which two students typically practiced the same number of hours, but had very different variations in their practice times?

_____

Hours of Practice per Week		
	Mean	Range
Sally	5	2
Matthew	9	12
Tim	5	12
Jennifer	5	3

5. Which two students had the same variation in practice times, but typically practiced a different number of hours per week?

_____

Problem Solving REAL WORLD

Use the table for Exercises 6–7.

6. The table shows the number of miles Johnny ran each day for two weeks. Find the median and the interquartile range of each data set, and use these measures to compare the data sets.

_____

_____

_____

_____

Miles Run
Week 1 2, 1, 5, 2, 3, 3, 4
Week 2 3, 8, 1, 8, 1, 3, 1

7. Is the mode a good description of the data for Week 2? Explain your reasoning.

_____

_____

8. **H.O.T. Sense or Nonsense?** Yashi made the box plots at right to show the data he collected on plant growth. He thinks that the variation in bean plant growth was about the same as the variation in tomato plant growth. Does Yashi's conclusion make sense? Why or why not?

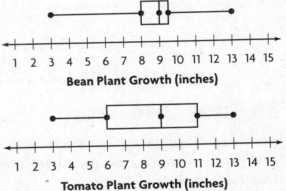

Bean Plant Growth (inches)

Tomato Plant Growth (inches)

_____

_____

_____

_____

9. ⭐ **Test Prep** Tommy analyzed data about the number of books his friends read each month. The table shows his results. Which two students typically read about the same number of books each month, but have different variation within their data?

Books Read per Month		
	Mean	**Range**
Mario	15	10
Jamal	11	10
Shakira	14	5
Sam	9	10

Ⓐ Mario and Sam

Ⓒ Shakira and Mario

Ⓑ Jamal and Sam

Ⓓ Sam and Shakira

FOR MORE PRACTICE:
Standards Practice Book, pp. P253–P254

Name _____

Describe Distributions

Essential Question How can you describe the distribution of a data set collected to answer a statistical question?

COMMON CORE STANDARD **CC.6.SP.2**
Develop understanding of statistical variability.

 **Activity**

Ask at least 20 students in your school how many pets they have. Record your results in a frequency table like the one shown.

Pet Survey	
Number of Pets	**Frequency**
0	
1	
2	
3	
4	

- What statistical question could you use your data to answer?

_____

_____

![key] **UNLOCK the Problem** REAL WORLD

You can graph your data set to see the center, spread, and overall shape of the data.

Make a dot plot or a histogram of your data.

- What type of graph will you use?

_____

- How will you label your graph?

_____

_____

Math Talk MATHEMATICAL PRACTICES
Explain why you chose the display you used.

© Houghton Mifflin Harcourt Publishing Company

Think about the overall distribution of your data.

- Are there any clusters?
- Are there peaks in the data?
- Are there gaps in the data?
- Does the graph have symmetry?

1. Describe the overall distribution of the data. Include information about clusters, gaps, peaks, and symmetry.

_____

_____

🔑 **Example** **Find the mean, median, mode, interquartile range, and range of the data you collected.**

STEP 1 Find the mean, median, and mode.

Mean: _____ Median: _____

Model: _____

STEP 2 Draw a box plot of your data and use it to find the interquartile range and range.

Interquartile range: _____ Range: _____

---

2. Which measure of center do you think best describes your data? Why?

_____

_____

3. Does the interquartile range or range best describe your data? Why?

_____

_____

4. What is the answer to the statistical question you wrote on the previous page?

_____

_____

Math Talk MATHEMATICAL PRACTICES
Compare your data set to the data set of one of your classmates. **Describe** how the data sets are similar and how they are different.

Name _____

Share and Show

Connie asked people theri ages as they entered the food court at the mall. Use the histogram of the data she collected for 1–5.

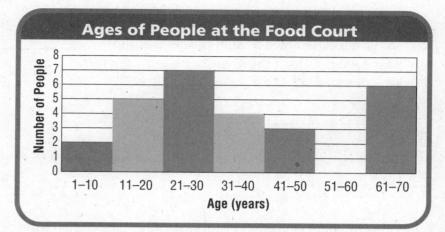

Ages of People at the Food Court

1. What statistical question could Connie ask about her data?

   _____

   _____

   _____

2. Describe any peak or gap in the data.

   _____

   _____

3. Does the graph have symmetry? Explain your reasoning.

   _____

   _____

On Your Own

4. The first quartile of the data set is 16.5 years, and the third quartile is 51.5 years. Find the interquartile range. Is it a better description of the data of the range? **Explain** your reasoning.

   _____

   _____

   _____

Math Talk MATHEMATICAL PRACTICES
Explain what, if any, information you would need to answer the statistical question you wrote in Exercise 1 and what calculations you would need to do.

5. The mode of the data is 16 years old. Is the mode a good description of the center of the data? **Explain**.

   _____

   _____

Problem Solving REAL WORLD

Use the dot plot for 6–10.

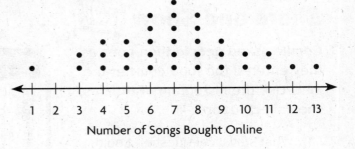

Number of Songs Bought Online

6. Jason collected data about the number of songs his classmates bought online over the past 3 weeks. Does the data set have symmetry? Why or why not?

_____

_____

_____

7. Does the data set have clusters? gaps? peaks? What is the overall shape of the data set? **Explain**.

_____

_____

_____

8. **H.O.T.** **Sense or Nonsense?** Jason claims that the median is a good description of his data set, but the mode is not. Is his statement sense or nonsense? **Explain**.

_____

_____

9. **H.O.T.** **Write Math** Trinni surveyed her classmates about how many siblings they have. A dot plot of her data increases from 0 siblings to a peak at 1 sibling, and then decreases steadily as the graph goes to 6 siblings. How is Trinnis dot plot similar to Jason's? How is it different?

_____

_____

_____

10. ⭐ **Test Prep** What is the interquartile range of Jason's data?

- **(A)** 0
- **(C)** 9
- **(B)** 4
- **(D)** 13

SHOW YOUR WORK

Name _____

Problem Solving • Misleading Statistics

Essential Question How can you use the strategy *work backward* to draw conclusions about a data set?

COMMON CORE STANDARD CC.6.SP.2
Develop understanding of statistical variability.

🔑 UNLOCK the Problem REAL WORLD

Mr. Owen wants to move to a town where the daily high temperature is in the 70s most days. A real estate agent tells him that the mean daily high temperature in a certain town is 72°. Other statistics about the town are given in the table. Does this location match what Mr. Owen wants? Why or why not?

Use the graphic organizer to help you solve the problem.

Town Statistics for the Past Year (Daily High Temperature)	
Minimum	62°
Maximum	95°
Median	69°
Mean	72°

Read the Problem

What do I need to find?

I need to decide if the daily high temperature in the town

_____.

What information do I need?

I need the _____ in the table.

How will I use the information?

I will work backward from the statistics to draw conclusions

about the _____ of data.

Solve the Problem

The minimum high temperature is _____.

The maximum high temperature is _____.

The median of the data set is _____.

Think: The high temperature is sometimes _____ than 70°.

Think: The high temperature is sometimes _____ than 80°.

Think: The median is the middle value in the data set.

Because the median is 69°, at least half of the days must have high temperatures less than or equal to 69°.

So, the location does not match what Mr. Owen wants. The median

indicates that most days _____ have a high temperature in the 70s.

Math Talk MATHEMATICAL PRACTICES Explain why the mean temperature is misleading in this example.

🔒 Try Another Problem

Ms. Green is buying a new car. She would like to visit a dealership that has a wide variety of cars for sale at many different price ranges. The table gives statistics about one dealership in her town. Does the dealership match Ms. Green's requirements? Explain your reasoning.

Statistics for New Car Prices	
Lowest Price	$12,000
Highest Price	$65,000
Lower Quartile Price	$50,000
Median Price	$55,000
Upper Quartile Price	$60,000

Read the Problem

What do I need to find?	What information do I need?	How will I use the information?

Solve the Problem

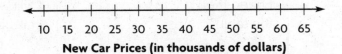

New Car Prices (in thousands of dollars)

- What would the box plot look like for a dealership that does meet Ms. Green's requirements?

_____

_____

Name _____

Share and Show

1. Josh is playing a game at the carnival. If his arrow lands on a section marked 25 or higher, he gets a prize. Josh will only play if most of the players win a prize. The carnival worker says that the average (mean) score is 28. The box plot shows other statistics about the game. Should Josh play the game? Explain your reasoning.

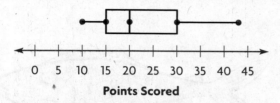

Points Scored

First, look at the median. The median is _____ points.

Next, work backward from the statistics.

The median is the _____ value of the data.

So, at least _____ of the values are scores

less than or equal to _____.

Finally, use the statistics to draw a conclusion.

_____

_____

2. **H.O.T.** **What if** a score of 15 or greater resulted in a prize? How would that affect Josh's decision? **Explain**.

_____

_____

3. A store collects data on the sales of DVD players each week for 3 months. The manager determines that the data has a range of 62 players and decides that the weekly sales were very inconsistent. Use the statistics in the table to decide if the manager is correct. **Explain** your answer.

Weekly DVD Player Sales	
Minimum	16
Maximum	78
Lower quartile	58
Upper quartile	72

_____

_____

On Your Own......................

4. Gerard is fencing in a yard that is 21 feet by 18 feet. How many feet of fencing material does Gerrard need? Explain how you found your answer.

_____

_____

5. **H.O.T.** Susanna wants to buy a fish that grows to be about 4 in. long. Mark suggests she buy the same type of fish he has. He has five of these fish with lengths of 1 in., 1 in., 6 in., 6 in., and 6 in, with a mean length of 4 in. Should Susanna buy the type of fish that Mark suggests? **Explain**.

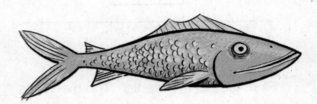

_____

_____

_____

6. **Write Math** The graph shows the number of stamps that Luciano collected over several weeks. If the pattern continues, how many stamps will Luciano collect in Week 8? **Explain**.

_____

_____

_____

_____

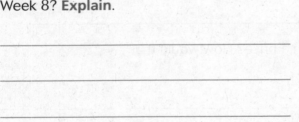

Stamps Collected

7. ⭐ **Test Prep** The table shows information about the distances between stops for two train lines. For which of the following are most stops at least 7 miles apart?

(**A**) Train A only   (**C**) Train A and Train B

(**B**) Train B only   (**D**) Neither Train A nor Train B

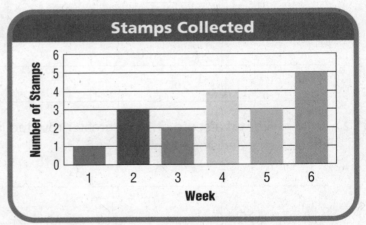

Train Stop Statistics (miles between stops)		
	Train A	**Train B**
Minimum	1	2
Maximum	12	16
Lower quartile	4	6
Upper quartile	11	13
Median	7	7

✓ Chapter 13 Review/Test

▶ Vocabulary

Choose the best term from the box to complete the sentence.

1. A _____ uses the median, quartiles, least value, and greatest value of a data set to show the data distribution. (p. 496)

2. The _____ of a data set is the median of the upper half of the data set. (p. 495)

3. A _____ is single value used to describe how spread out a set of data values is. (p. 503)

4. The overall shape of the graph of a data set is known as the

   _____ of the data set. (p. 517)

▶ Concepts and Skills

5. Amee's test scores are 55, 98, 83, 82, and 92. Marcus's test scores are 80, 84, 81, 83, and 82. Find the mean and range of each data set and use them to compare the data sets. (CC.6.SP.2)

   _____

   _____

   _____

6. The prices for the same DVD at several different stores are $19, $20, $19, $12, $19, and $19. Find the mean, median, and mode, and explain which best describes the data. (CC.6.SP.5d)

   _____

   _____

7. Sylvia's times in six races are 14, 12, 16, 13, 15, and 14 seconds. Find the range and interquartile range of the data and explain which better describes the data. (CC.6.SP.5d)

   _____

   _____

GO Online | **Assessment Options**
Chapter Test

8. Marcia is drawing a box plot of the data 17, 15, 21, 3, 23, and 11. Where should she draw the vertical segment inside the box? (CC.6.SP.4)

Ⓐ 3

Ⓑ 11

Ⓒ 15

Ⓓ 16

9. The table below shows the daily high temperatures, in degrees Fahrenheit, recorded at Chase's school last week. What is the mean absolute deviation of this data set? (CC.6.SP.5c)

High Temperatures (°F)						
Mon	Tue	Wed	Thu	Fri	Sat	Sun
70	74	68	69	68	68	73

Ⓐ 1 °F

Ⓑ 2 °F

Ⓒ 3 °F

Ⓓ 4 °F

10. Autumn's physical education teacher recorded the number of laps each student walked during class time and displayed the data in the dot plot shown. Which statement is not true about the data?
(CC.6.SP.2, CC.6.SP.5c)

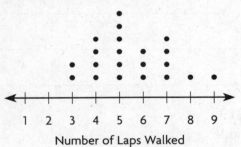

Number of Laps Walked

Ⓐ The median and mode are the same value.

Ⓑ There are no gaps in the data.

Ⓒ The range is 6.

Ⓓ The data has line symmetry.

11. What is the interquartile range of the data shown in the dot plot shown in the previous problem? (CC.6.SP.5c)

Ⓐ 3   Ⓒ 6

Ⓑ 4   Ⓓ 7

12. Which of the following data sets could be represented by the box plot below? (CC.6.SP.4)

Ride Passes Issued Per Hour

(A) 30, 80, 60, 10, 60

(B) 20, 65, 40, 70, 60

(C) 80, 70, 20, 60, 10

(D) 60, 20, 70

13. The data set below shows Mr. Long's last 6 bowling scores.

189, 163, 171, 165, 148, 155

What is the range of the data set? (CC.6.SP.5c)

(A) 41   (C) 26

(B) 34   (D) 24

14. What is the upper quartile of the data about Mr. Long's bowling scores in the previous problem? (CC.6.SP.5c)

(A) 155   (C) 171

(B) 164   (D) 180

15. The table shows data on the times it takes to load a page of photos at two websites during the past year. Which website has the least variability in load times, and why? (CC.6.SP.3)

Time to Load Photos (sec)		
	Website A	Website B
Minimum	3	1
Maximum	7	9
Lower quartile	4	6
Upper quartile	6	8
Median	5	7

(A) Website A, because its interquartile range is larger.

(B) Website A, because its range is smaller.

(C) Website B, because its interquartile range is smaller.

(D) Website B, because its range is larger.

16. A grocery store hands out discount coupons at checkout. The last five coupons handed out were for $1, $15, $2, $1, and $1 off the total bill. The store advertises that the mean savings per customer is $4. Explain why this statement could be misleading and tell which measure of center better represents the typical savings per coupon.

(CC.6.SP.5d)

_____

_____

▶ **Performance Task** (CC.6.SP.2, CC.6.SP.4, CC.6.SP.5c)

17. Coach Swanson is trying to decide which of two players should be on the starting lineup of the basketball team. She has her assistant coach collect data on the players' scores for the past 6 games and present them without the players' names so she can choose fairly.

> Player A: 10, 8, 12, 14, 10, 13
>
> Player B: 4, 26, 5, 10, 12, 13

A Find the median score of each player. Would the median scores help Coach Swanson choose? Explain.

_____

_____

B Draw box plots for each player.

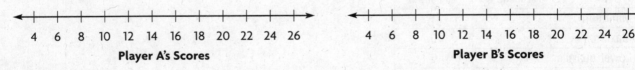

Player A's Scores   Player B's Scores

C The assistant coach says they should choose the player who has scored the highest number of points so far, but Coach Swanson wants the most consistent player. Which player does each person recommend? Use the box plots from Part B to justify your answer.

_____

_____

Glossary

Pronunciation Key

a	add, map	f	fit, half	n	nice, tin	p	pit, stop	û(r)	burn, term
ā	ace, rate	g	go, log	ng	ring, song	r	run, poor	yōō	fuse, few
â(r)	care, air	h	hope, hate	o	odd, hot	s	see, pass	v	vain, eve
ä	palm,	i	it, give	ō	open, so	sh	sure, rush	w	win, away
	father	ī	ice, write	ô	order, jaw	t	talk, sit	y	yet, yearn
b	bat, rub	j	joy, ledge	oi	oil, boy	th	thin, both	z	zest, muse
ch	check, catch	k	cool, take	ou	pout, now	<u>th</u>	this, bathe	zh	vision,
d	dog, rod	l	look, rule	ŏŏ	took, full	u	up, done		pleasure
e	end, pet	m	move, seem	ōō	pool, food	u̇	pull book		
ē	equal, tree								

ə the schwa, an unstressed vowel representing the sound spelled *a* in above, *e* in sicken, *i* in possible, *o* in melon, *u* in circus

Other symbols:
• separates words into syllables
′ indicates stress on a syllable

A

absolute value [ab′sə·lōōt val′yōō] **valor absoluto** The distance of an integer from zero on a number line (p. 115)

acute angle [ə·kyōōt′ ang′gəl] **ángulo agudo** An angle that has a measure less than a right angle (less than 90° and greater than 0°)
Example:

acute triangle [ə·kyōōt′ trī′ang·gəl] **triángulo acutángulo** A triangle that has three acute angles

addend [ad′end] **sumando** A number that is added to another in an addition problem

addition [ə·dish′ən] **suma** The process of finding the total number of items when two or more groups of items are joined; the inverse operation of subtraction

Addition Property of Equality [ə·dish′ən präp′ər·tē əv ē·kwôl′ə·tē] **propiedad de suma de la igualdad** The property that states that if you add the same number to both sides of an equation, the sides remain equal

additive inverse [ad′ə·tiv in′vûrs] **inverso aditivo** The number which, when added to the given number, equals zero

algebraic expression [al·jə·brā′ik ek·spresh′ən] **expresión algebraica** An expression that includes at least one variable (p. 257)
Examples: $x + 5$, $3a − 4$

angle [ang′gəl] **ángulo** A shape formed by two rays that share the same endpoint
Example:

area [âr′ē·ə] **área** The number of square units needed to cover a surface without any gaps or overlaps (p. 371)

array [ə•rā'] **matriz** An arrangement of objects in rows and columns
Example:

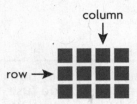

Associative Property of Addition [ə•sō'shē•ə•āt•iv präp'ər•tē əv ə•dish'ən] **propiedad asociativa de la suma** The property that states that when the grouping of addends is changed, the sum is the same
Example: (5 + 8) + 4 = 5 + (8 + 4)

Associative Property of Multiplication [ə•sō'shē•ə•tiv präp'ər•tē əv mul•tə•pli•kā'shən] **propiedad asociativa de la multiplicación** The property that states that when the grouping of factors is changed, the product is the same
Example: (2 × 3) × 4 = 2 × (3 × 4)

bar graph [bär graf] **gráfica de barras** A graph that uses horizontal or vertical bars to display countable data
Example:

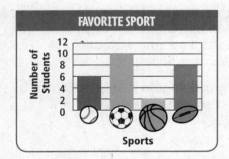

base [bās] (arithmetic) **base** A number used as a repeated factor (p. 249)
Example: $8^3 = 8 \times 8 \times 8$. The base is 8.

base [bās] (geometry) **base** In two dimensions, one side of a triangle or parallelogram which is used to help find the area. In three dimensions, a plane figure, usually a polygon or circle, which is used to partially describe a solid figure and to help find the volume of some solid figures. See also *height*
Examples:

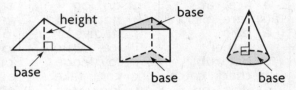

benchmark [bench'märk] **punto de referencia** A familiar number used as a point of reference

billion [bil'yən] **millardo** 1,000 millions; written as 1,000,000,000

box plot [bäks plät] **diagrama de caja** A graph that shows how data are distributed using the median, quartiles, least value, and greatest value (p. 496)
Example:

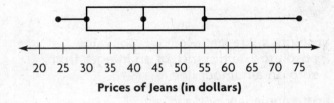

Prices of Jeans (in dollars)

capacity [kə•pas'i•tē] **capacidad** The amount a container can hold (p. 223)
Examples: $\frac{1}{2}$ gallon, 2 quarts

Celsius (°C) [sel'sē•əs] **Celsius (°C)** A metric scale for measuring temperature

closed figure [klōzd fig'yər] **figura cerrada** A figure that begins and ends at the same point

coefficient [kō•ə•fish'ənt] **coeficiente** A number that is multiplied by a variable (p. 262)
Example: 6 is the coefficient of *x* in 6*x*

common denominator [käm'ən dē•näm'ə•nāt•ər] **denominador común** A common multiple of two or more denominators
Example: Some common denominators for $\frac{1}{4}$ and $\frac{5}{6}$ are 12, 24, and 36.

common factor [käm'ən fak'tər] **factor común** A number that is a factor of two or more numbers (p. 17)

common multiple [käm'ən mul'tə•pəl] **múltiplo común** A number that is a multiple of two or more numbers

Commutative Property of Addition [kə•myōot' ə•tiv präp'ər•tē əv ə•dish'ən] **propiedad conmutativa de la suma** The property that states that when the order of two addends is changed, the sum is the same
Example: 4 + 5 = 5 + 4

Commutative Property of Multiplication [kə•myōot'ə•tiv präp'ər•tē əv mul•tə•pli•kāsh'ən] **propiedad conmutativa de la multiplicación** The property that states that when the order of two factors is changed, the product is the same
Example: 4 × 5 = 5 × 4

compatible numbers [kəm•pat'ə•bəl num'bərz] **números compatibles** Numbers that are easy to compute with mentally

composite figure [kəm•päz'it fig'yər] **figura compuesta** A figure that is made up of two or more simpler figures, such as triangles and quadrilaterals (p. 397)
Example:

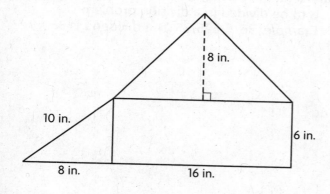

composite number [kəm•päz'it num'bər] **número compuesto** A number having more than two factors
Example: 6 is a composite number, since its factors are 1, 2, 3, and 6.

cone [kōn] **cono** A solid figure that has a flat, circular base and one vertex
Example:

congruent [kən•grōo'ənt] **congruente** Having the same size and shape (p. 375)
Example:

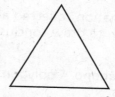 

conversion factor [kən•vûr'zhən fak'tər] **factor de conversión** A rate in which two quantities are equal, but use different units (p. 219)

coordinate plane [kō•ôrd'n•it plān] **plano cartesiano** A plane formed by a horizontal line called the *x*-axis and a vertical line called the *y*-axis (p. 123)
Example:

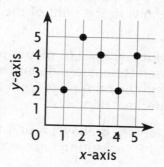

cube [kyo͞ob] **cubo** A solid figure with six congruent square faces
Example:

cubic unit [kyo͞o′bik yo͞o′nit] **unidad cúbica** A unit used to measure volume such as cubic foot (ft³), cubic meter (m³), and so on

data [dāt′ə] **datos** Information collected about people or things, often to draw conclusions about them (p. 451)

decagon [dek′ə·gän] **decágono** A polygon with 10 sides and 10 angles
Examples:

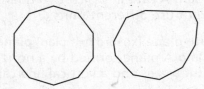

decimal [des′ə·məl] **decimal** A number with one or more digits to the right of the decimal point

decimal point [des′ə·məl point] **punto decimal** A symbol used to separate dollars from cents in money, and the ones place from the tenths place in decimal numbers

degree (°) [di·grē′] **grado (°)** A unit for measuring angles or for measuring temperature

degree Celsius (°C) [di·grē′ sel′sē·əs] **grado Celcius** A metric unit for measuring temperature

degree Fahrenheit (°F) [di·grē′ fâr′ən·hīt] **grado Fahrenheit** A customary unit for measuring temperature

denominator [de·näm′ə·nāt·ər] **denominador** The number below the bar in a fraction that tells how many equal parts are in the whole or in the group

Example: $\frac{3}{4}$ ← denominator

dependent variable [de·pen′dənt vâr′ē·ə·bəl] **variable dependiente** A variable whose value depends on the value of another quantity (p. 341)

difference [dif′ər·əns] **diferencia** The answer to a subtraction problem

digit [dij′it] **dígito** Any one of the ten symbols 0, 1, 2, 3, 4, 5, 6, 7, 8, 9 used to write numbers

dimension [də·men′shən] **dimensión** A measure in one direction

distribution [dis·tri·byo͞o′shən] **distribución** The overall shape of a data set (p. 516)

Distributive Property [di·strib′yo͞o·tiv präp′ər·tē] **propiedad distributiva** The property that states that multiplying a sum by a number is the same as multiplying each addend in the sum by the number and then adding the products (p. 18)
Example: 3 × (4 + 2) = (3 × 4) + (3 × 2)
3 × 6 = 12 + 6
18 = 18

divide [də·vīd′] **dividir** To separate into equal groups; the inverse operation of multiplication

dividend [div′ə·dend] **dividendo** The number that is to be divided in a division problem
Example: 36 ÷ 6; 6)‾36 The dividend is 36.

divisible [də·viz′ə·bəl] **divisible** A number is divisible by another number if the quotient is a counting number and the remainder is zero *Example:* 18 is divisible by 3.

division [də·vizh′ən] **división** The process of sharing a number of items to find how many groups can be made or how many items will be in a group; the operation that is the inverse of multiplication

Division Property of Equality [də·vizh′ən präp′ər·tē əv ē·kwôl′ə·tē] **propiedad de división de la igualdad** The property that states that if you divide both sides of an equation by the same nonzero number, the sides remain equal

divisor [də·vī′zər] **divisor** The number that divides the dividend
Example: 15 ÷ 3; 3)15 The divisor is 3.

dot plot [dot plät] **diagrama de puntos** A graph that shows frequency of data along a number line (p. 459)
Example:

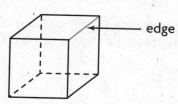

Miles Jogged

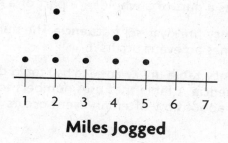

E

edge [ej] **arista** The line where two faces of a solid figure meet
Example:

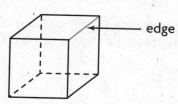

equation [i·kwā′zhən] **ecuación** An algebraic or numerical sentence that shows that two quantities are equal (p. 293)

equilateral triangle [ē·kwi·lat′ər·əl trī′ang·gəl] **triángulo equilátero** A triangle with three congruent sides
Example:

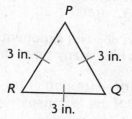

equivalent [ē·kwiv′ə·lənt] **equivalente** Having the same value

equivalent decimals [ē·kwiv′ə·lənt des′ə·məlz] **decimales equivalentes** Decimals that name the same number or amount
Example: 0.4 = 0.40 = 0.400

equivalent expressions [ē·kwiv′ə·lənt ek·spresh′ənz] **expresiones equivalentes** Expressions that are equal to each other for any values of their variables (p. 279)
Example: $2x + 4x = 6x$

equivalent fractions [ē·kwiv′ə·lənt frak′shənz] **fracciones equivalentes** Fractions that name the same amount or part
Example: $\frac{3}{4} = \frac{6}{8}$

equivalent ratios [ē·kwiv′ə·lənt rā′shē·ōz] **razones equivalents** Ratios that name the same comparison (p. 155)

estimate [es′tə·mit] *noun* **estimación (s)** A number close to an exact amount

estimate [es′tə·māt] *verb* **estimar (v)** To find a number that is close to an exact amount

evaluate [ē·val′yoo·āt] **evaluar** To find the value of a numerical or algebraic expression (p. 253)

even [ē′vən] **par** A whole number that has a 0, 2, 4, 6, or 8 in the ones place

expanded form [ek·span′did fôrm] **forma desarrollada** A way to write numbers by showing the value of each digit
Example: 832 = 800 + 30 + 2

exponent [eks′pōn·ənt] **exponente** A number that shows how many times the base is used as a factor (p. 249)
Example: $10^3 = 10 \times 10 \times 10$;
3 is the exponent.

Word History

Exponent comes from the combination of the Latin roots *ex* ("out of") + *ponere* ("to place"). In the 17th century, mathematicians began to use complicated quantities. The idea of positioning a number by raising it "out of place" is traced to René Descartes.

expression [ek·spresh′ən] **expresión** A mathematical phrase or the part of a number sentence that combines numbers, operation signs, and sometimes variables, but does not have an equal or inequality sign

face [fās] **cara** A polygon that is a flat surface of a solid figure
Example:

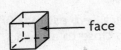
face

fact family [fakt fam′ə·lē] **familia de operaciones** A set of related multiplication and division, or addition and subtraction, equations
Example: 7 × 8 = 56; 8 × 7 = 56;
56 ÷ 7 = 8; 56 ÷ 8 = 7

factor [fak′tər] **factor** A number multiplied by another number to find a product

factor tree [fak′tər trē] **árbol de factores** A diagram that shows the prime factors of a number
Example:

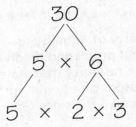

Fahrenheit (°F) [fâr′ən·hīt] **Fahrenheit (°F)** A customary scale for measuring temperature

formula [fôr′myoo·lə] **fórmula** A set of symbols that expresses a mathematical rule
Example: $A = b \times h$

fraction [frak′shən] **fracción** A number that names a part of a whole or a part of a group

frequency [frē′kwən·sē] **frecuencia** The number of times an event occurs (p. 459)

frequency table [frē′kwən·sē tā′bəl] **tabla de frecuencia** A table that uses numbers to record data about how often an event occurs (p. 460)

greatest common factor (GCF) [grāt′est käm′ən fak′tər] **máximo común divisor (MCD)** The greatest factor that two or more numbers have in common (p. 17)
Example: 6 is the GCF of 18 and 30.

grid [grid] **cuadrícula** Evenly divided and equally spaced squares on a figure or flat surface

height [hīt] **altura** The length of a perpendicular from the base to the top of a plane figure or solid figure
Example:

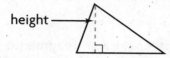

hexagon [hek′sə•gän] **hexágono** A polygon with six sides and six angles
Examples:

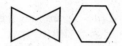

histogram [his′tə•gram] **histograma** A type of bar graph that shows the frequencies of data in intervals. (p. 463)
Example:

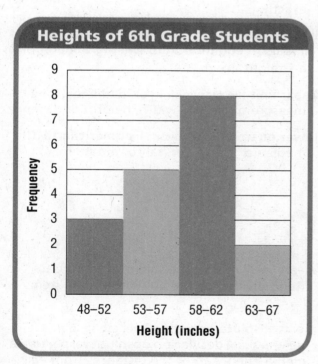

horizontal [hôr•i•zänt′əl] **horizontal** Extending left and right

hundredth [hun′drədth] **centésimo** One of one hundred equal parts
Examples: 0.56, $\frac{56}{100}$, fifty-six hundredths

independent variable [in•dē•pen′dənt′ vâr′ē•ə•bəl] **variable independiente** A variable whose value determines the value of another quantity (p. 341)

Identity Property of Addition [ī•den′tə•tē präp′ər•tē əv ə•dish′ən] **propiedad de identidad de la suma** The property that states that when you add zero to a number, the result is that number

Identity Property of Multiplication [ī•den′tə•tē präp′ər•tē əv mul•tə•pli•kāsh′ən] **propiedad de identidad de la multiplicación** The property that states that the product of any number and 1 is that number

inequality [in•ē•kwôl′ə•tē] **desigualdad** A mathematical sentence that contains the symbol $<$, $>$, $\leq$, $\geq$, or $\neq$ (p. 323)

integers [in′tə•jərz] **enteros** The set of whole numbers and their opposites (p. 97)

interquartile range [in′tûr•kwôr′tīl rānj] **rango intercuartil** The difference between the upper and lower quartiles of a data set (p. 503)

intersecting lines [in•tər•sekt′ing līnz] **líneas secantes** Lines that cross each other at exactly one point
Example:

inverse operations [in′vûrs äp•pə•rā′shənz] **operaciones inversas** Opposite operations, or operations that undo each other, such as addition and subtraction or multiplication and division (p. 305)

key [kē] **clave** The part of a map or graph that explains the symbols

kite [kīt] **cometa** A quadrilateral with exactly two pairs of congruent sides that are next to each other; no two sides are parallel
Example:

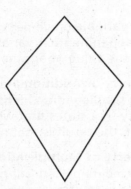

ladder diagram [lad'ər dī'ə•gram] **diagrama de escalera** A diagram that shows the steps of repeatedly dividing by a prime number until the quotient is 1 (p. 10)

lateral area [lat'ər•əl âr'ē•ə] **cara área** The sum of the areas of the lateral faces of a solid

lateral face [lat'ər•əl fās] **cara lateral** Any surface of a polyhedron other than a base

least common denominator (LCD) [lēst käm'ən dē•näm'ə•nāt•ər] **mínimo común denominador (m.c.d.)** The least common multiple of two or more denominators
Example: The LCD for $\frac{1}{4}$ and $\frac{5}{6}$ is 12.

least common multiple (LCM) [lēst käm'ən mul'tə•pəl] **mínimo común múltiplo (m.c.m.)** The least number that is a common multiple of two or more numbers (p. 13)

like terms [līk tûrmz] **términos semejantes** Expressions that have the same variable with the same exponent (p. 275)

line [līn] **línea** A straight path in a plane, extending in both directions with no endpoints
Example:

line graph [līn graf] **gráfica lineal** A graph that uses line segments to show how data change over time

line segment [līn seg'mənt] **segmento** A part of a line that includes two points called endpoints and all the points between them
Example:

line of symmetry [līn əv sim'ə•trē] **eje de simetría** A line that divides a figure into two halves that are reflections of each other (p. 128)

line symmetry [līn sim'ə•trē] **simetría axial** A figure has line symmetry if it can be folded about a line so that its two parts match exactly. (p. 128)

linear equation [lin'ē•ər ē•kwā'zhən] **ecuación lineal** An equation that, when graphed, forms a straight line (p. 359)

linear unit [lin'ē•ər yōō'nit] **unidad lineal** A measure of length, width, height, or distance

lower quartile [lō'ər kwôr'tīl] **primer cuartil** The median of the lower half of a data set (p. 495)

M

mean [mēn] **media** The sum of a set of data items divided by the number of data items (p. 473)

mean absolute deviation [mēn ab'sə•lōōt dē•vē•ā'shən] **desviación absoluta respecto a la media** The mean of the distances from each data value in a set to the mean of the set (p. 499)

measure of center [mezh′ər əv sent′ər] **medida de tendencia central** A single value used to describe the middle of a data set. (p. 471)
Examples: mean, median, mode

measure of variability [mezh′ər əv vâr′ē•ə•bil′ə•tē] **medida de dispersión** A single value used to describe how the values in a data set are spread out (p. 503)
Examples: range, interquartile range, mean absolute deviation

median [mē′dēən] **mediana** The middle value when a data set is written in order from least to greatest, or the mean of the two middle values when there is an even number of items (p. 473)

midpoint [mid′point] **punto medio** A point on a line segment that is equally distant from either endpoint

million [mil′yən] **millón** 1,000 thousands; written as 1,000,000

mixed number [mikst num′bər] **número mixto** A number that is made up of a whole number and a fraction
Example: $1\frac{5}{8}$

mode [mōd] **moda** The value(s) in a data set that occurs the most often (p. 473)

multiple [mul′tə•pəl] **múltiplo** The product of two counting numbers is a multiple of each of those numbers

multiplication [mul•tə•pli•kā′shən] **multiplicación** A process to find the total number of items made up of equal-sized groups, or to find the total number of items in a given number of groups; It is the inverse operation of division.

Multiplication Property of Equality [mul•tə•pli•kā′shən präp′ər•tē əv ē•kwôl′ə•tē] **propiedad de multiplicación de la igualdad** The property that states that if you multiply both sides of an equation by the same number, the sides remain equal

multiplicative inverse [mul′tə•pli•kāt•iv in′vûrs] **Inverso multiplicativo** A reciprocal of a number that is multiplied by that number resulting in a product of 1 (p. 76)

multiply [mul′tə•plī] **multiplicar** When you combine equal groups, you can multiply to find how many in all; the inverse operation of division

negative integer [neg′ə•tiv in′tə•jər] **entero negativo** Any integer less than zero (p. 321)
Examples: ⁻4, ⁻5, and ⁻6 are negative integers.

net [net] **plantilla** A two-dimensional pattern that can be folded into a three-dimensional polyhedron (p. 415)
Example:

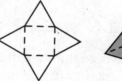

not equal to (≠) [not ē′kwəl tōō] **no igual a** A symbol that indicates one quantity is not equal to another

number line [num′bər līn] **recta numérica** A line on which numbers can be located
Example:

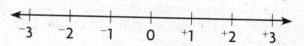

numerator [nōō′mər•āt•ər] **numerador** The number above the bar in a fraction that tells how many equal parts of the whole are being considered
Example: $\frac{3}{4}$ ← numerator

numerical expression [nōō•mer′i•kəl ek•spresh′ən] **expresión numérica** A mathematical phrase that uses only numbers and operation signs (p. 253)

obtuse angle [äb·tōōs' ang'gəl] **ángulo obtuso**
An angle whose measure is greater than 90°
and less than 180°
Example:

obtuse triangle [äb•tōōs' trī'ang•gəl] **triángulo
obtusángulo** A triangle that has one obtuse
angle

octagon [äk'tə•gän] **octágono** A polygon with
eight sides and eight angles
Examples:

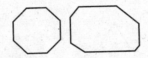

odd [od] **impar** A whole number that has a 1, 3,
5, 7, or 9 in the ones place

open figure [ō'pən fig'yər] **figura abierta** A figure
that does not begin and end at the same point

opposites [äp'ə•zits] **opuestos** Two numbers
that are the same distance, but in opposite
directions, from zero on a number line (p. 97)

order of operations [ôr'dər əv äp•ə•rā'shənz]
orden de las operaciones A special set of rules
which gives the order in which calculations are
done in an expression (p. 253)

ordered pair [ôr'dərd pâr] **par ordenado** A pair of
numbers used to locate a point on a grid. The
first number tells the left-right position and
the second number tells the up-down position.
(p. 123)

origin [ôr'ə•jin] **origen** The point where the two
axes of a coordinate plane intersect; (0,0)
(p. 123)

outlier [out'lī•ər] **valor atípico** A value much
higher or much lower than the other values in
a data set (p. 477)

overestimate [ō'vər•es•tə•mit] **sobrestimar**
An estimate that is greater than the exact
answer

parallel lines [pâr'ə•lel līnz] **líneas paralelas** Lines
in the same plane that never intersect and are
always the same distance apart
Example:

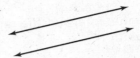

parallelogram [pâr•ə•lel'ə•gram] **paralelogramo**
A quadrilateral whose opposite sides are parallel
and congruent (p. 371)
Example:

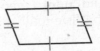

parentheses [pə•ren'thə•sēz] **paréntesis** The
symbols used to show which operation or
operations in an expression should be done
first

partial product [pär'shəl präd'əkt] **producto
parcial** A method of multiplying in which the
ones, tens, hundreds, and so on are multiplied
separately and then the products are added
together

pattern [pat'ərn] **patrón** An ordered set of
numbers or objects; the order helps you
predict what will come next
Examples: 2, 4, 6, 8, 10

pentagon [pen'tə•gän] **pentágono** A polygon
with five sides and five angles (p. 433)
Examples:

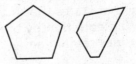

percent [pər•sent'] **porcentaje** The comparison of a number to 100; percent means "per hundred" (p. 187)

perimeter [pə•rim'ə•tər] **perímetro** The distance around a closed plane figure

period [pir'ē•əd] **período** Each group of three digits separated by commas in a multidigit number
Example: 85,643,900 has three periods.

perpendicular lines [pər•pən•dik'yōō•lər līnz] **líneas perpendiculares** Two lines that intersect to form four right angles
Example:

pictograph [pik'tə•graf] **pictografía** A graph that displays countable data with symbols or pictures
Example:

HOW WE GET TO SCHOOL	
Walk	✺ ✺ ✺
Ride a Bike	✺ ✺ ✺ ✺
Ride a Bus	✺ ✺ ✺ ✺ ✺ ◖
Ride in a Car	✺ ✺

Key: Each ✺ = 10 students

place value [plās val'yōō] **valor posicional** The value of each digit in a number based on the location of the digit

plane [plān] **plano** A flat surface that extends without end in all directions
Example:

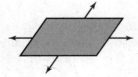

plane figure [plān fig'yər] **figura plana** A figure that lies in a plane; a figure having length and width

point [point] **punto** An exact location in space

polygon [päl'i•gän] **polígono** A closed plane figure formed by three or more line segments
Examples:

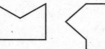

Polygons   Not Polygons

polyhedron [päl•i•hē'drən] **poliedro** A solid figure with faces that are polygons (p. 517)
Examples:

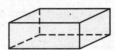

positive integer [päz'ə•tiv in'tə•jər] **entero positivo** Any integer greater than zero (p. 321)

prime factor [prīm fak'tər] **factor primo** A factor that is a prime number

prime factorization [prīm fak•tə•rə•zā'shən] **descomposición en factores primos** A number written as the product of all its prime factors (p. 9)

prime number [prīm num'bər] **número primo** A number that has exactly two factors: 1 and itself
Examples: 2, 3, 5, 7, 11, 13, 17, and 19 are prime numbers. 1 is not a prime number.

prism [priz'əm] **prisma** A solid figure that has two congruent, polygon-shaped bases, and other faces that are all parallelograms
Examples:

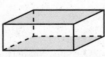

rectangular prism   triangular prism

product [präd'əkt] **producto** The answer to a multiplication problem

pyramid [pir′ə·mid] **pirámide** A solid figure with a polygon base and all other faces as triangles that meet at a common vertex
Example:

quadrants [kwä′drənts] **cuadranes** The four regions of the coordinate plane separated by the *x*- and *y*-axes (p. 127)

quadrilateral [kwä·dri·lat′ər·əl] **cuadrilátero** A polygon with four sides and four angles
Example:

quotient [kwō′shənt] **cociente** The number that results from dividing
Example: 8 ÷ 4 = 2. The quotient is 2.

range [rānj] **rango** The difference between the greatest and least numbers in a data set
(p. 503)

rate [rāt] **tasa** A ratio that compares two quantities having different units of measure
(p. 152)

ratio [rā′shē·ō] **razón** A comparison of two numbers, *a* and *b*, that can be written as a fraction $\frac{a}{b}$ (p. 147)

rational number [rash′·ən·əl num′bər] **número racional** Any number that can be written as a ratio $\frac{a}{b}$ where *a* and *b* are integers and *b* ≠ 0.
(p. 105)

ray [rā] **semirrecta** A part of a line; it has one endpoint and continues without end in one direction
Example:

reciprocal [ri·sip′rə·kəl] **reciproco** Two numbers are reciprocals of each other if their product equals 1. (p. 76)

rectangle [rek′tang·gəl] **rectángulo** A parallelogram with four right angles
Example:

rectangular prism [rek·tang′gyə·lər priz′əm] **prisma rectangular** A solid figure in which all six faces are rectangles
Example:

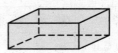

reflection [ri·flek′shən] **reflexión** A movement of a figure to a new position by flipping it over a line; a flip
Example:

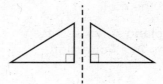

regroup [rē·groop′] **reagrupar** To exchange amounts of equal value to rename a number
Example: 5 + 8 = 13 ones or 1 ten 3 ones

regular polygon [reg′yə•lər päl′i•gän] **polígono regular** A polygon in which all sides are congruent and all angles are congruent (p. 393)

relative frequency table [rel′ə•tiv frĕ′kwən•sē tā′bəl] **tabla de frecuencia relativa** A table that shows the percent of time each piece of data occurs (p. 460)

remainder [ri•mān′dər] **residuo** The amount left over when a number cannot be divided equally

repeating decimal [ri•pēt′ing des′ə•məl] **decimal periódico** A decimal representation of a number that has one or more digits that repeat infinitely (p. 50)

rhombus [räm′bəs] **rombo** A parallelogram with four congruent sides
Example:

Word History

Rhombus is almost identical to its Greek origin, *rhombos*. The original meaning was "spinning top" or "magic wheel," which is easy to imagine when you look at a rhombus, an equilateral parallelogram.

right triangle [rīt trī′ang•gəl] **triángulo rectángulo** A triangle that has a right angle
Example:

round [round] **redondear** To replace a number with one that is simpler and is approximately the same size as the original number
Example: 114.6 rounded to the nearest ten is 110 and to the nearest unit is 115.

sequence [sē′kwəns] **secuncia** An ordered set of numbers

simplest form [sim′pləst fôrm] **mínima expresión** A fraction is in simplest form when the numerator and denominator have only 1 as a common factor

simplify [sim′plə•fī] **simplificar** The process of dividing the numerator and denominator of a fraction or ratio by a common factor

solid figure [sä′lid fig′yər] **cuerpo geométrico** A three-dimensional figure having length, width, and height (p. 415)

solution of an equation [sə•loo′shən əv an ē•kwā′zhən] **solución de una ecuación** A value that, when substituted for the variable, makes an equation true (p. 293)

solution of an inequality [sə•loo′shən əv an in•ē•kwôl′ə•tē] **solución de una desigualdad** A value that, when substituted for the variable, makes an inequality true (p. 323)

square [skwâr] **cuadrado** A polygon with four equal, or congruent, sides and four right angles

square pyramid [skwâr pir′ə•mid] **pirámide cuadrada** A solid figure with a square base and with four triangular faces that have a common vertex
Example:

square unit [skwâr yoo′nit] **unidad cuadrada** A unit used to measure area such as square foot (ft^2), square meter (m^2), and so on

standard form [stan'dərd fôrm] **forma normal** A way to write numbers by using the digits 0–9, with each digit having a place value
Example: 456 ← standard form

statistical question [stə•tis'ti•kəl kwes'chən] **pregunta estadística** A question that asks about a set of data that can vary (p. 451)
Example: How many desks are in each classroom in my school?

Substitution Property of Equality [sub•stə•tōō'shən präp'ər•tē əv ē•kwôl'ə•tē] **propiedad de sustitución de la iqualdad** The property that states that if you have one quantity equal to another, you can substitute that quantity for the other in an equation

subtraction [səb•trak'shən] **resta** The process of finding how many are left when a number of items are taken away from a group of items; the process of finding the difference when two groups are compared; the inverse operation of addition

Subtraction Property of Equality [səb•trak'shən präp'ər•tē əv ē•kwôl'ə•tē] **propiedad de resta de la igualdad** The property that states that if you subtract the same number from both sides of an equation, the sides remain equal

sum [sum] **suma o total** The answer to an addition problem

surface area [sûr'fis âr'ē•ə] **área total** The sum of the areas of all the faces, or surfaces, of a solid figure (p. 419)

tally table [tal'ē tā'bəl] **tabla de conteo** A table that uses tally marks to record data

terminating decimal [tûr'mə•nāt•ing des'ə•məl] **decimal exacto** A decimal representation of a number that eventually ends (p. 50)

terms [tûrmz] **términos** The parts of an expression that are separated by an addition or subtraction sign (p. 262)

tenth [tenth] **décimo** One of ten equal parts
Example: 0.7 = seven tenths

thousandth [thou'zəndth] **milésimo** One of one thousand equal parts
Example: 0.006 = six thousandths

three-dimensional [thrē də•men'shə•nəl] **tridimensional** Measured in three directions, such as length, width, and height

three-dimensional solid [thrē də•men'shə•nəl säl'id] **figura tridimensional** See *solid figure*

trapezoid [trap'i•zoid] **trapecio** A quadrilateral with exactly one pair of parallel sides (p. 383)
Examples:

tree diagram [trē dī'ə•gram] **diagrama de árbol** A branching diagram that shows all possible outcomes of an event (p. 9)

trend [trend] **tendencia** A pattern over time, in all or part of a graph, where the data increase, decrease, or stay the same

triangle [trī'ang•gəl] **triángulo** A polygon with three sides and three angles
Examples:

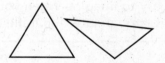

triangular prism [trī•ang'gyə•lər priz'əm] **prisma triangular** A solid figure that has two triangular bases and three rectangular faces

two-dimensional [tōō də•men'shə•nəl] **bidimensional** Measured in two directions, such as length and width

two-dimensional figure [tōō də•men'shə•nəl fig'yər] **figura bidimensional** See *plane figure*

underestimate [un•dər•es'tə•mit] **subestimar** An estimate that is less than the exact answer

unlike fractions [un'līk frak'shənz] **fracciónes no semejantes** Fractions with different denominators

unit fraction [yōō'nit frak'shən] **fracción unitaria** A fraction that has 1 as a numerator

unit rate [yōō'nit rāt] **tasa por unidad** A rate expressed so that the second term in the ratio is one unit (p. 152)
Example: 55 ml per hr

upper quartile [up'ər kwôr'tīl] **tercer cuartil** The median of the upper half of a data set (p. 495)

variable [vâr'ē•ə•bəl] **variable** A letter or symbol that stands for an unknown number or numbers (p. 257)

Venn diagram [ven dī'ə•gram] **diagrama de Venn** A diagram that shows relationships among sets of things
Example:

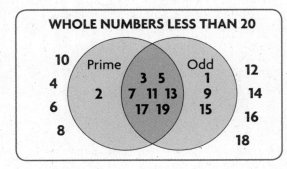

WHOLE NUMBERS LESS THAN 20

vertical [vûr'ti•kəl] **vertical** Extending up and down

vertex [vûr'teks] **vértice** The point where two or more rays meet; the point of intersection of two sides of a polygon; the point of intersection of three (or more) edges of a solid figure; the top point of a cone; the plural of *vertex* is *vertices*
Examples:

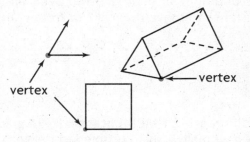

volume [väl'yōōm] **volumen** The measure of the space a solid figure occupies (p. 433)

weight [wāt] **peso** How heavy an object is

whole number [hōl num'bər] **número entero** One of the numbers 0, 1, 2, 3, 4, . . . ; the set of whole numbers goes on without end

x-axis [eks ak'sis] **eje de la x** The horizontal number line on a coordinate plane (p. 123)

x-coordinate [eks kō•ôrd'n•it] **coordenada x** The first number in an ordered pair; tells the distance to move right or left from (0,0) (p. 123)

y-axis [wī ak′sis] **eje de la y** The vertical number line on a coordinate plane (p. 123)

y-coordinate [wī kō•ôrd′•n•it] **coordenada y** The second number in an ordered pair; tells the distance to move up or down from (0,0) (p. 123)

Zero Property of Multiplication [zē′rō präp′ər•tē əv mul•tə•pli•kā′shən] **propiedad del cero de la multiplicación** The property that states that when you multiply by zero, the product is zero

Index

Perimeter
    changing dimensions, 401–404
    composite figures, 397–400

Pint, 223

Place value, 27

Polygons
    changing dimensions, 401–404
    on coordinate plane, 405–408
    regular, 393–396

Pose a Problem, 8, 38, 59, 63, 69, 70, 78, 82, 126, 158, 176, 190, 256, 268, 312, 352, 444, 466, 498

Positive numbers, 97–100

Pound, 227

Predictions
    making, 236

Prime factorization, 9–12
    defined, 9
    exponents, 9–11
    factor tree, 9
    ladder diagram, 10

Prism
    net, 419–422
    surface area of, 423–426
    volume of, 438

Problem Solving, In most lessons. Some examples are: 8, 20, 274, 286, 506, 520
    analyze relationships between quantities, 349–352
    apply greatest common factor, 21–24
    compare ratios
        use tables to, 159–162
    coordinate plane, 135–138
    data displays, 481–484
    draw a diagram
        applying greatest common factor, 21–24
        coordinate plane, 135–138
        data problems, 481–485
    equations with fractions, 317–320
    find a pattern
        analyze relationships between quantities, 349–352
        changing dimensions, 401–404
        compare ratios, 159–162

misleading statistics, 521–524
percents, 205–208
pose a problem, 38, 70, 78, 82, 126, 158, 176, 190, 256, 268, 444, 466
see Real World, Problem Solving
see Real World, Unlock the Problem
solve a simpler problem
    equations with fractions, 317–320
use a formula
    distance, rate, and time, 237–240
    geometric measurements, 441–444
use a model
    combine like terms, 275–278
    fraction problems, 87–90
    percent problem, 205–208
What's the Error?, 52, 70, 74, 104, 108, 112, 166, 194, 212, 222, 256, 268, 418, 422, 430
work backward
    data set, 521–524

Project, 2, 144, 246, 368

Properties
    of addition, 279
    Addition Property of Equality, 306
    Associative Property, 279
    Commutative Property, 279
    Distributive Property, 18, 21–24, 280
    Division Property of Equality, 313
    Identity Property, 279
    of multiplication, 279
    Multiplication Property of Equality, 314
    of operations, 279–282
    quadrilaterals, 406
    Subtraction Property of Equality, 305

Pyramid, 416
    surface area, 427–430

Q

Quadrants, 127

Quadrilateral
    on coordinate plane, 406–408
    trapezoids, 383–386

Quart, 223

Quartile
    lower, 495–497
    upper, 495–497

Quotients
    compatible numbers to estimate, 73–74

R

Range
finding, 504–506, 510, 514

Rates, 151–154
defined, 152
distance, rate, and time problems, 237–240
formula for, 237–240
unit rate, 152–154

Rational numbers, 105–108
absolute value, 115–118
compare and order, 109–112
on coordinate plane, 123–126

Ratios
defined, 147
equivalent
defined, 155
finding, 155–156, 173
graph to represent, 177–180
tables to solve, 163–166
model, 147–150
percent as, 191
rates, 151–154
tables to compare, 159–162
writing, 147

Reading
Connect to Reading, 122, 150, 236, 330, 348, 458

Real World
Problem Solving, In most lessons. Some examples are: 8, 20, 274, 286, 506, 520
Unlock the Problem, In most lessons. Some examples are: 5, 27, 275, 283, 513, 521

Reciprocals
fraction division, 76–77

Rectangles
area, 371–374
on coordinate plane, 405–408

Rectangular prisms
volume, 437–440

Rectangular pyramid, 416

Regular polygon
area, 393–396

Relative frequency table, 460

Remember, 9, 17, 28, 49, 53, 57, 58, 71, 102, 177, 192, 356, 434, 492

Repeating decimals, 50

S

Science
Connect to Science, 30, 42, 252, 396, 440, 494

Sense or Nonsense?, 33, 64, 82, 100, 207, 240, 278, 282, 304, 326, 358, 374, 378, 436, 454, 476, 494, 506, 516, 520

Share and Show, In every lesson. Some examples are: 6, 14, 277, 285, 505, 519

Show What You Know, 3, 47, 95, 145, 185, 217, 247, 291, 339, 369, 413, 449, 489

Simplifying
numerical expressions, 253–256
order of operations, 253

Solid figures, 415
pyramid, 416, 427–430
rectangular prisms, 437–440
rectangular pyramid, 416
surface area, 419
volume, 433

Solution of an equation, 293–296

Solution of an inequality, 323–326

Squares
area, 371–374

Statistical question
defined, 451
recognizing, 451–454

Statistics
misleading, 521–524

Student Help
Error Alert, 40, 62, 131, 156, 196, 220, 266, 298, 342, 419, 495, 514
Math Idea, 5, 14, 50, 54, 97, 101, 115, 210, 219, 234, 249, 257, 280, 293, 323, 371, 406, 459, 509
Math Talk, In every lesson. Some examples are: 7, 9, 275, 283, 517, 521
Remember, 9, 17, 28, 49, 53, 57, 58, 71, 102, 177, 192, 356, 434, 492
Write Math, 12, 20, 24, 35, 39, 52, 56, 69, 78, 81, 108, 112, 126, 130, 134, 149, 189, 230, 264, 274, 286, 303, 311, 312, 326, 334, 352, 377, 385, 404, 408, 418, 421, 435, 454, 461, 466, 471, 472, 480, 483, 493

Subtraction
decimals, 27–30
equations
solution, 305–308
order of operations, 253
solve addition and subtraction equations, 305–308
Subtraction Property of Equality, 305

Notes

Table of Measures

METRIC	CUSTOMARY

Length

1 meter (m) = 1,000 millimeters (mm)	1 foot (ft) = 12 inches (in.)
1 meter = 100 centimeters (cm)	1 yard (yd) = 3 feet
1 meter = 10 decimeters (dm)	1 yard = 36 inches
1 dekameter (dam) = 10 meters	1 mile (mi) = 1,760 yards
1 hectometer (hm) = 100 meters	1 mile = 5,280 feet
1 kilometer (km) = 1,000 meters	

Capacity

1 liter (L) = 1,000 milliliters (mL)	1 cup (c) = 8 fluid ounces (fl oz)
1 liter = 100 centiliters (cL)	1 pint (pt) = 2 cups
1 liter = 10 deciliters (dL)	1 quart (qt) = 2 pints
1 dekaliter (daL) = 10 liters	1 quart = 4 cups
1 hectoliter (hL) = 100 liters	1 gallon (gal) = 4 quarts
1 kiloliter (kL) = 1,000 liters	

Mass/Weight

1 gram (g) = 1,000 milligrams (mg)	1 pound (lb) = 16 ounces (oz)
1 gram = 100 centigrams (cg)	1 ton (T) = 2,000 pounds
1 gram = 10 decigrams (dg)	
1 dekagram (dag) = 10 grams	
1 hectogram (hg) = 100 grams	
1 kilogram (kg) = 1,000 grams	

TIME

1 minute (min) = 60 seconds (sec)	1 year (yr) = about 52 weeks
1 hour (hr) = 60 minutes	1 year = 12 months (mo)
1 day = 24 hours	1 year = 365 days
1 week (wk) = 7 days	1 decade = 10 years
	1 century = 100 years
	1 millennium = 1,000 years

SYMBOLS

$=$	is equal to	10^2	ten squared
$\neq$	is not equal to	10^3	ten cubed
$\approx$	is approximately equal to	2^4	the fourth power of 2
$>$	is greater than	$|^-4|$	the absolute value of $^-4$
$<$	is less than	$\%$	percent
$\geq$	is greater than or equal to	$(2, 3)$	ordered pair (x, y)
$\leq$	is less than or equal to	$^\circ$	degree

FORMULAS

Perimeter and Circumference

Polygon	$P =$ sum of the lengths of sides
Rectangle	$P = 2l + 2w$
Square	$P = 4s$

Area

Rectangle	$A = lw$
Parallelogram	$A = bh$
Triangle	$A = \frac{1}{2}bh$
Trapezoid	$A = \frac{1}{2}(b_1 + b_2)h$
Square	$A = s^2$

Volume

Rectangular Prism	$V = lwh$
Cube	$V = s^3$

Surface Area

Cube	$S = 6s^2$

Photo Credits

KEY: (t) top, (b) bottom, (l) left, (r) right, (c) center, (bg) background, (fg) foreground, (i) inset

Cover Front: (bg) Purestock/Getty Images; (deer) David W. Hamilton/Getty Images; (owl) Brian Hagiwara/Brand X Pictures/Getty Images; (leaf texture) Image Gap/Alamy.

Cover Back: (leaves) Studio Ton Kinsbergen/Beateworks/Corbis.

Title Page: (r) Brian Hagiwara/Brand X Pictures/Getty Images; (bg) Studio Ton Kinsbergen/Beateworks/Corbis.

Copyright Page: (tl) Danita Delimont/Alamy Images; (br) Don Hammond/Design Pics/Corbis.

Author Page: (tr) altrendo nature/Getty Images; (bg) (2 images) Purestock/Getty Images; (br) Daniel J. Cox/Getty Images.

Table of Contents: v Craig Tuttle/Corbis; vi (bg) Oleg Boldyrev/Alamy; vii Garry Gay/Alamy Images; viii (l) Jonathan Daniel/Getty Images; ix Michele Wassell/Alamy Images; x Oliver Gerhard/Alamy Images; Erin Paul Donovan/Alamy Images; xi Digital Vision/Getty Images; xii (l) Digital Vision/Getty Images.

Critical Area: 1 Craig Tuttle/Corbis; 2 (cr) D. Hurst/Alamy; (br) Foodcollection RF/Getty Images; (cl) Frederic Cirou and Isabelle Rozenbaum/PhotoAlto/Corbis; 8 PhotoDisc/Getty Images; 9 PhotoDisc/Getty Images; 13 (cr) C Squared Studios/PhotoDisc/Getty Images; 20 mediacolours/Alamy Images; 21 Corbis Super RF/Corbis; 22 Jean-Blaise Hall/Getty Images; 27 Rubberball/Alamy; 28 Lee Dalton/Alamy Images; United States Mint; 30 David R. Frazier Photolibrary, Inc./Alamy Images; 31 SW Productions/PhotoDisc/Getty Images; 34 Comstock/Getty Images; 35 Alamy Images; 38 Mike Kemp/Getty Images; 39 Brand X Pictures/Getty Images; 42 M. I. Walker/Photo Researchers, Inc.; 49 brandi ediss/Getty Images; 52 Don Mason/Corbis; 53 Craig Tuttle/Design Pics/Corbis; 56 PhotoDisc/Getty Images; 57 Anna Peisi/Corbis; 61 Bernhard Classen/Alamy; 64 (t) Judith Collins/Alamy; 71 Amos Nachoum/Corbis; 82 (t) Garry Gay/Alamy; 83 (cr) Getty Images; 87 (t) Plush Studios/Blend Images/Corbis; 90 (cr) ImageState/Alamy; 100 (t) Yellow Dog Productions/Getty Images; 101 (t) Visions of America, LLC/Alamy Images; 105 (t) Digital Vision/Getty Images; (tr) Getty Images; 110 (t) PhotoDisc/Getty Images; 112 (tr) imagewerks RF/Getty Images; 115 (tr) Corbis; 119 (tr) Tim Clayton/Corbis; 122 (tr) Jaak Nilson/Alamy Images; 131 (tr) Danita Delimont/Alamy Images; 136 (t) photoalto/Alamy Images.

Critical Area: 143 Tannen Maury/epa/Corbis; 144 Jonathan Daniel/Getty Images; 145 (br) Image Source/Corbis; 151 Daniel J. Cox/Corbis; 159 (t) Ron Chapple Stock/Alamy Images; 160 (t) Hill Street Studios/Getty Images; 163 Andersen Ross/Getty Images; 166 (t) Racing: Darryl Lenluk/Corbis; 172 (t) GK Hart/Vikki Hart/PhotoDisc/Getty Images; 177 (t) Nancy Hoyt Belcher/Alamy Images; 185 Cathy Maier Callanan; 187 MiRafoto.com/Alamy; 195 Victor Baldlzon/National Basketball Association/Getty Images; 198 J. Griffs Smith/Texas Department of Transportation; 209 Ronnie Kaufman/Larry Hirshowitz/Blend Images; 217 DLILLC/Corbis; 222 Vito Palmisano/Getty Images; 224 American School/The Bridgeman Art Library/Getty Images; 227 Bon Appetit/Alamy; 236 Ron Chapple Stock/Alamy; 237 Frank Krahmer/Getty Images.

Critical Area: 245 Michele Wassell/Alamy Images; 246 Tim Mainiero/Alamy Images; 249 Granger Wootz/Blend Images/Corbis; 252 Biomedical Imaging Unit, Southampton General Hospi/Photo Researchers, Inc.; 253 Herbert Kehrer/Corbis; 257 William Manning/Corbis; 261 (t) ableimages/Alamy; 264 Comstock/Getty Images; 265 Stock4B/Getty Images; 268 (t) Comstock/Getty Images; 271 Goodshoot/Jupiterimages/Getty Images; 274 (t) Digital Vision/Getty Images; (tc) Cheetah sprinting : C123/Corbis; (bc) Digial Vision/Getty Images; 275 Kevin Dodge/Corbis; 278 (tc) Artville/Getty Images; (b) Eyewire/Getty Images; (tr) Digital Vision/Getty Images; 283 (b) M & J Bloomfield/Alamy; Oleksiy Maksymenko Photography/Alamy; 291 Comstock/Jupiterimages/Getty Images; 293 Sports Illustrated/Getty Images; 296 NASA; 297 (cr) Concept by Beytan/Alamy Images; 300 Iain Masterton/Alamy Images; 304 Corbis; 305 Erik Isakson/Getty Images; 312 (t) Joseph Sohm/Visions of America/Corbis; 315 Image Source/Corbis; 317 Martin Sundberg/Getty Images; 320 Thinkstock/Jupiterimages/Getty Images; 323 jupiterimages/Getty Images; 326 Fuse/Getty Images; 327 Van Hasselt John/Corbis Sygma; 330 Bob Gibbons/Alamy Images; 331 Robert McGouey/Alamy Images; 334 Robert E Daemmrich/Getty Images; 341 Elena Elisseeva/Alamy Images; 344 Jaak Nilson/Alamy Images; 345 PhotoDisc/Getty Images; 348 Franco Vogt/Corbis; 349 Patti McConville/Getty Images; 351 Barry Austin/Getty Images; 359 Denis Scott/Corbis.

Critical Area: 367 Kelly-Mooney Photography/Corbis; 368 Nicola Angella/Grand Tour/Corbis; 371 Roman Soumar/Corbis; 378 (tr) fStop/Alamy; 379 Frank Whitney/Getty Images; 386 Elvele Images Ltd/Alamy Images; 390 Chuck Franklin/Alamy Images; 396 B.A.E. Inc./Alamy; 405 Toru Ysmanaka/AFP/Getty Images; 407 Tom Schierlitz/Getty Images; 413 (br) Andres Rodriguez/Alamy Images; 418 Harry Taylor; 419 Nikreates/Alamy; 426 NASA; 427 David R. Frazier Photolibrary, Inc./Alamy; 429 Terry Smith Images/Alamy; 430 (t) Peter Adams/Corbis; 433 Maciej Figiel/Alamy; 435 (b) Craig Lovell/Eagle Visions Photography/Alamy Images; 437 Studio Eye/Corbis; 440 (t) Comstock/Corbis; 443 Cephas Picture Library/Alamy; 449 Tony Garcia/Getty Images; 451 Chuck Franklin/Alamy Images; 452 AfriPics.com/Alamy Images; 454 David Wall/Alamy Images; 455 Greg C Grace/Alamy Images; 458 AF Archive/Alamy Images; 461 Ben Blankenburg/Corbis; 462 David Davis Photoproductions RF/Alamy; 463 AMPAS/FilmMagic/Getty Images; 465 Stockdisc/Getty Images; 466 Veronique Krieger/Getty Images; 472 (t) Camille Moirenc/Corbis; 476 (cl) PhotoDisc/Getty Images; 477 Corbis; 480 MLB Photos/Getty Images; 484 Golden Gate Bridge: Corbis; 489 (br) PhotoDisc/Getty Images; 491 WILDLIFE GmbH/Alamy Images; 492 Siaukia/Alamy Images; 494 Arco Images GmbH/Alamy Images; 495 Corbis; 496 Image Source/Getty Images; 502 Johner Images/Alamy Images; 503 (tr) Jim Lane/Alamy Images; 504 (tr) Corbis Super RF/Corbis; 512 Digital Vision/Getty Images; 514 (tr) Ocean/Corbis; 515 (br) Stockbyte/Getty Images; 519 (cr) Lee Foster/Alamy Images.

All other photos Houghton Mifflin Harcourt libraries and photographers; Guy Jarvis, Weronica Ankarorn, Eric Camden, Don Couch, Doug Dukane, Ken Kinzie, April Riehm, and Steve Williams.

© Houghton Mifflin Harcourt Publishing Company